MEHR Counselling Services
Mohammad J Nateghpour (Ph.D.)
Counselling, Psychotherapy,
Hypnotherapy

2nd edition

Social Research Methods

David Dooley

*University of California
at Irvine*

Prentice Hall
Englewood Cliffs, N.J. 07632

Library of Congress Cataloging-in-Publication Data

Dooley, David.
    Social research methods / David Dooley. -- 2nd ed.
        p.   cm.
    Includes bibliographical references.
    ISBN 0-13-818857-2
    1. Sociology--Research--Methodology. 2. Social sciences-
-Research--Methodology.   I. Title.
HM48.D66   1990
300'.72--dc20   89-38950
                                                        CIP

Editorial/production supervision and
  interior design: Marianne Peters
Cover design: Bruce Kenselaar
Manufacturing buyer: Ray Keating/Bob Anderson

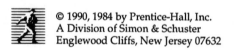
Printed in the United States of America
10 9 8 7 6 5 4 3

ISBN 0-13-818857-2

Prentice-Hall International (UK) Limited, London
Prentice-Hall of Australia Pty. Limited, Sydney
Prentice-Hall Canada Inc., Toronto
Prentice-Hall Hispanoamericana, S.A., Mexico
Prentice-Hall of India Private Limited, New Delhi
Prentice-Hall of Japan, Inc., Tokyo
Simon & Schuster Asia Pte. Ltd., Singapore
Editora Prentice-Hall do Brasil, Ltda., Rio de Janeiro

To My Son Kevin

Contents

Preface

This text is intended for students in their first social science methods course. Its goal is to introduce the whole array of social research approaches and validity threats. I was motivated to write this text to fill the need for a conceptually integrated and comprehensive approach to the basic methods course. As an instructor I found myself using several different texts—one for its coverage of experimental design and validity; another for its coverage of survey, qualitative, and correlational approaches; and a third to provide a brief review of statistics. The main drawback to this multitext approach is the lack of articulation of how different methods compared and contrasted on the same validity concerns. Comprehensive but conceptually unintegrated coverage leaves students unpracticed in comparing the results produced by different methods and unappreciative of their different advantages and disadvantages.

I assume that some readers will pursue graduate studies and research careers and that they will need to be aware of the whole range of social science methodologies in order to choose the one(s) best suited to their research problem. I assume that other students will pursue careers in areas other than professional research and that these students will almost certainly need to be effective consumers of research in whatever methodological form it takes. In both cases, I assume that the major social research problems will ignore traditional disciplinary boundaries and require multimethod approaches. In my view the best conceptual map for organizing these multiple methods came from the analysis of the different types of validity offered by Donald Campbell and his colleagues.

Although this second edition retains the organizational strategy of linking methodologies (designs and data collection procedures) with validity types, it differs in several ways from the first edition. The chapters are reorganized as well as updated with more recent examples. The ethics chapter (now Chapter 2) has been moved from near the end of the first edition to near the beginning of this one in order to raise the salience of values in human research. Moreover, subsections on ethics are included in several other chapters where relevant. Portions of the chapter on computer usage in the first edition are distributed among the other chapters, and others have been dropped to permit greater coverage of other matters. The major addition is the inclusion of a new chapter (Chapter 3) on library usage and report writing organized around the search for and interpretation of a particular brief study (which is reprinted for analysis). Theory and measurement are assembled in their own section (Chapters 4 to 6), and survey sampling and inferential statistics are joined in another section (Chapters 7 and 8). The design section ranges from true experiments to qualitative approaches (Chapters 9 through 13). The final section includes chapters on applied social research (Chapter 15) and on interpreting social research findings. This latter chapter (Chapter 14) both synthesizes the foregoing material on validity and design types and expands the coverage of literature review techniques.

I continue to be impressed by the extent to which the avoidance of math or statistics hinders undergraduates in their appreciation of research design. Although this book is not a statistics text, it is not possible to teach the reading of research articles without some minimal reference to statistics. Thus, the Appendix, reviewing basic statistics, is retained and expanded to help those students who either have not had a statistics course or who may require a brief review.

This edition would not have been possible were it not for the contributions of the many individuals who assisted in the first edition. Moreover, I am indebted to Julia Gelfand of the University of California, Irvine Library, for her assistance with Chapter 3 and to my students and colleagues throughout the years for their stimulation. Finally, I am indebted to the following reviewers for their written feedback about the first edition: James D. Becker, Kapiolani Community College; Steve A. Nida, Franklin University; and Ellen F. Rosen, College of William and Mary.

1

The Logic of Social Research

Ruling Out Rival Hypotheses

SCIENCE AS SYSTEMATIC DOUBTING

The Necessity of Skepticism

> Sir Cyril Burt. Could Margaret Howard or J. Conway who helped Sir Cyril in studies of the intelligence of twins or anyone else who knows them tel. (reverse charges) Oliver Gillie, Ol-485-8953.[1]

This advertisement appeared in the personal columns of the *London Times* on October 16, 1976. On the front page of the same paper on October 24, 1976, a news story by Oliver Gillie began, "The most sensational charge of scientific fraud this century is being levelled against the late Sir Cyril Burt, father of British educational psychology" (quoted by Hearnshaw, 1979, p. 235).

The Scandal. Burt was a social researcher. The scandal surrounding his research on the inheritability of intelligence was great, both because of his prominence and because of the influence of his research on social policy—specifically on the establishment of selective education in England and more generally on the debate about racial differences in intelligence.

Burt died a greatly esteemed scholar in 1971. He was called the "dean of the world's psychologists" (Dreger, quoted by Hearnshaw, 1979, p. 227). Burt was the co-founder of the *British Journal of Statistical Psychology* in 1947 and controlled or helped control it until 1963. His work was identified as a major support for the use of intelligence tests to decide the educational options of British schoolchildren.

Burt was studying a long-standing scientific puzzle: What contributes more to intelligence—genetic inheritance or rearing and environment? This is a knotty problem because genetics and environment are difficult to measure and control. Burt borrowed a method of research that takes advantage of a rare occurrence—identical twins reared apart. We know that identical twins have identical genes and that their intelligence levels are usually similar. However, environmentalists (those who think that the environment contributes more than genetics to intelligence) point out that twins usually have identical environments. Thus the similarity of identical twins' intelligence could be due either to their genes or to their shared environment. But when identical twins are separated and reared in different environments, environmentalists would argue that the twins should have different IQs to the extent that their environments are different. People who believe that genes cause intelligence would predict great similarity of identical twins' intelligence regardless of the environment.

To use the identical-twins-reared-apart method, you have to find many sets of such twins. Because of possible errors in measuring intelligence and in remembering aspects of child rearing, data from a few sets of twins might be misleading. Information from many sets of twins would be more convincing because chance errors in testing intelligence and in remembering the child rearing environment would cancel out.

Besides his other claims to fame (for example, his expertise in statistics and genetics), Burt was influential because he claimed to have found more identical twins reared apart than anyone else working in the intelligence area. After reporting on 15 such twin sets in 1943, he claimed 21 by 1955, twice that number by 1958, and 53 in his last report of 1966. Two other researchers also published separate reports on the Burt twins, confirming his conclusions. These researchers were Margaret Howard and J. Conway. These findings were the basis not only for Burt's defense of British educational policy but also, in part, for the controversial implication of racial differences in intelligence. Although Burt's conclusions favoring genetic over environmental causation were widely disliked and criticized during his lifetime, doubts about his scholarly integrity were not publicized until after his death.

Perhaps the first clue was that his published results were incredibly consistent over different reports based on increasingly large samples. A few such consistencies may occur by chance, but Burt's consistencies far exceeded chance. Since Burt could not explain these consistencies after his death, attention shifted to the other authors of reports based on Burt's twins—Howard and Conway. When neither Howard nor Conway stepped forward, reporter Gillie of the *Times* published his claim of fraud.

It now appears that Howard and Conway might have been unsalaried social workers who assisted Burt in some of his data collection in the 1920s and 1930s. However, his diary makes clear that he had no contact with them in the period after 1954, when they would have had to communicate with him to analyze his data. It seems that Burt himself wrote the articles attributed to them and got them published in the journal that he controlled in order to give the appearance of independent corroboration of his results.

An analysis of his correspondence indicates that he manufactured at least some of the twin data. He apparently worked backward from his published results to produce the raw data that he reluctantly provided other researchers interested in his findings.

The behavior of faking data and attributing false reports to others is the scholarly equivalent of embezzlement by bankers. Burt violated the unspoken pact that members of the research community have with each other—to report truthfully their observations.

Being a Critical Consumer. What is the moral of this story? First it should be emphasized that such fraud is the exception rather than the rule. This episode astonishes precisely because it ought to be and is exceptional.

One important lesson is that social research matters. Whether it is fraudulent, as in Burt's case, or not, it can address questions that have great social importance. By "importance" is meant not just theoretical importance (in the sense of being curious or interesting) but also practical significance in terms of affecting people's lives (for example, the thousands of British schoolchildren whose future careers were shaped by the testing program that Burt's research seemed to endorse).

Social research is powerful in a democracy because it is a persuasive source of information. We make many decisions independently for ourselves and many more in concert with others through our votes. Many of these decisions, whether personal or public , are influenced by social research. The Burt case should make it clear that you cannot believe everything you read. This is the other major lesson of the Burt affair—you should be doubtful or skeptical of everything you read. **Skepticism** is not an attitude of uniformly disbelieving everything. Effective skepticism is based on training that allows one to distinguish poor research, which deserves to be doubted or ignored, from excellent research, which deserves to be trusted.

In sum, you need to learn how to distinguish between good and bad research. This text provides the foundation for becoming critical consumers of social research. Whether you plan to consume research as a professional scholar or whether you want to be able to defend yourself as a private citizen from sales pitches disguised as social science, you will need to learn the principles of social research.

Burt, for all his failings, was a social scientist in that he provided data (fraudulent in his case) supporting his claims. The domain of social research includes rules of evidence for judging the credibility of any study. Burt's evidence could be and ultimately was evaluated according to these rules. In a sense, the Burt case testifies to the effectiveness of social research. It works best when people read it critically.

How Do We Come to Know?

Assertion, Authority, and Evidence. Social research typically results in assertions about causation, for example, the claim that *A* causes *B*. However, not all causal assertions are based on evidence. Unsupported assertions are easy to make and can be just as easily ignored. Either an assertion has supporting evidence or it does not. If evidence cannot be provided, one has to wonder why anyone should believe it or prefer it to a rival assertion based on evidence.

Sometimes assertions are supported by the authority, expertise, or rank of the source. If the authority bases the assertion on scientific evidence, we expect the evidence to be made public so that we may make our own independent evaluations of the data. As a frequently occurring example, we hear claims that a new treatment is successful in curing some previously incurable pathology (for example, schizophrenia, cancer, or heroin addiction). Scientists customarily ignore such claims unless and until they are documented. The motivation to recruit desperate, paying clients with claims of a miracle cure has all too often been the only basis for such claims. The authority, academic degree, or other claim to expertise of the source will not substitute for evidence.

Some authorities base their assertions entirely on faith, with no claims to scientific foundation. Confrontations of assertions based on faith with assertions based on evidence have made for some dramatic moments in history. Probably the most famous such confrontation was Galileo's heresy trial. In 1616, the Copernican model of the solar system, in which the earth moved around the sun rather than the sun around the earth, was evaluated by a Church court and was condemned as being contrary to the Bible. In 1632 Galileo published his *Dialogue on the Two Principal World Systems,* which seemed to favor the arguments for the Copernican view. He was summoned to Rome by the Inquisition, and as a result of his trial in 1633 he was forced to recant and his book was prohibited. He remained under house arrest for the remaining eight years of his life (see Hummel, 1986, for a description of these events).

Contrary to the popular view that this trial was a simple conflict of science versus religion, the matter was more complex, involving personal jealousies and power struggles. Redondi (1983/1987) even suggests that Galileo's trial was due to theological disputes other than his Copernicanism.

Although we may never know the full story of the trial, Galileo's defense of science was eloquent: "I do not feel obliged to believe that the same God who has endowed us with sense, reason, and intellect has intended us to forego their use" (quoted by Durant & Durant, 1961, p. 607). The centuries have vindicated Galileo. In 1757 the Church took books teaching mobility of the earth off the Index of Prohibited Books. In 1979, Pope John Paul II called for a reexamination of the Galileo case and admitted error in Galileo's trial. The Vatican has published its secret archives on the Galileo case and in effect said that the judges were wrong (Poupard, 1983).

One irony of this episode is that Galileo had many friends in the Church (including the pope) who advised him that he could avoid colliding with the Church if only he would not claim that his theory was proved. As it turned out, Galileo should not have claimed that his theory was proved since he was wrong in some respects (for example, in his theory of tides).

This episode is just one of many that demonstrate that, historically, assertions based on good evidence prevail over those based on authority and, in their turn, yield to better ones based on better evidence. This competition between rival explanations is the means by which the more plausible and useful explanation emerges.

Do We See Things as They Really Are?   Our skepticism about social research does not concern itself only or even mainly with rare instances of data fraud or unsupported assertions. Philosophers of knowledge, practitioners of **epistemology**, have long wondered how and even whether we can know about our world. Social research is, of course, **empirical** in the sense that it is based on experience of the world. But philosophers and scientists have raised doubts about how much confidence we can place in our observations.

What we usually mean by the notion of observation is that we are aware of sensations within us which we attribute to external causes. When I say, "There is a tree," I really mean that I have an inner visual sensation that corresponds to what I have learned is called a tree. But how can you or I be sure that a tree is really there? Perhaps I am having an hallucination; that is, the source of my inner sensations may not be a tree at all but rather some malfunction of my nervous system. This unavoidable indirectness of our relation to the world was well expressed by an important philosopher of science: "We do not actually see physical objects, any more than we hear electromagnetic waves when we listen to the wireless," (Russell, 1948, p. 311).

One branch of philosophy, called **ontology**, is concerned with the ultimate nature of things (that is, are there really external things out there to serve as sources of our sensations?). The view of ontologists who believe that there are such real sources is called **realism**. Although realism is not demonstrable (trying to prove the reality of an external source by reliance on suspect perceptions leads to an infinite regress), most scientists and laypeople act and talk most of the time as though they were realists. Nevertheless, it is worth noting that some philosophers of science have argued for another view, called fictionalism or instrumentalism. In this latter view, the supposed external sources of our perceptions are treated as fictions dependent on our observing instruments.

Selective Perceptions. Even if the sources of our perceptions are assumed to be real, there is little doubt that our observations are selective and subject to error. According to Thomas Kuhn (1970), normal science consists in solving puzzles within a framework made up of widely accepted beliefs, values, assumptions, and techniques. That is, scientists working on a given problem share certain basic assumptions and research tools that shape their observation of reality. This shared framework has been called a **paradigm**. Paradigms are like lenses through which we see the world.

According to Kuhn (1970), whole generations of researchers may engage in normal science within a paradigm before enough conflicting data are accumulated to force a **paradigm shift**. Such paradigm shifts or revolutions occur when existing theories can no longer be adjusted to handle discrepant observations. Paradigm shifts have been likened to gestalt perceptual shifts. Kuhn illustrates this phenomenon by a psychology experiment in which subjects were shown cards from a deck. In this deck there were some peculiar cards, such as black hearts and red spades, although the subjects were not told about them in advance. Most subjects required repeated exposures to the cards before noticing the peculiarities. It was as though the subjects looked at black hearts and "saw" red hearts because they believed that only red hearts existed. When they grasped the idea that there could be black hearts, it was as though someone threw a switch in their minds. Suddenly they could "see" the cards as they were. It would be well to reflect on the framework in which we think and do research and ask whether we would notice the black hearts and red spades if they were to show up in our data.

Another major critique of scientific observation is that by Karl Marx, who challenged its neutrality and comprehensiveness. For Marx, sensation is really more a matter of noticing, implying activity or motivation for some action (Russell, 1945). We only notice those relatively few things out of the universe of possible things as a part of the process of acting with reference to them. Marx thus located science in the context of political and economic activity, presumably driven by the self-interest of the participants who are themselves members of economic classes.

Can We Discover Causal Laws?

Faith of Science. There are other difficulties beyond our ability to perceive the world accurately. It is sometimes held that the mission of science is to discover the timeless laws governing the world. Implicit in this notion is what Bertrand Russell (1948) called the "faith of science" (p. 314). By this phrase he meant that we assume that there are regularities in the connection of events and that these regularities (or "laws") have a continuity over time and space. The great success of the physical sciences in the past two centuries lends credence to this assumption. For example, our lunar astronauts confirmed that physical relationships discovered on earth hold on the moon as well.

However, confidence in our capacity to discover timeless physical laws was shaken by the overthrow of Newtonian physics by Einstein early in this century (Stove, 1982). Social scientists have long been doubtful about their chances of imitating the success of the physical sciences. In the social domain, some scientists reject the assumption that there are knowable objective laws discoverable by observation. Rather, these critics hold, our understanding of the world is a social construction dependent on the "historically situated interchanges among people" (Gergen, 1985, p. 267).

Fallibilism. Assuming there are laws governing physical or social events independent of the socially constructed perception of them, philosophers of science warn us that they will be difficult to discover. One problem has to do with the essence of law discovery, **induction,** the extracting of an idea from observations and applying the idea to unobserved situations. Hume, writing in the 1700s, is usually credited with making the best case against such an inferential leap (Stove, 1982). Put simply, many repeated instances of an observation cannot guarantee its future repetition. However, most scientists and ordinary people would say that such repetition does increase the likelihood or probability of its happening again. Nevertheless, we must remind ourselves that we are liable to be mistaken sometimes, that is, that we are fallible in this regard. **Fallibilism** is the philosophical term for this posture of suspecting our own inductions.

In sum, the tools of our knowing, the operations of measurement and the induction of lawful relationships, are the products of human experience and therefore subject to flaw. We can assert a causal connection but only under warrant of (that is, limited by and no more valid than) our operations and criteria for judging causal connection. This limited and cautious approach to research is a topic of continuing debate about the philosophical foundations of social science (Gholson & Barker, 1985; Manicas & Secord, 1983).

The Strategy of Research

Theory as Testable Explanation. Social research is devoted to explaining social events, that is, to determining the causation of our social reality. What causes people to abuse their children, to become schizophrenic, to remain impoverished, to fail to learn to read and write, to engage in criminal acts? Besides our natural curiosity about how things work, we have a strong practical incentive to explain, predict, and (if we are successful) improve certain human conditions.

The social research domain includes a great variety of activities. Each of these activities can be located in one or another of three main clusters: tentative explaining, observing, and testing alternative explanations against observations. Each is necessary to social research. If all we did was imagine different explanations, we would never have a basis for choosing among them. On the other hand, proposing tentative explanations is vital to research because explanations make sense out of diverse observations and guide us in making still better observations. Tentative or preliminary explanations constitute **theory**.

Because there are usually two or more different theories to explain many social phenomena, we need to observe the phenomena carefully to find out which theory best fits reality. If our observations are to help us understand causation, they must be brought into contact with theory. For example, we may observe and describe the incidence of death by cholera or suicide. But merely counting and categorizing deaths, that is, **descriptive** research, does not explain them.

However, observing with possible explanations in mind becomes **causal** research. For example, John Snow suspected that contaminated water was involved in cholera. In the period from 1848 to 1854, he connected the different rates of cholera deaths to the different companies supplying London houses with water (see Lilienfeld, 1976, pp. 24–25). Similarly, Émile Durkheim, also working in the last century, associated changes over time in the rate of suicide with changing economic conditions (Durkheim, 1897/1951). Out of the unimaginably large number of social and environmental variables that these men might have considered, they were able to focus on water supply and economic conditions because their observations were guided by tentative explanations.

Finally, the match between theory and observation must be tested. The last step of the social research process is where choices are made. Does our tentative explanation fit the observations or does some other explanation fit better? How shall we decide? Real science is a process of repeated testings, of seeing whether observations confirm or disconfirm our tentative explanations. Popper (1987) made the point that it is too easy simply to look for confirmations. Rather, he argued, any "genuine test of a theory is an attempt to falsify it, or refute it. Testability is **falsifiabilty**"...(p. 141). As an example of **pseudoscience**, he offered astrology "with its stupendous mass of empirical evidence based on observation—on horoscopes and on biographies" (p. 139) but without the quality of refutability.

The fact that there are alternative or rival explanations means that we must have a rule for evaluating the fit of observations to any explanation. Since theories and observations are made public in the form of research reports, anyone can apply the rules of evidence. Anyone can look over the shoulder of the investigator and second-guess his or her conclusions.

Rules of Evidence. By what criteria do we identify a cause of some observed effect? How can we assess the causal claims of Snow and Durkheim about the causes of cholera and suicide? Traditionally, there are three criteria: (1) **covariation,** (2) cause prior to effect, and (3) absence of **plausible rival hypothesis** or explanation.

The first two of these criteria are simple and straightforward. If two things are causally related, observations of them should co-vary or be associated. If "bad" water causes cholera, we expect that more cholera cases should appear in houses supplied with bad water and fewer in houses supplied with good water. If rapidly changing economic conditions cause suicide, we should observe more suicides in changing economic times and fewer in stable economic times. The value of knowing that two things are associated is that we can rule out the conclusion of no relationship. However, covariation alone does not specify the type of causal relationship.

Hume, the philosopher who taught us to doubt our inductions from observations, also called our attention to another problem in discovering causal relations. He pointed out our habit of mind to attribute causation in the observed association of things. When two events repeatedly coincide, we come to expect one when we notice the other. This "prediction" often is taken as "causation." However, we must separate these two notions in our minds. Russell (1948) gives a clear illustration of this problem, called "Geulinex's two clocks." Both are perfect timepieces, perfectly synchronized, so that when one points to the hour, the other chimes. From this association we can derive prediction but not causation. That is, we would not claim that one clock causes the other to chime since both are caused by some prior event, the clockmaker. Thus we need additional criteria beyond simple association to judge causation.

The second criterion partially addresses this difficulty of distinguishing correlation from causation: If two things are causally related, the cause should precede the effect. Cholera cannot be caused by bad water if cholera appears first and the bad water is provided later. Evidence about the sequence of events can help us rule out one plausible direction of causation. But knowing that two events are correlated and that one comes before the other still does not settle the question. Recall Geulinex's two clocks, and suppose that one clock is set one second before the other so that its chimes are always heard before the other. Would we argue that it causes the other's chimes just because it occurs first?

Dealing with this problem is where the third and most complicated criterion comes into play. The third requirement for judging causation is the absence of any plausible (that is, reasonable or believable) rival explanations. What is "plausible"? This is a subjective matter. A rival explanation that seems implausible to the researcher who is conducting a study may later be judged to be plausible or even probable by others. Anything that can cause two events to be associated is a candidate for a plausible rival explanation.

A large part of what social researchers do is done to guard against such rival explanations. Social research is graded largely on the extent to which rival explanations are ruled out or made less plausible. Not all rival explanatory variables can be known in advance. Someone may think of a new and plausible counterexplanation years after a study is completed. Thus, the task of the social researcher is to state theory, collect data, and design and interpret studies in ways that minimize, as much as possible, present and future counterexplanations. To the extent that a researcher demonstrates covariation and temporal precedence and controls plausible rival explanations, we will be persuaded to accept his or her conclusion that A causes B.

The need to anticipate and guard against rival explanations is pervasive in social research and is a major theme of this text. Virtually every aspect of data collection and research design is shaped by the threat of counterexplanations. Whether as a consumer or as a producer of social research, you will need to learn to discriminate research on the basis of how well it controls and eliminates rival explanations of the findings.

Another major theme of this text is that social science can be and ought to be public for at least two reasons. First, as the Burt case illustrates, it must be conducted in public in order to be checked and kept honest. Public scrutiny of research is the best way of assuring that the research is conducted with integrity. Anyone willing and able may screen published research for errors or fraud.

Second, social research seldom provides definitive conclusions. Rather than providing laws of social behavior, it typically gives evidence for and against preliminary, would-be laws. This evidence requires interpretation. At any moment, you or I may have to choose one interpretation or explanation from several plausible rivals as the basis for action, even though we know that none of the explanations is certain and final. We are aware that future research may turn up new explanations that will replace the ones that are favored at the moment. Almost weekly, we hear tentative conclusions from researchers that, if taken seriously, would change our behavior (for example, evidence that coffee causes cancer or birth defects). In the same breath that these announcements are made, we are advised that the results are not conclusive pending further research and that it is up to us to make our own judgments about these data. Thus, in a very real way, each of us is a research consumer constantly weighing and evaluating the findings of social and other scientists in order to make difficult decisions under conditions of uncertainty.

USES OF SOCIAL RESEARCH AND RIVAL EXPLANATIONS

Personal Use of Research

Causal assertions based on evidence pervade our environment. We are advised to spend money on cars, toothpaste, cigarettes, political candidates, health habits, and a thousand other things based on brief references to data by the media. For example, you may have heard a news brief reporting a study of running and heart attacks. Perhaps it claimed that running helps prevent heart attacks because the evidence shows that there is a lower than expected rate of heart attacks among a sample of marathon runners. Although it may be true that running is good for the heart and prevents heart attacks, this evidence does not prove it. There is a very plausible rival explanation of these observations.

Assume that the evidence is true as reported and that marathon runners do have a better record of heart attacks than nonrunners. It is entirely plausible that marathon runners are different in some other respects from most people. A glance at a photo of a group of Olympic marathon runners lined up for the start of their event tells us that, taken as a group, these are relatively young, lean, small-boned people. Certainly, we would not mistake a marathon runner for a sumo wrestler. Maybe marathon runners have different body characteristics to begin with. Maybe they have stronger hearts or more efficient circulatory systems than nonrunners do. Such physiological advantages would help beginning runners succeed in running so that they would be encouraged to become devoted long-distance runners. The group of marathon runners we see lined up for the start of an important race are the highly selected few who remain after many others with fewer physical gifts have been screened out. In short, these runners may have been selected, indirectly, for their healthy hearts and resistance to heart attack (not to mention their long stride, motivation, and capacity for self-discipline).

The evidence seems to support two quite different assertions: (1) Running prevents heart attacks. (2) People resistant to heart attacks become runners. We may have or be able to find other evidence that helps determine which, if either, of these assertions is true. However, the evidence presented in the short news message cannot tell us. This is a common dilemma. Frequently, the available evidence suggests one causal assertion but cannot rule out a plausible rival explanation.

Thinking of rival explanations is very useful in a personal way because we are confronted with so many choices based on evidence. One of the handiest ways to assess the evidence for a choice is to see if it permits a plausible rival explanation. If it does, the evidence must be regarded as weak. If the decision is an important one and you cannot afford to make a wrong choice, you may want to look for another option based on more convincing evidence.

Professional Use of Research

The Cause of Schizophrenia. Most of us do not have the time or inclination to investigate all claims and advertisements for rival explanations. Perhaps the costs of a wrong decision are small in some personal decisions involving choices about goods, services, or personal behavior. For other kinds of choices, the costs are so high for wrong decisions and the evidence so complicated that we entrust the decision to professionals. In effect, we pay specialists to do the investigation and thinking about rival explanations for us. We may consult a physician for his or her assessment of the safety of a new high-endurance diet before trying it. We are thus trusting that this physician has been skeptical for us. Similarly, we trust mental health professionals, educators, criminal justice workers, social workers, and other human service professionals to evaluate the evidence on interventions in their areas of expertise and to provide us with guidance after critically and skeptically challenging claims based on evidence. One of the identifying characteristics of professionals is that they can and do make their own independent evaluations of causal assertions. If you plan a professional social service or academic career, you will need to learn how to make just the sort of evaluations of research evidence that are described here.

Unlike advertisers trying to persuade consumers with brief references to questionable evidence, professional researchers are expected to provide other professionals with detailed formal reports of their evidence. (Later in chapter 3 you will see a brief example of such a standard professional research report, which illustrates the way professionals communicate with each other.)

Just as a layperson evaluates a causal claim by looking for plausible rival explanations, so professionals challenge causal claims by hunting for rival explanations. Because they know their audience is sophisticated and critical, professional researchers make every effort to design their research to rule out rival explanations. It is a sign of the complexity of modern science that serious and sincere research efforts can still be vulnerable to rival explanations despite the best efforts of the researcher.

A good illustration of this difficulty in ruling out rival explanations comes from the research to find the cause of schizophrenia. Schizophrenia is the most important mental health problem in terms of occupied hospital beds. More than a mental health problem that wrecks the lives of individuals and families, it represents a major drain on the nation's health resources and accounts for a sizable share of the demand on the resources of the criminal justice system since abnormal behavior puts schizophrenics in jails and prisons.

Every few years our hopes are raised by the public announcement that a researcher has found the chemical key to schizophrenia. We are led to expect that in a few short years a vaccine or antidote will appear to wipe out schizophrenia in the same way polio was eradicated. Naturally there is great motivation to be the scientist who solves the riddle of schizophrenia, but unfortunately, such claims have always been premature.

A Breakthrough That Wasn't. The tale of one of these "breakthroughs" illustrates that evidence from professional research can be explained in more than one way. Solomon Snyder (1974) relates the story that began with a theory by two psychiatrists. Osmond and Smythies (1952) argued that schizophrenic behavior was produced by some toxic substance, which occurred naturally in the bodies of schizophrenics but which was not produced in the bodies of normal people. They suspected that this unknown toxic substance would be chemically similar to substances (such as mescaline) known to produce schizophrenic-like hallucinations in normal people. Finally, they reported a chemist's observations that adrenaline, which naturally occurs in human bodies, was structurally similar to mescaline. It seemed possible that some malfunction might produce a variant of adrenaline that would have the property of producing the symptoms of schizophrenia.

This theory gained support from the research of Hoffer, Osmond, & Smythies (1954), who reported two new pieces of evidence. First, they found adrenochrome (a breakdown product of adrenaline) in the blood and urine of schizophrenics but not in most normal people. Second, when adrenochrome was administered to normal people, they reported having psychedelic experiences like those of people under the influence of LSD. As Snyder says, "It would seem that the millennium of psychiatry had arrived" (1974, p. 56). Adrenochrome appeared to be the cause of schizophrenia. It remained only to find a way to control the production of this chemical and hundreds of thousands of schizophrenics could look forward to normal lives.

Unfortunately, Hoffer's two crucial findings could not be reproduced by any other researchers. The many failures of **replication** (that is, to reproduce the studies with the same results) led to efforts to find rival explanations for his evidence.

Why did Hoffer find more adrenochrome in schizophrenics than in normal people? Adrenochrome is produced when adrenaline is exposed to air. The longer the adrenaline is exposed to the air before being tested, the more it is converted to adrenochrome. Snyder (1974) suggests that Hoffer's samples from schizophrenics and normal people started out with the same low levels of adrenochrome, but the schizophrenics' samples were left exposed to air longer before testing. Thus, the evidence for differences between schizophrenics and normal people may have been created by the researchers' differential handling of the samples.

Why did Hoffer find that normal people given adrenochrome reported hallucinations? Snyder's rival explanation is that this observation was caused by **suggestion**. The subjects knew that they were being given a chemical that was thought to cause schizophrenic hallucinations, and this "suggestion" seems to have been carried out. The effect of belief on perception and behavior is well known in psychology and requires special experimental controls. The two causal assertions of the Osmond-Smythies theory and Snyder's rival explanations of Hoffer's findings are summarized in Figure 1–1.

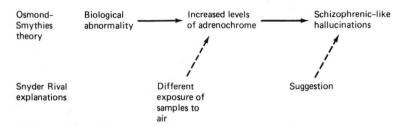

Figure 1.1 Osmond-Smythies theory and Snyder rival explanations.

In subsequent studies in which blood samples from schizophrenics and normal people were exposed to air for the same length of time, no adrenochrome differences were found. When subjects were kept from knowing whether they were receiving adrenochrome or some neutral substance, adrenochrome produced no hallucinations.

Although Hoffer's evidence was initially misleading, it had the ultimate effect of advancing the search for the cause of schizophrenia. As Snyder (1974) summarizes, "After the adrenochrome fiasco, psychiatrists became disillusioned and immensely skeptical about the drug-induced model psychosis approach to schizophrenia" (p. 57). Researchers closely rechecked the nature of schizophrenic symptoms and concluded that the psychedelic drugs did not really produce those symptoms. Consequently, the psychedelic drug approach to schizophrenia was seen as a dead end, and research resources were rechanneled along more promising lines. The search goes on for a new toxic substance or neural defect that might cause schizophrenic symptoms. New and improved theories resulted from this episode and are, ironically, our legacy from Hoffer, Osmond, and Smythies. In science, all interpretations are seen as tentative; nothing is ever "proved."

Political Use of Research

Busing for Desegregation. One reward for your investment in studying social research will be greater power to make personal decisions—that is, to analyze the assertions of those who would sell you personal goods and services. Beyond the benefits to your personal well-being, you must learn about research in order to enter certain professions. Unlike Snyder, your career interest may not be in curing schizophrenia. But a great many professions increasingly require a knowledge of how to critique research: criminal and civil law, the architecture of human habitations in accordance with the findings of environmental researchers, teaching with the latest "proven" techniques, practicing medicine, counseling drug addicts, conducting market surveys for business purposes, and so on. It is increasingly likely that your future career will require you to read and understand some sort of social research to obtain jobs at the highest professional levels.

Besides personal and professional reasons, you are obliged as an educated citizen to understand social research. Increasingly, significant social policy decisions are being based on causal claims that are supported (or not supported) by research evidence. Elected judges, members of Congress, and chief executives are making political decisions, partly on the evidence supplied by researchers. As a voting citizen, you exercise your ballot independently only if you can make your own assessment of the social research that is injected into policy debates.

One of the most dramatic examples of the influence of social research is the Coleman report (Coleman, et al., 1966). Coleman and his colleagues surveyed the educational opportunities and performance of a great many American students. They concluded among other things that black students did better in integrated than in racially isolated schools. This evidence became the most frequently cited social scientific evidence for the view that racially separate education was inherently unequal education and for the policy of busing for school desegregation. One reading of the Coleman report pointed to a causal assertion: Equalizing educational opportunity by desegregation would tend to equalize achievement.

A Reinterpretation.   The same data were reanalyzed by Jencks and his colleagues (1972), who pointed out a rival explanation for the benefits of integration. In Coleman's study, already-integrated blacks were compared with already segregated blacks. Opponents of desegregation could "argue that the high test scores of blacks in naturally integrated schools reflect the greater motivation or resources of black parents who put their children in desegregated schools" (Jencks, et al., 1972, p. 99). Thus the Coleman evidence may not apply to desegregation by public policy. If academic achievement is caused more by parental motivation than by school integration, busing would be expected to have little effect. Jencks argues that busing can produce small educational gains or losses depending on the specific conditions of the integration. He is more impressed with how little school conditions influence educational attainment and how little both school conditions and educational achievement influence later income levels. The dispute about the impact of education generally and of busing for integration specifically will continue in the realms of both science and politics. Just as we are still searching for the cause of schizophrenia, so we continue to ponder the relationship of education to social justice.

The point here is that evidence has been provided that can be used to support both sides of a major political question. You may be asked to decide at the polls which view you favor. If you have a closed mind on the question of busing, you can find some social scientist with evidence that supports your view. But if you want to support the best possible policy for this situation, you must do some work. You will need to know how to judge competing explanations of the data for yourself.

SUMMARY

The infamous Burt case illustrates the necessity for skepticism in using social research. Even in the absence of fraud, drawing causal inferences from social research can be difficult and uncertain. Social research proceeds by raising tentative explanations, making observations, and then testing how well alternative explanations fit the observations.

A tentative explanation that *A* causes *B*, for example, is supported by the observation that (1) *A* and *B* are associated, (2) *A* occurs before *B*, and (3) no rival hypothesis for the *A*-with-*B* association is plausible. By these rules of evidence, causal claims can be assessed in a public way. Causal claims based on such evidence have proven more convincing than claims based on faith or authority. Social research has implications for personal, professional, and public decision making. Because of its practical significance in each of these domains, it is important that everyone learn to read research critically.

EXERCISES

1. Find a newspaper or popular magazine article that claims a causal relationship. Check to see if the causal inference is supported by evidence or whether it depends on authority or faith. Check to see if the evidence shows an association of the two variables and that the causal variable comes before the effect. Finally, see if you can think of a rival explanation for this association. Repeat this exercise several times until you can do it quickly and automatically for any causal claim that you hear (for example, via television or professors).

2. For a handy collection of causal claims with alternative explanations, see the book *Rival Hypotheses* by Huck and Sandler (1979). Some of their 100 problems rely on common sense and a creative skepticism, and you should be able to solve them now. Others assume knowledge of topics that are covered in the following chapters. Try your hand at some of the problems now and again near the end of the course after you have read this text.

GLOSSARY

Causal: Pertaining to the generation of an effect.

Covariation: Association; level of one variable predicts the level of another.

Descriptive: Pertaining to the characterization of something or some relationship.

Empirical: Based on observation.

Epistemology: Branch of philosophy dealing with the nature of knowledge and our ability to know.

Fallibilism: In epistemology, the posture of doubting our own inductions.

Falsifiabilty: Aspect of an assertion that

makes it vulnerable to being proven false, an essential ingredient in the process of science.

Induction: Creation of general principles from specific observations.

Ontology: Branch of philosophy dealing with the ultimate nature of things.

Paradigm: Shared framework involving common theory and data collection tools in which researchers ordinarily approach scientific problems.

Paradigm shift: Revolution in assumptions about and perception of a research problem during which one paradigm is replaced by another.

Plausible rival hypothesis: Believable or possible alternative explanation for an observation.

Pseudoscience: Body of assertions that appears to be scientific because it involves observation but is not for lack of falsifiability, for example, astrology.

Realism: In ontology, the view that the sources of our perceptions are real and not fictions.

Replication: Repetition of a study to see if the same results are obtained.

Skepticism: Attitude of doubting and challenging assertions.

Suggestion: In social research, the effect on subjects of their beliefs about their situation.

Theory: Tentative or preliminary explanations of causal relationships.

NOTE

[1] These quotations, along with the details of the controversy surrounding Sir Cyril Burt, are found in Hearnshaw's biography of Burt (1979, pp. 227–261).

2

Ethics and Values

Protecting Human Subjects and Others

INTRODUCTION

Tuskegee Syphilis Study

On July 25, 1972, a news story by Jean Heller appeared in the *Washington Star*. Although overshadowed by political activities of the presidential election campaign, this article led to administrative actions that halted a research study of 40 years' duration. In addition, it began a process of legislative and administrative changes that greatly increased the protection of human subjects in medical and social research. In 1973, a U.S. Senate committee held hearings prompted by the revelation of the Tuskegee Syphilis Study. These hearings resulted in research guidelines for human research sponsored by the Department of Health and Human Services in 1981. These new ethical guidelines now effectively govern most social research in the United States. Thus, the present protections enjoyed by human subjects can be traced in large measure to the impact of the Tuskegee study (see Jones, 1981, for more details on this study).

The Beginning. In the 1930s penicillin, the present treatment of syphilis, had not yet become available. In 1929, the U.S. Public Health Service and the private Rosenwald Fund collaborated in supporting several demonstration programs for the control of syphilis. The Macon County, Alabama, project, one site in this series of syphilis control programs, ended in 1931. But as this demonstration project came to an end, an idea for an extended monitoring of the effects of untreated syphilis emerged.

With the funds for the screening and treatment demonstration program about to end, the Macon County project staff tried to think of ways to continue their involvement with this large, unsolved public health problem. These workers had discovered an incredible 36 percent rate of syphilis, much of it transmitted congenitally (that is, from an infected mother to her fetus), but an insignificant rate of treatment. The rationale for an extended monitoring was based on three objectives: (1) to study the untreated course of the disease in black people for comparison with an earlier study of a white population; (2) to raise the consciousness of the public to the problem of syphilis; and (3) to maintain the momentum of public health work in the area by sustaining the cooperative arrangements among state, local, and Tuskegee Institute medical personnel.

The monitoring of untreated syphilitics, which began on a short-term basis, was extended year after year and decade after decade into the 1970s. The study consisted of periodic checks of the untreated syphilitics, including the painful and sometimes dangerous lumbar puncture method for diagnosing neural syphilis.

Prevention of Treatment. By 1933, the research project had involved 412 syphilitics and 204 controls (all black males) and had become dedicated to following untreated cases to autopsy. The researchers actively worked to prevent the delivery of treatment to the identified cases. Unknown to these individuals, they had become subjects of a study dedicated to preserving their disease until death. To avoid "contaminating" the study with effective treatment, medicine with ameliorative but noncurative powers such as aspirin and iron tonic was administered. Families of the subjects were offered burial stipends in exchange for permission to perform autopsies on the deceased subjects.

A mobile Public Health Service unit was assigned to Macon County in 1939, but a nurse working on both this new mobile unit and the research project kept study subjects from receiving treatment. In World War II, the military draft identified some of the study's subjects in the registration process. Both state and federal laws were broken to keep such subjects from the treatment given to other men found diseased by draft screening. Even when penicillin became available in several clinics in Macon County in the 1940s, the research team continued the study and their efforts to deny treatment to the subjects. The investigators concluded that the penicillin treatment would be ineffective in the late stages of their subjects' disease and that the scientific benefits of studying the then elderly subjects justified continuation of the project.

Aftermath.   How did the Tuskegee study manage to escape detection and termination for four decades? Some of the reasons have to do with the powerlessness of the victims—impoverished, diseased blacks in the rural south at the mercy of the local and federal white medical power structure. In exchange for their participation, these subjects received some medicine and more medical attention in the form of regular medical checks than they might otherwise have received.

But to blame this project on the passivity of the subjects is to blame the victims. How can the actions of the researchers and the larger scientific community in condoning this project be understood? These investigators began as pioneers bringing medical care and public attention to a heretofore unattended medical problem with little incentive other than altruism and a proper scientific curiosity. In their dealings with their subjects, they were friendly and even affectionate. The investigators took pride in their work, regularly published and discussed their findings in the usual scientific channels, and even welcomed visiting scientists and interns. Despite their openness, the first complaints about the project from the scientific community did not appear until the mid-1960s. These early complaints came as a surprise and were either ignored or rejected as unfounded and ill informed. In retrospect, one is forced to conclude that well-intentioned scholars are not always adequately objective about their own research and that informal and unsystematic peer review from outsiders cannot be counted on to be either timely or effective in preventing abuse of human subjects.

The 40-year Tuskegee Syphilis Study began as a moral crusade to help the diseased poor through the advance of scientific enlightenment. It ended as a scientifically unjustifiable exercise, which will be remembered as a monument and symbol of research immorality. As of 1981, the Public Health Service had not made a public admission of wrongdoing, but an out-of-court settlement of a civil suit yielded $37,500 to each of the surviving syphilitics.

The scientific value of the study was negligible. Virtually none of the subjects was genuinely untreated. Because of the widespread use of penicillin for infections other than syphilis, most of the syphilitics received some penicillin for other problems over the years. The effort to prevent treatment succeeded only in preventing systematic treatment adequate to care for the subjects.

Ethical Philosophy and Practical Principles

If the Tuskegee Syphilis Study were unique we might be less concerned about ethical dilemmas in human research. Unfortunately, numerous examples of such violations in medical (Beecher, 1970, p. 17) and psychological research (Ad Hoc Committee on Ethical Standards of Psychological Research, 1973) have been documented. The impetus for revision of human research guidelines, which produced the National Research Act of 1974, stemmed from other major scandals besides the Tuskegee Syphilis Study. In the 1960s, live cancer cells were injected into humans without their informed consent in the Brooklyn Jewish Chronic Disease Hospital. Drug research without consent had been conducted in the Milledgeville State Hospital in Georgia also in the 1960s. Such incidents made it clear that something was needed to protect human subjects from researchers (Hershey & Miller, 1976).

Ethics. **Ethics** is that branch of philosophy that pertains to the study of right and wrong conduct. So central and practical is this branch of philosophy that theories of ethics have been produced throughout recorded history. For example, Plato held that proper conduct led to harmony. But we observe that the desires of people tend rather to conflict than to harmony. Thus the central ethical dilemma is how to reconcile two or more conflicting preferences. This dilemma is as old as the dialogues of Socrates and Thrasymachus, in which the latter says that "justice is nothing else than the interest of the stronger" (Plato, quoted by Russell, 1945, p. 117).

Later philosophers, unhappy with idealized but impractical ethics and with realistic ethics defined by brute force, tried to solve the dilemma by the more scientific-seeming method of **utilitarianism**. Utilitarianism seeks a rational assessment and balancing of costs and benefits of behavior. The proper behavior is that which produces the maximum benefit for the least cost, where the costs and benefits of all concerned are taken into account. Applied to human research, this method means that the benefits of the knowledge to be gained must be weighed against the costs, primarily those of the subject. Unfortunately, this utilitarian approach requires that someone place weights or values on the benefits and costs to be compared.

In terms of the Tuskegee study, what value can be placed on one man-year of forgone treatment for syphilis? What is the worth of the knowledge that was being sought about the differential development of syphilis in blacks and whites, which was the original justification for the study? As you can imagine, the placing of weights on such intangibles could prove quite difficult. Ultimately, the placing of values on costs and benefits becomes a political task.

In summary, the philosophical effort to discover proper behavior by logic and science has not succeeded. The ethical problems in human research can be understood as the outcomes of natural conflicts between parties with different interests. Researchers want to gain knowledge with minimal resistance. Human subjects want to protect their right to voluntary and informed consent in potentially risky endeavors such as research. Not surprisingly researchers and subjects will usually place different values on those different goals.

There are other naturally occurring conflicts in the research process that pose similar ethical dilemmas. For example, the researcher may falsify data or claim research conducted by another to obtain funding or status. These and other types of unethical behavior can be understood as the products of conflicting interests between researchers or between researcher and funder. Such conflicts, although serious, seldom produce the shocking moral tragedies of human subject abuse. Perhaps for that reason efforts to protect human subjects have produced a more detailed body of principles and procedures than the other ethical conflicts in research. Consequently, more of our attention will be given to reviewing these protection principles and the procedures designed to uphold them.

Principles. Utilitarianism illustrates the difficulty inherent in an objective scientific resolution of ethical dilemmas in research. By philosophical reasoning alone, we cannot arrive at a universally acceptable ethical system. Opposing self-interests and the difficulty of discovering objective weights for subjective values will necessarily require some neutral body to decide ethical conflicts.

The valuation of the society's and the subjects' costs and benefits will necessarily be based on the customary beliefs and the values of the culture with respect to the relative importance of the individual and the society. Some political body must resolve the research conflict by applying the appropriate cultural values to the opposing parties' costs and benefits.

Nuremberg Code: The First Legal Effort. Large-scale human research is relatively recent. Even in this brief history, different societies have disagreed on proper research conduct. The contrast of differing principles in the treatment of human subjects emphasizes the origin of such principles in different assumptions and values. For example, in World War II, human research was conducted under official German policy in various concentration camps. After the war, the cruelty of some of this research so shocked the victorious Allies that some researchers were tried by the Nuremberg Military Tribunal. To have a set of ethical guidelines for this tribunal (from the perspective of the Allied governments' values), the first legal effort to deal with such ethical problems was mounted. The result was the **Nuremberg Code** (see Table 2–1).

Table 2–1 The Nuremberg Code[*]

---

1. The voluntary consent of the human subject is absolutely essential. This means that the person involved should have legal capacity to give consent; should be so situated as to be able to exercise free power of choice, without the intervention of any element of force, fraud, deceit, duress, over reaching, or other ulterior form of constraint or coercion; and should have sufficient knowledge and comprehension of the elements of the subject matter involved as to enable him to make an understanding and enlightened decision. This latter element requires that before the acceptance of an affirmative decision by the experimental subject there should be made known to him the nature, duration, and purpose of the experiment; the method and means by which it is to be conducted; all inconveniences and hazards reasonably to be expected; and the effects upon his health or person which may possibly come from his participation in the experiments.
   The duty and responsibility for ascertaining the quality of the consent rests upon each individual who initiates, directs or engages in the experiment. It is a personal duty and responsibility which may not be delegated to another with impunity.
2. The experiment should be such as to yield fruitful results for the good of society, unprocurable by other methods or means of study, and not random and unnecessary in nature.
3. The experiment should be so designed and based on the results of animal experimentation and a knowledge of the natural history of the disease or other problem under study that the anticipated results will justify the performance of the experiment.
4. The experiment should be conducted as to avoid all unnecessary physical and mental suffering and injury.
5. No experiment should be conducted where there is a prior reason to believe that death or disabling injury will occur; except, perhaps, in those experiments where the experimental physicians also serve as subjects.
6. The degree of risk to be taken should never exceed that determined by the humanitarian importance of the problem to be solved by the experiment.
7. Proper preparations should be made and adequate facilities provided to protect the experimental subject against even remote possibilities of injury, disability, or death.
8. The experiment should be conducted only by scientifically qualified persons. The highest degree of skill and care should be required through all stages of the experiment of those who conduct or engage in the experiment.
9. During the course of the experiment the human subject should be at liberty to bring the experiment to an end if he has reached the physical or mental state where continuation of the experiment seems to him to be impossible.
10. During the course of the experiment the scientist in charge must be prepared to terminate the experiment at any stage, if he has probable cause to believe, in the exercise of the good faith, superior skill and careful judgment required of him that continuation of the experiment is likely to result in injury, disability, or death to the experimental subject.

---

[*]H. K. Beecher, *Research and the Individual: Human Studies* (Boston: Little, Brown, 1970), pp. 227–228.

The Nuremberg Code has spawned numerous sets of ethical principles for the protection of human subjects. The national and world medical and social science organizations that have devised these codes have tended to converge on similar principles, which maximize the protection of the subject's rights to safety and to informed consent. It is hoped that disseminating these rules will help reduce the ambiguity and disorder that had pervaded the researcher-subject relationship. However, it must be remembered that most of these codes (except the Nuremberg

Code) were intended not as laws but as guiding principles to which professional researchers would voluntarily conform.

CURRENT PROCEDURES FOR PROTECTING HUMAN SUBJECTS

If guidelines are to serve as more than wishful thinking, they must be backed up by sanctions and by external reviewers who can judge whether or not they have been violated. For example, point 6 of the Nuremberg Code permits a degree of risk to the subject up to the "humanitarian importance of the problem." This criterion, if left to the researcher, could lead to the subjective overestimation of the "importance" of the study and/or the underestimation of the subject's risk.

Two general approaches to enforcing these ethical principles are possible. The first approach is to discourage violations of ethical guidelines by penalties. The second approach consists of prior review of research proposals. Instead of punishing violations after their occurrence, the second approach denies the resources to carry out the proposed research.

Punishing Human Subject Violations

Legal Remedies. Even in the absence of codes for professional researchers and legislation requiring prior review, all citizens enjoy the protection of their lives and liberty to the extent guaranteed by state and federal laws. If a demented social researcher physically pulls you off the street and forces you to serve as a subject in his experiment, you can look to the criminal justice system for your liberation and the punishment of this violation of the kidnapping statutes. More likely to occur are research activities that are subject to civil justice. We have already seen the most famous example of such research—the Tuskegee study—which ultimately concluded with an out-of-court financial settlement of a class action civil suit. The federal government agreed to pay the subjects for the physical and mental stress caused by their participation in the syphilis project. Similarly, every social researcher is liable to lawsuit by human subjects who feel mistreated. Such suits are rare, but their possibility serves as one limit on researchers' misbehavior.

Both criminal and civil law provide two essential ingredients for sanctioning the punishment of investigators. First, a formal and neutral judge or jury determines whether a law has been violated or a personal injury has been caused. Second, a financial or other penalty is levied. However, before this judicial process can operate, a complaint must be filed. As illustrated by the Tuskegee study, making an effective complaint is often difficult or improbable for the least powerful and affluent subjects. In that particular case, civil action was prompted not by the subjects but rather by civil rights activists outraged by the revelation of the study. In less extreme cases of abuse, even well-informed and resourceful subjects may decide that the cost of seeking legal redress exceeds the discomfort or distress caused by their research experience.

Professional Associations. To provide better protection of human subjects and to do so while maximizing the independence of their members, professional associations and universities offer an extralegal (that is, outside the legal system) alternative. All major social research organizations (for example, the American Anthropological Association, American Psychological Association, and American Sociological Association) provide their members with ethical guidelines, violations of which can be challenged not only by the subjects but also by other professionals. Indeed the members of these associations are obliged not only to adhere to their association's standards but also to see that their fellow members adhere to them as well. These organizations and their members can back up their principles in various ways. One potential sanction is the denial of publication in association journals of reports of research based on unethical treatment of human subjects. Sometimes a public reprimand from the association or university will have the desired impact, threatening as it does continued employment and funding. The ultimate sanction that such voluntary organizations can impose is removal from the membership.

The human subject portions of the ethical guidelines of three professional associations are presented to illustrate the similarities and differences across different disciplines (see Tables 2–2, 2–3, and 2–4). The anthropologists' wide use of qualitative research methods leads them to special concern for their key informants and the protection of the general population being studied (often minority or Third World cultures). The psychologists' extensive use of experimental designs explains their special concern with such matters as deception. Psychologists also sometimes use animals in their research, and these subjects are also protected in the American Psychological Association's ethical guidelines (principle 10, not reproduced here). The sociologists' frequent use of archival records and surveys accounts for their emphasis on matters related to confidentiality.

Ideally, such principles as detailed in these tables are to be learned and internalized by students and members of these disciplines. As research is planned, these principles should help identify and eliminate threats to human subjects. Unfortunately, not all members of a discipline are so conscientious, nor are all these principles unambiguous. As a result, quasi-judicial procedures are occasionally necessary to enforce these rules within professional associations.

An example of such a quasi-judicial apparatus in a professional association comes from the American Psychological Association (APA). The Ethics Committee of the APA has the responsibility to review all complaints about members' violations of APA ethics and to report to the membership on trends in these complaints and their adjudication. Such complaints have risen from an average of about 57 per year in the 3 ½ years up to 1980 (Sanders & Keith-Spiegel, 1980) to 88 per year in 1986 and 1987 (Ethics Committee of the American Psychological Association, 1988). Despite its large membership (over 65,000 in 1987), there were no complaints about principle 9 (Research with Human Participants; see Table 2–3) in 1987 and only three complaints involving this principle in the period 1982–1987.

Table 2–2 Human Subject Guidelines of the American Anthropological Association*

Relations With Those Studied

In research, an anthropologist's paramount responsibility is to those he studies. When there is a conflict of interest, these individuals must come first. The anthropologist must do everything within his power to protect their physical, social and psychological welfare and to honor their dignity and privacy.

a. Where research involves the acquisition of material and information transferred on the assumptions of trust between persons, it is axiomatic that the rights, interests, and sensitivities of those studied must be safeguarded.

b. The aims of the investigation should be communicated as well as possible to the informant.

c. Informants have a right to remain anonymous. This right should be respected both where it has been promised explicitly and where no clear understanding to the contrary has been reached. These strictures apply to the collection of data by means of cameras, tape recorders, and other data-gathering devices, as well as to data collected in face-to-face interviews or in participant observation. Those being studied should understand the capacities of such devices, they should be free to reject them if they wish, and if they accept them, the results obtained should be consonant with the informant's right to welfare, dignity and privacy.

   1. Despite every effort being made to preserve anonymity it should be made clear to informants that such anonymity may be compromised unintentionally (November, 1975).

   2. When professionals or others have used pseudonyms to maintain anonymity, others should respect this decision and the reasons for it by not revealing indiscriminately the true identity of such committees, persons or other data (May, 1976).

d. There should be no exploitation of individual informants for personal gain. Fair return should be given them for all services.

e. There is an obligation to reflect on the foreseeable repercussions of research and publication on the general population being studied.

f. The anticipated consequences of research should be communicated as fully as possible to the individuals and groups likely to be affected.

g. In accordance with the Association's general position on clandestine and secret research, no reports should be provided to sponsors that are not available to the general public and, where practicable, to the population studied.

h. Every effort should be exerted to cooperate with members of the host society in the planning and execution of research projects.

i. All of the above points should be acted upon in full recognition of the social and cultural pluralism of host societies and the consequent plurality of values, interests and demands in those societies. This diversity complicates choice-making in research, but ignoring it leads to irresponsible decisions.

*Adopted by the Council of the American Anthropological Association, 1971 (dates of addenda indicated in parentheses).

From *Professional Ethics Statements and Procedures of the American Anthropological Association* (Washington, D.C.: American Anthropological Association, 1973; plus addenda, July 1979).

Table 2–3   Human Subject Guidelines of the American Psychological Association*

Research With Human Participants

The decision to undertake research rests upon a considered judgment by the individual psychologist about how best to contribute to psychological science and human welfare. Having made the decision to conduct research, the psychologist considers alternative directions in which research energies and resources might be invested. On the basis of this consideration, the psychologist carries out the investigation with respect and concern for the dignity and welfare of the people who participate and with cognizance of federal and state regulations and professional standards governing the conduct of research with human participants.

a. In planning a study, the investigator has the responsibility to make a careful evaluation of its ethical acceptability. To the extent that the weighing of scientific and human values suggests a compromise of any principle, the investigator incurs a correspondingly serious obligation to seek ethical advice and to observe stringent safeguards to protect the rights of human participants.

b. Considering whether a participant in a planned study will be a "subject at risk" or a "subject at minimal risk," according to recognized standards, is of primary ethical concern to the investigator.

c. The investigator always retains the responsibility for insuring ethical practice in research. The investigator is also responsible for the ethical treatment of research participants by collaborators, assistants, students, and employees, all of whom, however, incur similar obligations.

d. Except for minimal-risk research, the investigator establishes a clear and fair agreement with the research participants, prior to their participation, that clarifies the obligations and responsibilities of each. The investigator has the obligation to honor all promises and commitments included in that agreement. The investigator informs the participants of all aspects of the research that might reasonably be expected to influence willingness to participate and explains all other aspects of the research about which the participants inquire. Failure to make full disclosure prior to obtaining informed consent requires additional safeguards to protect the welfare and dignity of the research participants. Research with children or with participants who have impairments which would limit understanding and/or communication requires special safeguarding procedures.

e. Methodological requirements of a study may make the use of concealment or deception necessary. Before conducting such a study, the investigator has a special responsibility to: (a) determine whether the use of such techniques is justified by the study's prospective scientific, educational, or applied value; (b) determine whether alternative procedures are available that do not utilize concealment or deception; and (c) ensure that the participants are provided with sufficient explanation as soon as possible.

f. The investigator respects the individual's freedom to decline to participate in or to withdraw from the research at any time. The obligation to protect this freedom requires careful thought and consideration when the investigator is in a position of authority or influence over the participant. Such positions of authority include, but are not limited to, situations in which research participation is required as part of employment or in which the participant is a student, client, or employee of the investigator.

g. The investigator protects the participant from physical and mental discomfort, harm, and danger that may arise from research procedures. If risks of such consequences exist, the investigator informs the participant of that fact. Research procedures likely to

Table 2–3   (Continued).

Research With Human Participants

---

cause serious or lasting harm to a participant are not used unless the failure to use these procedures might expose the participant to risk of greater harm or unless the research has great potential benefit and fully informed and voluntary consent is obtained from each participant. The participant should be informed of procedures for contacting the investigator within a reasonable time period following participation should stress, potential harm, or related questions or concerns arise.

h. After the data are collected, the investigator provides the participant with information about the nature of the study and attempts to remove any misconceptions that may have arisen. Where scientific or humane values justify delaying or withholding information, the investigator incurs a special responsibility to monitor the research and to ensure that there are no damaging consequences for the participant.

i. Where research procedures result in undesirable consequences for the individual participant, the investigator has the responsibility to detect and remove or correct these consequences, including long-term effects.

j. Information obtained about a research participant during the course of an investigation is confidential unless otherwise agreed upon in advance. When the possibility exists that others may obtain access to such information, this possibility, together with the plans for protecting confidentiality, is explained to the participant as part of the procedure for obtaining informed consent.

---

*Principle 9 adopted by the Council of Representatives of the American Psychological Association, 1982.

From Committee for the Protection of Human Participants in Research, *Ethical Principles in the Conduct of Research with Human Participants* (Washington, D.C.: American Psychological Association, 1982), pp. 5–7. Copyright 1982 by the American Psychological Association. Reprinted by permission.

Given the large membership of the APA and the relatively intrusive experimental nature of much of psychological research, this record suggests little need for concern. However, another report based on a large sample ($n = 19,000$) of the membership yielded 5,000 descriptions of problematic human research studies (Ad Hoc Committee on Ethical Standards in Psychological Research,1973), which were used in formulating the present APA guidelines. The quantity and seriousness of many of these descriptions suggest that the adjudication procedure fails to hear many grave violations. One reason may be the reluctance of psychologists to report fellow psychologists for ethics violations; the percentage of complaints to the APA filed by psychologists fell from 32 percent in 1983 to 18 percent in 1987 (Ethics Committee of the American Psychological Association, 1988). Alternatively, it may be that research infractions common in the past are now being prevented.

Preventing Human Subject Violations

Federal Requirement of Prior Review.   Because of the apparent inability of the existing legal system and professional organizations to stop human subject violations, the federal government passed legislation to prevent research with

Table 2–4 Human Subject Guidelines of the American Sociological Association*

Respect For The Rights Of Research Populations

1. Individuals, families, households, kin and friendship groups that are subjects of research are entitled to rights of biographical anonymity. Organizations, large collectives such as neighborhoods, ethnic groups, or religious denominations, corporations, governments, public agencies, public officials, persons in the public eye, are not entitled automatically to privacy and need not be extended routinely guarantees of privacy and confidentiality. However, if any guarantees are made, they must be honored unless there are clear and compelling reasons not to do so.
2. Information about persons obtained from records that are open to public scrutiny cannot be protected by guarantees of privacy or confidentiality.
3. The process of conducting sociological research must not expose subjects to *substantial risk* or personal harm. Where modest risk or harm is anticipated, informed consent must be obtained.
4. To the extent possible in a given study, researchers should anticipate potential threats to confidentiality. Such means as the removal of identifiers, the use of randomized responses, and other statistical solutions to problems of privacy should be used where appropriate.
5. Confidential information provided by research participants must be treated as such by sociologists, even when this information enjoys no legal protection or privilege and legal force is applied. The obligation to respect confidentiality also applies to members of research organizations (interviewers, coders, clerical staff, etc.) who have access to the information. It is the responsibility of the chief investigator to instruct staff members on this point.

*Approved by the Council of the American Sociological Association, 1981.

From "Revised Code of Ethics," *Footnotes, 10*, no. 3 (1982), 10.

questionable practices. Since the federal government provides a large share of the funds for the conduct of social research, it can mandate guidelines for the protection of human subjects that will directly or indirectly influence most research. The federal regulations require that each institution that sponsors any research funded by the Department of Health and Human Services must establish local review committees to screen proposals. Even if a researcher could operate without federal funding, he or she usually still needs the permission of an institution to use its facilities, subject pool, and graduate assistants.

In 1974 the National Research Act was passed, leading to the establishment of the National Commission on the Protection of Human Subjects of Biomedical and Behavioral Research. Its recommendations in 1978 led the Department of Health and Human Services to issue final regulations in 1981.

Institutional Review Boards. In 1981, the current federal regulations were published in the *Federal Register*. These guidelines define the types of prior review minimally required of **institutional review boards (IRBs)**. Although mandatory only for projects with or seeking Department of Health and Human Services funds, these guidelines are customarily applied to all research at each institution. As part of the agreement, the institution is required to reveal how it will review nonfederally funded research. Voluntary agreement to apply the federal guidelines to nonfederally funded research is viewed favorably as an indicator of the institution's commitment to the protection of human subjects.

Human research proposals submitted for approval under the present federal guidelines fall into three categories: exempt, expedited, and full review. The first category, **exempt**, includes no or very low risk as judged by the investigators and applies to research not requiring formal review by the IRB. A researcher with a proposal that he or she judges to fall in the exempt category need only file an Exempt Registration Form with the the IRB showing evidence that the proposed research has been reviewed by the researcher's department chair or dean. To guide researchers, five characteristics of exempt proposals are identified by the government:

1. Research on "normal educational practices"
2. Use of "educational tests" if subjects can not be identified
3. Survey research except that in which all of the following are present:
   a. Subjects can be identified
   b. Subjects' responses could harm them legally or financially
   c. Topics are sensitive (for example, drug use, illegal or sexual behavior)
4. Observation of public behavior, including that by participants, except that in which all of the three above conditions are present (that is, 3a, b, and c)
5. Study of existing data if the data are publicly available or if subjects cannot be identified

The option of researchers to exempt their own research from review has raised some misgivings in those who desire maximum federal protection of human subjects (for example, Veatch, 1981). In contrast, others have noted some types of nonexempt research that they feel should have been exempted (see Thompson, Chodosh, Fried, Goodman, Wax, & Wilson, 1981). Finally, remember that the federal procedures define a minimum foundation of protection on which individual institutions and IRBs can erect higher standards.

If no exemption is claimed, the research proposal must be reviewed in some fashion by the IRB. **Full review** involves a formal evaluation by the entire IRB (or a quorum thereof). A speedier form of review is called **expedited review,** which is conducted by a single experienced member of the IRB (for example, its chairperson). Expedited review is judged suitable if the research method is considered to be of relatively low risk. The federal guidelines defining such low-risk methods pertain mainly to biomedical techniques (for example, collecting hair, nail clippings, sweat, small amounts of blood, and dental plaque). Social research techniques considered low risk for expedited review include noninvasive physiological recordings of adults (for example, testing sensory acuity); voice recordings; the use of existing documents; and nonstressful studies of group behavior, perception, and cognition.

Full review is required for those proposals judged not to fall in the exempt or expedited categories. In full review, the committee considers the risks and benefits of the proposed study (both to ensure no excessive risk of harm and to weigh the relationship of benefit to harm in the utilitarian sense), the adequacy of the informed consent procedure, and the protection of the subjects' identity where appropriate. Of special concern to the IRB is whether the subjects are capable of giving informed consent (for example, children and mentally disabled subjects) and whether there is any risk of coercion (for example, students or prisoners in a dependent relationship to the investigator).

Informed Consent. The key element in granting approval for research is often the matter of **informed consent.** Where the investigator can obtain such prior consent, the standards for the procedure are quite clear. Ordinarily, investigators are expected to provide the prospective subject with written information about the study and a waiver form to be signed by the subject. An example of such a consent form for exempt research appears in Table 2–5(a). The kind of information to be provided as the basis for this waiver request is detailed in Table 2–5(b). This information should cover the study's purpose and duration, subject identification or confidentiality procedures, risks and benefits, whom to contact for further details, and a statement that the participation is voluntary with no penalty for stopping at any time. After reading this information, the subjects are ordinarily asked to indicate their consent to participate in writing. This written consent does not waive any of the subjects' legal rights or release the researcher from liability for negligence in the research project.

Federal regulations recognize the right of IRBs to waive the requirements for written informed consent. Such waivers are given reluctantly and only for very good reason. Informed consent may be waived when the research cannot be carried out without the waiver. For example, experimental studies requiring deception would not be possible if the subjects were told of the deception in advance. Qualitative studies in which the participant-observer can gain entry only incognito would also be eliminated by prior informed consent. The IRB will grant such waivers only if the risk to the subjects is determined to be minimal and warranted by the benefits expected to be gained from the study. Usually, the researcher, in exchange for the waiver of prior consent, must provide full information to the subjects in the debriefing stage of the study.

The IRB's deliberations take place in the context of continuing debate between those who oppose deceptive experimental procedures on principle (Baumrind, 1985) and those who have found significant effects of such ethical requirements on research outcomes (Trice, 1987). Not surprisingly, IRB decisions have been shown to vary in response to the social sensitivity of the research topic. In one survey, IRBs were more likely to reject proposals (which were otherwise identical) dealing with socially sensitive issues such as racial or sexual discrimination (Ceci, Peters, & Plotkin, 1985). For further discussion of ethically problem-

Table 2–5(a) University of California Irvine Consent to Act as a Human Research Subject*

TITLE OF STUDY

NAME, DEPARTMENT AND TELEPHONE NUMBER OF INVESTIGATOR

You have been asked to participate in a research study which is exempt from review by a Human Subjects Review Committee. The purpose of this study, the terms of your participation, as well as any expected risks and/or benefits must be fully explained to you before you sign this form and give your consent to participate.
You should also know that:

1. Participation in research is entirely voluntary. You may refuse to participate or withdraw from participation at any time without jeopardy to future medical care, educational or employment status or other entitlement. The investigator may withdraw you from participation at his/her professional discretion.
2. If, during the course of this study, significant new information which has been developed during the course of the study becomes available which may relate to your willingness to continue to participate, this information will be provided to you by the investigator.
3. Confidentiality will be protected to the extent provided by law.
4. If at any time you have questions regarding the research or your participation, you should contact the investigator or his/her assistants who must answer the questions.
5. If, at any time, you have comments or complaints relating to the conduct of this research, you may contact the Human Subjects Committees Office, 145 Administration Building, University of California Irvine, Irvine, CA. 92717.
6. If this study is a medical investigation/experiment, you must also read and be given a copy of the Experimental Subjects Bill of Rights as well as a copy of this consent form to keep.

I consent to participate in this study.

SIGNATURE OF SUBJECT (Age 7 and older)   DATE

SIGNATURE OF PARENT/GUARDIAN (For Minor Subject—All persons under age 18)   DATE

SIGNATURE OF WITNESS (Optional)   DATE

Rev. 8/82

---

*Human Subjects Review Committee, University of California, Irvine.

Table 2–5(b) *UCI - Human Subjects Review Committee-General Campus Guide for Preparation of Written Informed Consent* *

The following information *must* be included in all written consent forms at UCI. Sections with an asterisk * are to be copied exactly as they appear below. Headings should follow the format as follows:

University of California Irvine
Title of Study
Name(s) of Investigator(s)
Investigator(s) Academic Unit(s) & Telephone Number(s)
Consent to Act as a Human Research Subject

Name of Subject	_____
Purpose of the Study	(Briefly state what the study is trying to discover)
Procedures & Duration	(Explain what the subject's participation consists of: completing questionnaire, being interviewed, etc. Include duration of participation: 1 hour, "X" time on several occasions, etc.)
Risks	(List any expected risks including physical, psychological, social, legal. Include any discomforts or inconveniences expected.)
Benefits	(Indicate any possible benefit(s) to the subject or to society or science.)
Compensation	(If the subject is to be compensated for participation (money, course credit), indicate amount, terms (e.g. does the subject have to complete the experiment to earn the compensation.)

*Confidentiality will be protected to the extent provided by law. If at any time you have questions regarding the research or your participation, you should contact the investigator or his/her assistants who must answer the questions.

*Participation in research is entirely voluntary. You may refuse to participate or withdraw from participation at any time without jeopardy to employment, educational or other entitlements.

*If at any time you have comments or complaints relating to the conduct of this research, you may contact the Human Subjects Committee's Office, 145 Administration Building, UC Irvine, Irvine, CA 92717.

I consent to participate in this study.

SIGNATURE OF SUBJECT (Age 7 and older)   DATE

SIGNATURE OF PARENT/GUARDIAN   DATE

*Children age 7 and older must sign the consent form, *assenting* to participation. Parent or guardian must sign, giving *legal consent*.

Additional signature lines may be added at the discretion of the investigator.

If non-English speaking subjects are to be included, call x 7114 for instructions for translation of consent forms.   9/82

---

*Human Subjects Review Committee, University of California, Irvine.

atic research that an IRB might evaluate, see the analytic strategy of Reynolds (1979, 1982).

OTHER ETHICAL CONFLICTS IN RESEARCH

The concern for the human subject in both legal procedures and professional associations' codes should not obscure several other important ethical dilemmas (for an overview of the variety of ethical issues that arise in socially sensitive research see Sieber & Stanley, 1988). Conflicts involving other figures in the research enterprise have stimulated additional guidelines. In some cases, these guidelines have been clearly established with little controversy. For other conflicts, the articulation of guidelines will be a continuing topic of public and professional debate.

The source of the ethical conflicts in research is the variety of players and their divergent self-interests and values. The major players include the investigator, the subject, the funder, and the society as a consumer of research. Other parties also figure in the process of science, including the professional associations, the research institutions such as universities, and the government in its regulatory role. The distinctions among these parties are not always clear cut since one may play two or more parts—for example, the government as funder, as consumer of research products, as regulator, and as investigator (as when it collects census data).

Each of these players can be expected to have different priorities. Since these priorities sometimes collide, ethical problems can arise between any two parties in the research enterprise. Competing interests from two or more directions seek to achieve their aims at the expense of the other parties involved.

Researcher Versus Researcher

Plagiarism.   As the first example of ethical conflict, consider perhaps the least controversial. Virtually all professional associations prohibit **plagiarism,** and the copyright laws provide additional remedies for stealing another author's published writing. Unfortunately, the explosive increase in scientific journals makes it difficult to catch plagiarized work, especially when published in obscure journals. One plagiarist actually published dozens of articles before being caught (the Algabti case, described in Broad & Wade, 1982).

Most plagiarism disputes are less clear-cut than using another's published work without permission. The faculty member who puts his or her name on a student's work illustrates how unpublished research can be "stolen" before the publication stage. In an era of large-scale team research, disputes can easily arise about authorship and the allocation of credit for creative contributions. Such disputes, unless prevented by agreements in the early stages of collaboration, can and do produce long-lasting hostility.

Research Peer Review. In contrast to the clarity of the rules against plagiarism, the ethical codes are less clear on another potential conflict between researchers. In employment and promotion decisions, in review of papers submitted for publication, and in grants of research funds, researchers are usually judged by their peers on the merits of their research. These decisions can govern which research reports will be published widely or not at all and which proposals will be funded or never carried out. Obviously, fairness and objectivity are vital requirements for such peer review procedures. The perception that the peer review mechanism is being abused could produce both interpersonal conflict and serious concern that the substantive direction of future research will be distorted if decisions favor certain types of research proposals and research careers over others.

The principal protection in the peer review process is the use of multiple reviewers. But whereas lawbreakers usually have the protection of 12-member juries, professional researchers are often judged by as few as two to five peers. Research on the peer review process in awarding grants has cast serious doubt on its reliability. Cole and colleagues had 150 National Science Foundation proposals reevaluated. They concluded that "the fate of a particular grant application is roughly half determined by the characteristics of the proposal and the principal investigator, and about half by apparently random elements which might be characterized as the 'luck of the reviewer draw'" (Cole, Cole, & Simon, 1981, p. 885). Similarly, research on peer review of manuscripts submitted for publication suggests low levels of reliability (Cicchetti, 1980) and only modest relationships between peer judgments of quality and later citation (Gottfredson, 1978). However, protection against sex, ethnic, or personal bias in manuscript review is offered by "blind" review techniques employed by many of the best journals.

Funder Versus Researcher

Fraud. As unpleasant and embarrassing as it is, scientists have had to admit that their colleagues sometimes engage in fraud. Of concern here is not financial fraud, looting the research grant to buy expensive cars and vacations, although perhaps that exists as well. The motivations to falsify data are subject to speculation, but the pressure to gain career success through publication is most often mentioned. The impact of such fraud can reach all the way to socially significant public policy.

Cases of documented fraud are rare historically but appear to be on the increase (see Broad & Wade's 1982 summary of 34 cases). In the 1970s and early 1980s, a rash of fraudulent research scandals broke in the biomedical sciences. In a recent case, a promising young cardiologist compressed a two-week experiment into a few hours. Suspiciously, he "got picture-perfect results, numbers so close to each other that their variability was 'too small to be real' [but] under scrutiny, he produced measurements that better reflected the imprecision normal for science, with numbers scattered around some average" (Begley, Malamud, & Hager, 1982,

p. 90). This case precipitated a blue-ribbon committee review of all of the cardiologist's published work (nearly 100 papers) and recommendations to prevent the reoccurrence of such incidents. These recommendations included both lessening the publication pressure ("to encourage the evaluation of young scientists on the basis of quality rather than numbers of publications") and better scrutiny of the primary data by other scientists (Broad, 1982).

Such fraud crops up in the social sciences as well, as evidenced by Sir Cyril Burt's falsification of test data (discussed in Chapter 1). However, Burt's is not the only such example and may underscore a general need to validate research by replication (Samelson, 1980). Recently, the National Institute of Mental Health (NIMH) reviewed the work of a young psychologist it had funded. This researcher had studied the effects of psychoactive drugs on the mentally retarded, and his recommendations had influenced treatment practices in some states. However, it was found that "only a few of the experimental subjects described in [some of the investigator's] publications and progress reports were ever studied." (Hostetler, 1987, p.12, quoting an NIMH draft report). Interestingly, some of the questionable reports were coauthored by respected researchers who, despite little or no involvement in the research, lent their names to the reports or whose names were added without their permission. The NIMH investigating panel recommended that this researcher be barred from additional NIMH funding for ten years and that the case be handed over to the Department of Justice, which subsequently indicted the researcher, the first such indictment in federal court. In a subsequent plea bargain, the researcher pleaded guilty, becoming subject to a maximum penalty of ten years in prison and $20,000 in fines; his institution had already reimbursed the funder more than $163,000, used by the researcher while he was there (Bales, 1988). What may never be known is the extent of harm done to thousands of retarded patients whose treatment was guided by these fraudulent findings.

Waste. Fraud can be thought of as a special case of waste in that the funder's resources have been squandered without the return of valid results. Another kind of waste can be alleged even when no fraud is involved. An instance of this conflict between funder and researcher is the Hutchinson versus Proxmire case (Kiesler & Lowman, 1980). Senator Proxmire, as part of his campaign to save taxpayers' money from being wasted on trivial research, publicized extreme cases of such waste with his Golden Fleece Award. One of various social and other scientists given this embarrassing award was Ronald Hutchinson in 1975 for his work on aggression in monkeys. Proxmire took credit for stopping Hutchinson's federal funding, and Hutchinson sued Proxmire. After the Supreme Court ruled in favor of Hutchinson's claim that he was not a public figure subject to Proxmire's public ridicule and remanded the suit back to a lower court for settlement, Proxmire settled out of court in 1980 for a public apology and $ 10,000.

Although Hutchinson may have won the battle, Proxmire may have won the war. The chilling effect of public ridicule and the power of legislators to restrict public research funds almost certainly will have an impact on what researchers can explore with public support.

No professional association's ethical guidelines define what is "significant" social research. Presumably, individual professionals are free, as they historically have been, to pursue their curiosity. Indeed, an honored intellectual tradition supports pure or basic research for its own sake regardless of its potential applicability. On the other hand, the taxpayers' representatives have an obligation to spend scarce public funds wisely.

The allocation of public funds to social and other research must, therefore, take into account the welfare of the entire society and not just the unbridled curiosity of researchers. But how should the conflict between the researcher's interests and the social interest be resolved? The researcher could make the claim that it is shortsighted to limit support to applied research. Since applied research is built on a foundation of theory and pure research, it will be weakened in the future if the funders stifle the curiosity of the pure researchers now. On the other hand, it is possible that there are misallocations of research funding because of certain societal arrangements and that we must explore these causes and think carefully about reordering our funding priorities (see Boulding, 1966, pp. 109–114).

But if the politicians guard us from trivial research, who guards against politicians awarding research grants in their political interest? When government research funds are awarded by peer review (fellow scientists) there is no guarantee that funds will be distributed evenly across congressional districts. Increasingly, federal research grants, especially for large projects, are being treated as pork-barrel opportunities to provide jobs in home states and districts (Clifford, 1987). In one publicized instance, a Massachusetts politician took credit for getting a $7.7 million research center for his home district over the recommendations of a technical review panel that favored another bidder, whose proposal would have cost the taxpayers $3.2 million less (Cordes, 1984).

Society (Public Interest) Versus Funder (Private Interest)

It is a truism that science is a part of and a reflection of society. Science is an institution that wittingly or not carries out the values of the society, or at least that part of society from which scientists come (for a sampling of perspectives in the sociology of science, see Barber & Hirsch, 1962).

That scientists see reality through the blinders of the society's values is a source of concern for those who want science to understand society in order to make it better. Human sciences, which seek data within the political and economic status quo, will necessarily be irrelevant, it is argued, for purposes of seeing beyond the status quo to a different future (Sarason, 1981).

Private Interests. In a complex and pluralistic society, it is inaccurate to think of a single homogeneous value set from which everyone approaches political and social problems. Rather, there are numerous competing private interests. The central government reflects those private interests that were on the winning side of the last election or coup. Thus, certain kinds of research funded in one administration may be eliminated by the next administration. For a not too imaginary example, consider research on psychological persuasion techniques as they might be studied in the birth control and abortion areas. Given the intense controversy about abortion, we would expect that public support for funding in this area would fluctuate with the political tides.

A more clear-cut type of private interest is the private firm that can sponsor research to serve its own ends. For example, a tobacco firm may decide to fund social research on public attitudes toward prohibition of smoking (for example, to defeat referenda to outlaw smoking in restaurants and other public places). Naturally, the funder has a vested interest in promoting results and techniques that would maximize profits by minimizing the adoption of such legislation. What effect does this natural self-interest have on the researcher's effort? To what extent should such privately employed researchers concern themselves with the "public interest"?

In recognition of this potential conflict, professional associations have provided guidelines regarding the recognition of research sponsorship. For example, the Revised Code of Ethics of the American Sociological Association calls for identification of all sources of research support or special relationships with sponsors. Moreover, the code says sociologists "must not accept grants, contracts, or research assignments that appear likely to require violation" of the principles of objectivity and integrity (American Sociological Association, 1982, principle I.A.7).

In recent years, universities have begun to add force to such requirements. Scientists are beginning to be required to report their associations with private industry and their funding from nonpublic sources. Such reporting will permit an assessment of possible conflict of interest, and local review boards can provide peer review and guidance in questionable cases.

Public Interest.   Although conflicts involving special interests may seem clear enough, the identification of the public interest appears much more difficult. What if the public interest of the nation supported social research that was, arguably, unethical? The most notorious example of this sort of dilemma was Project Camelot (Horowitz, 1973), a project intended to gauge the causes and forecast the occurrence of revolutions in the Third World. Supported by the U.S. military, it was supposed to provide techniques for avoiding or coping with revolutions. Survey and other methods were to be used in various developing countries after Camelot's conception in 1963.

The uproar over Camelot ignited in Chile. A Chilean sociology professor challenged the military implications of the project. The left-wing Chilean press and the Chilean senate viewed Camelot as espionage. This criticism resulted in U.S. Congressional hearings and the termination of Camelot by the Defense Department in August 1965.

With respect to such research projects as Camelot, Beals (1969) asks "whether social science should be the handmaiden of government or strive for freedom and autonomy" (p. 16). Since the "true" public interest may be in the eye of the beholder, a resolution of this matter will not be simple. Given the increasing importance of science in public policy and social welfare, scientists bear an increasing responsibility to consider the consequences of their work. Just how to anticipate the long-run consequences and how to weight the potentially different effects on different segments of society (for example, poor versus rich within a society or First World versus Third World nations) have not been worked out in any laws or professional codes. Perhaps for that reason, the movement of "public interest science" will continue as an educational and consciousness-raising force before it can be formulated by consensus (see Nelkin, 1979, for a review of the emergence of the public interest science movement).

SUMMARY

With the advent of large-scale, institutionalized social research came the increased risk of conflicts between different parties in the scientific enterprise. The most notorious examples of such conflict have been the abuse of human subjects, as in the Nazi medical experiments and the Tuskegee Syphilis Study. These scandals were not the only ethical violations in recent human research, but their publicity helped focus public and professional attention on the emerging problems of guiding research conduct.

Since philosophers of ethics have not been able to derive universal principles, the regulation of research conduct has been handled in political and professional institutions. Professional associations have attempted to preserve the autonomy of their members by helping them conform to ethical codes without external help. Criminal and civil legal procedures are also, in principle, available to protect human subjects and other parties in the research process.

However, these legal and professional procedures provide for punishment only after the fact and for only the relatively small proportion of ethical violations brought up for review. To guarantee more systematic and preventive protection of human subjects, the government now requires prior institutional review of research proposals. Under the jurisdiction of institutional review boards (IRBs), researchers must provide in their proposals for informed consent by their subjects and minimization or avoidance of risk to the subjects. Although informed consent can be waived, such waivers must be justified, and the protection of the unwitting subjects must be assured.

Besides the conflict between researcher and subject, other conflicts were noted, such as those between researchers, between funder and researcher, and between private interests and the public interest. In some cases, ethical codes already address these conflicts, as in the nearly universal prohibition against fraud and plagiarism. In other cases, ethical guidance is not so well articulated. We can expect continuing political and professional debate about some of these matters (for example, allocation of research resources in the public interest).

EXERCISES

1. Select a social research study with which you are familiar, such as one described in this text. Review this study from the standpoint of its protection of subjects. Identify any potential problem such as deception, risk of physical or mental stress, and protection of confidentiality. Judge the adequacy of the protection of the subjects and suggest any changes that would have improved this protection without damaging the research procedure.

2. Locate the IRB on your campus and obtain a copy of its application form. Sketch out an imaginary research proposal, preferably one with the potential for human subject violations (many examples of which can be found in the report of the Ad Hoc Committee on Ethical Standards in Psychological Research, 1973). Based on this proposal, fill out the IRB's application as though you were actively planning to conduct the research. Determine if your proposal would fall in the exempt, expedited, or full review category. If applicable, develop an informed consent form complete with description for briefing your prospective subjects and for soliciting their written consent. By the standards of your IRB and of relevant professional association codes, would your proposal be found acceptable in its treatment of human subjects?

3. Try to locate a research conflict, other than the protection of human subjects, that appeared recently in your local media (for example, a politician criticizing a researcher's work as trivial, a case of fraud or plagiarism, or concern about researchers concealing their support from private interests). Identify the parties to the conflict and how their interests are at stake (that is, what they hope to gain and what they risk losing). What laws, professional codes, or everyday moral principles, if any, apply to the conflict? What was the outcome of the conflict and was it a desirable outcome in your view? Be sure to spell out your judgment in terms of relative costs and benefits. If it was an undesirable outcome, what could be done to make sure the outcome is more satisfactory in future cases?

GLOSSARY

Ethics: Branch of philosophy that pertains to the study of right and wrong conduct.

Exempt: Category of IRB review in which the investigator judges the research to be of low risk and therefore exempt from further review except for clearance by an appointed administrator (for example, the chair of the investigator's academic department).

Expedited review: Category of IRB review in which the research is judged to be of sufficiently low risk that review can be hastened by assessment by one member of the IRB.

Full review: Category of IRB review in which the research proposal is analyzed by the entire committee.

Informed consent: Key element in human subject protection, usually required for IRB approval. The subject must be given adequate information and be able (that is, not a child, not mentally incompetent, and not coerced) to give voluntary written consent before participating.

Institutional Review Boards (IRBs): Committees established by U.S. federal regulations at each research institution to protect human subjects from abuses through prior review of research proposals.

Nuremberg Code: Statement of ethical guidelines for human research produced for the Nuremberg Military Tribunal, which judged war crimes after World War II.

Plagiarism: Falsely claiming credit for work authored by another.

Utilitarianism: Ethical approach that seeks a rational balance of costs and benefits of behaviors.

3

Finding and Interpreting Research Reports

Library Usage and Report Style

USING THE LIBRARY

When you attend class, where do you sit? If you arrive late to a crowded classroom, perhaps you have little choice. Or perhaps you give it no thought and sit wherever your friends sit. But is it possible that where you sit has an effect on how much you learn and how good a grade you receive?

Finding the answer to this question will illustrate some of the resources available to you in getting research information. The first part of this chapter deals with locating sources of information—finding relevant books and journals. This information search will be illustrated by a quest for an answer to the question just posed. The second part of the chapter presents a brief but complete journal article on the classroom seating question. This article both illustrates the typical format of a journal article and provides practice in interpreting such professional publications.

Catalogs for Finding Books

Although some libraries retain their traditional card catalogs, many college and university libraries have computerized their holdings. One benefit of such **online** electronic filing systems is that they can cost-effectively catalog very large libraries. This is especially important when a library's holdings are spread throughout different branches. For example, you may do most of your studying in the general library, but you would like to know that your campus is holding a needed book in the medical library. Large universities with several campuses may avoid duplicate collections on each campus. By using an online catalog for the entire system, you can identify the location of a needed book on a sister campus, and you may be able to acquire it by interlibrary loan in a matter of days.

Another advantage of many online library catalogs is that they can be accessed at all times (even when the library is closed) from remote computers, such as personal computers located in laboratories, homes, or dormitories. All that is needed is a **modem**, a device for linking your personal computer by telephone line to the host computer.

Such electronic file systems vary from college to college in the details of their use. Fortunately, their logic is more or less standard, making it possible to illustrate the general approach with any representative system. One of the the largest computer catalogs for college libraries is the MELVYL[1] system used throughout the nine campuses of the University of California (whose holdings are second only to the Library of Congress). The MELVYL catalog is similar to traditional card catalogs, in which holdings are entered alphabetically by each of several different indexes—author, title, and subject. Usually, the listings of an online catalog contain books added to the library since a certain date (for example, since 1977 for MELVYL). If you are unsuccessful in finding the book you want with the online catalog, you should consult the card catalog in case the desired reference was acquired earlier.

   If You Know Author or Title.   It is easy to find a book if you know its author or title. You might get the name of a likely author from a professor or a likely book title from the reference list in a textbook. The first step is to make a connection with the library's computer ("logged on" in computer jargon), a procedure that varies from system to system. The computer signals that it is ready for your use by giving you a particular kind of symbol, called a **prompt,** which also varies from system to system. You can then ask the computer about its holdings by following a simple procedure.

   The library's computer terminal is programmed to understand your request if you express it in a standard format. Typically, this format will include three components: a command, an index, and the key word(s) for which you are searching. If you are trying to find a book, your **command** will be "to find." In MELVYL, for example, you would type FIND (or F) to indicate that you wanted a search. Depending on whether you have the author's name or the title, you would then tell the computer to search under the appropriate **index**, that is, by author or title. This method is similar to the use of a card catalog in which separate file cabinets keep cards organized by author and/or by title. In MELVYL you could type PA, short for personal author (CA would stand for corporate or multiple authorship), or TW for title in the space for the index. There are other index terms that could be used, but these will serve to illustrate the general approach. The **key words** consist of the author's name or the book's title, depending on which index you are using. The computer can also be told to combine indexes by using what are called **Boolean operators**, which are logical connections that can be used to restrict or increase the search possibilities. For example, the operator "and" joining an author's name and some title words would narrow the search to those books that have both the indicated author and the indicated title. Other works by the same author would be ignored in the search.

   Suppose you wanted to find whether a copy of this text is available in your library. If you are using an electronic catalog that works like MELVYL, you could type any of the following statements after the prompt arrow:

```
F PA DOOLEY, DAVID <RETURN>
F PA DAVID DOOLEY <RETURN>
F TW SOCIAL RESEARCH METHODS <RETURN>
F PA DOOLEY, DAVID AND TW SOCIAL RESEARCH METHODS
<RETURN>
```

   To signal that you have completed your search instruction, you typically press the RETURN or ENTER key, usually represented in text by <RETURN> or <ENTER> The computer will then report whether it found any books with the indicated author or title. If it does, you can then ask for more detailed information by typing the DISPLAY command D.

If You Do Not Know Author or Title.   Perhaps you have no knowledge of the authors or titles related to your interest. In this case, you would use the same procedure, except that instead of the author or title index, you would use the index for subject, or SU in the search instruction. In this case, the key word or words depend on the topic you are exploring. To take the example from the beginning of the chapter, suppose you wanted to find out about the effects of classroom seating on grades. You could try inputting related terms following the command and index terms FIND SUBJECT (F SU), followed by the key words for the search.

If you try this method, you may find that the computer does not recognize your key words because most online catalogs use a **controlled vocabulary**. That is, to limit and make manageable the number of terms under which a subject could be filed, only certain officially designated synonyms are used. How do you know which terms are used and which are not? Typically, a standard terminology for subject headings is used. One such standard is the *Library of Congress Subject Headings* (Library of Congress,1986), which can be used with the MELVYL system. Whichever standard is used, you should be able to find copies of it conveniently close to the card or computer terminal catalog. Simply look up the terms that you have thought of and see whether they are acceptable search terms or whether alternative synonyms would be better. Such controlled terms as *classroom environment*, *spatial behavior*, *marking*, and *personal space* all appear in the *Library of Congress Subject Headings* and appear relevant to our question about the effect of seating location on grades.

Thus, we could use the following MELVYL command:

F SU CLASSROOM ENVIRONMENT <RETURN>

to locate any books on the subject of classroom environment. When this command was actually used, 31 different books were found in all of the University of California libraries (see the following reproduction of the terminal display):

→F SU CLASSROOM ENVIRONMENT

Search request: F SU CLASSROOM ENVIRONMENT
Search result: 8 records at Irvine
**   31 records at all libraries**

Type D to display results, or type HELP.

In the display (alphabetical by author) of these 31 titles, the seventh one, located in the library of the Santa Barbara campus (UCSB), appeared most pertinent:

7. Dicks, Robert Henry, 1946-
**   An investigation of the relationship between classroom distance**

and student outcomes / by Robert Henry Dicks. 1980.
UCSB Library   LB1084 .D534 1980

For a more detailed description, a long display of the Dicks book was requested:

→**D LONG AT ALL**
Search request: F PA DICKS, ROBERT HENRY
Search result: 1 record at UC libraries
1 record at all libraries
Type HELP for other display options.

1.
Author: Dicks, Robert Henry, 1946-
Title: An investigation of the relationship between classroom
distance and student outcomes / by Robert Henry Dicks. 1980.
xii, 158 leaves, bound : ill. ; 28 cm.

Notes: Vita.
Thesis (Ph.D.)—University of California, Santa Barbara, 1980.
Bibliography: leaves 131–138.
Typescript (photocopy)
Subjects: University of California, Santa Barbara—
Dissertations—
Education.
Interaction analysis in education.
Classroom environment.
Educational psychology.
School children—California—Santa Barbara County—
Psychology—Case studies.

Call numbers: UCSB Library   LB1084 .D534 1980

The last listing, **call numbers,** can be used to locate this particular volume on the shelves of the library at Santa Barbara. Although this PhD dissertation appears interesting, the descriptive terms in the longer display indicate that it deals with a population of schoolchildren rather than college students. In fact, the results of this and other searches using relevant terms turned up no book addressed to the particular question of seating location and grades in the college classroom.

Indexing and Abstracting Services for Journal Articles

Library catalogs can help you find volumes such as books, dissertations, or bound journals, but they cannot locate particular articles published in journals. Sometimes your question can best be answered by an article in a recent journal issue. There are numerous ways of accessing the periodical literature. Some of these tools simply index the literature, that is, provide minimal information such as author, title, journal reference, and perhaps some key words about the subject of the article. Other services go further and provide an abstract or summary of the article to help you decide whether it fits your needs.

Such indexing and abstracting services have been developed for different disciplines, for example, *Psychological Abstracts, Current Index to Journals in Education, Sociological Abstracts,* and *Index Medicus* (for a more detailed discussion of these and related services, see Reed & Baxter, 1983).

Using Psychological Abstracts. In the following sections, the use of one such periodical service will be illustrated—*Psychological Abstracts.* The details of using indexes and abstracts vary from service to service, but the procedure of *Psychological Abstracts* is representative. Moreover, this service covers hundreds of periodicals in the social sciences in many different languages from many different countries with, of course, special emphasis on psychological topics.

The *Psychological Abstracts* are kept in three media: as printed publications; as part of the online database called PsycINFO; and in the form of compact digital discs (CD-ROM) in the database called PsycLIT, readable on personal computers. The printed version is both widely available and free to library patrons and will be discussed first. There are three steps in finding an article's abstract in the printed version of *Psychological Abstracts*: (1) finding the key word or words in the controlled vocabulary or thesaurus; (2) finding an article's reference number in a monthly or seminannual subject index, and (3) finding the actual **abstract** in *Psychological Abstracts.* If you know the author's name and the year of publication, you can skip the first step and go directly to the author's index, which corresponds to the subject index and volume of abstracts.

The controlled vocabulary of the *Psychological Abstracts* is presented in the *Thesaurus of Psychological Index Terms* (American Psychological Association, 1988). We already have reason to suspect (from the library search based on the *Library of Congress Subject Headings*) that a likely key word for studies of seating and grades is *classroom environment.* Indeed, that term is found as an acceptable search word in the thesaurus, as seen in Figure 3–1(a).

The superscript *73* indicates the year in which this term was first included in this index system. *PN* refers to posting note, which is the number of occurrences of this term to date, and *SC* is the five-digit subject code. *SN* refers to the scope note, or definition of the term, which clearly includes the kinds of topics for which we are searching. *B* and *R* refer to broader and related terms respectively, which might be useful in considering alternative descriptors.

Having confirmed that *classroom environment* is an appropriate search term, we can now take the second step by turning to a subject index for *Psychological Abstracts. Psychological Abstracts* is published monthly, and each issue includes a brief subject index for the material abstracted in that issue. Every six months, a cumulative volume index is compiled and published. For purposes of this illustration, suppose we look up *classroom environment* in the index for the July-December 1981 volume. There are two references to classroom seating, outcomes, and college students (2143 and 6707); see Figure 3.1 (b) for 6707.

The third and final step consists of looking up the indicated abstract numbers in the appropriate volume, in this case, volume 66 of *Psychological*

Classroom Environment [73]
PN 1396   SC 09430
SN Physical, social, emotional, psychological, or
intellectual characteristics of a classroom, espe-
cially as they contribute to the learning process.
Includes classroom climate and class size.
   B   Academic Environment [73]
       Environment [67]
       Social Environments [73]
   R   Classroom Behavior [73]
       Classrooms [67]
       School Environment [73]

(a)

classroom seating position, grades & participation, college students,   pre
6707   tec

(b)

6707. **Levine, Douglas W.; O'Neal, Edgar C.; Garwood, S.
Gray & McDonald, Peter J.** (U California, Program in Social
Ecology, Irvine) **Classroom ecology: The effects of seating
position on grades and participation.** *Personality & Social
Psychology Bulletin,* 1980(Sep), Vol 6(3), 409–412. —Conducted
a 2 phase study to examine the effects of classroom seating
position on test scores and participation. When 209 undergraduates selected their seats (Phase 1), those in the front performed
better on the exam than did those in the rear. There was no
effect of proximity on participation. When Ss were randomly
assigned to seats (Phase 2), there were no differences in test
scores as a function of proximity; however, Ss in the front of
the class participated more than did those in the rear. Results
imply that the relationship between seating position and grades
is mediated by self-selection processes, while participation is
influenced by seat location per se. (8 ref) —*Journal abstract.*

(c)

Figure 3–1   (a) From *Thesaurus of Psychological Index Terms* (1988), entry for "Classroom Environment," p. 37;
(b) From *Psychological Abstracts Index* (July-December, 1981), section of p. 238 showing entry
6707; (c) From *Psychological Abstracts,* entry 6707, p. 700, vol. 66.   (This material is reprinted with
the permission of the American Psychological Association, publisher of Psychological Abstracts and
the PsycINFO Database. Copyright © 1967–1988 by the American Psychological Association. May
not be reproduced without prior permission of the publisher.)

Abstracts. See the abstract numbered 6707 (Levine, McDonald, O'Neal, & Garwood, 1980) in Figure 3–1(c).

Each abstract provides the following citation information: authors and
institutional affiliation of the first author (at the time the article is submitted);
article title; the journal in which it was published; and the date, volume, and pages
of this publication. The entire study is briefly summarized in the abstract. The
parenthetical information at the end of abstract 6707, *(8 ref),* indicates that the paper
cites eight other sources, and the final note, *Journal abstract,* indicates that the
abstract was the one printed with the article (as opposed to having been written
expressly for *Psychological Abstracts*). To find more details about this study, you

could look up the full article in the journal, using the citation information provided. Because this article is brief and typical of social science papers in its style, it is reproduced in its entirety later in this chapter.

Computerized Database Access.   As indicated earlier, it is possible to find such abstracts by computer. The electronic database PsycINFO includes the information in *Psychological Abstracts* from 1967 plus other material such as citations of dissertations in psychology and related disciplines. The electronic format offers some advantages over the manual search through printed versions of *Psychological Abstracts*. One obvious advantage is that the researcher need not consult the numerous volume indexes in order to cover longer time spans. However, because such an omnibus index would turn up many references on even relatively narrow topics, it may be necessary to focus the computer searches. This is conveniently done in PsycINFO and related databases by using combinations of search terms (the same kind of Boolean operator procedure described for book searches in online library catalogs), thus excluding all references that fail to meet all of the indicated keywords. For example, you could restrict your search to classroom environment *and* college *and* grades, thus eliminating studies of high school students and studies that did not include performance outcomes. The logic of such Boolean operators is illustrated in Figure 3–2, where the shaded area represents the overlap of all three descriptors.

You can also restrict searches in PsycINFO by excluding foreign language reports or limiting the search to a selected time period. Moreover, computer searches are not limited to the controlled vocabulary of the thesaurus but can also search words in the title and abstract to help locate relevant studies. Finally, one can access any identified abstracts immediately, without having to go to the relevant printed volume, and have them displayed on the computer monitor or printed.

Because the PsycINFO service requires connect time to a computer database, there may be a fee for its use. However, new technology in the form of

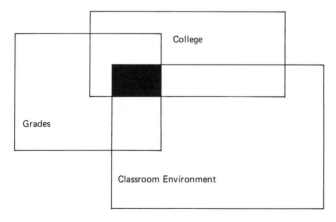

Figure 3–2 Studies of college, grades, and classroom environment.

CD ROM (compact disc, read only memory) products may bring down this cost. This technology permits the cumulative issue of PsycINFO database information in the form of a compact, laser-readable disc, which can be interpreted on a personal computer. This service is called PsycLIT and permits the same kind of focused searches (using Boolean operators) available through the online database.

In addition to PsycINFO, there are various other electronic databases serving other disciplines (for example, Sociological Abstracts, MEDLINE, and GPO Monthly Catalog for U.S. government documents). For more information on these computer search services, see Reed and Baxter (1983, chap. 8).

Citation Index.   One computer search service that deserves special mention is the Social SciSearch from the Institute for Scientific Information (ISI). This database is the electronic equivalent of the *Social Science Citation Index*. A **citation index** has the unique capability of searching for reports that cite a particular reference. This approach is valuable because it can locate any study in the context of all the related arguments, pro and con, about the interpretation of that study. Suppose you have found an article of special interest and would like to find later publications on the same question, especially those with commentary about the original article. You could search for such reports by using the technique summarized for *Psychological Abstracts*, but you would need to check the references listed in each discovered article to find whether it mentioned your primary report.

To facilitate this research, citation services, or citators as they are called, index articles by their references. Starting with just one article, one could easily multiply the number of pertinent references. Suppose you found that your primary article had been cited in ten subsequent publications. Using each of these ten newly discovered references as search keys, you could rapidly find all the other papers that cited any of them. If each of them was cited ten times, you would have acquired 100 potentially relevant references after just two iterations. Citators can also be used for author and subject retrieval. A related service of ISI is the publication of *Current Contents*. This weekly periodical displays tables of contents from thousands of current journals, providing a convenient way of locating pertinent articles even before they can be indexed and abstracted (for example, in *Psychological Abstracts*).

To follow our continuing example, a citation search was done on the Levine, McDonald, O'Neal, and Garwood (1980) article on seating and grades with Social SciSearch. By 1988, over seven years since it appeared in print, this report had been cited seven times. Of these citations, two appeared especially interesting because they indicated a debate about the merits of the original article:

CLASSROOM SEATING EFFECTS—ENVIRONMENT OR SELF-SELECTION— NEITHER, EITHER, OR BOTH
LEVINE DW; MCDONALD PJ; ONEAL EC; GARWOOD SG
PERSONALITY AND SOCIAL PSYCHOLOGY BULLETIN, V8, N2, P365–369, 1982

CLASSROOM SEATING LOCATION, ORDER EFFECTS, AND REACTIVITY
STIRES LK
PERSONALITY AND SOCIAL PSYCHOLOGY BULLETIN, V8, N2, P362–364, 1982[2]

Using the author index to *Psychological Abstracts*, it is a simple matter to locate the abstracts of these two reports to get a summary of the debate. As an exercise in your ability to use *Psychological Abstracts*, try finding these two abstracts. To get the full details, go directly to the two referenced articles and read the exchange. In the second part of this chapter, you will find a copy of the original article, which triggered this debate. You will have the opportunity to evaluate it yourself while becoming acquainted with the standard format of social science journal articles.

UNDERSTANDING SOCIAL RESEARCH REPORTS

Goals

Learning to Read Research.   The chief goal of this text is to enable you to read social science reports—that is, by the end of the text, you should be able to understand and critically evaluate most articles in most social research journals. One reason for this goal is to enable you to become a discriminating consumer of research. But being able to read research is also the first step on the way to conducting your own research. You will need to understand what has already been found before you can ask a new question or develop a new way of answering an old question.

Ability to read reports critically aids in planning and conducting research in another way. The weaknesses you will learn to identify in the reports of others' research are the same ones you will want to guard against in your own research. Scholars "read" their own research as they plan and conduct it in order to spot and correct potential problems. The product of a research project is a report to be read by others. You, as the author of such a report, will want to conduct your project so that the report will be as immune from criticism as possible. To do so requires that you serve as your own most severe critic by anticipating problems while they can still be corrected. Thus social research principles are equally applicable to the conduct of research and to understanding research reports.

Learning a New Language.   Reading research consists of two steps: translating and criticizing. Social research, as with any other specialized activity, has its own language or jargon. To gain access to the ideas of a report, the reader will have to be able to translate the jargon. There is nothing magical or mysterious about social science jargon any more than there is about a foreign language. A considerable part of this text consists of teaching social science language. Each chapter will define new terms and illustrate their use in typical contexts. Thus one of the secondary goals will be for you to expand your vocabulary to include the terms and symbols commonly encountered in social research reports.

Some readers feel blocked from reading social science research despite access to translations of technical terms. They believe they are incapable of understanding certain kinds of material. One of the most common examples of this belief has been called **math phobia**. Math phobics have had bad experiences with math and have developed the habit of avoiding anything mathematical. The sight of a mathematical symbol is enough to make the math phobic anxious and discouraged. When math phobics encounter social science statistics, they feel overwhelmed by the mathematical jargon and symbols. They may give up instead of patiently translating their way through the material. If you are math phobic, one goal is to learn to get past the block raised by the first hint of statistics.

Learning to Criticize. The second component in reading research is criticism. Criticism is crucial to science. Without it, the scientific system does not work well. Criticism helps ensure that research is conducted honestly and well, and it becomes a channel for pitting alternative ideas against each other. Thus, criticism is best when it is creative rather than merely negative. The critical process is at the core of scientific logic. An assertion is offered and evidence collected. The test is whether the evidence can be explained by the original assertion alone or can be explained as well by some rival assertion. Criticism by the author or by the readers provides the rival explanations and therefore is essential to the test. So fundamental is criticism to the shaping of research and research reports that authors typically invite criticism of their work before submitting it for publication. The publication process is itself largely a procedure for formal criticism of a research report by a jury of experts unknown to the author. Finally, in its published form, the research report is fair game for criticism by the readers, who may share their criticisms directly with the author or publicly through letters to the editor of the journal.

Critical analysis of research consists of trying to come up with rival explanations for the observed evidence. The identification and avoidance of rival explanations is a theme that runs throughout this text. As you will see, there are several types of rival explanations, which influence research designs and reports even when they are not mentioned. The threat of these rival explanations is (or should be) in the minds of researchers; that is, awareness of them shapes research. The researcher designs and conducts research to avoid the criticism of the work that will follow if someone else spots a plausible rival explanation left uncontrolled. The critical reader judges how well the researcher has succeeded in avoiding plausible rival explanations. Thus, another secondary goal will be for you to read research with the most important kinds of rival explanations constantly in mind as a means of discriminating the more from the less successful research.

The Form of Research Reports

Standard Report Styles. If you compare different articles from the same journal or from different journals in the same discipline, you will notice that they are similar in their style. For example, the references are detailed in the same way, the abstracts are about the same length, and the tables and abbreviations are consistent in their appearance. Such standardization gives a pleasing appearance to the report and, in substantive matters such as communicating citations or statistics, assures clarity. To achieve this standardization, the various social research disciplines publish rules to be followed by authors submitting papers for publication. Usually, these rules are briefly summarized in issues of the journals.

Some professional organizations have developed such extensive rules and examples to follow that they require separate publication. The *Publication Manual of the American Psychological Association* (American Psychological Association, 1983) is one of the more extensive and widely followed of these style systems. This text is following this publication manual when, in the body of the text, it refers to citations in parentheses as follows: (author, year). If you want to look up the full reference, you would go to the References, and find the author (listed alphabetically). If the same author has more than one citation, you would use the year to identify the particular one of interest. If the author has more than one reference in the same year, letters are used to avoid confusion (for example, Smith, 1987a and Smith, 1987b).

Most journals you will encounter in the social sciences follow a similar approach although there may be small differences on details. For example, the American Psychological Association requires the ampersand symbol (&) as an abbreviation for *and* in citations in parentheses of multiple authors (Smith & Jones, 1989), but the American Sociological Association uses the word *and* in the same situation. This is only one small example of the many rules governing everything from punctuation to paper selection. You will need to follow the appropriate guidelines in preparing a paper for a journal.

Sample Research Report. With minor variations, all social science reports have the same sections (perhaps with varying titles) in the same order. Research reports typically have four major sections: introduction, method, results, and discussion. Articles in most social science journals also have a brief summary, called the abstract, which precedes the introduction. Following is a very brief report that illustrates this format. Quickly scan this report before reading the commentary about it. Then return to the report and read it more carefully. The emphasis here will be on the goals of understanding, translating any jargon that you encounter, and grasping the outline of the report.

Commentary. The abstract typically condenses the whole article into less than 200 words. Busy readers use the abstract to get the gist of the whole study and to decide how much of the article they need to read or whether they need to

Classroom Ecology:
The Effects of Seating Position
on Grades and Participation[3]

Douglas W. Levine

University of California, Irvine

Peter J. McDonald

North Georgia College

Edgar C. O'Neal
S. Gray Garwood

Tulane University

A two-phase study was conducted to examine the effects of classroom seating position on test scores and participation. When students selected their seats (Phase 1), those in the front performed better on the exam than did those in the rear. There was, however, no effect of proximity on participation. When students were randomly assigned to seats (Phase 2), there were no differences in test scores as a function of proximity; however, students in the front of the class participated more than did those in the rear. These results imply that the relationship between seating position and grades is mediated by self-selection processes, while participation is influenced by seat location per se.

Recent investigations of classroom ecology have indicated a relationship between seating position and a number of classroom behaviors. For example, Becker, Sommer, Bee, and Oxley (1973) found that students' test scores decreased as a function of distance away from the front and center of the classroom. Similarly, other studies have shown that participation (Sommer, 1967) and attention (Breed & Colaiuta, 1974) increase as seating location becomes more proximate to the instructor.

The observed relationship in all of these nonexperimental studies, however, can be explained in at least two ways: (1) seat location per se, and (2) self-selection. It is possible that the location of the seat may lead to better grades, more participation, and so on, perhaps because of the high levels of eye contact with the instructor to which those in front seats are exposed (Argyle & Dean, 1965; Caproni et al., 1977; Goffman, 1963). It is also plausible

Personality and Social Psychology Bulletin, Vol. 6 No. 3, September 1980 409–412 that the more able and/or interested students may purposely select front seats and, thus, comprise a qualitatively different sample than those who choose seats in the rear (Sommer, 1967). The experimental studies (Caproni et al., 1977; Schwebel & Charlin, 1972) that could clarify this issue have not employed test performance measures. However, their results are congruent with a location explanation, at least for participation and attention behaviors.

In the present study, a two-phase approach was employed in an attempt to distinguish between the location and self-selection hypotheses. For Phase 1, students selected their seats in a large class setting, whereas for Phase 2 the same students were randomly assigned to seats. Exam scores and participation were recorded. If students in front seats perform better than do those in the rear in both phases of the study, support for the seat location hypothesis would be indicated, whereas the self-selection explanation would predict that seating position should affect performance only when students choose their seats. Furthermore, these effects should be accentuated in the center of the room.

METHOD

Subjects

The study was carried out in an introductory psychology class composed of 209 undergraduates, 132 males and 77 females. Students who indicated that they had visual or auditory handicaps (n = 2), who objected to being assigned a seat (n = 8), who were using a pass-fail grading option (n = 22), or who were auditing the class (n = 2) were not included in this study. Additionally, 16 students withdrew from the course, leaving a sample of 159 students, 95 males and 64 females. The instructor was a male senior faculty member who was unaware of the experimental hypothesis.

Classroom

The class met in an amphitheater-type room with 10 rows, each containing 25 seats. Each successive row was elevated approximately one foot (.30 m) above and one and one-half feet (.46 m) behind the row in front of it. The instructor stood on an eight-inch (10.32 cm) raised platform approximately eight feet (2.44 m) in front of the first row.

Procedure

During the first week of classes, the instructor informed the students that they would be participating in an experiment within the classroom which would require them to select a seat which they would retain until instructed otherwise.

Four weeks later, after their first examination, students were randomly assigned to seats. Again, they were instructed to remain in the assigned seats. Following the second exam, which was given four weeks after the first, students were told the purpose of the experiment and permitted to sit wherever they chose.

Seat selection was employed before seat assignment to maximize the impact of the manipulation. It is possible that if the students had been assigned seats on the first day of class and then told a month later that they could sit wherever they chose, few would have moved (DeLong, 1973).

Each examination was composed of 50 multiple-choice items. Test scores were determined simply by the number of items answered correctly. Participation data were collected by two observers. Participation was defined as a single occurrence of voluntary initiation of discourse with the instructor. If the discussion continued beyond the initial question or comment, it was recorded as only one participation.

For purposes of analysis, seating positions in the classroom were divided into six areas based on two levels of proximity (front and rear) and three levels of centrality (left side, center, and right side). The two levels of proximity were obtained by dividing the class into two equal parts between the fifth and sixth rows; the three levels of centrality were obtained by dividing the class along the two aisles.

RESULTS

Phase 1

When students selected their seats, those in the front (M = 33.99; n = 72) performed better on the exam than did those in the rear (M = 31.66; n = 87). A 2 x 2 x 3 (sex x proximity x centrality) unweighted means ANOVA indicated the proximity effect was significant $F(1, 147) = 5.33$, $p<.03$. Neither sex nor centrality was reliably related to test score, nor did any of the variables interact.

For participation, the only significant effect was a sex difference, $F(1,147) = 4.29$, $p<.05$, with males (M = .25; n = 95) participating more than did females (M = .03; n = 64).

Phase 2

After students were randomly assigned to seats, the proximity effect on test scores evident in Phase 1 was no longer obtained. Students assigned to the front (M = 32.23; n = 83) did not score better than those assigned to the rear (M = 32.89; n = 76), $F(1, 147) = .05$, n.s. Proximity did, however, affect participation, with students in the front (M = .15) participating more than did those in the rear (M = .01), F(1, 147) = 3.95, p<.05.

Correlations

Scores on the two exams were found to be significantly related, r(157) = .66, p<.01, while participation across the two phases was not, r(157) = .03, n.s. Somewhat surprisingly, no relationship between test scores and participation was evident, either when students selected their seats, r(157) = .13, n.s., or when they were assigned to them, r(157) = .08, n.s.

DISCUSSION

In interpreting the results of the present study, it would seem essential to distinguish between test scores and participation as indicators of "performance" in the classroom, even though it has often been assumed that they function as parallel measures (Becker et al., 1973). The test score data corroborate the findings of Becker et al. (1973) and provide support for the self-selection hypothesis, rather than the seat location explanation. On the other hand, the participation data appear to be more congruent with the location hypothesis. The significant correlation between the two exams and the lack of relationships for participations across phases lends additional support to this conclusion. Specifically, it seems that "better" students select front-row seats and perform better on examinations. They do not, however, appear to participate any more than do the other students. In fact, the lack of an effect of proximity on participation in Phase 1 implies that the "better" students are relatively immune to pressures to participate because of location. Conversely, when the students in the front and the rear sections of the classroom are comparable because of random assignment, location per se affects participation. This finding is congruent with the experimental evidence indicating that eye contact from the instructor increased participation rates (Caproni et al., 1977).

The lack of centrality effects in either phase of the study was somewhat unexpected and at variance with the results of Becker et al. (1973) and Sommer (1967). This could be due to any of a number of reasons, including class size, classroom configuration, or the relative weakness of the centrality "manipulation." The fact that the present study did involve an extremely large class at the introductory level necessitates caution in generalization. It remains to be determined if these results apply in smaller classes or with more advanced students.

REFERENCES

ARGYLE, M., & DEAN, J. Eye-contact, distance and affiliation. *Sociometry*, 1965, *28*, 289–304.

BECKER, F. D., SOMMER, R., BEE, J., & OXLEY, B. College classroom ecology. *Sociometry*, 1973, *36*, 514–525.

BREED, G., & COLAIUTA, V. Looking, blinking, and sitting: Non-verbal dynamics in the classroom. *Journal of Communication*, 1974, *24*, 75–81.

CAPRONI, V., LEVINE, D., O'NEAL, F., McDONALD, P., & GARWOOD, G. Seating position, instructor's eye contact availability, and student participation in a small seminar. *Journal of Social Psychology*, 1977, *103*, 315–316.

DELONG, A. J. Territorial stability and hierarchical formation. *Small Group Behavior*, 1973, *4*, 55–63.

GOFFMAN, E., *Behavior in public places*. Glencoe, Ill.: Free Press, 1963.

SCHWEBEL, A., & CHARLIN, D. L. Physical and social distancing in teacher-pupil relationships. *Journal of Educational Psychology*, 1972, *63*, 543–550.

SOMMER, R. Classroom ecology. *Journal of Applied Behavioral Science*, 1967, *3*, 489–503.

Douglas W. Levine is a graduate student in the Program in Social Ecology at the University of California, Irvine. His research interests include nonverbal behavior, helping behavior, and self-awareness.

Peter J. McDonald is an Assistant Professor of Psychology at North Georgia College. His major research interests are in the area of social motivation.

Edgar C. O'Neal is Professor of Psychology and department chairman at Tulane University. His research interests include aggression and person perception.

S. Gray Garwood is an Associate Professor of Psychology at Tulane University. His research centers on the cognitive underpinnings of social development.

read the article at all. The abstract presents the main question(s) to be answered, the basic design and measures used to answer the question, and the nature of the results. Professional readers of research studies do not necessarily read all parts of each report of interest to them. For example, once the reader finds from the abstract what answer the study arrives at, he or she may turn directly to the method section to see how the answer was reached. Perhaps a scholar is trying to review all studies on a particular topic. He or she might use the abstract to make sure that the study applies to the topic and then turn directly to the results section to find out exactly what answer the study found to the question. For the experienced reader, the abstract serves as a kind of table of contents. By knowing what kind of material will be treated in each section of the report, the reader can skip quickly to the part that he or she most needs to read.

The introduction raises the question or problem to be studied. The background to the problem is presented, including previous studies on the issue. The theory or theories that predict what the answer will be are summarized or referenced. The reader learns here what makes this study significant—that is, what is intellectually original or socially important about it. The authors may have created a new theory or explanation that their study will test. Or they may have identified two or more existing explanations of the same evidence.

The conflict between competing explanations may provide the motivation for the study. This is the case in the reprinted article. The authors cite several studies showing that students seated closer to the front of a classroom perform better academically. But they also observe that this result could be due to either of two reasons: (1) Better students choose to sit up front or (2) sitting up front makes students better. The authors' original contribution is to design a study that will tell which of the two explanations is better. Their design is spelled out in the method section.

The method section is the heart of a research report. It tells how the study was done so that others can check it. One way of checking is to inspect the method section for possible rival explanations that were not ruled out by the design. Another way of checking a study is by actually repeating it. The method section must give enough detail so that anyone can independently perform the study. When the same type of study is repeated by different researchers, including skeptics with no vested interest in the outcome, we are more convinced than by just one study.

The method section tells how measurements were made and details the study's **design**. As in the reprinted study, it is common to begin by telling about the subjects—how many males, how many females, how many dropped out (note that the symbol n stands for number of subjects). The method section also defines how different concepts are measured. For example, how is "participation" defined by Levine and others? (Hint: See the third paragraph under Procedure.)

In experimental studies such as this, the researchers do more than just observe and measure; they also do things to observe the reaction of the subjects. In this case, the researchers did two things. First, they let students pick their own seats, which they were required to keep for a period, in order to see what kinds of students chose to sit up front. Then the experimenters assigned seats, to see the effect of being made to sit up front. There are many different patterns or designs for grouping subjects, assigning manipulations (that is, doing things to subjects such as assigning seats) to different groups, and then observing their reactions. Design, like measurement, is an important source of possible rival explanations.

The results section tells the outcome of the study in numerical terms. This section is often difficult reading for those with little statistical background. Even without such a background, however, it is possible to learn to make sense of the results section.

Statistics fall into two main categories. Descriptive statistics, as their name implies, describe the subjects on one or more measurements. Take as an example the first sentence of the reprinted results section. The 72 students ($n = 72$) who chose to sit up front are described in terms of their exam scores. They received an average score of 33.99 (M = average = 33.99). The 87 students sitting in the rear received an average test score of 31.66. These averages are descriptive in that they tell us about each of these two groups as a whole. We know that a representative member of the "front" group is described by a score of 33.99.

Inferential statistics deal with another matter. Do the values 31.66 and 33.99 seem very different to you? Would you infer that students in other courses or other universities would show the same result, that is, that those sitting up front would get better grades than those sitting in back? Since 33.99 is larger than 31.66 by only 2.33 points, perhaps the difference occurred by chance. Thus we have a rival explanation of the findings—maybe the students that were studied are not representative of all other students. To infer that their findings generalize to others and thus to rule out the alternative explanation of chance, the researchers calculated an inferential statistic called an F statistic. The F statistic for the proximity effect (that is, sitting closer is related to higher grades) was 5.33. What are the chances that this value of F could have occurred by chance? The probability (p) of getting this F value was less than (<) 3 percent (.03). Thus the expression $F = 5.33$, $p < .03$ is the basis for the researchers to infer that the proximity effect reached **statistical significance** (that is, was not a fluke). When p is not less than .05 it is customary to say that the finding is "not significant," symbolized by "n.s." Although this is not a statistics text, there will be some material in later chapters to help you make sense of descriptive and inferential statistics.

The discussion section presents the conclusions that the authors draw from their study. This section not only summarizes these conclusions but also indicates how much confidence can be placed in them. This estimate of confidence is based on the authors' own inspection for rival explanations. To the extent that one or more rival explanations are judged plausible, confidence in the authors' assertion is low. If the authors have succeeded in eliminating or making implausible all explanations but one, they will be justifiably confident in their conclusion. When the authors identify remaining problems or doubts about their finding, they typically finish by speculating about avenues for further research.

SUMMARY

The first step in social research is often that of finding out what is already known. Because of the increase in social research publications, it is necessary to learn how to use the most efficient search procedures, several of which are described in the first part of this chapter. A representative computer-based procedure for locating items in a library is illustrated by the MELVYL system. The procedure for finding a journal article on a particular topic was represented by *Psychological Abstracts*.

Once a relevant article or chapter has been located, it is necessary to read the study critically. Fortunately, social research journals follow a fairly standard format, which makes it easy to follow the argument. A brief research report on the relation of class seating position and grades is reprinted in the second part of the chapter to illustrate the typical format: abstract, introduction of the theoretical question, methods of measurement and design, results of the statistical analyses, and discussion of causal conclusions. Each of these aspects of research (theory, measurement, design) is a topic for extended treatment in upcoming chapters.

EXERCISES

1. If you are not already familiar with your library's system for locating books by title, author, or subject, plan to become so now. Often libraries offer brief introductions to their procedures with hands-on instruction if computer terminals are a part of the indexing system. Sign up for such introductory instruction or review the library's printed guidelines for searching for a book. Then, as an exercise, pick a topic of interest to you and try to find one or more books in your library on that topic.

2. Once you are familiar with your library's indexing system, get acquainted with one of the standard journal indexing or abstracting services. If you are interested in a psychological topic, try finding a journal article on the subject through *Psychological Abstracts*, following the procedure illustrated in this chapter. Or with your librarian's help, pursue a subject with another indexing service.

3. Once you have found a journal article of interest to you, review it critically. Locate each of the major sections identified in the article reprinted in this chapter. Challenge the main assertion of each section, trying to think of rival arguments. You should become so familiar with this standard format that you can go directly to the particular section of any article to the information you want—the question being tested, the measures being utilized, the numerical results, or the conclusions reached.

4. Obtain a copy of a publication manual for the social science discipline to whose journals you most frequently refer. If appropriate, try casting your next paper in the format prescribed by that manual.

GLOSSARY

Abstract: Brief article summary that appears at the beginning of most social research reports or which can be retrieved by an abstracting service such as *Psychological Abstracts*.

Boolean operators: Connecting words such as *and* or *or*, which can identify overlapping or nonoverlapping sets of information, for example, to find all the books by an author named Jones *and* about the subject of density.

Call number: Identifying code of numbers and letters by which an item can be located in a library.

Citation index: Database of publications searchable by the references or citations included in the articles.

Command: In the context of an online catalog search, the part of the user's instructions that tells the computer what action is desired, for example, FIND.

Controlled vocabulary: Set of terms officially designated and recognized by a catalog or file system.

Design: In research, the arrangement of subjects, experimental manipulation, and observation of results.

Index: In the context of an online catalog search, the part of the instructions that tells the computer what type of file is to be searched—by author, title, or subject or some combination of these.

Key words: In the context of an online catalog search, the part of the instructions that tells the computer the specific term to search for, for example, the author's name or the book's title.

Math phobia: Fear and consequent avoidance of math-related subjects.

Modem: Device for linking computers by telephone line, the word being an abbreviation for *modulator-demodulator*.

Online: Connected to a computer for direct interaction with the electronic database.

Prompt: Symbol on a computer screen indicating readiness for the next step in the procedure.

Statistical significance: In inferential statistics, the judgment that a finding was not due to chance.

Statistics: Numerical summaries of observations. For example, descriptive statistics describe single variables or associations among variables, whereas inferential statistics pertain to the inference or generalization from small groups of subjects to other groups of the same kind of subjects.

NOTES

[1]Registered Trademark of the Regents of the University of California. Copyright 1984 The Regents of the University of California. All rights reserved.

[2]Copied with the permission of the Institute for Scientific Information, 1988.

[3]Levine, D. W., McDonald, P. J., O'Neal, E. C., & Garwood, S.C. (1980). Classroom ecology: The effects of seating position on grades and participation. *Personality and Social Psychology Bulletin*, Vol. I, No. 6, pp. 409–12. Copyright 1980 by Sage Publications, Inc. Reprinted by permission of Sage Publications, Inc.

4

Theory

From Concepts to Measures

INTRODUCTION TO THEORY

Diagramming Theories

A Model of Academic Achievement. Theories are conceptual systems; they state suspected relationships among concepts. Figure 4–1 presents a picture of one theory in the area of academic performance (Maruyama & McGarvey, 1980). The words inside the circles are the names of concepts, and the arrows represent beliefs about causal relationships. Thus the arrow pointing from academic ability to academic achievement indicates that ability causes achievement.

More accurately, we should say that the arrow from ability to achievement indicates that ability is thought to cause achievement. It is conceivable that achievement causes ability or that each causes the other or that the two are completely unrelated. Each of these possible relationships would have made a different theory from the one we see in Figure 4–1.

The possibility that concepts are unrelated or are related in unexpected ways reminds us of the most important thing about theories—they are tentative and preliminary. We are not sure about them, and that is why we call them theories instead of laws or facts. Theories are preliminary to laws in that they are working models subject to change and improvement. The theoretician might come back to the model in Figure 4–1 and erase an arrow, reverse the direction of an arrow, add an arrow, add another concept, or remove a concept. Theories are like artists' sketches. They are not painted in oil or sculpted in marble on the first try. Rather, the artist makes a preliminary sketch in pencil or in clay. This sketch is frequently adjusted or fitted to the reality that the artist sees or remembers. In a sense, the

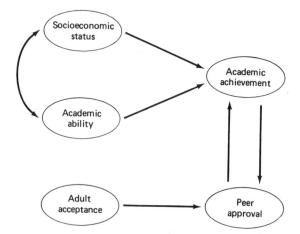

Figure 4–1   Diagram of a sample theory for causation of academic achievement. (Based on G. Maruyama, and B. McGarvey, "Evaluating causal models: An application of maximum-likelihood analysis of structural equations.") From *Psychological Bulletin*, 1980, *87* 502–522. Copyright 1980 by the American Psychological Association. Adapted by permission of the authors.

sketch is tested against the visual reality before the artist is ready to set it permanently in oil or marble.

   Constructs.   What are the elements of theory called concepts? Consider the theory in Figure 4–1, which consists of five concepts and their relationships. **Concepts** are abstract aspects of reality. They are aspects or properties of things, people, or events that we perceive or imagine. Sometimes concepts are obvious and seem quite concrete or tangible. For example, color and weight are familiar aspects of things that we are used to seeing or feeling. Among the first words that children learn are the names for different colors. Although babies are not expected to be able to define the concept of color, they can grasp that one aspect of all objects is color. Similarly, without being formally told, we all grasp the idea that some objects are light enough to be lifted and others are too heavy to move.

   Sometimes concepts are more complex or less obvious than color or weight. They are imaginings or constructions of our minds that are not universal or obvious to everyone. For example, empathy (understanding another person by taking his or her point of view) is an aspect of human social behavior that is not directly seen or felt, as is color or weight. Empathy is not easy to measure because it has to be inferred indirectly from observations of behavior. As an exercise, think for a moment of the two people you know who illustrate extremes of empathy—the one with the most empathy and the one with the least. How did you determine these levels of empathy; that is, what did you see or hear that told how these two people differed on this one aspect? We will call such complex, inferred concepts **constructs**, although the terms *concept* and *construct* are commonly used interchangeably in social research.

   The five concepts in Figure 4–1 are all constructs in the sense that they are complex, inferred aspects of persons or social relationships. Socioeconomic status reflects the social class or rank of the individual's parents (as indicated by the parents' occupation and education). Academic ability refers to natural cognitive ability or intelligence. We will not be concerned right now with how such constructs are measured; this will be a topic for later discussion. Assume, for now, that measures or estimates of these characteristics are available and that different people get different scores on these measures. That is, a person could be high or low on each of these constructs, and the measures of these constructs would reflect this value by yielding correspondingly high or low scores. When a theoretical construct or concept is measured and the measurement can yield different or varying values, we call it a **variable**. Although the term *variable* is sometimes used interchangeably with *concept* and *construct*, *variable* is reserved here to mean an indicator or measure such as grades in school, and **theoretical variable** refers to an abstract or unmeasured concept or construct such as academic achievement. This is an important distinction, which you should understand clearly: *Concepts, constructs,* and *theoretical variables* all refer to abstract, unmeasured aspects of people or things, which we imagine in our mind's eye; *variables* are the concrete, measured representations of these aspects, which we can count, categorize, or otherwise assign numerical values.

Socioeconomic status and academic ability are characteristics of individuals that, according to the theory in Figure 4–1, existed before their academic achievement. Status and ability are presumed to be caused by still earlier constructs. But a theory has to start somewhere. Some theories are more ambitious and extensive than others in that they try to explain the relationships among more concepts. Nevertheless, there are always some concepts that are taken as starting points and are supposed to cause other concepts but whose own causes are unknown. Such a "starter" construct is sometimes called an **exogenous construct** because its causes originate from outside the theoretical model. Exogenous theoretical variables have straight causal arrows leading away from but not to them. In their measured form, such causal variables are sometimes referred to as **independent variables** since their levels are independent of and not caused by the other variables or concepts in the theory.

Status and ability are observed to be related to each other; that is, high parental status is known to be associated with higher ability. Since no effort is made in this theory to explain the causal connection of status and ability to each other, their association is signified by a double-headed curved arrow. This sign symbolizes association without any indication of causal direction.

Status and ability are thought to cause achievement, as indicated by the straight, single-headed arrows in Figure 4–1. School grades are known to be associated with status and ability. The theory suggests that these associations are causal. Achievement—the effect in this causal relationship—is an **endogenous construct** since its causes are stated within the model. Effects or endogenous variables are commonly called **dependent variables** because their values or levels are thought to depend on (that is, to be caused by) the independent variable(s). The relationships of status to achievement and of ability to achievement are examples of simple **direct causal paths**. These particular direct causal paths are not especially interesting because they are neither new nor controversial. We expect students with high ability and/or with the advantages of high socioeconomic status to have high achievements. Of course, we know that not all high-ability or high-status students will have high achievements, and we may be interested in measuring the strength of these causal relationships. The theory does not say how strong these causal connections are; it only says that they exist, that is, that the connections are strong enough to be detected.

What is most interesting in this theory is the pair of causal relationships suggested between achievement and peer approval (see Figure 4–1). The arrow from peer approval to achievement suggests that being liked by same-age people influences accomplishment. It is assumed that most students value high academic achievement. If a student is accepted by his or her classmates in such a classroom, the peer group's desire for achievement will be adopted by the individual. Thus, approval is thought to cause achievement through the individual's conformity with prevailing expectations that people should try harder. Of course, this scenario is based on the assumption of high-achievement values. If the dominant classroom value is anti-high achievement, the influence model would predict a decrease in achievement as the student adopted the prevailing values. As you can see, just one causal arrow in the diagram is shorthand for a number of assumptions and logical connections.

The right-hand arrow from achievement to approval suggests a quite different kind of causal relationship. Sometimes referred to as the "star model," this arrow suggests that successful achievement causes approval (again assuming an environment that places a high value on achievement). High achievers are rewarded with peer popularity.

The presence of both arrows in the diagram indicates that both the social influence and the star models are at work. Suppose a low-achieving student is transferred from a low-achievement to a high-achievement school. The two causal processes might operate as follows: The student begins to become acquainted and may adopt the harder work habits and achievement motivation of his or her new friends, following the influence model. Harder work may produce improvements in achievement, which in turn gain the student wider acceptance, following the star model. The new popularity may involve acceptance by an elite, high-achieving inner group, whose more intensive work habits are then adopted. The new work habits lead to still greater achievement, which in turn causes still greater popularity by our rising star. This alternating sequence of two causal processes is an example of **reciprocal causation**.

The fifth concept is adult acceptance, the degree of approval of the student by important adults such as parents and teachers. Since adult acceptance has an arrow going from it but none to it in Figure 4–1, it is an exogenous variable. In this model, it is thought to have a causal impact on peer approval. Greater acceptance by adults is expected to lead to greater acceptance by peers. Since peer approval may be a cause of achievement, adult acceptance affects, by **indirect causation**, academic achievement. When one variable indirectly causes another variable, there is a third variable that is the effect of the first and the cause of the second. This variable in the middle is called an **intervening variable**. Peer approval intervenes between adult acceptance and academic achievement.

Why Have Theories?

Action. It has been said that nothing is so practical as a good theory. Of course, not everyone thinks of theories as practical. The word *theory* connotes impractical things, ivory towers where theoreticians take flights of fancy that have little to do with real life or average people. If there are such impractical theories, they are hard to justify. Just as training in social research should help you discriminate between good and bad research, so such training should help you to discriminate between more and less useful theories.

What are the uses of a theory? There are at least two major ways in which theories serve us. First, theories meet our need to act even when we are uncertain.

The necessity to act often forces us to guess about how the world works. Until our guesses can be replaced by laws, we want our guesses to be the very best that they can be. Theories are sophisticated generalized guesses. Good theories are coherent, that is, logical and internally consistent. More than that, good theories integrate existing knowledge and observations—both established laws and the newest hints and clues from research. Well-researched and well-argued theories are more persuasive than wild guesses. To the extent that theories are believable, they can contribute to very important social policy decisions. For example, one relationship in the theory of Figure 4–1 contributes to the policy of school integration. The arrow from peer approval to academic achievement, the social influence path, suggests that moving students from low-achievement to high-achievement schools would produce better academic performance by disadvantaged students.

Research. The second way in which theories prove useful is in their guidance of research. Empirical research consists of collecting precise observations in order to answer questions. But the world poses a great many questions. How does one focus on a particular one? Theory serves to identify the critical questions. The better the theory, the better are the questions to which it points, that is, those that are worth answering and that are answerable. Questions that are worth answering are ones that have not already been answered and that are not trivial in either a scientific or social sense. To answer an already answered question is to engage in a redundant exercise. Such research does not make an original contribution. It is important to distinguish redundant research, which addresses a question that has been answered, from essential research, which repeats and checks a study that purports to have answered a question still in doubt.

Answerability is another important criterion of good questions. One characteristic of answerable questions is that they are manageable. Such questions as "What causes poverty?" or "What causes war?" are socially significant, unanswered questions, which are too large to answer in any single study with our present knowledge and methods. Just as one would not expect to climb Mt. Everest alone in a day, so researchers are resigned to dividing great social questions into smaller questions in teamwork with other researchers. Good theories provide manageable tasks, which together will build up to the solutions to the great puzzles.

Another characteristic of answerable questions is that they are based on propositions that can be disconfirmed. Good theories produce clear predictions, which can be supported or contradicted by observations. For example, one proposition from the theory in Figure 4–1 is that peer approval raises academic achievement, at least in achievement-oriented schools. This assertion leads to a question: In such schools, will students who are accepted by their peers make greater academic progress than students not so accepted? Since the researcher should be able to measure the concepts in this question, such as "academic progress," we should be able to get a clear yes-or-no answer. If the answer is no and the research has been conducted fairly and accurately, we take this answer as evidence for doubting the theory stated in Figure 4–1. In sum, we can falsify or cast doubt on theories, if we can find observations that contradict them (Popper, 1987). Good theories have to run this risk of being shown wrong. Theories that do not run this risk are not proved as laws by virtue of being irrefutable; they are simply bad theories. On the other hand, evidence consistent with a theory does not assure us that some future test will not go against it. Thus, one or even a few observations in support of the theory is not taken as conclusive proof.

How can one tell if a theory can be disconfirmed? Platt (1964) has suggested a key question:

> It consists of asking in your own mind, on hearing any scientific explanation or theory put forward, "But sir, what experiment could disprove your hypothesis?"; or, on hearing a scientific experiment described, "But sir, what hypothesis does your experiment disprove?" (p. 352)

Bad theories can be difficult to disconfirm for different reasons. Sometimes the concepts in the theories are so vague that they cannot be measured. Other times, theories fail to give clear predictions. Such theories are so "flexible" that they can be manipulated to explain any answer to any question put to them.

Research without theory is possible but inefficient. Theory serves to organize research. Independent researchers working on the same problem can coordinate their studies within the framework of a shared theory. Guided by theory, a researcher can build a program of research that is greater than the sum of its individual studies. Theory can provide a context that makes each study more meaningful by linking it to others converging on the same theory.

Nomothetic Versus Idiographic Approaches. The role of theory just described can be called the **nomothetic** approach. The term *nomothetic* refers to the science of general laws, and the nomothetic approach strives to discover general relationships that hold in different times and places. Social scientists are hesitant to elevate one of their theories to the status of law even after repeated supportive findings. Nevertheless, researchers in the nomothetic tradition operate as though there were general, lawful relationships for which their methods might find some evidence.

In contrast, other social researchers adopt the **idiographic** approach. This approach focuses on the particulars of the individual person, place, or time under study without trying to generalize or discover universal laws that apply elsewhere. In this text, as in the social sciences generally, the predominant approach is nomothetic. That is, we will assume that research is guided by a theory that applies to more than one person or situation. Nevertheless, it should be remembered that some social researchers use the idiographic approach, and this perspective will be given more attention in the chapter on qualitative research (Chapter 13).

THE PROCESS OF THEORY-BASED RESEARCH

Steps in Making and Using Theory

Theory is one part of the research process. Theory-based research consists of a few repeating steps: induction, deduction, and tests. After testing, the results are fed back to the first step, and the sequence begins again. These four steps are illustrated in Figure 4–2.

Induction. By induction is meant the creation of general principles or relationships from specific observations, anecdotes, or research results. This is the process of theory construction. What are the origins of the general principles that theorists use to explain or organize particular observations? The origins may be earlier theories, analogies borrowed from other disciplines, or new insights invented by the theorist.

In Figure 4–2, the inductive process is symbolized by the arrows from data to the conceptual system. The illustration of a theory is an abbreviation of the theory shown in Figure 4–1. From actual observations of achievement, peer and adult acceptance, status, and ability, the theorist states relationships that can be expected to apply generally to all students in all schools. Thus, the theory serves the very useful purpose of summarizing many separate observations.

Theory need not simply summarize observed relationships. Theory can also express the theorist's imagination or intuition about unobserved relationships. The theorist may invent new concepts and predict new associations between concepts. Thus, theory is partially grounded in data and is partially a function of speculation. Different theories are blends of different proportions of facts and imagination.

How do theorists select areas about which to theorize? The theorist's special interests and training will help orient him or her toward one or another

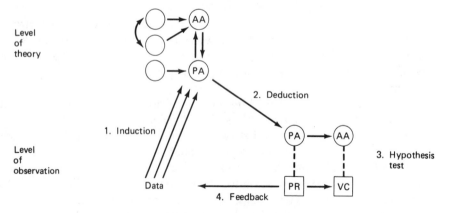

Figure 4–2 Steps in social research.

broad area. But within an area, a theorist will probably be attracted to a **paradox**—a situation in which existing theories and existing data seem to clash. The theorist attempts to explain apparently divergent observations within a more comprehensive theory, which includes and integrates seemingly conflicting prior explanations. The result is a set of constructs and their causal relationships, which may fit reality better than prior theories.

Deduction.   The next step in theory-based research is **deduction,** which is the process of specifying assertions or propositions from general theoretical principles. More than one proposition can be drawn from a theory that has many constructs and causal paths. Figure 4–2 illustrates the deductive step by the selection of just one relationship from the theory portrayed in Figure 4–1: the causal path from peer approval (PA) to academic achievement (AA). These two constructs and their relationship constitute a proposition diagrammed as two circles and a joining arrow. This proposition is presumed to be general. If the proposition holds generally for all students in all schools, we expect it to hold for any sample of students from any school.

Hypothesis Testing and Operationalization.   To assess empirically a theory or any of its propositions, we must measure the constructs of each proposition for some particular subjects. When a construct is measured, the construct is said to have an **operational definition**. In this example, we can follow standardized procedures to get measures of peer approval and academic achievement for a sample of students from a particular school. The procedures or operations that are followed may consist of self-report questionnaires, structured interviews, or standardized observations by trained raters. In fact, there is usually more than one way to define any construct operationally. The resulting measures or indicators are symbolized by squares in Figure 4–3, which is an enlargement of a section of Figure 4– 2.

When a proposition is operationalized (that is, its constructs are translated into indicators), it becomes a hypothesis. A **hypothesis** is a testable proposition. It is a prediction about the relationships among indicators. Since most constructs can be measured in more than one way and in more than one sample, any proposition

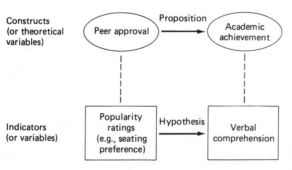

Constructs (or theoretical variables)

Indicators (or variables)

Figure 4–3 Testable hypothesis from theoretical proposition.

can be translated into many hypothesis tests—one for each combination of different operational definitions and samples. Thus, the general proposition in Figure 4–3 could be translated into a very specific hypothesis or prediction. For example, for students enrolled in achievement-oriented schools, we might hypothesize that students rated as popular (defined as those students whom other students say they want to sit beside in class) will score higher on the standard achievement test employed in the school (for example, verbal comprehension).

The third basic step in social research is the test of the hypothesis. **Hypothesis testing** is the procedure whereby theory and reality are brought face to face with each other. If the observed data are inconsistent with our hypothesis, we are inclined to reject it and to doubt the proposition and the theory from which it was deduced. Since theories are general, they should apply generally. Thus any inconsistency of data with theory tends to diminish our confidence in the theory (that is, falsifies the theory), assuming the hypothesis test is well conducted. Of course, it is always possible that the test is defective in some way.

On the other hand, an instance of a good fit of data and theory does not "prove" the theory. Since theory is general and should hold for all cases (within the theory's domain), only a test of the theory in all relevant cases would prove the theory conclusively. It is always possible that the next hypothesis test will turn up a sample or an operationalization of the constructs that the theory does not fit. This problem points up the asymmetry of hypothesis testing: A finding against the theory strikes a heavier blow than a finding for the theory provides support. Nevertheless, assuming that the hypothesis test was well conducted, data that are consistent with the hypothesis are taken as support for it.

Since a single hypothesis test cannot prove the truth of a proposition and its parent theory, hypothesis testing is often repeated several times for the same proposition. Different researchers, using different samples of subjects and similar or different indicators of the constructs, can each test hypotheses based on the same proposition. These repeated hypothesis tests or replications provide information not only about the generality of the findings (Is the proposition supported in different samples?) but also about the quality of the hypothesis test (Is the construct operationalization and research design of each test sound as compared with the other tests?).

This text is largely concerned with hypothesis testing. Different replications or hypothesis tests aimed at the same proposition frequently give different results. Consequently, researchers spend a great deal of their time trying to understand how differences in the designs of hypothesis tests cause these different results, to determine which hypothesis tests are most convincing, and to design still better hypothesis tests. Different hypothesis tests may have in common the same theoretical variables and the same expectations for the direction of causation from independent to dependent variables. But these hypothesis tests can vary enormously in their operationalization of constructs and in the way causal direction is demonstrated. Evaluating the quality of measurement and the quality of research design will be the major task of the remainder of this book.

Feedback. The fourth and final step is the feedback of the results from hypothesis testing to the inductive process of supporting or revising theory. Theory serves as a kind of running scorecard for hypothesis testing. As results emerge from hypothesis tests, they become part of the observational database on which theory is founded. New findings may require adjustments in theory. Of course, theories are not revised after or because of each study. In time, a preponderance of evidence from sound and replicated studies will have to be reflected in the theory. New inductive work will have to be done if the new findings are at odds with the old theory.

Commonly, a new finding that is both convincing and inconsistent with prevailing theory will be accommodated by a small adjustment in the theory. Suppose that the hypothesis that greater peer approval leads to increased academic achievement was repeatedly and convincingly disconfirmed. These findings could be reflected in the theory shown in Figure 4–1 by removing the arrow from peer approval to academic achievement. The other arrows and all the constructs could remain in place until such time as new research required their adjustment.

Guidelines for Theory.   Aside from consistency with the data, theories are commonly shaped by two concerns. The first concern is for **parsimony,** which may be understood in this context as efficiency. A parsimonious theory or explanation is one that makes use of the fewest constructs and relationships necessary to explain the phenomenon of interest. If two theories are equally successful in accounting for the data, we generally prefer the more parsimonious one. If a complex theory is only slightly more explanatory, we might still prefer the simpler theory on grounds of parsimony. This preference is not just a matter of convenience to save theorists and researchers the trouble of working with extra concepts. Scientists who prefer parsimonious explanations share a faith that underlying causal mechanisms are relatively simple. Nevertheless, some realities, especially social realities, do not seem very simple, and our evidence may force us to complicate our theories with more concepts and relationships.

The other concern that shapes our use of feedback in revising theory is **generality**. Theorists continually try to stretch their theories to explain more and more data. Indeed, theory is supposed to make sense out of otherwise separate and isolated observations. The more observations that can be explained by the theory, the more general and useful it is. In the absence of theory, our science would consist simply of lists of unrelated facts and observations. The benefit of a general theory is that it can be used to predict what will happen in circumstances that have never been encountered. Before we had a theory of gravity, humanity made do with a great many unrelated observations of how different objects fell from different heights. But with a general theory of gravitational attraction, it became possible to predict and, therefore, control the falling or orbiting behavior of objects on places no person had ever been before (for example, the Apollo lunar landings). For this reason, theorists strain to extend the generality of their explanations.

Generality and parsimony are not necessarily compatible. To extend the theory of Figure 4–1 regarding achievement and approval to cover low-achievement environments, it may be necessary to add more constructs and causal propositions. The price of greater generality may be greater complexity. Nevertheless, it is conceivable that we may someday arrive at a theory that achieves both parsimony and generality. Such a combination of simplicity and power is called elegance. The elegant theory not only is very functional but also has a kind of beauty. For further discussion of social research theory, see Dubin (1978) or Marx (1965).

An Example of Theory

Where Are Theories Found? Statements of theory are everywhere. We find them explicitly stated in the introductions of most research reports, since it is theory that provides the rationale for conducting most studies and that points to the variables and questions being studied. Theory is also implicit in method and results sections since the measurement of concepts and the design of the study must serve the hypothesis test drawn from theory. Finally, theory is often explicitly reconsidered in the discussion section of research articles. Here the work of feeding back the results of the study to the theory-revision process is begun. Thus, most data-based or empirical studies make references to theory throughout their reports. Such studies illustrate in miniature each of the research steps.

Theory can also be represented in pure form without any hypothesis tests or presentations of new data. Such theory statements are devoted entirely to the articulation and defense of theory, drawing on and reviewing existing data. Such theory statements may require long journal articles or even whole books. There are even some journals devoted entirely to the presentation of such theory (for example, *Psychological Review*) or theory and review articles (for example, *Psychological Bulletin*). Other journals present a mix of theory and empirical articles (for example, *American Sociological Review*).

Social Causation and Mental Disorder. Consider the following summary of a theory drawn from Wheaton (1980). The basic theoretical problem involves the long-standing observation that low socioeconomic status (SES) is associated with high rates of mental disorder. Different theories have arisen to account for this observation. One theory, called the social causation model, has the causal path leading from poverty to mental disorder. Another, the social drift model, has the path leading from disorder to poverty (that is, abnormal behavior leads to job failure and to poverty). Wheaton offers a variant of social causation theory. For a summary of his theory, see Figure 4–4. You should be able to apply many terms introduced in this chapter to this figure.

Concepts or constructs are illustrated in the top row by the three terms *success/failure, attribution tendency,* and *adaptation potential.* Success/failure refers to the idea that people experience some ratio of positive experiences and accomplish-

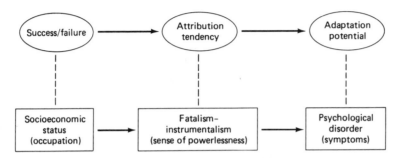

Figure 4–4   A social causation theory of mental disorder. (Adaptation of figure 1 in Wheaton, B. The socio-genesis of psychological disorder, *Journal of Health and Social Behavior*, 1980, *21*, 100-124.

ments to negative experiences and defeats. The arrow from *success/failure* to *attribution tendency* indicates that this ratio of experiences affects one's customary style for explaining (that is, attributing) events—assigning blame or credit to oneself versus to the rest of the world. Finally, this attribution tendency is thought to affect adaptation potential (that is, one's ability to adapt or respond to stressful events). The more a person believes that he or she has no effect, the less well he or she will cope with life's challenges.

These theoretical variables or constructs have to be operationalized or measured in order to test the theory. The vertical dashed lines match each construct with its operationalized counterpart (in boxes). Thus Wheaton believes that one's ratio of successes to failures is linked to one's economic situation, which is operationalized by occupational status. Similarly, attribution tendency is operationalized by questions about one's sense of powerlessness. These items measure a range of attitudes from fatalism (belief that one's fate is out of one's hands) to instrumentalism (belief that one is an instrument of one's own destiny). Finally, adaptive potential is thought to be reflected by the degree of one's psychological disorder as measured by the number of symptoms.

You should be able to identify the independent, or exogenous, variable (socioeconomic status) and the dependent, or endogenous, variable (psychological disorder). Remember that exogenous variables have no arrows leading to them, but they have arrows leading from them to other variables. What kind of variable is fatalism-instrumentalism? Since it "intervenes" between status and disorder, it is called an intervening variable.

Having identified the parts of this sample theory, try stating one proposition in terms of its constructs and then restating it as a testable prediction or hypothesis. For example, you might select the proposition that attribution tendency affects adaptive potential. In the form of a testable hypothesis, this could be stated as follows: *A person who agrees with items reflecting a greater sense of fatalism will also report having more symptoms of psychological disorder.* Note that this hypothesis is expressed in terms of measured or measurable variables. Also note that it consists of a prediction that could be found either true or false. The finding that it is false would tend to disconfirm (weaken our belief in) the theory as stated.

SUMMARY

A theory is a collection of assertions about causally related constructs that helps guide research and which, in turn, is modified and clarified by research. Research, in this view, proceeds in steps: The researcher first draws theory from observations and speculation (induction), then selects a specific causal proposition from a theory (deduction), and finally operationalizes relevant constructs in the form of variables to check the fit of the expected relationship to the observed relationship (hypothesis test).

Variables can be independent (also called exogenous if they have no causes themselves in the theory), or they can be dependent (also called endogenous). If a variable seems to link an independent to a dependent variable, it is called intervening. Operationalizing variables and arranging (designing) research studies to test hypotheses are the central concerns of most of the rest of this text.

EXERCISES

1. Find a newspaper or popular magazine article that implicitly or explicitly states a theory. Identify the cause and effect constructs. Are there any other kinds of constructs that intervene between the cause and effect variables? Now, for each construct, state a variable that operationalizes or measures it. Finally, diagram the theory at both the construct and measured variable levels (as in Figure 4–4) by joining the names of the variables by arrows indicating the supposed causal direction.

2. When you can diagram such simple theories, find more elaborate theories in the professional research literature. Search professional journals in your area of interest. Find either a report that tests a theory (for example, Wheaton, 1980 or the article by Levine, McDonald, O'Neal, & Garwood, 1980, reprinted in Chapter 3) or an article stating a theory without any test (for example, Patterson, 1976). In the former case, identify the constructs (by placing them in circles) and their associated variables (by placing them in boxes) for the key propositions. In the latter case, where there is no operationalization of the theory, select a proposition from the theory and translate it to hypothesis-testing terms. In both cases, use arrows between boxes or between circles to show the causal direction expected from the theory.

3. Practice making the distinction between constructs and variables by listing constructs or theoretical variables that come to mind, for example, length, intelligence, and academic achievement. Then beside each construct write several possible operationalizations or measured variables, for example, for length: feet and inches measured by a ruler, light years measured by astronomical methods, and microns measured by an electron microscope. Then reverse the process, and make a list of measured variables followed by matching constructs. This is a good

exercise to do with a partner, where one of you provides the construct, for example, and the other provides the variable.

GLOSSARY

Concept: Abstract aspect, attribute, or property of people, things, or events.

Construct: Complex, inferred concept, often used interchangeably with concept.

Deduction: Drawing of specific assertions from general principles.

Dependent variable: In hypothesis tests, a variable that is supposed to be caused by one or more other variables, that is, is dependent on them.

Direct causal path: In a theory, a simple one-way causal connection between two constructs.

Endogenous construct: In a theory, a construct that is caused by one or more other constructs, exogenous or endogenous, within the theory.

Exogenous construct: In a theory, a construct that causes other constructs but which itself has no cause specified within the theory.

Generality: Attribute of a theory of being widely applicable, that is, of being able to account for many different observations.

Hypothesis: Prediction, usually drawn by deduction from a theory.

Hypothesis testing: Procedure by which a hypothesis is checked for its fit or agreement with observations.

Idiographic: Research approach that tries to understand persons or situations for their unique characteristics without trying to generalize (as opposed to nomothetic approach).

Independent variable: In hypothesis tests, a variable that is supposed to cause one or more other variables that is not caused by them, that is, is independent of them.

Indirect causation: In a theory, a set of two or more causal connections by which one construct causes a second indirectly via one or more intermediate constructs called intervening constructs.

Intervening variable: Measured variable in a hypothesis test or a theoretical variable in a theory that is the effect of one variable and a cause of another.

Nomothetic: Pertaining to the science of general laws (as opposed to the idiographic approach).

Operational definition: Procedure by which a construct is made observable.

Paradox: Apparent contradiction between two different theories, between two different observations, or between a theory and observations.

Parsimony: Attribute of a theory of being simple or sparing of constructs and relationships.

Reciprocal causation: In a theory, a two-way causal connection between two constructs in which each causes the other.

Theoretical variable: Concept or construct as distinct from a variable that is measured.

Variable: Measure or indicator thought to represent an underlying construct or concept and produced by an operational definition of the construct or concept.

5

Measurement Theory
Toward Construct Validity

INTRODUCTION TO MEASUREMENT

A Case of Measurement

The N-Ray Affair.   Measuring things that are hard to see is crucial to the advance of both the social and physical sciences. The difficulty of measuring the invisible is illustrated by an episode in physics although, as you will see, this story is more about social and psychological processes than physical reality.

In 1903, a French physicist published his discovery of a new kind of radiation, which became known as N rays (Klotz, 1980). The discoverer's name was René Blondlot, a highly respected member of the French Academy of Science. He was working in an era of scientific expansion, triggered by Roentgen's generation of X-rays in 1895. Physicists were working at the frontier of the discovery of untold new forms of radiation such as alpha rays, beta rays, and gamma rays, each exhibiting new properties and potential for scientific advance and practical application.

The key to detecting and then exploring a new radiation was the development of a good measure. The concept of N rays had to be operationally defined, that is, researchers needed a standard, observable indicator of the presence of N rays. Only then could work on the new ray proceed rapidly and independently in various laboratories. Blondlot provided a technique for detecting the N ray.

Figure 5–1 is a diagram of Blondlot's spark gap apparatus used to detect N rays. A great variety of objects were claimed to emit N rays: electric discharge tubes, the sun, certain types of gas burners, and even cold steel. Blondlot suspected that such radiation would have the effect of reinforcing the energy of an electric spark thus making it brighter.

When a spark discharged between the points of two wires carrying electricity from an attached battery, its brightness could be observed directly or photographed. Typically, the spark gap detector was enclosed in a light-tight box

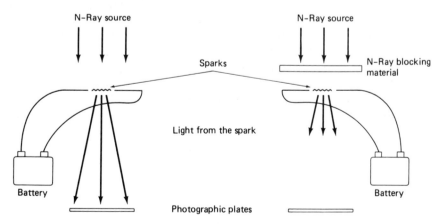

Figure 5–1   Spark gap detector for N rays.

to keep out the confounding effects of visible light. The brightness of the spark should be greater when an N ray source was present than when the source was absent or blocked off. Thus Blondlot had contrived to make the invisible visible.

Blondlot's success in identifying N rays was followed by a host of related discoveries. For example, a respected medical physicist named Charpentier announced his discovery that N rays were produced by the human body and could be used to improve exploration of living human organs (for example, measuring the human heart while it was beating). In less than a year, several investigators were competing for the honor of having discovered this promising new form of radiation. Publications in the *Annals of the French Academy of Science* about N rays jumped from 4 in the first half of 1903 to 54 in the first half of 1904 (versus only 3 about X-rays, for example).

After the sudden emergence of published scientific research about N rays in 1903 and 1904, there was not a single report on them in the Academy's Annals in 1905. What had happened to N rays? What happened was an American physicist and practical joker named R. W. Wood, a professor of physics at Johns Hopkins University. One of Wood's hobbies was the pursuit of frauds such as spiritualistic mediums. When he tried and failed to observe N rays in his lab by using Blondlot's procedure, he became skeptical. He arranged to visit Blondlot's lab at the University of Nancy.

Blondlot and his colleagues very hospitably demonstrated for Wood their various measurement approaches to N rays. For example, they showed him photographs taken in the procedure, illustrated in Figure 5–1. The photographic images of the spark exposed to the N-ray source were distinctly brighter than those taken when the N-ray source was removed or blocked off. But Wood noticed that the technique of making these photos was seriously flawed. The photographic plates were exposed for five seconds per trial for repeated trials in order to amplify any difference indicating the presence of N rays. Unfortunately, the researchers may have favored the N-ray source by leaving the photographic materials for a longer total time when the source was exposed than when it was covered.

In another experiment in a darkened room, Blondlot's staff demonstrated N-ray effects that they claimed were visible to the naked eye. When Wood could not see the effects that others in the same room claimed to be seeing, he devised a very practical joke. The source of the N rays was supposed to be a piece of steel. Unknown to the other observers, Wood substituted a similarly shaped piece of wood, not believed to be a source of N rays. When Blondlot's staff continued to "see" the N rays, Wood concluded that their belief in N rays was deluding them.

In 1904, Wood published his exposé of N rays and effectively ended that line of research outside of France. Before the N-ray bandwagon was stopped, 20 French scientists had in 1903 and 1904 confirmed the existence of this new form of radiation. As Klotz (1980) reports,

> When only French scientists remained in the N-ray camp, the argument began to acquire a somewhat chauvinistic aspect. Some proponents of N rays maintained

that only the Latin races possessed the sensitivities (intellectual as well as sensory) necessary to detect manifestations of the rays. It was alleged that Anglo Saxon powers of perception were dulled by continuing exposure to fog and Teutonic ones blunted by constant ingestion of beer. (p. 175)

Most of the French scientists who verified N rays did so in the vicinity of Nancy, suggesting some sort of sociopsychological contagion or persuasion. To protect the honor of French science, *Revue Scientifique*, a scientific journal, challenged Blondlot to prove once and for all his ability to identify and measure N rays. The challenge consisted of preparing two identical boxes, one with a "known" N-ray source such as steel and the other with an equal weight of a non-N-ray source such as lead. The boxes would be identified by numbers known only to the staff of the *Revue Scientifique* and sent to Blondlot. He could use any and all of his techniques to determine which was the N-ray source box. After considerable delay, Blondlot wrote back in 1906 to decline the challenge.

The moral of the N-ray affair is that the measurement of even the most neutral and objective of physical realities is subject to human distortion. How much more vulnerable to misperception and mismeasurement are the subtle and emotion-laden constructs of the social sciences. Blondlot's experience shows that humans can see what they want to see and that they can persuade others to see what they want them to see. We do not so much believe what we see as we see what we believe. That this problem is a persistent one is illustrated by a more recent dispute between Jacque Benveniste, the head of a French allergy laboratory, and the British journal *Nature*. Doubting the claims of Benveniste, *Nature* sent an observation team that included the professional magician James ("The Amazing") Randy to study the French laboratory's procedures. The review team concluded that the researchers were not sufficiently objective because when the identity of the samples was masked from the researchers, the experiment failed (Maugh, 1988).

The Threat of Mismeasurement. The fragility of measures of complex social constructs must be kept constantly in mind. An ever-present rival explanation in social research is that the construct under investigation was mismeasured. If the indicator we are using does not truly reflect the construct of interest, any results from the study cannot bear on the proposition and theory in question.

Social research constructs are often intangible and as hard to "see" directly as Blondlot's N ray. But we can hope to have some indirect sign or measure of the construct just as Blondlot hoped that an electric spark would flare up in the presence of N rays. The spark's flare was not an N ray itself but was thought to be a visible indicator of its presence. Similarly, social scientists hope that their measures will reflect the presence and magnitude of such abstractions as social status, empathy, or criminal tendencies.

Unfortunately, an indicator may measure nothing at all, or it may measure something other than the construct of interest. We now know that there are no such things as N rays to make the spark flare. Blondlot's indicator was measuring, if anything, the belief or hope that N rays existed. N rays were always absent, but Blondlot's indicators showed their presence to believers and their absence to nonbelievers. This was and is an interesting phenomenon, but it belongs in the realm of social research rather than physics.

Measuring Measures

As we have seen with the N-ray affair, measures do not necessarily do a good job of reflecting the construct for which they are intended. As a result, in planning or judging research, one must evaluate all measures used or to be used. It has become customary to judge the quality of measures on two dimensions: reliability and validity. Both will be discussed in more detail later, but each can be given a preliminary definition here.

Reliability. **Reliability** refers to the degree to which observed scores are "free from errors of measurement" (*American Psychological Association*, 1985, p. 19). As will be seen, reliability can be judged by the consistency of scores. Is there agreement between parallel forms of a measure or between different parts of the same measure or between different raters using a measure?

Validity. **Validity** "refers to the appropriateness, meaningfulness, and usefulness of the specific inferences" made from the measures (*American Psychological Association*, 1985, p. 9). Thus validity is not inherent in a measure but is a function of the fit between measure and label.

Judging and improving the reliability and validity of psychosocial measures is a special research area in its own right called **psychometrics**. Psychometricians have invented ways of measuring measures and assigning them scores. These scores are called reliability and validity coefficients, and they tell us how much confidence we can place in the measures. (For more thorough treatment of psychometric issues, see J. P. Campbell, 1976, or Nunnally, 1978.)

Measures are rarely perfect and are occasionally worthless. The utility of a measure depends not only on its reliability and validity but also on its specific purpose. Thus a measure with moderate reliability and validity may be adequate for a preliminary research study but inadequate for making an important decision about a particular person. Because of the importance of measuring research measures, different disciplines have developed standards for reporting new tests and measurement procedures (for example, *American Psychological Association*, 1985). These standards and the psychometric procedures on which they are based derive from measurement theory.

Measurement Theory

Decomposing Observations. The foundation of measurement theory is the recognition that any observation, test score, or outcome of a measurement procedure is imperfect. It is useful to think of the **observed score** (also called fallible score) as the sum of two general components: **true score**, which is a perfect representation of the characteristic to be observed, and **error**, the difference between the perfect score and what is actually observed. This relationship can be expressed simply for any individual's observed score (X) as

$$X = T + E$$

where T = *true score* and E = *error*.

The goal of measurement is to assign numbers to objects or individuals that reflect the true quantity of the attribute of interest. Unfortunately, we cannot know exactly how much of any particular observed score (X) is due to T and how much is due to E. In order to help resolve this dilemma, the error, or E component, is defined as random. This definition is crucial because it makes it possible to estimate the relative shares of observed scores contributed by true scores and error for a whole group of scores. Defining measurement error as random implies the following: Measurement error is unpredictable, is as likely to be positive as negative for any observation, and is expected to add up to zero over a large number of observations. That is, error may favor an individual on one item or test, but over many tests the bad luck should balance the good.

Random Errors Cancel. Consider an example of measurement error that you have probably experienced. Suppose you are enrolled in a course in which weekly ten-item quizzes are given. Each item is of the true/false type. To correct for guessing, the instructor subtracts one point for each incorrect answer. Now imagine the results of a typical quiz on which you got a score of 8 but knew only seven of the ten answers. That is, in all frankness and off the record, you would have to admit that you guessed on the three items you did not know. You got two of the three right by chance and one wrong. As a result your score consisted of the following components:

8 = 7 (true score) + 1 (error: 2 right – 1 wrong)

Now suppose that on the next quiz you get an observed score of 5. Again let us assume that on reflection, you knew the correct answer on seven items. But this time, of your three guesses, only one was right. This would represent an error of -1 (1 right - 2 wrong). In addition, you discover that you skipped one of the questions to which you knew the answer because you failed to read it or to put down an answer. This is another kind of chance error and so will be added to the error component: (-1) + (-1) = -2. This time your observed score of 5 consists of the following components:

5 = 7 (true score) – 2 (error)

Besides guessing and skipping items, other sources of error include misunderstanding items, chance variations in performance levels due to the occasion of the test (for example, having a headache on test day), chance variations in grading (for example, grader has a headache while grading your exam), and chance variation in the difficulty of the items.

This seems to leave us with a dilemma. We want to measure true scores but inevitably find ourselves with fallible scores. Worse yet, each time we take a test, the amount and direction of error is unpredictable. There are probably occasions when the errors on a particular test or item are very small or cancel out entirely, but we cannot know when these occasions occur. This is the point at which the assumption of randomly distributed errors comes to our rescue.

Suppose that all of your quiz scores could be broken down into true (reliable) and error components. Table 5–1 illustrates what ten such quizzes might look like, on the assumptions that the reliable score is always 7 and that the random errors sum to zero over 10 quizzes.

On the assumption that measurement errors cancel out (add to zero), the sum and average of observed scores equals the sum and average of true scores. Of course, ten quizzes may not be enough for random errors to cancel each other completely. However, the sum of many observed scores should be close to the sum of true scores—which is why grades are based ideally on many quizzes or on exams with many items.

As will be seen in a later section, random error is the fundamental cause of unreliability. The greater the proportion of random error in each observation, the less reliable is the measure. Ways of measuring reliability and of increasing reliability will be discussed later.

Table 5–1   Observed, True, and Error Scores for Ten Imaginary Quizzes

Quiz Number	Observed Score	True Score	+ Error
1	8	= 7	+1
2	5	= 7	-2
3	10	= 7	+3
4	8	= 7	+1
5	3	= 7	-4
6	5	= 7	-2
7	8	= 7	+1
8	10	= 7	+3
9	7	= 7	0
10	6	= 7	-1
Sum	70	70	0
Average	7	7	0

Bias.   Observed scores can include other components besides true score and random error. One such component is **bias,** which consists of nonrandom error. A simple example of bias in the measurement of height is the use of an overly long "yardstick." Suppose that you used a meter stick (measuring 39 3/8 inches), mistaking it for a yardstick. Everyone you measured would seem to be 3 3/8 inches shorter than they really were (39 3/8 inches - 36 inches). Thus your observed height measurements would consist of the true heights plus any random error plus this bias, or in symbolic form, where $B =$ bias, $X = T + B + E$.

This kind of systematic bias presents less of a problem when all subjects of a study have the same biased measure. If everyone's height is mismeasured by 3 3/8 inches, everyone will still stand in the same relation to everyone else. The tallest person will still have the greatest observed height, and the shortest person will have the smallest observed height. For many statistical purposes, the bias will have no effect. However, if the absolute level of a measurement is used to make a decision (such as diagnosing a patient based on a test score) or if observations with different biases are combined, it is essential to minimize the bias or to compensate for its effect.

Biases in measurement come from various sources. Bias can come from the rater or judge (called rater bias). Individual differences among raters can cause consistent differences in their observations. For example, two teaching assistants may differ slightly in their grading standards. The "hard" grader will give consistently fewer points than the "easy" grader for each subjective test answer. Biases can also be produced by situational differences between different testing occasions. We would expect a difference in performance between groups if one section of students had to take their quizzes under conditions of noise or exhaustion and the other section always took the same quiz under more tranquil and restful conditions.

How can we make sure that measures are applied uniformly so that differences in observations are not due to measurement bias? The best way is to standardize measurement so that all methods and raters operate in the same way. **Standardization** serves to assure us that any differences in observed scores are due to real individual differences or to random error, that is, that any bias is constant from observation to observation.

The word *standardization* implies not only uniformity but also the existence or possibility of a standard or referent against which to compare each local version of the measure. One example is the standardization of time. If we are concerned that a clock is too fast, it could be compared with a standard time measure kept by an astronomical observatory.

More Than One True Score.   Another unwanted component of observed scores comes from genuine, nonrandom individual differences other than those associated with the construct that is supposed to be measured. In other words, the true score component of an observation can be divided into two parts: Tx (the part that relates to the concept of interest) and Tnx (the part that relates to any other theoretical variable that happens to be associated with the measure).

As an example, imagine an IQ test with very simple questions, which just about everybody over the age of six could answer correctly without guessing. Now suppose that this easy test were translated into Latin and administered to a sample of adults with normal intelligence.

Some people would get very low scores because they could not make sense out of the Latin questions. Some who had studied Latin could be expected to get all the answers right. Others who had studied some Latin-based language such as Spanish might get some correct answers to the extent that they could understand the Latin questions. Thus there would be individual differences in scores and these differences would be fairly dependable (that is, consistent or nonrandom). If another similar elementary test were administered in Latin translation, individuals would get scores similar to the ones they received the first time.

The problem is to decide what individual characteristic is being measured by the test. It might seem that the test was measuring intelligence since it was labeled an intelligence test. If this were the case, the true score for the target construct (Tx) would measure intelligence. But it should be clear in the preceding example that the scores varied from high to low not because of differences in intelligence but because of differences in familiarity with the Latin language.

It seems that this "IQ" test is not measuring intelligence but rather something else. We can label this something else nx to stand for any true score for a construct other than that for which the measure is intended or named. In this case, the observed score X comprises more of the true score due to knowledge of Latin (Tnx) than to the true score associated with the target variable of intelligence (Tx). The point is that the true score component of the observed score consists of two parts and the name of the test does not necessarily tell us which part is dominant. Whether a test measures the concept for which it is named is the question of validity.

Distinguishing Invalidity and Unreliability.   Disregarding the component of bias (B), our symbolic representation of an observed score (X) would be as follows: $X = Tx + Tnx + E$.

One major question to be asked of a measure is whether it is unreliable. This question really asks how large the error component (E) is relative to the true score components ($Tx + Tnx$), which accurately reflect some aspect(s) of the individuals being measured. If X is entirely due to E, nothing is being measured. This situation ($X = E$) is illustrated in Figure 5–2(a). If we assume that our observations contain no true scores (Tx or Tnx), we are simply measuring random, meaningless noise. Imagine a true/false test written in code or in a very cryptic language with which no one has any familiarity. Since no one taking the test has any idea what the questions mean, everyone simply guesses on all the items. Since it is a true/false test, everyone might as well flip coins: heads true and tails false or vice versa. Some members of the group will be a little more lucky or a little less lucky. But such lucky high scores and unlucky low scores are undependable. Since they are due to the chance flips of the coins and not to any characteristic of the individuals, these high or low scores are not likely to be repeated.

this case, the observation is measuring something. Some dependable characteristics are systematically or reliably producing the high and low observed scores. The circled construct (labeled with a "?" to indicate that we do not know whether it is Tx or Tnx) is connected to the measure in the square in Figure 5–2(b).

In the research literature, we seldom see examples of case 5–2(b), that is, perfectly reliable measures. Most measures have some combination of true and error components. The relative proportions of these two components govern the degree of reliability of the measure.

The second major question is whether the measure is valid. To be valid, a measure has to be reliable. Validity means that the measure taps the characteristic it is supposed to tap. An unreliable measure is unrelated to any characteristic. Thus it does not make sense to ask whether a totally unreliable measure taps any particular characteristic.

An invalid measure may be highly reliable, as illustrated in Figure 5–2(c). If $X = Tnx$, there is no measurement error. In this case, the measure is doing a good job of measuring. Unfortunately, it is measuring the wrong construct. This measure is misnamed. If we could discover what it is measuring, that is, what nx is, we could make this measure very useful by renaming it. The key point here is that validity of measurement must always be in reference to some particular concept. A yardstick is an invalid way of measuring weight but a valid way of measuring height.

Finally, Figure 5–2(d) illustrates a valid measure because the observed score corresponds to the target construct. Validity is the most important aspect of measurement. High validity implies high reliability and close correspondence of

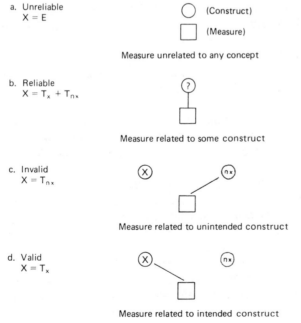

a. Unreliable
   $X = E$

   ◯ (Construct)
   ☐ (Measure)

   Measure unrelated to any concept

b. Reliable
   $X = T_x + T_{nx}$

   ⓘ

   Measure related to some construct

c. Invalid
   $X = T_{nx}$

   Ⓧ   ⓝ

   Measure related to unintended construct

d. Valid
   $X = T_x$

   Ⓧ   ⓝ

   Measure related to intended construct

Figure 5–2 Reliability and validity: Measurement components and construct operationalization.

measurement. High validity implies high reliability and close correspondence of the measure with the target construct. If a measure is reliable but invalid, a rival explanation of any findings becomes plausible. The observed relationship is not pertinent to the theory and constructs to which the hypothesis test was addressed.

RELIABILITY

Estimating Reliability

Reliability Coefficient. How can reliability be measured? Ideally, the reliability measure should be large when there is no error and small when there is little but error. A statistic that satisfies these conditions is called the **reliability coefficient,** the ratio of two numbers both of which are measures of variation. One of these numbers is the amount of variation (or variability) of the true score component of the observed score. This number is divided by the second number, which is the variability of the observed score (which includes both true and error components). If there is no error, the variability in the true score will equal the variability in observed scores, and the reliability will equal a perfect 1 (a number divided by itself = 1). But if there is no true score, true score variability will be zero and the reliability will also be zero. For intermediate amounts of error, the reliability coefficient takes on values between 0 and 1, rising with the proportion of true score variability.

How do we measure the variability of the true score component since all we actually know are the observed scores, in which true and error components are mixed up? Fortunately, the reliability coefficient can be estimated by the degree of association of two measures of the same variable (Nunnally, 1978). The degree of association is measured by a correlation coefficient (see the Appendix for a review of correlation). This statistic approaches +1 if the measures agree (that is, tend to be high together or low together) and zero if the two measures have no correspondence.

Uses of Reliability Estimates. The most common use of reliability information is in evaluating a measure. If the reliability coefficient is very low, the measure is assigning scores in a random, meaningless way. Measures with low reliability are best avoided.

Another implication of low reliability is that any relationship of the measure with another variable will be underestimated. This effect of lowering correlations is called **attenuation.** One practical use of knowing the reliability coefficients of measures is to correct for the attenuation due to unreliability (for the details of this procedure, see Nunnally, 1978).

Another practical benefit of reliability estimates is in the estimation of true scores. An individual's estimated true score (expressed as the difference from the group's average) is the observed score (also expressed as the difference from the group's average) multiplied by the reliability coefficient. There is an important principle implicit in this formula. Since reliability is almost always imperfect (less than 1), the estimated true score is almost always going to be nearer the average of all scores than the observed score. A test score above the mean (for example, +10 where the mean is 0) when multiplied by the reliability coefficient (say .7) will yield a smaller estimated true score (10 × .7 = 7). This implies that the error in this case was positive (estimated error = observed - estimated true = 10 - 7 = +3). If you work through this same formula for a low observed score (for example, -10), you will find that the low-scoring person is credited with having had negative error or bad luck.

What is interesting about this pattern is that there is a kind of bias operating in measurement error. Above-average observed scores will, typically, have gained from error and below-average observed scores will have lost. The evidence for this principle comes from a comparison of scores from earlier tests and later tests for the same persons. On the average, first-test high scorers will get lower scores on the second test. The extent of this change depends on the test's reliability. The more reliable the test, the smaller the change. Since this principle applies to low scorers on the first test as well, their second test scores can be expected to move upward to the mean. This phenomenon of test score change is called **regression toward the mean,** which is of special concern for studies based on repeated measures of the same subjects (Nesselroade, Stigler, & Baltes, 1980.)

Types of Reliability Measures

Within-Test Consistency. Many measures in social research consist of tests or questionnaires with multiple items such as intelligence tests, achievement tests, attitude scales, and health and mental health symptom scales. A reliable test should exhibit consistency among its own items.

How could we measure interitem consistency? One of the simplest ways is to split the test into two parts and correlate one half with the other half. This is called the *split-half* method or the *odd-even* method (after the most common way of dividing a test into two halves—odd-numbered items and even-numbered items). Thus, on a ten-item multiple-choice quiz, two scores could be calculated: the sum for items 1, 3, 5, 7, and 9; and the sum for items 2, 4, 6, 8, and 10. These two scores could be correlated over the individuals who took the test. The resulting correlation would estimate the reliability of either five-item subtest. But split-half estimates of reliability are not ideal because in short tests, any half of the items drawn at random might not represent the whole test very well.

A more systematic and widely used way of measuring interitem consistency uses the average correlations of each item with every other item. For example, item number 1 of a ten-item test could be correlated with item number 2 over all the persons taking the test, then with item number 3, and so on. The average of all these correlations summarizes the consistency of the average item on the test. This average interitem correlation only describes the reliability of any single item, not the reliability of the whole ten-item test, which takes all the items into account.

One of the most important discoveries in psychometrics is that the sum of items is more reliable than any one item. In general, the more items on the test, the more reliable it is. If you recall the example in Table 5–1, errors in each quiz tend to cancel out over many tests. The same principle applies to multiple-item tests. Random errors on each item are expected to cancel out over many items. Thus the average item reliability of a test must be adjusted upward to take into account the number of items on the test. The most common length-adjusted estimate of test reliability based on the consistency among all the items (with three or more answer options) is called **coefficient alpha**. A related coefficient called KR-20 can be applied to items of the two-answer or true/false type (for more detail see the discussion of the Spearman-Brown Prophecy Formula, in Nunnally, 1978).

The interitem reliability coefficient estimates how well the test would correlate with an equal-length test composed of similar items administered under the same conditions. Since this reliability coefficient depends both on the interitem consistency and on the length of the test, it can be improved in two ways. The test could be made more reliable if items with greater intercorrelations are substituted for the existing items. The test could also be made more reliable if more items could be added even if their intercorrelations are not greater than the existing items. Unfortunately, substantially raising the reliability of a test made up of unreliable items can require the addition of a great many new items. Thus, there is a trade-off between the reliability of a test and its length. The researcher usually accepts an adequately but imperfectly reliable measure that is of practical length.

Other Reliability Coefficients. If all measures consisted of multiple self-report items and the only source of error in testing came from within the test, we would not need other reliability measures. Some measures depend not on multiple items graded by a single rater but on multiple judges counting selected behaviors (for example, the number of times a professor smiles at his or her class while trying to establish rapport during their first ten minutes together). For such observational measures, an important source of error is the way different judges rate the same reality. Measuring reliability when between-rater error can be large requires a type called interrater reliability.

Even if the measure consists of multiple test items, there are sources of error other than those occurring within a test. Other errors can occur when the same test is administered on different occasions, called between-occasion error. For example, the individual may have felt ill on the first test and well on the second. Or the individual may have been assigned an uncomfortable or noisy location the first time but a comfortable and quiet one the next time. Differences between occasions cannot be attributed to true score since they have nothing to do with the individual's ability or knowledge.

Such between-occasion error is not taken into account by reliability coefficients based only on interitem consistency for one occasion. If a person performs badly on one test because of temporary illness, the performance reflects his or her true score and his or her illness on that occasion. There is no way to separate true ability from other factors operating during one session. Thus the effect of illness (or noise or an uncomfortable chair or a faulty pen) that operates only in that session shows up as a true score rather than error in within-test reliability coefficients. Only when test results from more than one occasion are compared can we identify between-occasion error.

Remember that reliability is the proportion of variability in observed scores due to true scores. If you shift some variability away from the true score component and assign it to error, this proportion (and thus reliability) will decline. For this reason, we do not expect all kinds of reliability estimates to be equal. Typically, we expect an interitem reliability coefficient to be larger than one that includes both interitem and between-occasion or interrater error. Three of the most common methods of estimating between-rater or between-occasion reliabilities are test-retest, parallel form, and interrater.

Test-Retest Reliability. The correlation of scores from two administrations of the same test estimates test-retest reliability, which is often reported as evidence of the stability of the trait being measured. High agreement in scores of the same people on the same test is used to demonstrate that the characteristic in question is unchanging. Unfortunately, the reuse of the same test does not necessarily support this interpretation. Since individuals may remember their answers from the first test and may want to appear consistent over time, they may get the same retest score for reasons other than trait stability.

Parallel Test Reliability. The correlation of two different but similar tests over the same individuals estimates parallel test reliability. Parallel tests are made up of similar or interchangeable items. If two parallel tests are administered on the same occasion, we would expect them to correlate as well as two halves of the same test. In such a single-occasion case, the correlation of two parallel forms would reflect mainly interitem reliability. If the two parallel tests are administered on two different occasions, say two weeks apart, we would expect a lower correlation, reflecting the added error due to differences between occasions.

When the same (test-retest) or parallel tests are used on two or more occasions, consideration must be given to the possibility of development. Suppose two tests are relatively uncorrelated after an interval of one year. Does this result prove the unreliability of the test (if the test is reused in the test-retest approach) or tests (if parallel forms are used)? Not necessarily—both the first and second administrations of the test may accurately measure the characteristic at the time of measurement. The low correlation over occasions could reflect genuine developmental changes. Thus when reliability is measured by the parallel test method, you must consider whether the characteristic being measured is subject to developmental changes and whether enough time has elapsed between administrations to permit such changes.

Interrater Reliability. The correlation of scores provided by two observers based on the same behavioral sample estimates interrater reliability or the equivalence between the raters. For example, the two observers could be counting the number of smiles produced each minute by the same professor during the same ten-minute sample. The correlation between the raters could be calculated over each of the minutes of observation. When there are more than two raters, the interrater reliability is often reported as the average among all possible pairwise interrater correlations.

Another, simpler estimate of interrater reliability is commonly reported, that of rater agreement expressed as a percent. Suppose the observers were judging a gymnastics performance. For each competitor, any two judges could be said to agree (if they assigned the same score, say 9.5) or to disagree (say one gave a 9.5 and the other gave a 9.6). A measure of their agreement would be the percentage of gymnastic performances on which they agree (say they agree seven of ten times, or 70 percent).

Unfortunately, there are several problems with using percent agreement as an estimate of reliability. If exact agreement is required, this measure fails to give credit to near misses (often called adjacencies). Even if credit is given for adjacent as well as exact agreements, the procedure fails to allow for chance agreements. If there are only a small number of categories in the rating system (say good versus bad gymnastic performance), we can expect a certain amount of agreement by chance (in the case of two categories, we expect 50 percent agreement by chance). Even if allowance is made for chance agreement, the system fails to allow for similarity among those being rated. If everyone in a highly select group is clearly very good, the raters might achieve a 100 percent agreement without really demonstrating that they could make accurate distinctions in a reliable way. Remember that our basic definition of reliability is the ratio of true score variability to total observed score variability. If there is no variability in the true or observed scores, reliability has no meaning. For additional discussion of interrater reliability estimation, see S. K. Mitchell (1979) and Tinsley and Weiss (1975).

Different Errors, Different Reliability Estimates. Different approaches to reliability estimation reflect different sources of error, as summarized in Table 5–2. Each reliability measure has its advantages and disadvantages. The research situation will determine which kind of reliability is best for purposes of drawing a particular conclusion. If the measure in question depends heavily on subjective ratings from several judges, interrater reliability would be the coefficient of choice. If the study employs parallel forms of the same test, the

Table 5–2 Types of Reliability Coefficients and Sources of Error

Type	Measured by Correlation	Source of Error	Potential Problems
Interitem (also called "consistency")	Among items within test	Within test	May not generalize across raters
Test-retest (also called "stability")	Between two administrations of the same test	Different occasions as well as within test	Confounded by memory of first test and real development
Parallel forms	Between two forms of the test	Different occasions and forms as well as within test	Confounded by real development
Interrater (also called "equivalence")	Between raters	Differences in raters as well as within test	Beware of interobserver agreement percentages

parallel forms correlation would be the reliability coefficient of choice. In sum, the choice of reliability coefficient depends on the situation—a combination of occasion(s), test form(s), and judge(s). One reliability theory is based on the recognition of the different facets of the measurement situation. Since each facet (occasion, rater, item, and form) can contribute error that affects a measure's reliability, different combinations of these facets may have to be considered. For more detail on the approach to the generalizability of measurement reliability, see Cronbach, Gleser, Nanda, and Rajaratnam (1972).

Just as there is no single best type of reliability coefficient for all situations, so there is no generally agreed on minimal level of reliability. High reliabilities (in the .90s) are always desirable. Lower reliabilities in the .80s, .70s and even .60s are seen in the scientific literature and may be appropriate depending on the research. The danger of using measures of low reliability is not that of finding support for nonexistent relationships but rather of failing to find support for relationships that do exist (see the earlier discussion of attenuation).

Standardization. How can one make measures more reliable? The most general answer is standardization. For each source of random error in a test score, standardization will tend to reduce that error and increase reliability. Interitem differences can be reduced by asking questions in a similar manner (standardizing format and instructions) and about similar content (intentional redundancy).

Standardization also applies to raters, forms, and occasions. Rater training reduces rater errors (both within and between raters) by eliminating individual differences in the way raters make judgments. Identical test instructions and inclusion of equivalent items serve to standardize different forms of a test. Similarly, test occasions can be partially standardized by use of identical test instructions and similar or identical test environments (for example, same room, same time of day, and same noise and heat level).

VALIDITY

Estimating Validity

The Use of Validity Assessment. Validity is the extent to which a test measures what it is supposed to measure. The validity of a measurement determines the plausibility of one ever-present rival explanation of research findings. This rival explanation argues that observed relationships among a set of variables have no bearing on the theory in question because at least one of the measured variables is invalid (that is, fails to represent its conceptual counterpart in the theory).

Most measures consist of some true score for the target construct, some true score for other constructs, and some error. Validity estimation consists in judging the degree to which X measures the intended rather than unintended characteristics, that is, that the measure is correctly named.

Response Styles and Sets. What kinds of variables are apt to intrude into social science measures, to contribute unwanted true score components? There are two major types of such variables that are thought to affect self-report measures: response styles and response sets.

Response style refers to a person's manner of responding to test items, independent of item content. One common response style is called acquiescence, or yea-saying. Acquiescence is defined as "a generalized tendency to be agreeable" (Rorer, 1965, p. 151). Operationally, the acquiescence style is usually defined as a disposition to agree with test items, that is, to answer "yes" or "true." Response style is believed to be a personality trait, which will appear on different tests regardless of content. Other response styles include nay-saying, or the tendency to say "no," and the extreme response style, or the tendency to select the more extreme of the available answers. Because response style is not random but rather a consistent tendency of individuals, it could contribute an unwanted reliable score component to test scores and would thus tend to lower the validity of a measure. A score reflecting response style is, in effect, measuring the response style instead of or in addition to the characteristic it is supposed to measure.

Efforts to measure response style directly have tended to lower our concern about the effects of a general response style. Content-independent measures of response styles have not been found to agree with each other, casting doubt on the meaningfulness and generality of the concept. Nevertheless, test builders usually guard against a yea-saying or nay-saying style by balancing item wording, so that items are not always scored in the yes or in the no direction.

Response set refers to the tendency of the respondent to answer items in a way, conscious or unconscious, that gives a preferred image of himself or herself. A common response set is called social desirability, or defensiveness, which is the tendency to answer items in a way that is socially desirable. For example, the socially desirable answer to the item "I have never told a white lie" is "true" even if the honest answer is "false." On measures of personally sensitive topics such as mental adjustment or illegal behavior, the social desirability set would be expected to influence test scores. Since some people are consistently more defensive than others, this variable may contribute a substantial component to the observed scores. Indeed, the issue is not whether social desirability contributes to self-report tests but "whether a sufficient amount of independent variance [due to Tx] remains in the self-inventories to produce other strong factors" (Nunnally, 1978, p. 557).

One approach to the social desirability problem is to make self-report items that are neutral on this characteristic or to write alternative answers that are equal on social desirability. Unfortunately, these items and answers are difficult to write. Another approach is to measure social desirability and remove this component statistically. Because social desirability appears to be a complex variable, which includes components caused by the respondent's actual adjustment, self-awareness, and honesty, its statistical removal from observed scores may remove some true score component. Fortunately, recent research indicates that "in most applications, attempts to correct scores for defensiveness or SD do not enhance validity," (McCrae & Costa, 1983, p. 886).

Types of Validity Measures

Various approaches to measuring the validity of measures have been suggested, but most of these can be grouped into three types: criterion-, content-, and construct-related (*American Psychological Association*, 1985, p. 9). However, the distinctions among these types are not always clear-cut, and some have argued that validation is better thought of as the single process of hypothesis testing (Landy, 1986). Nevertheless, it is useful to understand the differences in the approaches and when each type is most appropriately used.

Criterion Validity. Just as with reliability, different methods of assessing validity have different applications and limitations. One of the most common approaches to validation is called **criterion validity** or criterion-related validity. A criterion is an existing measure that is accepted as an adequate indicator of the characteristic of interest. That is, a criterion is a measure that is assumed or defined to be valid. Criterion validation consists of correlating the criterion with the new measure that is being assessed for validity. The correlation of the new measure with the criterion measure is the criterion **validity coefficient**. This coefficient reaches +1 if the new measure and the criterion correspond perfectly. If the two are uncorrelated ($r = 0$) or weakly correlated, the new measure is said to be invalid.

Criterion validity has a number of variants. If, as is commonly the case, the new test is measured before the criterion, this method is called *predictive validity*. For example, suppose the criterion is success in law school as measured by law school grade point average (GPA). The Law School Aptitude Test would be validated if it predicted the criterion (that is, law school GPA). Predictive validity is especially useful in evaluating tests that are used for decision-making purposes such as admission to graduate school.

If the criterion and the measure being validated are collected at the same time, the method is called *concurrent validity*. If the criterion is collected before the measure, the method is called *postdictive validity*. Concurrent and postdictive validity coefficients are commonly used in judging whether the two measures can be substituted for each other. If the criterion measure is costly or time-consuming, it would be desirable to find a brief, inexpensive substitute. Suppose there were a highly accurate but costly blood test for screening a disease. Such a blood test might not be practical for use on millions of persons in a short time. A brief, self-report test that correlated highly with the blood test would make a desirable substitute.

The criterion validity method has the advantage of providing single, easily interpreted coefficients. Unfortunately, the simplicity of the criterion validity approach is based on the fundamental assumption that the criterion is valid. If the criterion really does represent the intended construct, criterion validity is appropriate for decision making. However, the validity of the criterion is sometimes debatable. Consider length of stay on the job as the criterion for job performance. If maximizing the employee's time on the job is really the most important goal of the personnel director, this measure is a proper criterion for job placement tests. But staying on the job may not measure performance on the job. If people who stay are also lazy or inefficient, testing to the criterion of length of stay could be a mistake for the employer.

Content Validity. Not all measurements have criteria, that is, agreed-upon standards. In the absence of a criterion, you can always assess a measurement's validity by inspecting its content, its **content validity**.

Tests can be thought of as samples of larger domains. For example, an achievement test in economics is supposed to indicate how much knowledge of economics the student has gained. No one expects the test to cover the entire domain of economics. In that case, the test would have to be as long as the course itself. Rather, the test is supposed to ask a sample of questions that fairly represents the domain of all possible questions. We assess the content validity of such a test by judging how well the test's sample of questions represents the domain.

Since this approach depends on the subjective judgment of the domain, a quantitative coefficient is not ordinarily produced by content validation. Although content validity is appropriate for many achievement tests (for example, course exams), it is often too subjective and imprecise for many scientific purposes.

Another problem with content validity is that items with content validity tend to be obvious in their intent, and items that "give away" tests may lead to incorrect measurement. For example, if a test is used to select applicants for a very desirable training program (say, pilot school in the military), obvious items would be answered by all applicants in a way that increases their chances of being selected. It would be better if such a screening test included items that predicted future success as a pilot (that is, criterion validity) but did not obviously indicate which answer would help the candidate get admitted.

Construct Validity. The third form of measurement validation, and the one emphasized throughout this text, is called **construct validity**. In construct validation, the question is how well the test measures the underlying construct (Cronbach & Meehl, 1955). The abstract nature of the target construct makes this approach complicated and the results uncertain. Construct validity can no more be definitively and finally established than theories can be proved. Rather, evidence is gathered that tends to strengthen or weaken our confidence in the construct validity of the measure. Several kinds of evidence can be brought to bear on the question of construct validity: the relations among items on a test, the relation of the test to other supposed measures of the same construct, and tests of the relationships among different constructs.

A major way of assessing the construct validity of a measure based on observed variables is the statistical procedure called *factor analysis* (Kim & Mueller, 1978). Recall that the validity question is whether a test measures the intended construct or instead measures some other construct(s). Factor analysis identifies how many different constructs (called factors) are being measured by a test's items and the extent to which each item of a test is related to ("loaded on" in the jargon of factor analysis) each factor. Factor analysis uses the correlations among all the items of a test to identify groups of items that correlate more highly among themselves than with items outside of the group. Each such group of items is said to be highly loaded on and to define a common factor. A measure made up of items sharing just one factor is said to be unidimensional (that is, to measure just one characteristic or construct).

Factor analysis aids in answering one part of the validity question: Is the test measuring one construct or more than one construct? Even if a test is designed with factor analysis to measure a single construct, we are still not sure that this construct is the one we want to measure. We could assess the content covered by the items that load on a common factor, but such an assessment is really content validation (see the previous discussion).

A second approach involves correlating the test to be validated with other measures thought to reflect the same construct. Suppose we have a new test that we think measures empathy (defined as the extent to which a person displays accurate understanding of another person). An empathy measure should correlate with other tests believed to measure empathy, but it should not correlate with tests thought to measure other constructs, such as athletic skill. If the several different empathy measures agree with each other and with our new test, we have a kind of construct validity called *convergent validity* (so named because of the convergence of several different tests). If our new empathy test disagrees with the several tests believed *not* to measure empathy, we have additional construct validation called *discriminant validity* (since our empathy measure is discriminated from nonempathy measures, as it should be).

One important reason for concern with discrimination is the risk of **method effects.** *Method* here refers to "everything that the investigator does to obtain an array of measurements" (Fiske, 1987, p. 286). Sometimes the measurement method contributes a systematic effect that is not germane to the construct of interest. As a result, measures using the same method but targeted at different constructs may inappropriately converge. Their agreement with each other will be due to their sharing the same method (that is, reflecting some method effect). For example, if we measure empathy and athletic skill with a paper-and-pencil self-report questionnaire, we may find that people tend to rate themselves high on both or low on both despite our belief that these two constructs should not be highly related. The reason may be some effect of the self-report method, perhaps a tendency of people to rate themselves consistently favorably or unfavorably depending on their self-esteem. A good way to check for the presence of method effects is to measure different constructs with several different methods. This approach has been formalized as the *multitrait-multimethod matrix* (Campbell & Fiske, 1959). The term *matrix* refers to the set of correlations resulting when each of the constructs is measured by each of two or more methods. If a measure is relatively free of a method effect, it will correlate well with other measures of the same construct using different methods (convergence) and will not correlate well with measures of different constructs based on the same method (discrimination).

This method of correlating two or more measures resembles the type of criterion validity called concurrent validity. The difference is that in criterion validity the criterion is assumed to be valid, but in construct validity the existing measures are not assumed to be valid. If the intercorrelations among measures of the same construct prove small, doubt is cast equally on the validity of all of the tests. In such a case, further evidence is required to identify which, if any of the tests, is the valid one. Such disagreements (failure to find convergence) among like-named tests do happen from time to time (for example, the failure to find convergence among several empathy measures by Kurtz and Grummon, 1972).

Even if a test is shown to be unidimensional by factor analysis and to have convergent and discriminant validity, we still cannot be sure that the measure has construct validity. It is conceivable that each of the tests showing convergence measures the wrong construct. Just such misleading convergence occurred in the case of the measurement of N rays. How can we judge whether the intended construct is being measured?

The third approach to construct validation is to assess the relationship of the measured construct to other constructs in the context of theory. Remember that constructs are elements of theories. A test with construct validity should measure the concept as it is defined and understood in its parent theory. The test of a construct's validity is thus related to the truth of the theory itself.

Suppose we have two nonconvergent measures each of which purports to measure the same construct. How can we use the theoretical interrelationships between this construct and others to identify which measure has the better construct validity? To make this problem more graphic, suppose the nonconvergent measures are of the construct empathy as understood in C. R. Rogers's theory of psychotherapy (1957). This theory is summarized in Figure 5–3.

According to Rogers, high therapist empathy should lead to client improvement (arrow 3 in the figure). The construct validity question is whether the concept of empathy is operationalized better by measure A or measure B (that is, we must choose between relationships 1A and 1B in the figure). The only evidence we have are the observations about relationships 2A and 2B. Assuming the theory (arrow 3) is correct and that measured client change is a valid measure of the concept of therapeutic change by client (relationship 4 in the figure), observations of 2A and 2B can help us choose between 1A and 1B. If 2A is strong and 2B is weak, we are led to conclude that measure A is a more valid measure of the empathy construct as employed in this particular theory than is measure B. The reason for this conclusion is that measure A has the kind of relationship expected by the theory. In summary, this method of construct validity determines how well the measure being validated conforms to the theory. Just as criterion validity is based on the assumption that the criterion is valid, so construct validation is based on two assumptions: that the theory is correct and that the measure of the other construct in the theory is valid.

The three main types of measurement validation are summarized in Table 5–3. As with reliability assessment, there is no single right way to validate a measure. The situation determines the most appropriate type of validity. The three types of validity have in common a reliance on assumptions. That is, the validation of a measure cannot be made independent of some belief about the validity of other measures, of theory, or of the content domain of the construct.

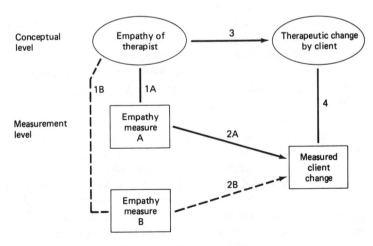

Figure 5–3 Construct validation.

Table 5-3 Summary of Measurement Validity Types

Type	Method
Construct	Extent to which the measure reflects the theoretical concept it is supposed to measure.
Convergent-discriminant	The measure should agree with other measures of the same construct and disagree with measures of different constructs.
Theoretical-experimental	The measure should be related to other variables in a study in a way consistent with the theory.
Factor analysis	The measure should have the theoretically expectable factor structure (usually unidimensional).
Criterion	Extent to which measure agrees with some other measure believed to be a direct and accurate reflection of the behavior or characteristic in question.
Predictive	Relationship of measure to later criterion (often for selection or forecasting purposes).
Concurrent	Relationship of measure to simultaneously available criterion (often for test equivalence of less expensive measures to existing diagnostic or categorizing criterion measure).
Postdictive	Relationship of measure to previously measured criterion (often for same purpose as concurrent criterion validation).
Content (or Face)	Extent to which measure tests or covers the requisite topics, usually based on expert judgment and applied to assessment of achievement tests.

SUMMARY

This chapter has introduced two important ways of assessing social science measures: reliability and validity. Reliability assesses the extent to which a measure measures something. Validity assesses the extent to which the something that is being measured is the intended construct, criterion, or content domain. Both reliability and validity can be understood in terms of the decomposition of observed scores. Reliability decreases as the amount of random error in the score increases. Validity increases in proportion to the amount of the score that reflects the intended true score component.

Reliability can be measured in several ways, including interitem, test-retest, parallel forms, and interrater correlations. Similarly, validity can be assessed in several ways, including construct, criterion, and content methods.

Validity is more important than reliability. If a measure has high validity, it must also have high reliability. If it has low validity, it is misnamed and misleading regardless of its reliability. Of the three types of validity discussed here, construct validity is the most important for social research because of the threat that the intended concept is not reflected by its measures.

EXERCISES

1. Find a newspaper or popular magazine article that reports a social research study. Identify one test or measure employed in the study and assess its reliability and validity. Consider the extent to which random error could creep into this measure's scores and what could have been done to keep it out. Consider the extent to which this measure might really measure something other than its intended construct. Can you think of some other construct that it might be tapping and why this might be the case? How difficult was this task of estimating the reliability and validity from nonprofessional publications?

2. You probably found the first exercise difficult because little is said about measurement details in the popular press, although the measures are the foundations of the reported research. Now find a professional study that describes the development and analysis of a measure. This report should contain explicit discussions of reliability and validity assessment methods and results. Such articles are concentrated in journals specializing in instrumentation and measurement and also are scattered throughout much of the social research literature. If you have difficulty finding such a report try one of these examples: (a) a measure of loneliness by Russell, Peplau, and Cutrona (1980); (b) a measure of test anxiety by Suinn (1969).

GLOSSARY

Attenuation: Effect of measurement error or unreliability in reducing the apparent magnitude of association of two variables. Statistical correction for attenuation is possible if the reliability of the variables is known.

Bias: That part of the deviation of the observed score from the true value of the construct or constructs being measured that is unchanging (as distinct from randomly varying error). Such bias may stem from faulty measurement procedures as in method bias or rater bias.

Coefficient alpha: Commonly seen coefficient of length-adjusted, interitem, or within-test consistency or reliability appropriate for multi-item tests when the items have three or more answer options (KR-20 is an appropriate substitute when the items have two answer options).

Construct validity: Approach to measurement validity that is most important to theory-based research because it assesses the extent to which the measure reflects the intended construct; different approaches depend on the relationships among observed variables (for example, factor analysis and convergent-discriminant construct validity) or on the fit of observed associations with theory.

Content validity: Approach to measurement validity that rests on the judgment that the content of the test (for example, an achievement test) is an adequate sampling or representation of the domain of the material being covered.

Criterion validity: Approach to measurement validity that correlates the measure to be validated with another, called a criterion, which is accepted as an adequate indicator of the characteristic to be measured. Depending on whether the criterion is measured after, at the same time as, or before the measure being validated, the procedure is called predictive, concurrent, or postdictive criterion validation.

Error: In measurement theory, that part of the deviation of observed scores from true scores that is random or unpredictable.

Method effects: Source of construct invalidity in which measures of different constructs using the same measuring procedure fail to diverge.

Observed score: Also called fallible score, the value obtained by the measurement procedure and assumed to contain some degree of error.

Psychometrics: Research area devoted to evaluating and improving reliability and validity of social research measures.

Regression toward the mean: When the same measure is applied more than once, the subsequent scores will, on the average, move toward the mean (that is, initial high scores will tend to move lower), but the greater the reliability (that is, the less the error), the smaller will be this change.

Reliability: Extent to which a measure reflects systematic or dependable sources of variation rather than random error.

Reliability coefficient: Estimate of the share of the variation in observed scores that is due to the true score component; usually arrived at by correlating two or more measures of the same type—for example, interitem, interrater, parallel form, or test-retest (see Table 5–2).

Response set: Tendency of a person to answer items in a way designed to produce a preferred image (for example, social desirability is the response set of answering to give a favorable impression), which can reduce construct validity.

Response style: Person's habitual manner of responding to test items that is independent of item content and can reduce the construct validity of the measure (for example, acquiescence, or yea-saying).

Standardization: Arrangement of measurement procedures so that they will be identical (or nearly so) when applied to different subjects, at different times, or by different raters; contributes to the reliability of the measurement and reduces bias and the chance of differential bias across conditions of the study.

True score: That part of the observed score that reflects genuine individual differences in the subjects or objects being assessed; it can pertain to the construct of interest; to other extraneous, even unknown constructs; or to both.

Validity: Extent to which a measure reflects the intended phenomenon (for example, construct, criterion, or content domain).

Validity coefficient: Estimate of the agreement of the measure being validated with another believed to represent the criterion (criterion validity) or the target construct (convergent-type construct validity); usually presented as a simple correlation but not appropriate for all types of validity, for example, content validity (see Table 5–3).

6

Types of Measures
Finding and Using
Them

CATEGORIZING MEASURES

Introduction

Measuring Intimacy. Take a moment to consider how you would go about measuring the intimacy of a stranger's communication to you. (By intimacy is meant the extent to which something personal or secret is disclosed.) For scientific purposes, the procedure must follow some clear rules so that any other researcher could obtain the measure in the same standard way. Moreover, the measure has to have reasonable reliability and validity.

To be valid, the measure may well have to be somewhat hidden or disguised. If someone is asked to assess the intimacy of his or her own communications, we are apt to hear what the person thinks is appropriate or desirable rather than a frank assessment. Even if all persons in our study were perfectly frank, it is likely that different individuals would have different definitions of intimacy or different levels of self-awareness of their intimacy.

Handwriting Samples. Zick Rubin (1975) provides a clever procedure for sampling communications without revealing that the topic is intimacy. Rubin's assistants approached strangers in airport departure lounges. Adults, seated alone, were asked to give a sample of their handwriting for a class project in handwriting analysis. The assistant provided a sheet and a pen. On the sheet was a sample of the assistant's handwriting and a space for the subject's writing sample. The assistant's writing sample was provided in the guise of allowing a comparison between the assistant's and the subject's writing style. The real purpose was to introduce an experimental manipulation. The assistant's "sample" was a stimulus that was intentionally varied in intimacy of self-disclosure. After reading the assistant's writing sample, the subject was asked to write one or two sentences. The resulting sentences were the observations on which intimacy measures could be based.

To assign measures of intimacy to these "handwriting samples," Rubin defined five intimacy levels ranging from little or no disclosure (that is, shifted away from self) to intimate disclosure (that is, clearly intimate information on such topics as sex, religion, or other central life concerns). Two judges independently rated the most intimate part of each sample on this five-point scale. The interjudge correlation was a satisfactory .77. Their two ratings were added together (ranging from 2 to 10) to yield the intimacy rating.

Such ratings of intimacy are a subjective matter. The correlation of .77 indicates that despite reasonably good agreement, these two raters did occasionally disagree in their judgments. Rubin considered the possibility that a simpler, more objective indicator might also reflect disclosure intimacy. He counted the number of words in each handwriting sample and found that this measure correlated moderately with intimacy rating ($r = .56$).

Rubin's (1975) study also provided evidence on the construct validity of these measures. One of the most common findings in the literature on verbal openness is that of reciprocity, the view that the more intimate the disclosure of one person, the more intimate the response of the other person. Rubin found that both intimacy rating and number of words behaved as expected. They both increased with the intimacy of the writing sample provided as a stimulus by the research assistants.

Two Dimensions of Measures

This chapter will introduce the main types of **quantitative measurement**. Rubin's intimacy rating and number of words are examples of quantitative measures, standardized procedures for numerically characterizing behaviors. There is another approach to research that is based on *qualitative methods*, which is considered in a separate chapter (Chapter 13). There are so many quantitative measures that only a few examples can be mentioned. The goal here is to help you locate and evaluate measures as you may need them. Two important dimensions will be used to organize the discussion of measures: (1) **verbal versus nonverbal measurement**; and (2) **obtrusive versus unobtrusive measurement**.

Verbal Versus Nonverbal. Verbal measures include written or spoken verbal communications from the subject of the study. Nonverbal measures include physiological measures and visual judgments of nonverbal behaviors. Responses to a questionnaire are verbal, but measures of heart rate or categorizations of facial expression are nonverbal measures. Rubin's intimacy rating was based on written self-description and thus falls into the verbal category.

Obtrusiveness. Obtrusive measures are those that intrude to a greater or lesser degree into the awareness of the subject undergoing measurement. Unobtrusive measures are made without the awareness of the subject and may be made by an invisible judge or from verbal records or physical traces produced by the subject but analyzed later or elsewhere. An interviewer or experimenter necessarily enters into the awareness of the interviewee or subject. Such research thus falls in the category of obtrusive measurement. A rater who secretly counts social interactions in a public place or who analyzes public data such as mortality records engages in unobtrusive measurement. Although Rubin's handwriting samples were obtained with the awareness of the subjects, their purpose was secret. His intimacy rating thus could be considered relatively unobtrusive. The use of unobtrusive methods raises ethical issues, which will be noted later.

These two 2-level dimensions provide a convenient four-way breakdown of measurement types, as shown in Table 6–1. Of course, the distinctions between these four categories are less clear than the table implies. For example, it is customary to label as unobtrusive measurement such records as unemployment rates and census data. Although many archival records are unobtrusively collected (for example, birth and death statistics), the data in our census and unemployment

Table 6–1 Types of Measures

	Obtrusive	Unobtrusive
Verbal	Questionnaires	Content analysis
	Projective tests	Process analysis
Nonverbal	Physiological measures	Traces
	Visual ratings	Archives

records come from questionnaires and interviews, which are, by definition, obtrusive. For simplicity in presentation, such records are treated together here as unobtrusive.

Reactivity. One aspect of a measurement method that particularly threatens research studies is **reactivity**. Reactivity refers to the reaction or behavior change caused by the research measurement. The degree of reaction to a measure depends on the topic being assessed. For example, questions about sexual behavior are presumed to be more sensitive than questions about political views. In addition, two other factors influence reactivity.

First, reactivity varies with the extent to which the studied behavior is under the control of the subject. In general, verbal behaviors are presumed to be more highly controlled by the subject than are nonverbal responses. For just this reason, law enforcement agencies tend to put more faith in lie detector results (based on physiological responses) than in self-reports.

Second, reactivity varies with the extent to which the subject is aware of being studied. In general, the less obtrusive the measurement, the less concern we need have about the threat of measurement reactivity. You can now see the point of sorting measures into categories according to their verbal-nonverbal and obtrusive-unobtrusive characteristics. As illustrated in Figure 6–1, measures can be thought of as falling on a continuum of reactivity ranging from high reactivity (obtrusive, verbal self-report) to low reactivity (unobtrusive, nonverbal observation).

In the following sections, each of the four types of measurement methods will

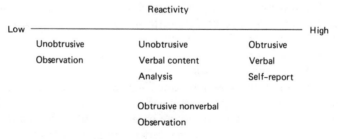

Figure 6–1 Reactivity of measurement types.

be discussed and illustrated briefly. The emphasis will be on assessing the measures in terms of reliability, validity, and reactivity. As indicated in the previous chapter, it is desirable to use more than one method to measure each construct (Campbell & Fiske, 1959). For lists of additional measures and more detail about particular measures, you will be referred to several measurement guides.

OBTRUSIVE, VERBAL MEASURES

Interviews and Projective Tests

The Interview. Absent from the typology of measurement types (Table 6–1) is one of the earliest and still most common procedures in human research—the interview. The omission was intentional because interviewing is one of the most complex measuring techniques and could arguably be located in three of the four categories. The interviewer might make judgments about the subject's number of eye contacts or physical condition, in which case the measurement would fall into the obtrusive, nonverbal rating category. Alternatively, the interviewer might focus on the the speed, loudness, or interruptive aspects of the person's speech pattern, in which case the measure would fall into the unobtrusive, verbal category (although in this case it is obtrusive since the subject is aware of being observed by the interviewer).

The most common use of the interview is to obtain answers to questions, and the procedure is usually considered verbal and obtrusive. The interviewer may follow a more or less structured program of questions and record the answers. If the interview is highly structured, with every question asked in the same words and in the same order, the interviewer is, in effect, administering a questionnaire. Such questionnaires can be administered in various formats with varying involvement of the interviewer. This is not to say that the interviewer makes no difference. The medium of the questionnaire (in person, by phone, or by mail) can affect the results. The presence of an interviewer and the rapport between interviewer and interviewee have important implications for the way the questionnaire is completed.

Measuring Type A Behavior by Interview. One construct that can be assessed by interview is Type A behavior pattern (TABP), the label given to a personality **trait** associated with coronary heart disease. Type A people are more aggressive, ambitious, and competitive; have a greater chronic sense of time urgency; and are more likely to experience coronary heart disease than their behavioral opposites, called Type Bs (see Powell, 1987, for a detailed review of TABP measurement issues).

The earliest procedure for assessing coronary-prone behavior was the structured interview (SI), conducted and evaluated by trained judges. Subjects are evaluated in this interview not just on the content of their answers but also on the emotional tone of their responses as evidenced by such behaviors as interrupting the interviewer during deliberately slow questions. Since a trait is understood to be an enduring aspect of a person's behavioral style, we would expect people to be rated similarly on this construct over time. In a ten-year follow-up using the structured interview, 67 percent of the subjects were given similar A or B ratings (Carmelli, Rosenman, & Chesney, 1987). There are other methods of measuring this construct than by personal interview, and some of these alternative approaches will be illustrated in later sections.

Projective Tests. There are two major strategies for obtaining information about people through structured interviews. The one more commonly used in social research and to which most of this section will be devoted is called nonprojective testing. In contrast, projective testing is infrequently used in social research but is commonly employed in psychodiagnosis and is seen occasionally in published mental health research, particularly case reports.

Projective tests are standardized procedures for eliciting responses to ambiguous stimuli. They are designed to provide tasks that are vaguely defined or unstructured. Such tasks allow the subject to see, say, or do what he or she wishes with minimal guidance or restriction. Projective techniques are so named because the subject is assumed to "project" his or her unconscious thoughts and feelings onto the "screen" provided by the unstructured task. Because of their emphasis on the unconscious and their origin in the Freudian movement, most projective techniques are identified with psychoanalytic theory. Nevertheless, the projective method is not inherently limited to the measurement of analytic concepts.

Probably the best-known projective technique is the Rorschach inkblot. Rorschach was a Swiss psychiatrist who administered many different inkblots to subjects representing different diagnostic categories. The Rorschach method presently consists in showing ten standard inkblots to the subject. The subject is asked to describe what he or she sees, and the test administrator copies down every word of this description. This verbatim record or protocol is then analyzed. There are several different scoring systems for analyzing Rorschach protocols, based on the characteristics that differentiate the responses of different diagnostic groups. To provide modern, psychometrically adequate projective techniques, efforts have been made to interpret Rorschach protocols by computer and to create an inkblot system with parallel forms that can be group administered (Holtzman Inkblot Test). Despite these advances, the inkblot projective approach is still not widely accepted for social measurement outside the clinical setting.

Other common projective techniques include the Thematic Apperception Test (TAT), word-association and sentence completion tests, and expressive tests such as the Draw-A-Person Test (DAP). Generalizations about projective tests are limited by the considerable differences among projective techniques both in method and in sophistication. Measures of reliability are difficult to apply to projective tests and have yielded mixed findings when they have been applied. Measures of the validity of projective tests have also been impeded by methodological obstacles. Criterion validation has been studied by comparing diagnoses based on complete case history information (the criterion) with those based on projective test protocols alone. Such comparisons seem to show greater than chance agreement only for experienced clinicians, and even their agreement rates are far from perfect.

Projective techniques have the advantage of being relatively disguised and therefore nonreactive compared with nonprojective, obtrusive self-report measures. The subject, unless well read in projective testing, cannot infer what answers will produce the desired impression. However, the underlying assumption of projective measures has been cast in doubt. Called the projective hypothesis, this assumption is that "the individual's responses to the ambiguous stimuli presented to him reflect significant and relatively enduring personality attributes" (Anastasi, 1976, p. 584). The evidence suggests that the information about enduring personality traits is considerably obscured by information about the subject's temporary state and by random noise produced by the ambiguity of the procedure. In sum, projective techniques are widely regarded as unsatisfactory on the usual psychometric criteria and are much less frequently used than questionnaires.

Questionnaires

One motivation for using questionnaires in research is their ease of use as illustrated by the measurement of Type A. Since the Type A interview approach (SI) requires special training to administer, it would be an authentic public health benefit to develop a simpler, more automated procedure for identifying Type A persons. Several self-report questionnaires have been developed by focusing on the answers to the SI. The best known and most widely used of these questionnaires is the Jenkins Activity Survey (JAS), which features computer scoring. The JAS correctly categorized Type A behavior patterns in 73 percent of the cases, using the SI as the criterion in one study (Jenkins, Zyzanski, & Rosenman, 1971). Unfortunately, such questionnaires, despite their reliability and ease of use, miscategorize a substantial number of individuals. We are reminded that a 70 percent agreement rate with the SI must be judged against a 50 percent chance agreement for a two-category classification (Mathews, 1988). Apparently questionnaires fail to capture some aspects of the complex phenomenon that is TABP (Byrne, Rosenman, Schiller, & Chesney, 1985), and we will return to these other aspects later in this chapter.

Because of their ease of use, questionnaires dominate social science measurement of the obtrusive, verbal type. They have been designed to measure demographic characteristics, aptitude, achievement, attitude, personality, social relationships, and social environments, to name just a few of the most common topics. The next four subsections will illustrate a few of the thousands of paper-and-pencil tests designed to measure these characteristics. The fifth will discuss the problem of and resources for locating existing questionnaires that you may wish to use.

Demographic Measures. Demographic measures reflect fixed characteristics of persons, such as gender, age, and ethnicity, and are usually straightforward and highly reliable. For example, most people can be easily categorized as male or female, but even this item can produce some errors, as when a telephone interviewer incorrectly records a respondent as a male based on a deep-sounding (but actually female) voice.

More complex demographic items pertain to theoretical constructs for which the respondents themselves may not have ready answers (for example, social class). Typical of the standardized social status measures is the Hollingshead Two Factor Index of Social Position (Hollingshead & Redlich, 1958). The respondent is counted in one of seven occupational levels (ranging from higher executives of large concerns, proprietors, and major professionals to unskilled employees) and one of seven educational levels (from graduate professional training to less than seven years of school). The numerical codes corresponding to the assigned categories (ranging from 7 to 1) are then multiplied by predetermined coefficients: Occupational level is multiplied by 7, and educational level is multiplied by 4. The resulting products are summed to produce the index of social position (ranging from 11 to 77). Based on this score, the respondent can be assigned to one of five social class groups. Hollingshead has subsequently revised this index to account for the fact that household status is increasingly a function of two working spouses (Hollingshead, 1975). Another more widely used status measure is Duncan's Socioeconomic Index, which ranks occupations on the basis of prestige, education, and income (see D. C. Miller, 1977, pp. 211–230).

Aptitude and Achievement Tests. The parent of all present measures of an individual's intellectual aptitude is the Binet-Simon scale developed early in this century. Alfred Binet was asked by the French Minister of Public Instruction to study the education of retarded children. Binet and Simon produced a set of 30 problems or tasks arranged from easy to hard, with the difficulty of each problem determined empirically by administering the test to normal children. Certain tasks on the test could be identified as falling, for example, in the 7-year-old level if 80 to 90 percent of normal children at least 7 years old could perform the task. A child who could pass the 7-year-level parts of the test but not the 8-year-level parts would be assigned the mental age of 7.

The Binet was revised for use in the United States by Alfred Terman of Stanford, and this version became known as the Stanford-Binet. Along with this version, the concept of *intelligence quotient* (IQ) was introduced. The IQ is the mental age, as determined by the test, divided by chronological age. If a child has a mental age of 7 and is in fact 7 years old, his or her IQ would be 7/7 = 1. Traditionally, the IQ is expressed as this ratio multiplied by 100, so that an IQ of 100 indicates normal intelligence for one's age.

Perhaps the most widely used of the individually administered intelligence tests are those developed by David Wechsler for adults (Wechsler Adult

Intelligence Scale, or WAIS), children (Wechsler Intelligence Scale for Children, or WISC), and preschoolers (Wechsler Preschool and Primary Scale of Intelligence, or WPPSI). These scales all sample vocabulary, arithmetic, spatial perception, comprehension, and related verbal and nonverbal performance abilities. Reliabilities for the full scales vary in the .90s, although individual subtest reliabilities are typically lower. The WAIS IQs have been found to correlate in the .40s and .50s with college grades and to predict subsequent release rate and work adjustment for institutionalized retardates. Of group-administered intellectual aptitude tests, college students are most familiar with the Scholastic Aptitude Test (SAT) of the College Entrance Examination Board.

One complaint against aptitude tests is that they are confounded with achievement. Aptitude tests are sometimes assumed to measure native ability to learn. But most intelligence tests award points for achievement, such as knowledge of vocabulary. Thus one's apparent aptitude or ability to learn can be made to seem greater by past tutoring, which may give some social groups unfair advantage. Achievement tests, in contrast, are intended to assess one's level of acquired knowledge or skill. No pretense is made that all candidates have had an equal opportunity to acquire the skills. All that is required is that all candidates have the same conditions in which to display their acquisitions.

You are familiar with achievement tests in the form of midterms and finals. Such achievement tests are designed by your instructors to assess material in their particular courses. There are many published tests intended to measure achievement and advanced aptitude in large populations. One such nationally administered test is the Graduate Record Examination (GRE). College students applying for graduate education are frequently required to take the verbal and quantitative aptitude tests and one of the 20 advanced achievement tests of the GRE corresponding to their major, or the counterpart tests for law school (Law School Aptitude Test, or LSAT) or medical school (Medical College Aptitude Test, or MCAT).

Personality Tests. Personality tests measure constructs such as emotions, motivations, values, and other enduring features of one's psychological makeup. Personality tests can include measures of attitudes and opinions—that is, the individual's orientation to or assessment of other persons or things. Such attitudes may be used to draw inferences about personality, since such attitudes may reveal something about one's perceptual style.

Personality questionnaires can range from single items to elaborate, multiscale *instruments* (which is another name for a paper-and-pencil measure, not electrical hardware). When the answers to more than one item are combined, the result is called a scale score and the set of items is called a *scale*. Multi-item scales have the advantage over single-item measures of greater reliability, as discussed in the previous chapter. There are numerous techniques for deriving single scores from multiple items (or scaling), and they differ considerably in complexity. (More will be said about some of the most commonly used scales in the chapter on survey methods, Chapter 7.)

The multiple-item personality questionnaire is illustrated by the widely used Internal-External Scale (I-E Scale) of Rotter (1966). Rotter explains behavior as a function of the belief that it will engender a reward. According to Rotter, individuals differ in their generalized expectancies. That is, an important trait or characteristic of persons is their belief or expectancy about the locus (source) of control of reinforcement. Presumably there are I-type people, or "internals," who believe strongly that they control their own fate; E-type people, or "externals," who believe that they are not in control of their own fate; and many people who fall between these two extremes. Rotter's I-E Scale is a 29-item paper-and-pencil test (including 6 filler items designed to conceal the purpose of the test, that is, to lower its reactivity). Each item consists of a pair of statements of belief about the locus of control. The subject selects one statement from each pair that is most consistent with his or her own general point of view and receives one point for each answer scored in the external direction.

Internal consistency reliability for the I-E Scale has ranged in the .60s and .70s. Test-retest reliability (interim period of one to two months) has ranged from the .50s to the .70s. The I-E has been found to be negatively correlated with measures of social desirability to a moderate degree (the external locus of control belief statements appear to be less socially desirable than the internal belief statements). To test its construct validity, researchers have administered the I-E to people known independently to differ on the construct of alienation. Rotter's theory predicts that externals would feel more alienated or powerless. Compared to externals, internals, as measured by the I-E, are more likely to show signs of being actively aware of and involved in their environment. For example, they are more likely to know about and ask doctors about their diseases (in the case of patients with tuberculosis), more willing to take part in civil rights marches and freedom rides (in the case of black college students during the early 1960s), and more likely to be an active member of a labor union (in the case of Swedish workers).

Personality questionnaires can be constructed in different ways. One approach includes or excludes items depending on how well the items agree with each other. This approach employs **factor analysis** to make sure that a common factor underlies all of the items of the scale. If an item fails to agree with this common factor, it is excluded in favor of one that does. An example of such a factor-based scale is Eysenck's introversion-extraversion scale from the Eysenck Personality Inventory, or EPI (Eysenck, 1973). Eysenck believes that compared to outgoing extraverts, shy introverts experience a chronically higher level of mental arousal or responsiveness. By factor analysis it has been shown that the 24 yes/no extraversion (E) items are loaded on (correlated with) the extraversion-introversion factor. That is, each of these items shares or measures something in common with the other items.

A major alternative to the factor analytic approach to scale construction is the **empirical criterion approach**. In this approach, items are selected according to their ability to discriminate previously identified groups of subjects. An example is the development of the Minnesota Multiphasic Personality Inventory (MMPI). The answers to the 550 MMPI questions are used to produce scores on ten standard diagnostic scales and three validity scales designed to check whether the respondent has answered the questionnaire carefully, honestly, with comprehension, and without any response tendency such as social desirability. Eight of the ten diagnostic scales were composed of items that discriminate normal people from one or another of eight clinical groups. Each clinical group consisted of about 50 cases diagnosed at the University of Minnesota hospitals. For example, a group of individuals diagnosed as paranoid was contrasted with a group of normal controls. Items that were answered one way by the paranoids but the other by normals were included in the paranoia scale. Items that failed to discriminate were omitted.

Two diagnostic scales were created to discriminate between different types of normal groups. For example, the MMPI masculinity-femininity scale items were chosen to discriminate normal males from normal females. This scale illustrates the limitations of the empirical criterion method: The items were chosen to discriminate males and females in the 1940s in the state of Minnesota. The reference group hardly represents the population of the United States in the last decades of the twentieth century. For example, normal college males currently score "abnormally" high on the femininity scale because their interest in cultural activities is more similar to the interests of 1940 Minnesota females than to those of 1940 Minnesota males.

Measures of the Social Environment.   Self-report measures can be used to assess a person's social environment as well as his or her personality. An early approach to measuring the social environment was **sociometry** (Moreno, 1960). This approach asks respondents to name other persons with whom they have special contact or closeness and is conducted with all members in a small closed group, such as a grade school class or the residents of an apartment building. A typical item asks each respondent to name the three persons in the group whom they would like to invite to a party. A person's choice score consists of the number of other respondents who chose him or her. The sociometric method can thus provide data about a person's standing in the social environment independent of his or her own belief or attitude about that standing. The disadvantage of the sociometric method is that the choice scores may not generalize outside of the closed group in which the measures are taken. For example, an apartment dweller may have a circle of family or friends outside of the apartment community. A low choice score for such a person may not reflect his or her available social support or level of socializing.

Another approach to measuring social environments has been mounted by Rudolph Moos. He has developed scales for assessing the social climate of nine different environments, including families (Family Environment Scale, or FES) and college dormitories (University Residence Environment Scale, or URES). Each environment is conceptualized as having a unique "personality." Just as individuals can be characterized as more or less supportive or controlling, so environments can be thought of as being high or low on different dimensions. For example, the URES is administered to college students living in residence halls, fraternities, and sororities. The respondents answer true/false questions about their residence, and the resulting answers produce ten scales such as emotional support, competition, academic achievement, and student influence.

As evidence for the validity of Moos's social ecological approach, Moos and Van Dort (1979) reported results from a study of 1,164 freshman college students living in 52 living units. A subset of 12 items from the URES was identified as a special Physical Symptom Risk Scale. This special scale reflected lack of cohesion or togetherness among residents, lack of emotional support, an excess of competitiveness, and a sense of student powerlessness in the living unit. Living units with high scores on this scale in the fall had greater than expected average health problems by the following spring. A later study also found that URES predicted academic performance, but with different patterns for dormitory versus fraternity groups (Schrager, 1986).

Finding Self-Report Measures. Each researcher should begin the empirical study of a construct by searching for the best existing tests and measures for that construct. One practical reason for using existing measures is the savings in test development time. Another more substantive reason is that this practice enables the comparison of different studies that use the same measures. When the same measure is used, differences in results between studies can be traced to design and sample differences rather than to measurement differences.

Two good starting points are books by Reed and Baxter (1983) and D. C. Miller (1977). Chapter 9 of the former lists and discusses a variety of indexes to psychological tests. About half of the latter is devoted to descriptions of measures broken down by topic, including actual questions and answer codings, along with information on reliability and validity and references to the measure's original publication. Miller also presents a useful inventory of all measures utilized in the *American Sociological Review* (the principal journal of the American Sociological Association) from 1965 to 1974 by topic. Finally, he lists over a dozen compilations that are devoted to listing or reviewing social measures (for example, Bonjean, Hill, & McLemore, 1967). There are comparable indexes for measures in the psychological literature (for example, Chun, Cobb, & French, 1975). A series of three volumes by John Robinson and colleagues provides considerable detail about measures, including the items or samples of items and introductory chapters comparing measures of the same constructs. Each volume covers a different research area: political attitudes (Robinson, Rusk, & Head, 1968), occupational attitudes and characteristics (Robinson, Athanasiou, & Head, 1969), and social psychological attitudes (Robinson & Shaver, 1973). The compendium that presents the most thorough critical analysis is the *Buros Mental Measurement Yearbooks*. Although the name implies that it appears annually, in fact, just eight such "yearbooks" were produced by Buros between 1938 and 1978 (Buros, 1978). One of the special benefits of the Buros series is that the same measure can be followed through several yearbooks, which provide updates on the perception of the measure in the field as well as updated references to its applications.

OBSERVATION MEASURES

Unobtrusive, Verbal Measures

Communication is the transmission of information from a sender to a receiver and can proceed on several different channels simultaneously: speech, body movements (called kinesics), touch, odor, body placement (called proxemics), facial expression, and eye movement and contact (called gaze). Since communication behavior is such a crucial part of being human and being social, it represents a large share of social research. This section deals with the study of speech and writing, using content and process analytic methods. The goal of this research is to draw inferences about the thoughts and feelings of communicators from the form of their messages.

The analysis of verbal communication can be applied to recorded samples of communication. To the extent that communicators are unaware that recordings of their communication are being analyzed, this research is unobtrusive even though the communication is produced under the control of the communicator. For this reason, content and process analyses of communication are often regarded as unobtrusive research methods. Many of the language components studied are not typically controlled consciously by communicators but are stylistic habits. For this reason, content and process analysis, even when they are obtrusive, are regarded as less reactive than self-report questionnaires.

Content Analysis. The term **content analysis** has become an umbrella label for procedures that count occurrences of selected verbal features in samples of text or speech. One use of content analysis appears in journalism research, where the emphasis given to certain kinds of content can be quantified by counting the occurrences of words referring to the content or by measuring the length of articles devoted to selected topics (for example, in inches or lines of print). Such quantifications could then be used to draw inferences about some underlying aspect of the communication not otherwise obvious.

An example of this approach grew out of the "white flight" controversy of 1975. In the spring of 1975, James Coleman announced his conclusion that compulsory busing for school desegregation produced the undesirable outcome of white exodus from the inner cities to the suburbs. Subsequently, Coleman's conclusions were challenged and debated in the social science literature. Two researchers wondered whether the popular print media accurately reflected the criticisms and doubts raised about Coleman's claims as well as they publicized his initial argument (Weigel & Pappas, 1981). They scanned 200,000 pages of print in 20 periodicals over six months from April through September 1975. The 69 articles referring to "white flight" were copied and content analyzed. For each article, a word count was performed for each of three types of content: uncritical of Coleman, qualified criticism of Coleman, and critical of Coleman. The results showed that over 26,000 words were devoted to uncritical presentations of Coleman's conclusions about white flight against less than 6,000 words of qualified critical or critical reports.

Process Analysis. Content analyses often study words—those units that carry the substantive meaning or topic. But language can also be studied in units such as the sentence or phrase, which can be categorized in terms of form or process rather than topic or content. In addition, verbal communication includes nonlanguage or *paralanguage* aspects, such as voice quality, pauses, and vocalizations without linguistic meaning. Analysis of such behaviors may be more aptly named **process analysis.**

There are numerous coding systems for process analysis of communication. All such procedures must address the same methodological issues, such as defining the unit of analysis (the clause, the sentence, the statement, and so on), the representative sampling of communication (for example, the location of samples from early, middle, or late in the conversation or relationship; length and number of samples; random versus nonrandom drawing of samples), and the training of judges to be reliable coders (the criterion of reliability and the nature and length of training).

An example of a process analytic system designed for studying small groups is R. J. Bales's (1950, 1969) 12-category Interaction Recorder. Verbal behaviors in groups are conceived of as problem-solving behaviors and are coded in such response mode categories as showing solidarity, giving suggestions, asking for opinions, showing antagonism, and so on. Numerous process analytic systems similar to Bales's have been created to focus on one special type of communication—psychotherapy (see Kiesler, 1973, for a compendium of these approaches).

A representative example of a paralinguistic process analytic system is the Interaction Chronograph method of counting and timing such verbal behaviors as silence, speaking, and interrupting (Chapple, 1949; Matarazzo, Matarazzo, Saslow, & Phillips, 1958). When an individual's interaction behaviors are timed from a recording of a standardized interview, they are found to be stable across interviews. Because of this stability, such paralinguistic speech characteristics are thought to be indicators of individual personality and ability differences. Speech characteristics have been correlated with paper and pencil test results for mental patient and nonpatient groups. For example, "initiative," the proportion of possible times that the interviewee communicates again following his or her own last utterance (avoiding silence), correlates positively with self-reported anxiety.

Application to Type A Behaviors. Is it possible that paralinguistic or nonverbal behaviors in the standardized interview are better, less reactive indicators of Type A than the answers to the questions of the structured interview or the Jenkins Activity Survey? One study compared self-report answers with paralinguistic process measures of Type A (Schervitz, Berton, & Leventhal, 1977). For the criterion of Type A behavior pattern, the researchers obtained standardized interview ratings by a trained interviewer. They then subjected the audiotapes of these interviews to analysis by two auditors. These auditors obtained high agreement rates (90 to 92 percent) in judging three types of paralinguistic process: speaking speed, answering speed, and emphasis. Finally, JAS questionnaire scores were gathered from the same subjects. The best combination of the three speech characteristics correlated better with the SI than did JAS.

Finding Content and Process Measures. Because they are so time-consuming in their development, rater training, and application phases, process and content analytic procedures have not multiplied as have self-report questionnaires. Nevertheless, it is a wise policy to scan the existing procedures before developing a new and possibly redundant system. Unfortunately, there are few indexes to content and process systems. The classic *Unobtrusive Measures* (Webb, Campbell, Schwartz, & Sechrest, 1966) refers to numerous studies of unobtrusive language behavior and conversation sampling (see especially pp. 127-134). Three general guides to content analysis are those by Berelson (1952), Holsti (1969), and Weber (1985). A useful guide to therapy-relevant process analytic systems is found in Kiesler (1973).

Obtrusive, Nonverbal Measures

Nonverbal observation methods are either obtrusive or unobtrusive, depending on whether the subject is aware of being observed. Two major categories of observed behavior are covered in this section: ratings of nonverbal behavior and physiological measures. Some of these measures could be obtained unobtrusively, and their inclusion in this section is somewhat arbitrary. For example, behavior could be observed unobtrusively from behind a one-way mirror, making it impossible for the subject to know if he or she is being observed. However, if the one-way mirror is in a social science laboratory, we must assume that the subject is aware of the potential presence of observers. In contrast, an extreme case of obtrusive measurement would be physiological monitoring, in which the subject is physically linked to mechanical measuring instruments.

Application to Type A Behavior. As noted in previous sections, Type A behavior can be measured by structured interview, questionnaire content, and paralanguage. Interestingly, it can also be indicated by such nonverbal signs as greater arm movements, sitting still less, spending more time in exploration, and more frequent gesturing (Hughes, Jacobs, Schucher, Chapman, Murray, & Johnson, 1983). Just as there are rating systems for verbal content and process analysis, so observational procedures have been developed for various nonverbal behaviors.

Examples of Nonverbal Behavior Ratings. Since Darwin, scientists have tried to judge human emotion from facial expression. Perhaps the most elaborate of recently developed systems is Ekman and Friesen's Facial Action Coding System (FACS). This procedure is based on underlying facial anatomy as well as on cross-cultural studies of facial expression of emotion. The FACS is so elaborate that over 7,000 different combinations of facial actions can be identified (Ekman & Friesen, 1978). As one example of the FACS numerical coding procedure, the code 6 + 12 means cheek raiser and lip corner puller, that is, smiling. The goal of such research is to measure emotion for which the verbal expression may be suppressed intentionally or cannot be verbalized (for example, in preverbal infants) but which might "leak" out through nonverbal channels such as the face.

Within the area of the face, visual contact behavior has been the most studied single feature. The measurement of such behaviors as mutual gaze or breaking eye contact can be judged with adequate reliability across judges (see Vine, 1971). Individuals seem to be consistent across partners in their looking behavior, and there are large differences between individuals (Ellsworth & Ludwig, 1972).

Visual behavior and facial expressions are only the beginning of observable human expressions. Just as facial expression can be coded and gazes counted, so can the other body movements be tabulated. The study of communicative body motion is called **kinesics**. As theorized by Birdwhistell (1970), the kinesthetic channel is just one of several more or less continuously operating communication channels along with the speech channel. Head, arm, and other body motions communicate in a system of signals with shared meaning within a society. These signals transmit information by themselves as gestures and in conjunction with other channels as kinesic markers and stress indicators. As an example of one notational system for recording body motion, forward body lean is symbolized by "/" and a head nod would be indicated by "H" (Birdwhistell, 1970). In some cases, it may be possible to record body motions electromechanically, for example, by using pressure-sensitive switches mounted in chairs to count the number of times children leave their seats in a study of classroom disruption (Foster & Cone, 1980).

Another body of literature has grown up around interpersonal spacing, or **proxemics**. The distance between interacting persons can be observed in a laboratory, where a person is asked to approach another up to the point at which discomfort is felt. Similarly, unobtrusive observations can be made by estimating the distances between people in a natural setting. To capture the context in which proxemic behavior is observed, an anthropologist has developed a notational system for recording the gender, posture, orientation, body odors, touching behavior, and voice loudness, among other characteristics, of the observed persons (Hall, 1965).

An Application to the Job Interview.   An example of the use of nonverbal ratings appears in a study of the interaction of race and interview behavior. Naive white job interviewers (college students) were observed interviewing black and white high school students who were actually trained confederates of the experimenter (Word, Zanna, & Cooper, 1974). The confederates were coached to perform similarly in the interview and to answer questions in a way that made them appear equally qualified. Two judges, behind one-way mirrors, rated four nonverbal behaviors of the interviewers that were thought to reflect "immediacy." Immediacy was defined as the extent to which behaviors reflect and enhance positive attitudes between two people in interaction. These four immediacy behaviors were (1) physical distance in inches (proximity), (2) forward lean in 10-degree units of angle from the vertical, (3) eye contact measured as a proportion of time spent looking at the job applicant's eyes, and (4) shoulder orientation in 10-degree units from parallel to the shoulders of the applicant. The reliability correlations of the judges' ratings ranged from .6 for shoulder orientation to .9 for distance. These measures were combined into a single measure of total immediacy. The results showed that black applicants received less behavioral immediacy, largely because the interviewers placed themselves farther from black than from white applicants. Compared to whites, the blacks also got shorter interviews and received higher rates of speech errors from the interviewers (as judged from audiotape by two additional raters).

In a second experiment, 30 white college students (the subjects) were divided into two groups to be interviewed for jobs. Those in the immediate group received the treatment received by white applicants in the first study—close proximity, longer interviews, and fewer speech errors. The nonimmediate group received the treatment given blacks in the earlier study—greater distance, shorter interviews, and more speech errors. The interviewers in each case were confederates of the experimenters who had been trained to produce these different styles of interaction. Videotapes of the interviews were judged by trained observers. The students in the nonimmediate condition were judged significantly less adequate for the job and less calm and composed. These nonimmediate subjects also rated their interviewers as less friendly.

Psychophysiological Measures.   Many psychophysiological measures have been used to reflect underlying attitudes and emotions that would otherwise have to be inferred from rater observations or from self-reports. Such physical measures typically require specialized hardware and specialized training to operate reliably. Several of them depend on the activity of the autonomic nervous system, which controls a host of peripheral (as opposed to central or brain) functions in the body. The **autonomic system** is divided into two subsystems—the sympathetic and the parasympathetic. The sympathetic system tends to dominate during intense emotions such as rage or fear. Autonomic signs of emotion include changes in salivation (for example, dryness of the mouth during stage fright), in heart rate and blood vessel constriction, in sweat gland activity and electrical skin conductance (for example, sweaty palms), and even in dilation of the pupils of the eyes.

Measuring pupil changes with precision requires special equipment and room arrangements. Typically, a subject is seated facing a screen. A first slide is shown to allow the pupil to adapt itself to the brightness of the reflected light and to provide a base-level pupil size with a neutral stimulus. Then another slide is shown at the same brightness but with more arousing content. The subject's eyes are photographed with a movie camera while he or she is looking at each slide. When the film is later projected, the experimenters can measure in millimeters the size of the pupils on the screen. The difference in pupil size between neutral and arousing slide conditions can be taken as an indicator of emotional response. As validation of this measure, it has been shown that hungry subjects will show greater pupil dilation than recently fed subjects in the presence of slides of food (Hess, 1973).

Changes in electrical skin conductance (related to sweat gland activity) constitute the galvanic skin response (GSR). The GSR is measured from electrodes attached to the skin and is one of the principal measures of the "lie detector." False answers are expected to produce greater autonomic arousal.

Another autonomic indicator measures heart rate and blood pressure. A practical application of such measures is illustrated by a study of the effects of traffic congestion (Stokols, Novaco, Stokols, & Campbell, 1978). Employees of a suburban company were measured for heart rate and blood pressure and reported their daily commuting time and distance. The physiological measures were associated with both distance and time. The results are consistent with ratings of commuting stress as reported by the subjects on questionnaires.

Autonomic nervous system activity stimulates the adrenal gland, which secretes hormones such as epinephrine and norepinephrine into the blood system. These hormones affect various organs of the body, which are also directly affected by the autonomic nervous system. These hormonal secretions can be picked up by blood assay and thus serve as another, still more obtrusive, indicator of emotion or stress. One study attempted to reduce Type A behavior by several different procedures and evaluated the outcome not only with the usual paper-and-pencil questionnaires (for example, JAS) but also with before and after blood assays (Levenkron, Cohen, Mueller, & Fisher, 1983). At each test point, two blood samples were drawn, before and after a stress-inducing task. The samples were measured for change in plasma-free fatty acids (ΔFFA) believed to reflect sympathetic nervous system arousal. In partial support of the researcher's theory, it was found that this outcome declined in the treated groups.

Besides the autonomic system, another large category of human physiological response is the electrical activity of the brain and muscles. The brain generates changing voltages, which can be measured as wave patterns by the *electroencephalogram* (EEG). Plate or needle electrodes are placed on the surface of the scalp at locations near selected brain structures. The electrical activity is then amplified and displayed on a video screen or as lines on a moving paper. Some common patterns of brain activity have been identified, such as the 8 to 12 cycles per second (CPS) alpha waves, which are the signature of the resting brain with the eyes shut. Different stages of alertness and sleep can be identified through EEG analysis, thus offering a tool for the objective study of unconscious (that is, sleeping) internal experience. The EEG has also been widely used in the study of abnormal conditions such as epilepsy.

Electrical activity is also produced by muscular activity and can be measured by the *electromyogram* (EMG). As with EEG measurements, EMG measures are obtained from electrodes placed on the skin near the muscles of interest. The resulting EMG is thought to measure "mental work." For example, the EMG from the right arm increases if a right-handed subject imagines lifting a weight. Since thinking involves linguistic processing, it is not surprising that EMGs from the facial area near the lips increase during silent thought. This method has been used to monitor the effort of cognitive processing during the presentation of a message that attacks an important set of beliefs, permitting physiological studies of attitude change (Cacioppo & Petty, 1981).

Finding Nonverbal Measures. Two helpful handbooks for nonverbal measurement systems are those of Scherer and Ekman (1982) and Siegman and Feldstein (1987). Also see the review of notation systems for nonverbal behavior by Rozensky and Honor (1982). The specific techniques of physiological measurement depend on the particular model of apparatus used. Thus step-by-step guidance for such measures are best obtained from the instructional manuals accompanying the equipment.

Unobtrusive, Nonverbal Observations

The least reactive measures are ones that are made without the knowledge of or verbal reports from the subject. There are three general types of such unobtrusive, nonverbal observations. One is the observation of nonverbal behavior that has already been discussed. This section will consider two other types of unobtrusive measures: physical traces and archival records.

Traces. Physical **traces** include both *accretions* of and *erosions* in some physical substance. The principle of erosion measurement is that people leave evidence of themselves by wearing down surfaces. For example, museum managers have identified the most popular exhibits by the wear on the floor's surface near the exhibits (see Webb, Campbell, Schwartz, & Sechrest, 1966).

Measures of accretions follow the same logic. Numbers, locations, and behaviors of people can be measured by their leavings. Erosion can be difficult to measure with precision, since weeks or months of wear may produce only barely noticeable erosion. In contrast, accretions are easily counted or weighed. An example of a frequently measured type of accretion is litter. Since litter removal costs hundreds of millions of dollars per year and since litter poses fire and health hazards, there is great practical benefit to measuring and researching littering behavior (Geller, 1980). As with any other measure, the accretion-of-litter measure must specify the unit of measurement. For example, how small a piece of litter will be counted—as small as a cigarette stub or only as small as a soft drink can? Moreover, the area of analysis must be well defined so that the same amount of coverage or observation is provided at different times.

One approach illustrates this method of trace measurement. The Photometric Index (PI) utilizes photographic enlargements (for example, of picnic grounds), which are then studied by magnifying glass within segments defined by a grid overlay. Such litter counts can be subjected to the usual reliability estimation procedure for different counters or for the same counter for different occasions with the same photos. Reliability can be quite high with such methods as the PI. Since litter is the criterion in such research, validity concerns are minimal.

Unfortunately, trace measures are subject to sources of error and constant bias, which need to be adjusted for or controlled. For example, is the museum exhibit with high floor wear located near the entrance, so that many visitors would be expected to pass by on their way elsewhere? Was the measure of littering adjusted for the time of observation (for example, higher picnic use on holidays, weekends, and warm-weather days)? With proper controls for such extraneous sources of variation, trace measures can be very persuasive.

Archival Records. **Archives** are the ongoing records kept by society for other than scholarly purposes. Archival records include vital statistics (for example, births and deaths) as well as the quantitative history of events in such social systems as health, law and criminal justice, journalism, and politics. Many such archives consist of records obtained unobtrusively, in the sense that the events were recorded routinely by some public agency without the subjects being aware that the data would or could serve as research observations about them. On the other hand, some archival records are collected in an obtrusive, verbal way, although they will be considered in this section because of their methodological similarity to other archives. The prime example of such an obtrusively collected archive is the census.

Besides their relative nonreactivity, archival data offer several other advantages. They are usually convenient and inexpensive. The costs of collecting, storing, and indexing them have typically already been paid by the collecting agency. Other kinds of archives such as discontinuous ancient records (for example, cuneiform tablets) have to be found, unearthed, sorted, restored, translated, and classified before substantive analysis is begun. Obviously, such archaeological, anthropological, or historical archival work proves costly and time-consuming.

Another advantage of archival records is their extensiveness. They tend to be based on entire populations rather than on samples and to be longitudinal rather than cross-sectional. For example, the suicide statistics for a state are based on all death certificates of state residents, not just a sample of a few neighborhoods or cities. Moreover, to the extent that laws and coroners define suicide in a consistent way, the suicide records can be used over many years rather than just one month or one year. These qualities often make archival records the only measure suitable for answering certain kinds of questions (for example, has the suicide rate changed over the past 40 years?).

Still another advantage of archival records is their reliability and validity. The routine nature of many archival data collections implies standardized procedures, which are presumed to be applied in the same way over time and location. For example, laws and court rules should be similar across jurisdictions within a state, so that annual figures on the number of convictions for burglary should be both accurate and comparable between districts and over time. Even when the definitions of archival measures change, the data collectors will sometimes collect both the old and the new version of the variable (for example, unemployment rate) for a period of time to permit comparison of the two versions. Archival measures often are the criterion measures for the construct of interest. For an epidemiologist studying mortality due to lung cancer, the records of death by lung cancer are often the most valid as well as the most practical indicator available.

There are so many different kinds of archival measures that scholars have used them not only to study the obvious theoretical constructs (for example, using records of traffic fatalities to study the safety of freeway interchange design) but also as surrogates for other unmeasured constructs. For example, Phillips (1979) used single-car fatalities as a stand-in for suicide on the grounds that some one-car "accidents" are actually misclassified suicides. Thus government records on economics, politics, education, crime, and weather can be used as measures of abstract concepts such as "quality of life" and other social indicators.

Despite all their advantages, archival analyses can pose some knotty problems. The first problem is locating the proper data set. By definition, archival data are collected for purposes other than research. When these other purposes are satisfied, collected data may be stored, forgotten, and all too often lost. The fact that your first inquiries do not discover the data you want does not mean that the data did not exist or do not still exist. It may only mean that you have not found the right place or the right archivist.

Even though the data have been collected, the feasibility of their use may depend on the storage format. For example, data on paper forms may have to be transferred to computer format before analysis, with all the costs of retrieving the forms, keypunching the data into the computers, and refiling the forms. If the data are already in computer form, are they sufficiently summarized or detailed for your purposes? You may have to discover data providers who can present the data to you in the format you can afford to analyze.

Although archival data are potentially standardized, reliable, and valid, they are not necessarily any of these things. Your job as an archive analyst is to discover the errors or changes that have crept into the records system. For example, it is safe to assume that a record system involving multiple reporting sources using new forms or data-handling procedures will not perform as planned in the beginning phases. Some reporting units adopt and learn the new procedures early. Other reporting units with less motivation may never fully cooperate in the building of the archive. You should always wonder "what's in it" for the front-line data gatherers. What is their incentive and their supervisors' incentive to produce comprehensive, accurate records? How well are the data screened before being deposited in the central information file? How vigorously are the formal criteria and definitions of the data applied? Even when records are collected in the letter and spirit of the formal archival procedures, they are subject to the usual data-handling errors such as miscoding on the original forms, misrecording into computer or other file formats, and mishandling in the subsequent aggregations or analyses.

Sources of Trace and Archival Measures. Both trace and archival measures are discussed in *Unobtrusive Measures* (Webb, Campbell, Schwartz, & Sechrest, 1966, pp. 35- 52 and 53-111). Few trace measures are created for standardized use across studies (the PI measure of litter is one exception). Thus most investigators develop such trace measures for one-time use in a particular study. Archival measures are so numerous that an exhaustive index would be enormous. However, a handy guide is D. C. Miller (1977). This volume mentions several statistical source books (see pp. 67-68 and 98-139), with special attention given to U.S. census data. A good general strategy is to approach the librarians of the nearest government publications center, often available in your university library. Other increasingly important sources of social research data are the sample surveys collected by social scientists and political, consumer, and economic opinion pollsters, who sometimes make their data available for secondary analysis (see D. C. Miller, 1977, pp. 99-103). Many colleges and universities have joined together so that faculty and students of the member schools can obtain access to data collected elsewhere.

ISSUES IN USING MEASURES

Ethical Issues

Guidelines for Test Makers and Givers. Ethical principle 9 of the American Psychological Association cautions researchers to protect their subjects' well-being both by seeking their informed consent and by protecting the confidentiality of any information gained from the study's measures (Committee for the Protection of Human Participants in Research, 1982). The APA's ethical principles also warn against the misuse of assessment whether in research or not (Principle 8). For example, some APA members have been asked to stop marketing a battery of tests that were found to be deficient in meeting technical standards for test construction (*American Psychological Association*, 1987, p. 113). To protect the rights of test takers (whether in research, in clinical testing, or in schools), there are a number of standards including the right of test takers to an explanation of test results (*American Psychological Association*, 1985, p. 85).

Testing As a Social Issue. Group-administered aptitude tests have taken on increasing social significance. Aptitude tests were originally intended to diagnose individuals in order to provide appropriate training and care for the retarded. Now, group tests are used to screen hundreds of thousands of candidates for admission to higher education and to jobs. For example, 90 percent of all four-year colleges require some kind of entrance exam such as the Scholastic Aptitude Test (SAT), but some critics argue that such tests are misnamed achievement measures (Jencks & Crouse, 1982). Ralph Nader's consumer protection group has argued that the testing industry exercises unregulated power and that its products should not be passively accepted as fair and accurate predictors of educational or career success (Nairn, 1980). Increasingly, legislative and judicial restrictions are being imposed on group testing to protect the rights of individual citizens.

The most explosive controversy about group intelligence testing has been produced by results indicating significant IQ differences between racial groups. These findings have led to acrimonious debate about the heritability of intelligence and charges of cultural testing bias. From its inception as a tool to aid the mentally disadvantaged, intelligence and aptitude tests are now seen in some quarters as instruments for perpetuating ethnic and social class disadvantages. (For a sample of this debate, see Cleary, Humphreys, Kendrick, & Wesman, 1975; Cronbach, 1975; Scarr & Weinberg, 1976.)

Sometimes tests give offence not by their interpretation but by their content. In one instance, the answer sheets to six personality and youth attitude tests given to 5,000 ninth-graders were burned in response to complaints from parents and the press (Nettler, 1959). The school board found no benefit in such items as "I enjoy soaking in the bathtub" and judged that they might undermine a child's moral character. Fears of invasion of privacy or of psychological harm from survey questionnaires should be anticipated and may require active public relations efforts to still (Eron & Walder, 1961).

Computers in Measurement

Coding the Data from Measures. Once data are collected, they must be put in a form suitable for analysis, usually by computer. The first step in data management is developing a **codebook**. The codebook names each variable for which data are being recorded, briefly describes it, and tells its location or sequence. Each individual subject is termed a **case**, and each case or unit of analysis will have a number representing that individual's score for each variable or measure. The resulting database consists of a table of individual names or identification codes (cases) by variables. Your instructor's grade sheet probably resembles such a table, with students' names in the left-hand column and each student's scores on tests and exercises running from left to right in the appropriate row. Such a table can be easily entered into a computer file and then analyzed statistically.

Computers in Collecting and Scoring Measures. Although computers are most often thought of as a means for storing and analyzing the results of measuring procedures, they can also play other roles in data collection. One function is to gather data directly from the subjects. For example, some of the physiological measures described earlier in the chapter can involve the continuous flow of information such as pulse rate or brain wave frequency. It is often most efficient to have such data fed directly into computer storage, where it can be linked second to second with other measures and with any special event markers desired by the researcher (for example, indicating the timing of different experimental stimuli). Computers can also facilitate the scoring of paper-and-pencil questionnaires. For example, the 550-item MMPI can be machine scored and the results analyzed by computer. One such analysis is to compare the MMPI profile of any subject with profiles of previously studied subjects in order to determine which diagnosis best fits.

SUMMARY

Because of the threat of method effects (two measures giving the same results because of shared method rather than shared construct), it is desirable to use more than one method in measurement. To help organize them, measures are categorized by two dimensions: verbal versus nonverbal and obtrusive versus unobtrusive. Verbal, obtrusive methods include projective tests and nonprojective questionnaires. Verbal, unobtrusive measures include communication analyses such as content and process analysis. Nonverbal, obtrusive measures can include ratings of nonverbal behavior and psychophysiological measures. Nonverbal, unobtrusive measures include trace (erosion or accretion) and archival records.

Every measure can be assessed in terms of reliability, validity, and reactivity—the extent to which the measuring procedure produces a change in the behavior under study. For each of the four categories of measures, indexes are cited that list and assess measures in these terms. Such indexes should be consulted to find the best existing measure before undertaking the time-consuming task of creating and validating a new measure.

EXERCISES

1. Select a measure to be evaluated in terms of its reliability and validity. Then look it up in an appropriate index. For example, you might check a test that you yourself might have to take, such as the GRE (see J. V. Mitchell, 1985, vol. I, pp. 622-626).

2. Define a construct to be measured in an imaginary study. Then try to identify four different measures of that construct, one from each of the four categories of Table 6–1 by using the suggested indexes and your own creativity.

Compare the measures that you identify in terms of reliability, validity, reactivity, and suitability for different kinds of research.

GLOSSARY

Archives: Ongoing records kept by institutions of society.

Autonomic system: Human nervous system, which includes two subsystems, the sympathetic and the parasympathetic, the former of which controls certain body responses indicating emotion.

Case: Unit of analysis, usually an individual subject, for each of whom measures are collected on each variable.

Codebook: Index that names the variables and specifies their location in the data set.

Content analysis: Procedure for measuring the occurrences of selected lexical or vocabulary features in speech or text.

Empirical criterion approach: Measurement construction approach that selects items according to their ability to discriminate groups known to differ on the dimension to be measured.

Factor analysis: Statistical approach to measurement construction that measures the extent to which test items agree with a common underlying dimension or factor.

Kinesics: Pertaining to body movements, especially the study of the communicative aspects of such movements.

Obtrusive versus unobtrusive measurement: Dimension of measurement that separates observations known to the subject from those occurring outside of the subject's awareness.

Process analysis: Procedure for measuring selected grammatical or nonlexical forms in speech or text.

Projective tests: Measurement procedures by which subjects respond to ambiguous stimuli; presumed to reflect significant personality characteristics.

Proxemics: Pertaining to interpersonal spacing, especially the study of communicative aspects, causes, and effects of spacing.

Quantitative measurement: Collecting and reporting observations in such a way that the data can be characterized numerically.

Reactivity: Extent to which a measure causes a change in the behavior of the subject.

Sociometry: Measurement approach that describes a person's social relationships from the number of "choices" of that person made by others.

Traces: Physical records based either on wear or erosion or on leavings or accretions.

Trait: Personality characteristic or behavioral style, for example, Type A, or coronary-prone behavioral style.

Verbal versus nonverbal measurement: The dimension of measurement that separates observations of verbal communication (for example, self-report or ratings of speech behavior) from observations of other kinds.

7

SURVEY DATA COLLECTION

Issues and Methods in Sample Surveys

This chapter and the next deal with two aspects of an important problem of social research—drawing conclusions about the many based on a sample of a few. This chapter discusses the procedure of estimating population characteristics based on samples from that population, that is, survey methodology. The next chapter covers the statistical inference to a population from sample data, whether those data are collected in a survey or in an experiment.

INTRODUCTION TO SURVEY RESEARCH

A Case of Sampling Bias

Literary Digest Poll of 1936. A survey is a method for collecting information from a **sample** of people by the administration of a questionnaire. Perhaps the most infamous survey is that conducted by the periodical *Literary Digest* in 1936 to predict the winner of the presidential election. As with the surveys in previous presidential election years, the sample was chosen from telephone directories and car registrations, and as a result, the *Literary Digest* predicted that Alfred Landon would defeat Franklin Roosevelt by a wide margin. This error has been cited by critics of sample surveys and has given heart to politicians behind in the polls ever since.

Despite the paradox of judging the whole from a small part, all of us use just this method virtually everyday. When served a bowl of steaming hot soup, the commonsense thing to do is to taste a fraction of a spoonful of the soup to determine how hot the entire bowl is. That is, we measure a sample in order to draw an inference about the whole. Of course, we may exercise some care in drawing our sample. Perhaps we stir the bowl well so that a spoonful from one part of the bowl is much like a spoonful from any other part.

The *Literary Digest* poll in 1936 erred in part because it failed to draw a representative sample of the voters. In 1936, the United States was in the depths of the Great Depression. Many poor voters would be motivated by the economic crisis in their lives, yet they were underrepresented in telephone directories (because they could not afford phones) and in automobile registries (because they could not afford cars). In failing to ask their opinions, the pollsters underestimated Roosevelt's popularity.

Problem of Error. Sampling bias is just one of several different kinds of error that threaten survey research. That such errors can be and have been controlled, however, is evidenced by the growing confidence placed in political surveys. Political polls can be corrected by, among other things, drawing respondents that are representative of all segments of society. Inappropriate respondents (for example, below voting age, unregistered to vote, or unmotivated to vote) can be excluded after their identification by careful questioning.

The effect of late trends in voter opinion can be handled by conducting surveys right up to the day of the election—even interviewing voters after they have stepped out of the voting booth but before the polls are closed and votes counted.

Such improvements in political survey designs have led to impressive accuracy in recent elections. Some people have expressed concern that polls are too accurate. In the presidential election of 1980, small samples of voters were polled after they left the voting booths by the national electronic media. Based on these postvote, precount surveys, the media predicted the victory of Ronald Reagan over Jimmy Carter hours before the polls closed in the western time zone, and Carter conceded the election before the balloting was complete. Days later, the vote tallies confirmed the accuracy of the surveys and the confidence that people placed in them. However, some observers and politicians wondered if the survey-based prophesies were not self-fulfilling since they may have demoralized some of Carter's supporters and kept them from going to the polls in the western states. In 1984, Congress voted to request the national media to refrain from projecting the election winner until the polls closed everywhere.

Rationale for Survey Research

Feasibility. It is fortunate that sample surveys can be so accurate because the alternatives are either a **census** (that is, a survey in which the sample is 100 percent of all targeted respondents) or no information at all. The census is impractical for social scientists since only the national government has the resources to contact everyone and the legal mandate to require that everyone cooperate.

Even the federal government attempts such national censuses only once every ten years. Although the decennial census is supposed to reach everyone, it fails to an unknown degree. The census is an invaluable source of descriptive data about the population and can be used as a standard against which to gauge the representativeness of sample surveys. However, when social scientists go beyond demographics to measure sociological and psychological constructs, they are forced to conduct sample surveys. Fortunately, samples need not be very large relative to the population. For example, political pollsters typically sample only a few thousand voters to represent many tens of millions of voters. As a result, survey research plays an important role in the social sciences and in consumer market studies as well as in political forecasting.

Errors and Validity. Surveys can be threatened by several types of errors. Construct validity is threatened by measurement errors in the self-report question-naire. A validity problem that is of special concern in research based on samples is statistical inference validity, which is covered in the next chapter: Do the responses to the survey represent the beliefs, feelings, and attitudes of the larger population to which the survey is to be generalized?

DESIGNS, MEDIA, AND ERRORS

Design Types

Before considering the problems of errors and biases, we must identify the basic types of surveys. First, we will consider types of designs, and then we will address the medium of contact—mail, phone, or face-to-face interviews. Each design has different strengths and weaknesses. The most important distinction in survey designs is between those surveys that measure at one time and those that measure at more than one time.

Cross-sectional versus Longitudinal Designs. If a survey is conducted at one time, it is said to be a **cross-sectional survey**. Cross-sectional findings can be safely generalized to the sampled population only at the time of the survey. A political opinion poll taken two weeks before an election could be an accurate representation of voter sentiment at that time, but we could not assume that the results represent opinion on election day since events could swing voter sentiment in a matter of a few days.

A **longitudinal survey** is conducted over time, with two or more administrations of the same or similar instrument. Longitudinal surveys are commonly divided into three categories: panel, trend, and cohort, all of which have the benefit of measuring changes over time.

Panel Surveys. When data are gathered at different times from the same respondents, the survey uses the panel design, and the respondents are collectively called the panel. The major advantage of the **panel survey** is that changes in particular individuals can be followed over time.

A major difficulty for panel surveys is reaching and reinterviewing respondents. In general, the longer the lag between initial and later interviews, the greater the risk of losing respondents. This loss of respondents is called **attrition,** which can occur because respondents move, change their minds about cooperating, fall ill, die, or go on vacation. If such attrition is related to the variables under study (for example, health), it may significantly affect the inferences that are drawn. For example, the degree of change between the average symptom levels in a first and a later interview may be due in part to the effects of health on the dropout rate.

A second problem with panel studies, **pretest sensitization,** is that the experience of the first interview may cause changes in the second. For example, a health survey may raise respondents' self-consciousness about health symptoms (say, chronic cough) or health habits (say, smoking). This sensitization by the first interview could lead to behavioral change (decreasing smoking) by the time of the second interview.

Another problem in comparing survey measures over time applies to all longitudinal surveys, not just to panel surveys—the problem of changes in measures over time. Interviewers may change their interviewing behavior as they gain experience, or new interviewers may join the survey team. Results showing changes in the respondents might really be due to changes in the interviewers.

Typically, panel survey designs employ a short time lag between interviews to protect against these problems. However, at least one 20-year follow-up panel has been conducted. The original Midtown Manhattan Study surveyed 1,660 Manhattan residents from 20 to 59 years of age (Srole, Langner, Michael, Opler, & Rennie, 1962). A reinterview of this same group was attempted in 1974, thus converting a cross-sectional design to a panel design (Srole, 1975). Of the 1,660 candidates for reinterview, 858 were alive and located, and 695 of these were successfully reinterviewed.

The unique benefit of the panel design is illustrated by the comparison of mental symptoms in the 695 respondents who were interviewed 20 years apart. In 1954, 16 percent of the respondents (age 20 to 59) had sufficient mental symptoms to be judged "impaired." In the 1974 study, these same respondents were 20 years older, now 40 to 79, and 18 percent were judged to be impaired. These two proportions of impaired are about the same, and one might guess that the same individuals who were impaired in 1954 were still impaired in 1974. But the panel design permits a comparison of 1954 and 1974 mental status by individual. Srole (1975) reports that over half of those judged impaired in 1954 had actually improved in 1974, and that some persons not judged impaired in the first interview had become impaired by the second.

Panel designs need not be restricted to just two interviews, as seen by the Panel Study of Income Dynamics. It began in 1968 and continued with annual reinterviews with the heads of households containing individuals from the original sample of families. The alternate name of this study suggests the magnitude of this continuing project: Five Thousand American Families (Hill, Hill, & Morgan, 1981). The special power of this study is illustrated by its test of the hypothesis that those who are poor now have been poor in the past and will remain poor in the future. Cross-sectional survey designs can reveal only the extent of poverty at one time but not movement into and out of any social class. The Five Thousand American Families study has shown "that there was not only far more year-to-year change in economic status than anyone had thought, but that there were substantial demographic differences between the very small group of families who were persistently poor and the much larger group who were only temporarily poor..." (Duncan & Morgan, 1981, p. 2). Although subsequent analyses of these same data have reported higher estimates of the persistence of poverty (Bane & Ellwood, 1983; W. J. Wilson, 1987), it is clear that such panel survey data provide the best opportunity to answer such questions.

Trend Surveys. In the panel design, the original sample of respondents is drawn to represent the population at the beginning of the study. Although the population may change subsequently, the same panel is reinterviewed repeatedly. In contrast, the **trend survey** keeps up with changes in the population by drawing a new sample at each measurement point. A common application of trend studies is in the measurement of political attitudes. Monthly or weekly estimates of the percentage of the voting population favoring a candidate are typically based on new samples, which together constitute a trend design.

One of the chief advantages of the trend design is that previously interviewed respondents need not be relocated, thus avoiding the problem of attrition. Highly mobile types of persons would be underrepresented in reinterviews in the panel design since such people would be more likely to drop out of the panel. But in a trend design, a new sample is drawn that includes highly mobile persons who happen to be in the area at the time of the survey.

Another important advantage of the trend design is that it avoids the test reactivity problem of the panel design. Some kinds of survey content are rather sensitive (for example, questions about mental and physical health or suicidal thoughts) and may raise the respondent's self-awareness of these problems. Interviewers in such studies are sometimes asked for help by their respondents. Ethically, the interviewer has an obligation to provide at least minimal information (for example, the telephone number of an appropriate service agency). Thus the initial interview may cause a subsequent change in the respondent. In the trend design, sensitive questions can be asked and appropriate help offered without fear that later responses will be distorted. The price of these advantages is the lack of precision in comparing different groups over time. Differences in trend samples cannot be traced to changes in particular individuals.

The trend survey design is exemplified in another study of American mental health, which took almost 20 years to complete. In 1957, 2,460 adults were interviewed (Gurin, Veroff, & Feld, 1960), and a new sample of 2,267 respondents was interviewed in 1976 (Veroff, Douvan, & Kulka, 1981). Although this design could not tell how the mental symptoms of particular individuals had changed, as could the Midtown Manhattan Study, it could reflect something of the changing social climate. For example, the trend survey indicated that the 1976 population was more likely to deal with unhappiness by seeking informal social support and less likely to use prayer than the 1957 population (Veroff, Douvan, & Kulka, 1981).

Cohort Designs.   A special case of the trend design is the **cohort survey,** which measures fresh samples, each drawn from the same subpopulation as it moves through time. The subpopulation is called a cohort, and the most common way of defining a cohort is by birth year.

The cohort survey has special value for researchers in human development. Suppose a developmental researcher wanted to study personality traits, such as achievement, in adolescents. One could sample and test at one time a cross section of young people ranging in age from 12 to 17. Suppose differences were observed between 17-year-olds and 14-year-olds. A natural interpretation would be that the observed differences are due to agewise development. Unfortunately age is not the only factor on which these adolescents differ. They belong to different birth cohorts. Seventeen-year-olds and 14-year-olds would have had different experiences as a function of growing up in somewhat different social eras. In other words, age and cohort are confounded and inseparable in this cross-sectional design.

To separate age and cohort effects, a series of cohort studies can be conducted. For example, cohorts born in 1955, 1956, 1957, and 1958 could each be surveyed in 1970, 1971, and 1972. Then it would be possible to assess each cohort's progress over time. The cohort effect is the difference between different cohorts measured at the same age, and the age or developmental effect is the difference between different age groups within the same cohort. As an example of a cohort effect, one study revealed that adolescents aged 14 in 1970 had higher achievement scores than those aged 14 in 1972 (Baltes, Cornelius, & Nesselroade, 1979).

Such multiple-cohort sequential analyses have been stimulated by Schaie's (1965) General Developmental Model for separating age, cohort, and time of measurement or period effects. As Adams (1978), Baltes, Cornelius, and Nesselroade (1979), Kosloski (1986), and others have pointed out, such sequential strategies can provide descriptive but not definitive causal information. In the preceding example, the 1956 birth cohort was 14 in 1970 and the 1958 cohort was 14 in 1972. These two cohorts, controlling for age (14 years old) differ in two respects—their birth cohort (which is related to social and cultural differences in the eras in which they grew up) and their period of measurement (which is related to the current events at testing, 1970 versus 1972). Thus measured differences between these two sets of 14-year-olds could be due to birth cohort or to period. In conclusion, cohort designs, especially multiple-cohort sequential designs, permit useful insights into developmental processes, but cohort and period remain confounded even when developmental age is controlled.

Media Types

The term *medium* refers here to the method of gathering data from surveyed respondents—by mail, phone, or face to face. Each of these media presents special advantages and disadvantages in cost, sampling method, success in gathering data from the sample, type of content, and format of the questions. These different media will be briefly discussed here and referred to again throughout the remaining sections. For more detailed treatments of these survey media, see Dillman's (1978) analysis of mail and telephone surveys and Groves and Kahn's (1979) comparison of telephone and face-to-face surveys.

Face to Face. Although still common, the face-to-face medium is becoming prohibitively expensive. Reaching people at their residences is becoming increasingly difficult in an era in which both spouses work. More frequent callbacks to find someone at home are compounded by inflating costs of personnel and transportation.

Nevertheless, face-to-face surveys are thought to maximize trust and cooperation between interviewer and interviewee. Face-to-face contact may permit questioning on more intimate topics and decrease refusals. In-person contact also allows the use of special aids such as cards showing the questions or answer options. The personal interview permits the interviewer to see and evaluate the respondent's nonverbal behavior and habitat. Finally, face-to-face interviews can be conducted with respondents who do not have phones or the ability to read a mailed questionnaire. Were it not for limited resources, face-to-face interviewing would probably be more widely used than at present. With personal survey methods priced beyond the reach of many social scientists and their funders, the realistic options are often phone or mail surveys.

Telephone. The telephone interview costs approximately half what a face-to-face interview costs (Groves & Kahn, 1979). Interviewers need not waste their time driving many miles to a residence only to find no one at home. The callback to the absent respondent requires only a redial rather than another long trip. Moreover, telephone interviewing permits unique control and supervision in that all of the interviewers can be monitored because they work inside a single complex.

With phones now so widely distributed in society (in excess of 90 percent of all households in urban areas of the United States), relatively few people cannot be reached by phone. Unfortunately, those few are probably different from and, therefore, not represented by those with phones. On the average, those without phones are poorer, younger, less educated, nonwhite, and female heads of household (Tull & Albaum, 1977).

Another potential problem is that many people (20 to 40 percent in some areas) elect not to list their phone numbers in telephone directories (Rich, 1977). Unfortunately for these persons but fortunately for the success of the telephone survey method, such unlisted numbers are easily reachable through the procedure of **random digit dialing** (RDD). In RDD, telephone numbers are composed by a random process, usually by computer. Thus a phone number is just as likely to be generated and called if it is unlisted as if it is listed. One potential problem with RDD is that the identity of the respondent is not known when the call is placed, and the respondent has the option of remaining anonymous even if the interview is completed. Although not a problem for cross-sectional research, such anonymity impedes follow-up interviews required in panel designs. However, one nationwide RDD study was able to reinterview 78 percent of the original sample three years later, indicating that even panel designs can be carried out by phone (Booth & Johnson, 1985).

Once a household is contacted by phone, one household member is typically chosen for the interview, usually randomly or quasi-randomly (Troldahl & Carter, 1964). Although telephone surveys tend to underrepresent some segments of the population, such underrepresentation may not be so serious for some purposes as to rule out the approach. It should be remembered that even face-to-face surveys tend to underrepresent some population segments. Thus the choice is not between perfect and imperfect media, but between media with different degrees of effectiveness.

Another concern with telephone interviewing is that it may not yield the same answers as face-to-face interviews, particularly on more intimate and sensitive items. It is feared that respondents may more easily terminate the interview, decline to answer certain items, or give a false answer to a stranger on the phone than to a new acquaintance sitting in their living room. Several studies have compared phone and personal surveys by using the same questions, and some of them have found small differences in response style. For example, telephone interviewees produce more missing data on income questions, more acquiescence (tending to agree), more evasiveness, and more extreme response bias (tending to select extreme answers such as "very satisfied" or "very unsatisfied" rather than moderate answers such as "slightly satisfied"). However, average item scores were generally not significantly different in the phone and personal interviews (Jordan, Marcus, & Reeder, 1980). When asked their preference, respondents indicated that they prefer personal to phone interviews and that they are more likely to agree to be interviewed in person than by phone (Groves, 1979).

In other research, data obtained by phone have been found comparable to those collected face to face (T. F. Rogers, 1976). For example, one study compared phone and personal surveys of criminal victimization (Tuchfarber & Klecka, 1976). The surveys were compared on demographic characteristics of the respondents, reports of victimization, and attitudes toward crime-related matters. The authors concluded that in "each instance, the bulk of the evidence supports the contention that RDD yields data of equal, if not superior, quality and reliability to those data collected by a traditional personal interview" (pp. 63-64). The telephone interviews actually yielded higher rates of some crimes (for example, 39 percent greater for household crimes), suggesting a greater willingness to be frank on such sensitive topics on the phone than in person. It is now widely accepted that the telephone medium is a viable alternative to the face-to-face medium and can be used successfully for sensitive, complex, and lengthy interviews.

Mail. Return rates are notoriously low for mailed questionnaires, typically in the 20 percent to 30 percent range for the initial mailing (Nederhof, 1985). Think of how many times you have thrown away the postage-paid, self-addressed return envelope or card begging you to answer a few short questions. Although the mail return rate can be increased to the 60 to 70 percent range by repeated mailings (three or more attempts), the increasing cost of postage tends to eat into the initial cost advantages of this method. More important for measurement validity, with mail questionnaires there is no control over substitution of respondents. For example, the designated respondent may hand the questionnaire to another person. In general, tight control of the administration of the questionnaire is sacrificed in the mail medium.

High return rates have been reported for specialized samples for whom the mail survey may be suitable (Dillman, 1978). For general population surveys, most social scientists tend to limit their choices to personal and phone media, although mail contacts may play an important supplementary role. Appointments for or announcements of impending home visits or phone calls could be sent by mail. Complicated questionnaire materials such as answer cards could be sent by mail prior to the actual contact by telephone interviewers. Once a respondent has been involved in a longitudinal survey by an initial personal or phone contact, reinterviews could be conducted by mail. Telephone contacts also have been used in similar supplemental ways in surveys in which the primary data collection medium is either mail or personal contact.

Types of Errors

As with any social measurement, survey research is subject to various kinds of error. It will be convenient to organize our review of survey errors along two dimensions. The first dimension includes the two categories of error: random error and bias (nonrandom error). The second dimension includes the two major components of the survey process: the sampling phase and the data collection or measurement phase. In combination, these two dimensions give four types of errors as summarized in Table 7–1.

Random Error. Variable and unpredictable, **random error** has the effect of making estimates based on surveys less precise than they would otherwise be. First, consider **sample error**. Several different samples of the same size from the same population would almost certainly disagree because small samples rarely represent the entire population exactly. By chance, any given sample is likely to slightly over- or underestimate the true value in the population. Such sample-to-sample variation is called random sampling error.

In general, if many samples were collected from the same population, they would tend to converge around a central point. If the estimates of all these samples were bunched tightly together, we would say that there is little sampling error. In that case, almost any sample we chose would provide a good estimate because all estimates were so close together. But if the estimates of these many samples were widely different from each other, we would say that there is a great deal of sampling error. In that case, we would be much less confident in believing any of the survey estimates. In summary, the issue of random sampling error pertains to

Table 7–1 Types of Survey Error and the Problems They Present

Source of Error	TYPE OF ERROR	
	Random	*Bias*
Sampling	Lack of precision of survey estimates	Directionally wrong estimates
Data collection	Lack of reliability of measurement	Lack of validity of measurement

the extent to which different samples yield estimates that agree (less error) or disagree (more error).

Random error also appears, as discussed in Chapters 5 and 6, in data collection. Once a person has been identified by some sampling procedure, it is necessary to contact and interview the respondent. Error that enters this data collection process contributes to what has been called unreliability of measurement. For example, a sampled respondent might give unpredictably different responses to the same item on different days or to different interviewers. Errors can arise from interviewers' mistakes, from variations in how respondents interpret ambiguous questions, and from mistakes in recording or tabulating the answers. **Data collection error** adds to sampling error to increase the disagreement among independent survey estimates of the same population characteristic.

Bias. When errors behave systematically to push the survey estimate consistently above or below the true value, they are called **bias**. Random sample errors and random data collection errors are as likely to miss the true population value in either direction. If we had only random error to deal with, we could trust the average of many survey estimates as the best overall estimate of the population value because negative and positive errors should cancel each other out. If bias is present, averaging will not provide a good estimate of the population value. If all the sample estimates are biased by some amount, the average of all these estimates will differ from the population value by this same amount.

Sample bias occurs when the sampling procedure is not representative. Suppose a jar were filled with marbles, half red and half blue. If you picked out ten marbles blindfolded, you would expect to get an average of five red and five blue marbles. But suppose that someone arranged to put all the blue marbles on the bottom, so that you were more likely to select the red marbles from on top. Naturally, your samples would be unrepresentative.

The same sort of bias occurs in real surveys when one type of person has a greater chance of being sampled than another type. In the case of the *Literary Digest* survey, Republicans had a better chance of being sampled because of their overrepresentation in the telephone books and car registration files.

Even if the original sample is drawn in a representative or unbiased way, the final estimate may still become distorted by **data collection bias**. We know that there are individual differences in response set that can lead to biased answers (for example, social desirability). Sometimes such bias can be checked. For example, in the original panel survey following an experimental alcoholism treatment, many subjects claimed to be able to drink moderately. However, checks of official records from jails and hospitals seemed to contradict these apparent successes (Pendery, Maltzman, & West 1982; see Heather & Robertson, 1983, for a rejoinder). Data collection bias in the interview stage of the survey is referred to as **observation bias**.

Another nonsampling bias can occur in the process of contacting sampled individuals. For example, young people and males may be less likely to be found at home than older people and females. Even when the sampled individuals are reached, not all contacted people may be willing to be interviewed. And among those willing to be interviewed, there may be some types of respondents who will decline certain questions (especially about private or sensitive matters such as income). The result is that an unbiased sample may yield a biased set of respondents on one or more items. This type of data collection bias is referred to as **nonobservation bias**.

Total Survey Errors.   The sum of all errors, bias and random, from sampling and data collection is difficult to measure. **Total survey error** is the difference between the estimate produced by a sample survey and the true or population value. Unfortunately, the population value is unknown and, in general, unknowable. Thus total survey error can only be estimated by considering each source of error. One component of data collection error is observation bias—for example, claiming falsely to have a library card. An estimate of the existence, direction, and magnitude of this particular error can be obtained by verifying card ownership with the library. Similarly, other sources of error could, in principle, be measured and summed to provide an estimate of total survey error.

In practice, estimates of total survey error are difficult to generate and rarely attempted (Andersen, Kasper, Frankel, & Associates, 1979; *Sociological Methods and Research*, 1977). Some ongoing, large-scale surveys, however, do attempt to estimate total error. These include the census (Bailar, 1976) and *The Current Population Survey* (Bureau of the Census, 1978). Survey researchers attempt to design the sampling and data collection procedures so as to minimize error and to provide opportunities to check some of the more likely sources of bias or random error.

SAMPLING

Sampling Terminology and Designs

Basic Terms.   It is common to hear reports of surveys qualified by some statement such as "The survey estimate [for example, of the percentage of voters favoring a politician in an upcoming election] is within plus or minus 3 percent of the true population value with 90 percent confidence." Another way of saying it is that if the same survey were repeated 100 times, the estimates from 90 of these surveys would fall in the range of 3 percent above or below the correct value. Much of what sampling experts do is design sampling methods that provide estimates with ever smaller errors at greater levels of confidence. The sampling theory by which this result is accomplished uses several basic terms.

An **element** is the unit from or about whom survey information is collected, usually an individual person. The total of all potential elements to whom survey results are to be generalized is called a **population**—for example, the population of current residents of the United States who are working or seeking employment. To estimate the American unemployment rate, we would select a sample of elements in such a way that they represent the population of American job holders and job seekers.

To draw a sample in a representative way, we ideally would like to begin with a list or **enumeration** of all the elements in the population. In practice, complete population lists are seldom available. Consequently, one must work with some incomplete list called a **sampling frame**. For example, a sampling frame might consist of a list of residential addresses in a city. Since the sample is drawn from this sampling frame, any generalizations can be made only to the frame. If the frame is unrepresentative of the population (for example, if some homeless job seekers do not have residential addresses), the sample will be unrepresentative of the population.

Sample Stages. *Single-stage* samples are those drawn in one step from a sampling frame. *Multistage* samples are drawn in a sequence of two or more **sample stages,** only the last of which identifies the elements to be interviewed. For example, a two-stage sampling procedure might be used to represent the population of college students. First, a sample of colleges might be drawn from the population of colleges. The sampling frame for the population of colleges might consist of the list of all colleges accredited by all of the regional accrediting organizations. Then a sample of students might be drawn from the students enrolled in the colleges drawn on the first step. The sampling frames for this second stage might consist of the lists of registered students provided by the campus registrars of the sampled colleges.

A **sampling unit** consists of either the element (for example, college student) or a group of elements (for example, college) that is selected at a sampling stage. Sampling units consisting of groups of elements are called **clusters**. Clusters are defined in terms of existing groupings, usually areas (blocks, cities) or organizations (industrial plants, colleges). *Multistage cluster sampling* designs involve several steps: selecting initial sampling units or clusters, enumerating or listing the elements within the selected clusters, and selecting elements from the chosen clusters. Multistage cluster sampling is economical because instead of enumerating all of the elements in the population, the survey researcher need only enumerate the elements in the selected clusters. By concentrating the interviewing in certain geographically limited clusters, survey travel and personnel time are minimized.

Elements may, alternatively, be categorized by **stratification**. A stratum consists of all the elements that have a common characteristic. For example, the variable sex would define two strata—males and females. Strata differ from clusters in that one must begin with an enumeration of all elements from which a stratum can then be defined. In contrast, one can identify a cluster such as a block or a college without knowing the elements it contains.

Depending on one's research goals, one could sample in one or more stages from selected clusters or strata or from stratified clusters. For example, clusters consisting of colleges could be stratified according to such variables as private versus public, unisex versus coed, large versus small, or urban versus rural. Colleges could then be drawn from each stratum before sampling students (elements) from the chosen colleges. The choice of sampling strategy represents a balance of feasibility (including available knowledge about the population, such as the existence of an enumeration) and purpose (including the required measurement precision and hypothesis). For a more detailed treatment of survey sampling methods, consult standard texts such as Babbie (1973), Sudman (1976), or Williams (1978).

Probability Sampling. There are two overriding goals of sampling—to provide unbiased samples and to provide sample estimates with the smallest sampling variability. First, we will consider the problem of bias and its solution—probability sampling. In a later section, we will see that probability sampling also helps with the problem of sampling variability by facilitating its measurement.

Sampling bias, as illustrated by the *Literary Digest* survey, is produced by sampling procedures that consistently miss some elements while overrepresenting other elements. The method of sampling from car registrations and telephone listings illustrates sample-frame bias. That is, the population of voters was not enumerated fully, and the convenient but incomplete listing was biased in favor of Republicans and against Democrats.

Bias is avoided when every element has an equal chance of being sampled. In the case of the *Literary Digest* survey, a different frame would have been required, one that did not systematically exclude certain kinds of elements. Beyond defining an unbiased sampling frame, the actual selection of elements from the frame must be done in a way that gives the elements in the frame an equal probability of selection. Such a sample method is called **probability sampling**.

Theoretically, the best way of achieving probability sampling is by **random sampling**. One example of random sampling is a lottery in which every contestant is represented by a ticket. A blindfolded person draws out the winning ticket from a box containing all the tickets. This random selection is fair because each ticket has an equal chance of being chosen.

More commonly, **systematic sampling** is used instead of random sampling. Copying every single element and putting all the elements into a mixing drum can be tedious when the frame is large (say, the telephone directory of a large city). To simplify the process, systematic sampling draws every nth element from an existing list beginning at a randomly determined point (every 100th person in a telephone directory starting with a randomly chosen person on a randomly chosen page).

In the case of multistage sampling, the researcher may have to select later-stage samples from different-sized clusters—for example, large colleges versus small colleges. To draw 100 respondents from a university with 25,000 enrolled students and 100 students from a small college with 2,500 students would not give every student an equal chance of being selected. One way of preserving equal probability across all elements in the population is to use the method of **probabil-**

ity proportionate to size (PPS). With PPS, the number of respondents drawn from each cluster is proportionate to the size of the cluster. In the example, we might draw 100 students from the larger university but just 10 from the smaller.

On the other hand, when the purpose of the study is not to represent all elements but to compare and contrast subpopulations, PPS may be inappropriate. If the goal is to compare satisfaction with teachers across the range of different-sized colleges, the sample might appropriately **oversample** in smaller colleges to provide adequate numbers of respondents from all types of campuses. Nevertheless, within each subpopulation, strata, or cluster, probability sampling would be retained by use of random sampling or systematic sampling with a random start. If we later wanted to combine the results for such non-PPS samples into an estimate for the whole population, we could statistically correct for any disproportionate sampling—a procedure called **weighting**. Thus if students from large colleges were only one-tenth as likely to be selected as their small-college counterparts, the responses of large-college respondents could be multiplied by ten.

Nonprobability Sampling. The alternative to probability sampling is **nonprobability sampling,** which includes any method in which the elements have unequal chances of being selected. A common nonprobability method is **convenience sampling,** which as the name implies depends on the convenient availability of respondents. In effect, subjects select themselves. Laboratory experiments commonly sample by convenience from the population of college students eligible or required to participate as human subjects. Students typically volunteer for available studies depending on their timing and the interest of the experiment's subject matter. The experimenter typically takes the first students who sign up and makes little or no effort to check the representativeness of the volunteers.

Usually, the experimenter is not interested in estimating any population characteristic from the sample. Rather, the goal is to split the original group of volunteers into two or more experimentally different groups. This division of the original group into subgroups may be done by random assignment, which should be distinguished from random sampling, which selects a group from a population.

Other nonprobability sampling procedures include purposive sampling and quota sampling. In **purposive sampling,** respondents are chosen because of certain characteristics. For example, unemployment is suspected of being a risk factor for certain stress disorders but is relatively rare in the population and is not enumerated. With a 5 percent unemployment rate, a general survey of the work force would have to reach 10,000 persons to collect a sample of 500 unemployed. If such a large survey is not feasible, the researcher may resort to purposive sampling, for example, by interviewing all people applying for unemployment compensation or all people fired from a closing factory. Unfortunately, there is no way of knowing whether the 500 unemployed contacted by purposive sampling are representative of all unemployed, including those who do not seek unemployment compensation or who were not employees in declining industries.

In **quota sampling,** the researcher tries to create a sample that matches the demographic profile in the population or fits some predetermined demographic profile. For example, if it is known that 54 percent of the adults of a community are female, and the researchers want 100 total respondents, the first 54 females and the first 46 males could be selected by quota to match the population profile. Often quota sampling is a special case of convenience sampling, for example, selecting the 100 respondents from those persons doing business at a shopping center. Even if the quota procedure is highly detailed so that respondents are selected to fit several different criteria such as sex, age, or ethnicity, there is no guarantee that the sample will be unbiased on some overlooked but important dimension. For example, if the shopping center is located in an affluent neighborhood with a high Republican registration, the sample drawn there would not give an accurate reading on political opinion in the population as a whole.

Random Sample Error

Defining Sample Error.   Since some sample error is unavoidable, the term *error* can be misleading because it suggests some sort of mistake. What is commonly called sampling error is nothing more than sampling variability. More precisely, sampling error is another name for the square root of the sampling variance (for a review of measures of variability, see the Appendix). The sampling variance is the average of the squared differences between each different sample and the average of all the samples. This variance can be calculated easily whenever multiple samples are drawn from a population. However, multiple samples are rarely taken, and sampling variance must often be estimated from a single sample.

One way of estimating sampling variance is to divide a single sample into a number of subsamples. The variance among the subsamples describes the variability or sampling error for a sample of the size of each of the subsamples. However, larger samples (such as the size of the original sample) are less variable than smaller samples. You need only think of sampling from your present class in order to represent your class's average grade. A sample of 20 or 30 has a better chance of representing the entire class average than a small sample of 2 or 3. Accordingly, the sampling variance for the set of small subsamples must be adjusted downward by dividing by the number of subsamples in order to describe the sampling variance of the larger original sample.

Sampling Variability and Sample Size.   The principle that larger sample sizes make for better estimates of population values is called the **law of large numbers.** Intuitively, it makes sense that the larger the sample size, the better the chances that unrepresentative elements (those much higher or lower than the average for the group) would cancel each other out. This principle is useful in estimating sampling error directly from an undivided sample.

In an earlier section, we saw that probability sampling had the advantage of providing more representative, less biased samples. Another benefit of probability sampling is that it aids in the measurement of sampling variability. In simple (one-stage) random sampling, all elements in the sample frame have an equal chance of selection. Given this information, the variance of elements in the sample can be converted into an estimate of the sampling variance for all samples with the same sample size.

This sampling variability estimate based on one undivided sample is called the **standard error of the mean,** which is estimated from a single sample as the standard deviation of the sample (square root of the variance) divided by the square root of the sample size. This is a very useful fact because it tells how much improvement in sampling precision can be expected from an increase in sample size. For example, quadrupling the sample size will cut sampling error only in half. The essential points to remember are that sampling variation or error decreases as sample size increases and that bigger and bigger samples yield diminishing returns for precision.

Confidence Interval of Samples. The standard deviation of the sample can tell us how much confidence to place in a sample estimate. Even without selecting and interviewing all possible samples from a population, we know something important about the estimates from many such samples—their distribution. Suppose we took all such samples and plotted their values, for example, unemployment rate. We could think of each sample estimate as an individual observation and plot the number of samples that yielded that value. The result would be a frequency distribution such as we ordinarily plot for a single variable measured in a group of subjects. Since each observation is from a sample, the distribution of sample estimates is called a sampling distribution. An idealized sampling distribution is illustrated in Figure 7–1.

In the illustration, the sampling distribution takes the shape of a normal (bell-shaped) curve. By a mathematical theorem called the **central limit theorem,** the sampling distribution approaches normality as the number of samples increases. Most sample means congregate near the middle of the distribution, with fewer and fewer sample means at greater distances from the middle. The average

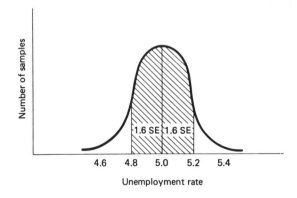

Figure 7–1 Sampling distribution for unemployment rate: Assumed normal distribution with standard error = .11, 90 percent confidence interval (shaded area), and population unemployment rate of 5 percent.

of the samples is the best estimate of the population value, in the present imaginary case, 5 percent unemployment.

The special benefit of the normal curve is that its shape is well defined. We know that about two-thirds of all sample means fall within plus or minus 1 standard error of the population mean and that 90 percent of the sampling estimates fall in the range between plus and minus 1.6. The large-scale survey used to estimate the U.S. unemployment rate has a standard error of the monthly unemployment level of .11 (National Commission on Employment and Unemployment Statistics, 1979). Thus, assuming the true population level of unemployment was 5 percent, nine out of ten samples of the same size would fall in the range 4.82 to 5.18 percent (5 percent plus or minus 1.6 × .11).

Of course, we do not know the population value of unemployment, and we are forced to use our sample estimate as the best guess of the population value. However, we can specify a **confidence interval** for any desired degree of confidence. If we want 99 percent instead of 90 percent, we must expand our confidence interval to include 99 percent of the samples. Since 99 percent of all sample estimates fall within plus or minus 3 standard errors of the population value, our 99 percent confidence interval would be plus or minus 3 × .11, or .33 for unemployment. If our sample had 5 percent unemployment, our best point estimate of the unemployment in the population would also be 5 percent, and we would be 99 percent confident that the population unemployment would be in the interval of 4.67 to 5.33.

In summary, sample size and confidence interval width are closely related. As sample size goes up, the standard error goes down. As the standard error goes down, the confidence interval becomes narrower.

Determining Sample Size. Because sample size is related to the confidence interval, one could, in principle, select the sample size to yield any given interval. Formulas exist for calculating the required sample size as a function of the desired degree of confidence, the desired precision or width of the confidence interval, and the population variance as estimated by the sample (Williams, 1978, p. 219).

Unfortunately, there are several problems with this approach. The formulas require information that is not usually known until after the survey has been conducted, such as the estimated sampling variability. Moreover, the formulas rest on such assumptions as the normality of the sampling distribution. Practical problems arise as well. Most surveys measure several different variables, each of which may require different levels of measurement precision and thus different minimal sample sizes. Even if the largest minimum size could be determined, the actual sample size may be constrained by another severe limitation—feasibility within the available budget.

Survey sample size is often maximized within the constraints of the survey design (including the number of trend samples or panel reinterviews, length of questionnaire, medium, and number of callbacks to complete the interviews) and total research resources. Survey planners often make decisions in a zero-sum situation, in which any increase in sample size must be compensated for by resource savings in other areas. How much precision and certainty is worth purchasing becomes a problem in the valuation of knowledge. This problem is beyond the scope of this chapter, but it has been treated elsewhere (Sudman, 1976, chap. 5).

In the absence of precise estimates of required sample size and within the constraints previously noted, most sample sizes are set by rule of thumb and guesswork. For example, the sample size can be set by reference to earlier surveys of a similar kind. If subgroup comparisons are especially important, the overall sample size can be set to achieve some minimal representation of the smallest subgroup of interest.

DATA COLLECTION

Although sampling is the design component unique to survey research, it is not the only source of error. Recent research suggests that nonsampling measurement error typically exceeds sampling error and should, therefore, be given great attention (Assael & Keon, 1982). Bias and random error can be produced in each of several parts of the data collection process, and each has a possible remedy. In the following sections, we will consider respondent contact and cooperation, interviewer training and rapport, and questionnaire construction and processing.

Contact and Cooperation

Completion Rates. An unbiased sample can yield biased results if some of the sample elements are either not contacted or are contacted but not interviewed. The extent to which a sample is successfully reached and persuaded to cooperate is measured by the **completion rate**. A low completion rate raises concern about possible nonobservation bias. If the uncontacted or uncooperative members of the sample differ in some systematic way from those who are contacted and cooperative, the survey will be biased.

The effect of noncompletions on random error is simpler than it is on bias. Although noncompleters reduce the size of the completed sample, which will tend to contribute to sampling error, this problem can be compensated for by drawing a sample large enough to yield the required number of completed interviews. Unfortunately, a sample made adequate in size by this approach will still be at risk of bias. If the attitudes of the kinds of people who dislike surveys are to be known, the uncooperative must be persuaded to cooperate.

The completion rate can be defined in different ways. In face-to-face surveys, the completion rate is often defined as the number of completed interviews divided by the number of respondents eligible for interview, that is, the sum of those interviewed plus those known to be living at the contacted address but never home or cooperative. In telephone interviewing with random digit dialing, the number eligible is difficult to define since an unanswered number may indicate that an eligible respondent is not at home or that the number is in a vacant house or is a pay phone. Since most phone numbers that are unanswered after many calls (say 12 or more) are known to be ineligible, unanswered phone numbers are commonly excluded from the calculation of completion rates. Recent urban telephone surveys have achieved completion rates in the range of 50 to 90 percent (Groves, 1979; Jordan, Marcus, & Reeder, 1980; O'Neil, 1979; Tuchfarber & Klecka, 1976). Face-to-face surveys using the same instruments as those used in telephone surveys tend to achieve slightly better completion rates.

Checking and Avoiding Bias.   Low completion rates may be due to low *contact* rates (sampled respondents not at home), low *cooperation* rates (refusals), or both. Noncontact bias has been measured by comparing respondents who are interviewed on early attempts with respondents interviewed on later attempts (that is, who could not be contacted initially and who resemble, presumably, the kinds of people who are never contacted). Respondents requiring more contacts to reach are younger, have more education, live in central cities, and have higher incomes (Dunkelberg & Day, 1973). Unfortunately, the tendency to be at home and available for survey contact has been declining steadily over recent years (Weeks, Jones, Folsom, & Benrud, 1980). The noncontact bias can be at least partially overcome by increasing the level of effort—that is, making many callbacks at different hours, especially on weeknights and on weekends.

Cooperation is in part a function of interview content and of interviewer style (topics to be treated later). Cooperation is also a function of the respondent's characteristics and of the data collection medium. Respondents typically prefer face-to-face interviews to telephone interviews and are less likely to refuse a person than a phone interviewer (Groves, 1979). Information about the personal characteristics of noncooperators comes from a comparison of initial cooperators with initial refusers who later cooperated or about whom some other data were available. Uncooperative urban interviewees are reported to be lower in education and income and to be older (O'Neil, 1979). In a nonmetropolitan study, noncooperators had less education, more residential stability, and smaller households (Comstock & Helsing, 1973).

Unlike bias due to noncontact, bias due to noncooperation is not controlled merely by increasing the number of callbacks. Initial refusers can occasionally be persuaded to relent and cooperate, but the effort devoted to such attempts to "convert" respondents is limited by ethical guidelines. People have a right not to participate in research. Improvements in rater training and in questionnaire design may be the best methods for improving cooperation. With cooperation rates on the decline, research to improve cooperation in surveys will become increasingly necessary.

Interviewer Effects and Training

Rapport.   In mail surveys, there is no interviewer, and the respondent must decide, based on the written materials, how honestly and thoroughly to answer the questions. In face-to-face and phone surveys, the interviewer can play an important part in the respondent's decision to cooperate, to answer honestly, and to complete every item. Since the interviewer can influence the completion rate and the validity and reliability of the answers, he or she must try to create a friendly and trusting atmosphere. When the interviewer gains the respondent's confidence and achieves good two-way communication, he or she is said to have established **rapport** with the respondent.

Several behaviors can contribute to establishing rapport. A well-groomed and appropriately dressed interviewer has the best chance of getting a foot in the respondent's door. A pleasant manner and a clear and competent-sounding voice will help avoid an early termination of the interview. The interviewer's goal is to obtain the respondent's sincere cooperation. The interviewer should be friendly, respectful, and honest while carrying out the interview. Arguments and persuasion should be avoided; the respondent's ideas, opinions, and beliefs are to be observed, not changed.

Random Error.   Random error occurs in the interviewing situation when mistakes are haphazardly introduced by the interviewer. Errors can occur when the questions are misread or the answers are misrecorded. The extent of such errors has been monitored by tape-recording interviews for later analysis. In one study of very carefully selected interviewers, an average of three reading errors occurred in every ten questions, and some sort of nonprogrammed speech behavior was found in over half of all questions (Bradburn, Sudman, & Blair, 1979). Although the interviewers' errors in this study did not significantly distort the responses, such errors have the potential to decrease measurement reliability.

The general solution recommended for avoiding such errors and to increase reliability is training. The goal is to standardize behavior by instruction and rehearsal. Most professional survey organizations conduct training for their interviewers and provide detailed written instructions in the form of a manual (Guenzel, Berckmans, & Cannell, 1983; Survey Research Center, 1976). The required training will vary in length, depending on the complexity of the questionnaire and the interviewer's experience. For example, for *The Current Population Survey,* 50 to 60 hours of training are provided for new interviewers in their first three months and two to three hours for experienced interviewers before each monthly survey (National Commission on Employment and Unemployment Statistics, 1979).

Bias.   Interviewers can bias their survey in various ways. An interviewer may ask certain questions differently or probe more intensively with some respondents than with others based on knowledge of the study's hypotheses. For example, interviewers who expected that their respondents would underreport certain behaviors (for example, gambling) did indeed obtain lower reported levels of such behaviors (Bradburn, Sudman, & Blair, 1979).

Interviewers can also introduce bias by their personal characteristics. Interviewer effects can be studied by comparing the average responses gathered by different interviewers. In an analysis of surveys of economic outlook, it was found that male interviewers obtained more optimistic reports than did female interviewers (Groves & Fultz, 1985). Although training might help correct bias due to interviewers' expectations, only interviewer selection can reduce bias due to fixed characteristics.

Questionnaire Construction

Questionnaire construction is another stage in survey research design at which bias and error can enter. In this section, we will briefly address three aspects of questionnaire construction: individual item clarity, item order and scaling, and questionnaire format (also see Sudman & Bradburn, 1982).

Item Construction. Items that are unclear or badly worded introduce random error because respondents are forced to interpret such items. Since different people will place different meanings on the same ambiguous questions, variations in answers will be due to random interpretation as well as to genuine differences between respondents.

There are several common problems in composing items. One is the **compound item,** which squeezes more than one question into a single item. Consider the following item written to evaluate a course: "Do you like the content and the lecturer's style?" This item should have been divided into separate questions, one about content and one about the lecturer's style so that respondents with different views on the two topics are not forced to choose which question to answer.

A second common problem occurs with **closed-ended questions,** that is, ones that give the respondent fixed answers from which to choose. The respondent can become confused if the provided answers are incomplete (that is, if they omit one or more possible answers) or overlapping (that is, if they are not mutually exclusive). The following item illustrates both problems: "How often do you feel depressed? (1) once a year or less; (2) one to four times per month; (3) once per week; (4) more than once per week." The person who feels depressed four times per month must choose between answers 2 and 3, both of which include the respondent's answer. The person feeling depressed 2 to 11 times a year has no suitable answer.

A third common problem is vagueness. Vague terms force the respondent to guess at the question's meaning. For example, if asked, "Have you recently changed your residence?" the respondent might wonder how recent is "recent." A fourth problem concerns wording. If the item is very long, uses difficult vocabulary, or is composed with negative or convoluted phrasing, many respondents will misunderstand. A fifth problem is posed by items to which the respondent has no answer. Some respondents will attempt an answer even though it is based on a fading memory or on guesswork unless given the clear option to say they do not know.

Item composition can also affect the validity of the questionnaire insofar as it increases or decreases the chance of bias. The most obvious source of bias is the nonneutral wording of questions. For example, in questions about whether respondents favored more assistance for the needy, the choice between the words *welfare* and *poor* had a significant impact on the results. The term *welfare* resulted in less generous responses, apparently because it had the connotation of waste and bureaucracy (Smith, 1987). For further discussion of how to write survey questions, see Converse and Presser (1986).

Questions about some topics are inherently frightening, and they tend to be refused or to be answered in a biased way. For example, "Have you ever underreported your income on tax returns?" Such items typically yield underestimates of the true level in the population. One solution is to omit items that are judged too threatening since they may not only produce biased results but also lead to increased terminations or refusals. Another approach is to phrase the questions to minimize the threat even at the cost of precision (for example, asking for income levels in large categories rather than in exact terms). A third strategy attempts to estimate the true population rate from threatening survey items. One such approach, called the random response method, lowers but does not eliminate bias on threatening items (for experiments on the random response method see Bradburn et al., 1979, and Locander, Sudman, & Bradburn, 1976).

Order Effects.   Virtually all surveys include more than one item. Different items may measure different attitudes or beliefs, or several different items may be combined to measure a single variable. The reliability of the measurement increases with the number of items used. The limit to the number of items is set by the resources of the researcher (since longer questionnaires require paying interviewers for more hours of labor) and by the patience of the interviewees. Since the patience of the interviewees varies with their interest in the topic, there is no fixed limit on the length of questionnaires. Very boring or very threatening questionnaires may be too long at ten minutes. On the other hand, questionnaires lasting an hour or more have been successfully used without fatal harm to the completion rate.

One concern in multiple-item questionnaire construction is that each item may be influenced by earlier items. That is, respondents may answer in a biased way, depending on the preceding items. This problem is especially important in the comparison of answers to the same item across different surveys. Unless the questionnaires are identical, different average responses to the same item could be due either to differences in the samples or to different item orders. To test the order effect, item order can be reversed on different versions of the same questionnaire. When this step was taken with two abortion attitude items, one specific (in response to a strong chance of a serious birth defect) and the other general (at the mother's choice because she does not want more children), significantly different answers were obtained (Schuman, Presser, & Ludwig, 1981). Respondents expressed up to 17 percent higher agreement with the general proposition favoring legal abortion when that proposition was asked before rather than after the more specific item. This finding has not only been replicated but also been shown to depend on the context of the other questions surrounding the items (Bishop, Oldendick, & Tuchfarber, 1985).

One possible solution to the order problem is to randomize the order of items within a survey (that is, different respondents would get the same items but in randomly different orders). However, this approach does not guarantee that "true" responses are produced, only that the extent of the bias is reduced to an unknown extent in some random orders. It appears that order effects are strongest for general or summary items because their interpretation is most subject to the influence of prior specific items. Thus it might be advisable to avoid general items or to isolate them from more specific items.

Item order may also be manipulated to maximize cooperation and smooth progression through the questionnaire. It is probably desirable to open a questionnaire with less threatening and more interesting items to ensure cooperation in the crucial early stage. Questions on related topics or those that **branch** from each other (that is, questions that follow up other questions depending on the earlier answers) are most efficiently grouped together.

Combining Items.   By far the most common method of creating a composite score from multiple items is to sum the responses. The most commonly seen approach uses items with Likert-style wording. A Likert-style item consists of a statement followed by a number of possible levels of agreement (for example, from "strongly agree" to "strongly disagree"). If there are seven possible levels of agreement, each would be given a value in equal intervals from 1 to 7. The respondent thus receives a score between 1 and 7 on each item, and these item scores can easily be summed over all related items to produce a summary score. Such a sum of scores constitutes an index.

The summing of Likert-style items is based on equal weighting of each item. Composite scores can also be derived from sets of items that have unequal weights, for example, the Thurstone scale. Thurstone scales are not commonly seen in surveys because they are difficult to construct. Each Thurstone-type item has been selected from a large pool of items and preclassified in intensity by a large panel of judges. Each final Thurstone item is chosen because the judges agree on the location of the item at some point on an equal-interval scale. For example, you might want to measure willingness of a respondent to disclose intimate information. In the Thurstone approach, a set of topics would be selected to represent different degrees of intimacy (for example, from disclosures about politics to those about sexual behavior). The respondent would indicate each topic on which he or she would be willing to disclose. The scale score would be a function of the weights of the checked items. In theory, the respondent should check all topics at and below the level of their most intimate disclosure level and none of the items rated higher in intimacy. Unfortunately, there is no guarantee that respondents will interpret the items in the same way as the judges. Thus, a respondent who chooses many less intimate topics may get as high an average intimacy score as someone who chooses the most intimate topic but few others.

A related approach combines items that empirically form a **scalar structure**. A scalar structure exists if harder or less frequently chosen items are chosen only if easier or more frequently chosen items are also chosen by each respondent. When a set of items satisfies this criterion, it is called a Guttman scale. If more than a few responses differ from the scalar pattern, it will be impractical to score the responses as a Guttman scale. The Guttman scale score is based on the pattern of responses and the intensity structure of the items. Thus a scale score might consist of the value of the "hardest" item chosen since the scalar structure implies that all easier items are also chosen. However, if some respondents diverge from the scalar structure, such a scoring procedure would be misleading. In that case, the same items would produce different scale (value of hardest item chosen) and index (sum of all checked items given equal weight) scores. The choice of composite index or scale scoring will have an impact on item selection, wording, and organization.

Format and Response Recording.   After wording and ordering the individual items, it is necessary to choose the format of the questionnaire and to provide for coding and processing the answers. Obviously, the questionnaire should be visually uncluttered. Tiny print, small margins, and multiple items per line can all contribute to reading and recording errors unless the interviewer is well trained. The design must also provide for smooth progression from item to item and for the recording of responses in a way that facilitates later data management.

Many questionnaires contain some items that are inappropriate for some respondents. It is not just that the respondent cannot answer or must answer "don't know"; such items would be confusing for and waste the time of certain respondents. For example, there may be 20 items asking about perceptions of one's job. Such items could prove both irrelevant and embarrassing to someone who has recently become unemployed. To skip such items, questionnaires utilize branches. For example, the items about the job would ordinarily follow an item asking about current employment status. Respondents who are employed would be taken through the job items. Unemployed respondents would take a different branch, skipping ahead to the next section of the questionnaire. Such skips can be confusing and lead to random errors unless the branching decision is well defined. Ideally, the fork should be well labeled and require no subjective decision or recall of earlier items on the part of the interviewer.

Recording answers depends on question format. Closed-ended questions come complete with all possible answers. The respondent (in mail questionnaires) or the interviewer will simply mark the code number associated with the chosen answer. Since a respondent may elect to make no answer, there should be answer codes for each possible type of nonresponse (for example, "don't know," "could not say," "refuse to answer," or "other"). As an example of a questionnaire using closed-ended questions and branching, see *The Current Population Survey* items reproduced in Figure 7–2.

Open-ended questions, by definition, require the respondent to compose the answer and the interviewer to record it. The format for open-ended questions must include ample recording space. If the open-ended question is difficult, the interviewer may have to probe (that is, ask the same question more than once with variations in the wording). An example would be the question "What kind of work was [the respondent] doing?" which is number 23C in Figure 7–2. The list of all possible types of work would be too long to include as fixed answer alternatives. The respondent may not immediately think in terms of the kind of categories sought by the question (note the examples in parentheses to help focus the respondent and to discriminate the question from those surrounding it).

Although open-ended questions can produce rich and interesting answers, the results require extra time and effort to code. Answer coding means the assignment of answers to one or more of a number of categories, each of which can in turn be recorded as a brief number code. Only thorough training, precise and detailed coding guidelines, and frequent supervisory checks can ensure reliability and validity in this step.

Computers in Survey Research. Once an answer code has been recorded, usually directly on the questionnaire, the next step is data processing. Analyses of large surveys almost always require computer assistance. If an answer is recorded as a pencil mark on paper, it can be transferred to a computer-readable format manually. In that case someone must read the answer and type it into computer memory. Alternatively, the answer can be recorded by the interviewer on a machine-readable questionnaire form, where pencil marks can be photoelectrically scanned (as on the questionnaire in Figure 7–2), thus saving the manual retyping step.

Still more advanced, the **computer-assisted telephone interview** (CATI) allows answers to be recorded by the interviewer directly into a computer. This technique not only avoids some data transfer errors but also avoids certain questionnaire administration errors. The interviewer reads the questions not from a printed sheet but from a computer terminal located at his or her phone station. As each answer is entered into the computer, the appropriate skips and branches are performed automatically so that the interviewer is fed the appropriate next question based on the previous answer. Because of its promise for reducing various kinds of errors and the economies of telephone surveys, CATI has become very widely used (Groves, 1983; Palit & Sharp, 1983; Sudman, 1983).

SUMMARY

In this chapter, we have considered both the design of surveys to fit different research problems and the conduct of surveys to minimize bias and random error.

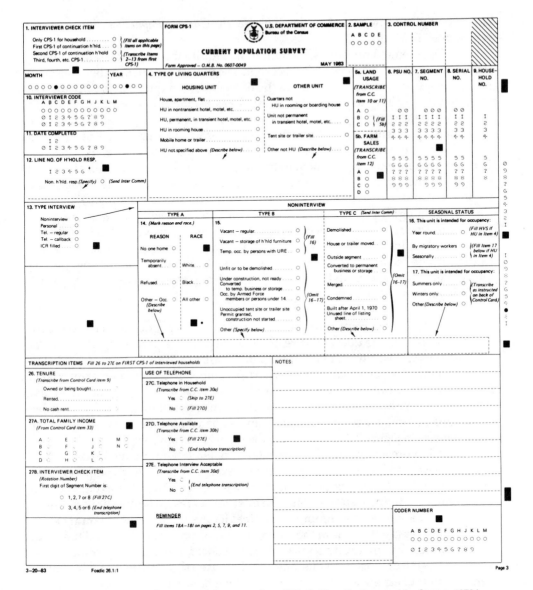

Figure 7–2   Current population survey (form CPS-1). (From the Bureau of the Census, 1978.)

The points made in this chapter are pertinent both for the researcher who is planning a survey and for the consumer who is evaluating the results. For example, the researcher will want to utilize probability sampling and to maximize completion rate in order to minimize the bias found in sampling and data collection. Similarly, the reviewer of a reported survey will want to check whether probability

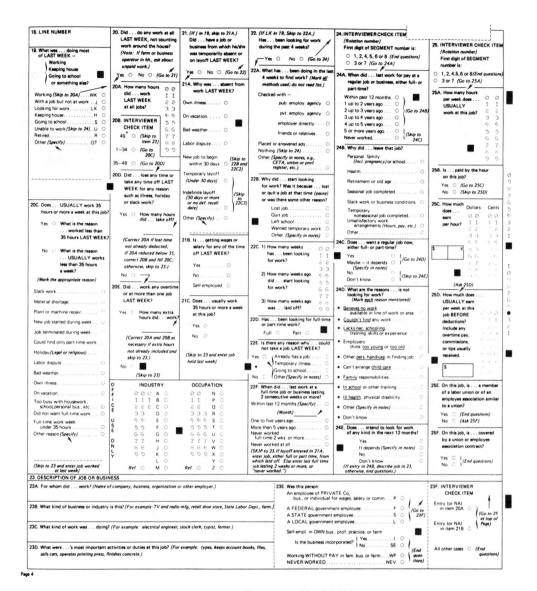

Figure 7–2 (Continued.)

sampling was used and how high the completion rate was in order to judge how much credence to place in the findings.

Some of the issues to consider both in planning and in judging a survey are summarized in Table 7–2. For each problem area, potential difficulties or choices are indicated, along with possible solutions or diagnostics.

EXERCISES

1. Pick a topic you can explore in a brief questionnaire (for example, evaluation of the instructor's performance in class). Design an appropriate survey plan (that is, cross-sectional versus longitudinal), construct a suitable questionnaire, draw a sample from the class, and collect the data. Briefly summarize those aspects of the study that a reader would need to know to assess the risk of error or bias in your results.

2. Reports of surveys vary greatly in their detail. Reports in published articles are necessarily abbreviated, with only a few paragraphs telling about the methodology of the survey. Find a published report with as much detail about the survey method as possible and, following the sections of Table 7-2, evaluate both the information presented and the information omitted. An interesting description of an important survey can be found in Hunt (1985, chap. 3).

Table 7–2 Summary of Common Survey Problems and Solutions or Diagnostics

Problem Area	Problem Nature	Solution or Diagnostic
Design selection	Cross-sectional versus longitudinal. Medium: phone, person, or mail.	Does design satisfy inferential requirements of the hypothesis? Is medium appropriate to topic, design, precision requirements?
Sampling error	Random misestimation of population value by sample.	Is the sample size adequate to provide required precision in the required confidence range? (Check sampling error.)
Sampling bias	Constant misestimation of population value by sample.	Is the sample selected randomly from a representative sampling frame?
Data collection error	Interviewers make random reading or recording mistakes.	Are interviewers trained and is questionnaire well formatted?
	Questionnaire has too few items, or items are poorly worded.	Are items clear, well scaled, and sufficient in number? (Check reliability of measurement.)
	Data are miscoded or carelessly managed.	Are data checked for accuracy?
Data collection bias	Respondents with completed interviews are unrepresentative of original sample.	Is completion rate high? Do incompletes or refusals differ from the completes?
	Interviewers, item wording, or item order influence answers.	Are interviewers trained to avoid bias? Are items worded neutrally and ordered to avoid bias?

GLOSSARY

Attrition: Loss of subjects from a study over time, which is especially troublesome in long panel surveys.

Bias: Deviation that consistently distorts in one direction (that is, the type of error that does not sum to zero).

Branch: Technique by which irrelevant questions can be skipped and the interviewee directed to the next appropriate item.

Census: Survey of the entire population.

Central limit theorem: Principle that the sampling distribution approaches normality as the number of samples increases.

Closed-ended questions: Items that can be answered from a few predetermined choices.

Cluster: Sample unit consisting of a group of elements.

Cohort survey: Special type of trend survey design in which fresh samples are drawn and interviewed from the same subpopulation as it ages. As a group, the subpopulation is known as a cohort and is usually defined by year of birth.

Completion rate: Proportion of the sample that is successfully contacted and interviewed.

Compound item: Question that consists of two or more components.

Computer-assisted telephone interview (CATI): Technique in which the telephone interviewer is fed appropriate questions by a computer-controlled monitor and inputs the interviewee's answers directly to the computer.

Confidence interval: Range of values around the sample estimate within which we can expect the population value to fall at some level of confidence.

Convenience sampling: Nonprobability sampling method that depends on self-selection.

Cross-sectional survey: Survey conducted at one time.

Data collection bias: When procedures for collecting survey data lead to a consistent distortion from the true value of the sample.

Data collection error: Random inconsistencies produced in gathering survey data.

Element: Unit from whom survey information is collected, usually a person.

Enumeration: List of all elements in the population; usually not available.

Law of large numbers: Principle that larger sample sizes allow for better estimates of population values.

Longitudinal survey: Survey conducted at two or more times (for example, panel, trend, and cohort longitudinal survey designs).

Nonobservation bias: Data collection bias that occurs in the stage of contacting sampled respondents (for example, the tendency to fail to contact or get cooperation from certain types of respondents).

Nonprobability sampling: Method of sampling in which the elements have unequal chances of being selected.

Observation bias: Data collection bias that occurs in the interviewing or measurement stage (for example, the tendency of respondents to give answers that are socially desirable).

Oversample: To draw a disproportionately large number of elements to assure an adequate number of representatives from small clusters or strata.

Panel survey: Longitudinal survey design involving multiple interviews with the same subjects; as a group, such subjects are known as a panel.

Population: Collection of all elements to whom survey results are to be generalized.

Pretest sensitization: Production of changes in later interviews by the experience of a prior interview.

Probability proportionate to size (PPS): Method of preserving equal probability of sampling across all elements in the population by which the number of elements drawn from each cluster is proportionate to the size of the cluster.

Probability sampling: Sampling method in which all elements have an equal probability of being drawn.

Purposive sampling: A nonprobability

sampling method that involves choosing elements with certain characteristics.

Quota sampling: A nonprobability sampling method that creates a sample matching a predetermined demographic profile.

Random digit dialing (RDD): A method of drawing a sample of respondents for telephone interviews in which phone numbers are composed randomly, thus reaching phone subscribers with unlisted numbers.

Random error: Random deviation, which tends to average to zero over numerous sample subjects or items.

Random sampling: Probability sampling method in which all elements have an equal chance of being drawn by virtue of the random procedure.

Rapport: Relationship between interviewer and interviewee characterized by trust.

Sample: Subset of individuals selected from a larger population.

Sample bias: When numerous samples are on the average unrepresentative of the population.

Sample error: Unavoidable deviations of different sample estimates from each other.

Sample stages: Single-stage samples drawn in one step from a sampling frame while multistage samples are drawn in a sequence of two or more steps.

Sampling frame: Available list of elements from which samples can actually be drawn; usually not a complete enumeration. Systematic differences between enumeration and sampling frame are a source of sampling bias.

Sampling unit: Either the element or grouping of elements that is selected at a sampling stage.

Scalar structure: Hierarchical pattern in a set of items in which harder or less frequently chosen items are chosen only if easier or more frequently chosen items are also chosen by most respondents.

Standard error of the mean: Sampling variability estimate based on the standard deviation of the sample, which is divided by the square root of the sample size.

Stratification: Categorization of elements having some common characteristic. The group of all elements having such a common characteristic is called a stratum.

Systematic sampling: Probability sampling technique in which every nth element is sampled from an existing list of available elements.

Total survey error: Sum of all bias and errors from sampling and data collection (that is, the total difference between the estimate produced by a sample survey and the true or population value).

Trend survey: Longitudinal survey design involving a series of cross-sectional surveys each based on a different sample.

Weighting: Statistical adjustment that compensates for disproportionate sampling.

8

Inferential Statistics

Drawing Valid Conclusions from Samples

The previous chapter dealt with the problems of drawing samples to represent populations and then measuring variables in those samples. This chapter deals with the problem of making the leap from information about a sample to an inference about the population. To help us judge the confidence we can place in that leap, we employ inferential statistics. If you are not already familiar with descriptive statistics, you should review the appendix before proceeding with this chapter.

PURPOSE AND MEANING

Example: Academic Performance, Anxiety, and Biofeedback

$t = 4.66$, p < .01.   Symbols and numbers such as these appear in virtually every social research report based on quantitative measures. The t is the name of a particular kind of inferential statistic. The number 4.66 is the value of the t statistic in this example. The **p** stands for *probability*. The expression < .01 means that such a large value of t as 4.66 is expected to occur by chance less than 1 percent of the time. The purpose of this expression and its meaning in social research will be discussed in this chapter.

The particular expression "$t = 4.66, p < .01$" can be found in an actual study, which evaluated some methods for improving the academic performance of college students (Stout, Thornton, & Russell, 1980). These researchers hypothesized that a reduction in anxiety would lead to improved grades. To test this hypothesis, students were randomly assigned to three groups: (1) anxiety reduction by biofeedback (BF), (2) anxiety reduction by progressive relaxation (PR); and (3) no treatment (NT). In the BF condition, students learned to relax through the use of feedback from a machine (electromyograph) that measured their muscle tension. The PR students were taught relaxation by taped instruction but without feedback from the electromyograph. The NT subjects were given no relaxation training.

Suppose you were considering whether to use biofeedback to improve your ability to relax and to raise your academic performance. In asking this question you would be trying to draw an inference about the whole population of college students of which you are one member from the small sample of college students studied by Stout, Thornton, and Russell. To draw a conclusion from this study, you would need to ask at least two questions about its results. The first question is whether the BF group achieved better grades than the NT group. The answer to this question is conveniently given by **descriptive statistics** (that is, those that summarize information about groups). The scores in a group will differ from student to student. Of the various ways to summarize a group of such varying scores in a single number, one of the most commonly used is the mean. The mean is simply the sum of the scores divided by the number of subjects in the group. To answer the first question, we find that the mean of the BF group (90.33) exceeded the mean of the NT group (79.83); that is, the biofeedback group performed better than the control group *in this sample*.

The second question you need to ask is the one that is answered by **inferential statistics**: Does the difference between the BF and NT groups hold for other similar college students? In this particular study, there were just 15 BF and 12 NT students. Is it possible that these two groups were, in some unknown way, unrepresentative of all students?

Generalizing a conclusion from small samples to large populations requires a leap of faith, or an inference. If every student had been tested, there would be no need for an inference or for an inferential statistic. Unfortunately, a sample may not represent a population very well. Imagine that every one in your present class would be given the same grade. Further suppose that this grade would be determined not by how well every student did but how well only a few students did—say just two. Thus, if the two sampled students were both A students, you and everyone else in your class would get an A. If the two sampled students were failing students, you and everyone else would get an F. Would you be willing to be graded in this way?

In the same way, there is a risk that the sample of 15 BF students in the preceding study misrepresents the population of college students who might receive BF (or that the 12 NT students misrepresent all possible untreated students). This risk is one of the major threats to the validity of social research—that findings may be due to an accident of sampling. To check this threat, we use inferential statistics, and the type of validity addressed is called **statistical inference validity**.

Variability and Inference. To understand how an inferential statistic is derived (such as $t = 4.66$), you need to understand the importance of **variability**. A group's performance can be described not only in terms of its mean (or other such measures of **central tendency**) but also by its variability, that is, the spread of scores within a group. In groups that have a lot of variability, members are spread far apart, both above and below the mean. This idea is easily grasped from the frequency distributions in Figure 8–1. A **frequency distribution** is simply a way of summarizing and organizing the scores from a group by showing how

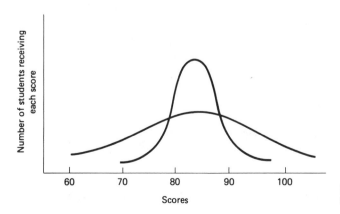

Figure 8–1 Broad and narrow distributions.

many members of the group received each possible score. In Figure 8–1, you see two distributions—one with much variability and the other with little.

The variability within groups as well as the difference between the means of two groups help us in judging whether the difference is "real" (that is, holds for the population) or "accidental" (that is, holds only in the sample). To see this relationship, imagine two different ways in which the biofeedback data might have been distributed (see Figure 8–2).

A comparison of the two parts of Figure 8–2 reveals that there is much less overlap when the distributions are narrow. That is, nearly every student in the biofeedback group did better than any student in the no-treatment group. That the relaxation treatment improved student performance can hardly be doubted in the case of Figure 8–2(a). In contrast, if the distributions are wide, as in Figure 8–2(b), the results are much less clear. Many students in the control group did as well as the average student in the BF group. In this case, the difference between the two groups might have occurred accidentally. Perhaps the BF condition was assigned a few more students from the high range, whereas the NT group received a few more from the low range.

a. Narrow distributions

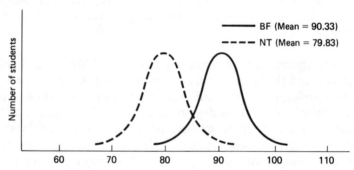

b. Broad distributions

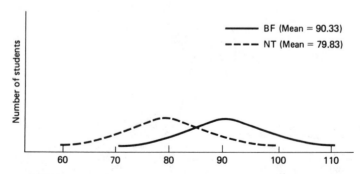

Figure 8–2 Alternative distributions for the biofeedback (BF) and no treatment (NT) groups.

The problem of statistical inference is that of deciding whether the data look more like Figure 8–2(a) or Figure 8–2(b). When the data are as extreme as pictured in Figure 8–2, most of us could decide merely by seeing the distributions. However, many times the results will be less clear-cut; the two groups are likely to have more overlap than in Figure 8–2(a) but less than in Figure 8–2(b). In most cases, we need a more precise method of summarizing such results.

Inferential Logic

Effect-to-Variability Ratio. The essence of the problem illustrated in Figure 8–2 is weighing the difference between the two groups (the apparent effect of biofeedback) by the variability of the groups. Just as the effect can be summarized as the difference between two groups (90.33 − 79.83), so the variability of the groups can be summarized by descriptive statistics. One of the most commonly used measures of variability is the standard deviation (SD). This measure of variability depends on the distance of each score from the average score or mean. If most students' grades are close to the mean, as in Figure 8–2(a), the standard deviation for each group will be small. If most grades are far from the group means, as in Figure 8–2(b), the standard deviations will be greater. The standard deviations for the actual groups were reported as 5.0 for the BF group and 6.3 for the NT group.

Given measures of effect (difference of two means) and variability (standard deviations for two groups), we can summarize their relationship in a single number: **effect-to-variability ratio** (that is, effect divided by variability). Since the two groups have different standard deviations, these will have to be combined or pooled before calculating the ratio.[1] One form of this ratio is called the *t* statistic or Student's *t* after the pen name (Student) used by Gossett, who developed this statistic. Student's *t* has very desirable properties. As the difference between groups becomes larger relative to the variability, the *t* statistic becomes larger. As the difference between the groups shrinks or the variability increases or both, *t* becomes smaller. Thus *t* summarizes the graphic information such as that in Figure 8–2 in a single number. It should be large for situations such as those pictured in Figure 8–2(a) and small for those illustrated in Figure 8–2(b).

If inferential statistics only summarized the relationship of the size of effect to variability, they would not do the job required of them. The inferential statistic *t*, when calculated for the data in the biofeedback example, is 4.66. Is 4.66 sufficiently large so that we can conclude that the BF and NT groups look more like Figure 8–2(a) than Figure 8–2(b)?

Certainty and Confidence. One answer to these questions is that no magnitude of *t*, no matter how large, can make us absolutely certain. As long as we have only sample evidence, we cannot be certain of the whole population. Statisticians do not speak of certainty or proof. Rather, they work in terms of probability, risk, and confidence. If we cannot eliminate uncertainty, we can at least limit it.

Inferential statistics help us choose between two rival hypotheses. One hypothesis is that the observed difference is due to chance (likely when the effect is small compared to the variability). This hypothesis is called the **null hypothesis** (abbreviated H_0). The null hypothesis implies, in our example, that BF has no effect because there is no real difference between the populations from which the samples were drawn. The other hypothesis is that the difference observed in the samples signifies a real difference in the populations (likely when the effect is large relative to the variability).

Suppose for a moment that H_0 were true and that our observed difference (which results in $t = 4.66$) is a fluke. In this scenario, two unrepresentative groups were drawn by chance, yielding a difference that is not really true for the populations. Had other groups been drawn from the pool of all students and given the same treatments, their comparison would show no difference on the whole. What are the chances of drawing such unrepresentative samples that t is equal to 4.66 when H_0 is true? Probability theory provides an exact answer to this question. The chances of drawing unrepresentative samples are small, and the chances of drawing extremely unrepresentative samples are extremely small. Given the information from our samples, it is possible to estimate just how likely or unlikely it is that a given value of t would be found if H_0 were true. The expression "$t = 4.66, p < .01$" can be translated as follows: Samples yielding such an effect-to-variability ratio as $t = 4.66$ are drawn by chance less than 1 percent of the time from populations that have no real difference. In simpler terms, it is improbable that the difference observed is due to sampling error.

Can we be certain that the observed difference is real and not due to sampling? No; if we were to reject H_0 as false and assume that there was a real difference, we would be in error about one time in a hundred. This particular kind of error is called a **Type I error**, which occurs when the null hypothesis is rejected despite being true. In statistics, this kind of error cannot be avoided altogether, but its risk can be limited. The opposite kind of error is not rejecting the null hypothesis when it is wrong—a **Type II error**. These types of errors are summarized in Table 8–1.

The risk of making a Type I error can be determined before a study begins. The maximum risk of a Type I error is set by the researcher and is called **alpha** (α). The most commonly used alpha level is .05 (see Cowles & Davis, 1982, for the origins of this convention). An inferential statistic (for example, a t value) with

	Null Hypothesis is Correct	*Null Hypothesis is False*
Null hypothesis is not rejected	Correct	Type II error
Null hypothesis is rejected	Type I error	Correct

Table 8–1   Errors in Inferential Statistics

$p < .05$ is commonly said to be statistically significant. A finding with **statistical significance** is one that is believed to be representative of a real pattern in the pool of all subjects from which the sample was drawn. Of course, researchers or readers can set the alpha level as they please. Sometimes, data are reported with $p < .10$ and sometimes with $p < .01$. The risk of making a Type I error is higher when $p < .10$ (10 times in 100) than when $p < .01$ (1 time in 100).

On the other hand, the chances of making Type II errors move in just the opposite direction as alpha is made smaller and smaller. Type II errors are inferences that H_0 is true when it is really false. Samples can understate the true difference or relationship just as they can imply a relationship or difference that does not exist. Social scientists tend to emphasize Type I errors and set alpha to avoid them at some precise low level. However, Type II errors are also of concern, and that is why alpha is not set at some extreme level such as .00001. For a discussion of the optimum level of statistical significance, taking into account the costs of both Type I and Type II errors, see Nagel and Neef (1977).

Finding Critical Values. How do we know whether a particular value of t (or other inferential statistic) is statistically significant at some alpha (for example, .05)? An essential requirement of an inferential statistic such as t is that it has a known **probability distribution**. That is, the probability of occurrence of each value of t (on the assumption of no difference in the population) has been calculated from its known distribution and can be found displayed in tabular form. The numbers in such a table are called **critical values** of the statistic because each is the value that the observed t must exceed if it is to be judged statistically significant at the chosen alpha level. To look up the critical values of an inferential statistic, one needs to decide on the alpha level and the **degrees of freedom** (based on the number of subjects or the number of data points, such as cells of cross-tabulation tables) used in calculating the inferential statistic. The reader of a research report need not calculate the degrees of freedom and look up the significance level of the inferential statistic—this step is nearly always performed by the author. Each inferential statistic has its own probability distribution, which is used in a similar way to determine the significance of the calculated statistic (for example, F, or chi square).

As an illustration of this general approach, Table 8–2 gives the critical values of the t statistic. The left-hand column lists the degrees of freedom from 1 to 100. Degrees of freedom larger than 100 are not listed because they change little, as seen by the listing for infinite degrees of freedom (last row). The degrees of freedom for the t statistic in our continuing example are the sum of the subjects in the two groups minus 2. Since the BF group had 15 members and the NT group had 12, the degrees of freedom are 15 + 12 - 2 = 25. Degrees of freedom can be thought of as the amount of free information left after calculating the statistic. You will sometimes see degrees of freedom reported in parentheses, as $t(25) = 4.66$, or as subscripts, as $t_{25} = 4.66$. In the table of t values, for each number of degrees of freedom, you will find a row of critical values of t corresponding to various alpha

	t_v .25 t_v (.5)	t_v .2 t_v (.6)	t_v .15 t_v (.7)	t_v .1 t_v (.8)	t_v .05 t_v (.9)	t_v .025 t_v (.95)	t_v .01 t_v (.98)	t_v .005 t_v (.99)
1	1.000	1.376	1.963	3.078	6.314	12.706	31.821	63.657
2	.817	1.061	1.386	1.886	2.920	4.303	6.965	9.925
3	.765	.978	1.250	1.638	2.353	3.183	4.541	5.841
4	.741	.941	1.190	1.533	2.132	2.776	3.747	4.604
5	.727	.920	1.156	1.476	2.015	2.571	3.365	4.032
6	.718	.906	1.134	1.440	1.943	2.447	3.143	3.707
7	.711	.896	1.119	1.415	1.895	2.365	2.998	3.500
8	.706	.889	1.108	1.397	1.860	2.306	2.896	3.355
9	.703	.883	1.100	1.383	1.833	2.262	2.821	3.250
10	.700	.879	1.093	1.372	1.813	2.228	2.764	3.169
11	.697	.876	1.088	1.363	1.796	2.201	2.718	3.106
12	.696	.873	1.083	1.356	1.782	2.179	2.681	3.055
13	.694	.870	1.079	1.350	1.771	2.160	2.650	3.012
14	.692	.868	1.076	1.345	1.761	2.145	2.624	2.977
15	.691	.866	1.074	1.341	1.753	2.132	2.602	2.947
16	.690	.865	1.071	1.337	1.746	2.120	2.583	2.921
17	.689	.863	1.069	1.333	1.740	2.110	2.567	2.898
18	.688	.862	1.067	1.330	1.734	2.101	2.552	2.878
19	.688	.861	1.066	1.328	1.729	2.093	2.539	2.861
20	.687	.860	1.064	1.325	1.725	2.086	2.528	2.845
21	.686	.859	1.063	1.323	1.721	2.080	2.518	2.831
22	.686	.858	1.061	1.321	1.717	2.074	2.508	2.819
23	.685	.858	1.060	1.319	1.714	2.069	2.500	2.807
24	.685	.857	1.059	1.318	1.711	2.064	2.492	2.797
25	.684	.856	1.058	1.316	1.708	2.060	2.485	2.787
26	.684	.856	1.058	1.315	1.706	2.056	2.479	2.779
27	.684	.855	1.057	1.314	1.703	2.052	2.473	2.771
28	.683	.855	1.056	1.313	1.701	2.048	2.467	2.763
29	.683	.854	1.055	1.311	1.699	2.045	2.462	2.756
30	.683	.854	1.055	1.310	1.697	2.042	2.457	2.750
31	.683	.854	1.054	1.310	1.696	2.040	2.453	2.744
32	.682	.853	1.054	1.309	1.694	2.037	2.449	2.739
33	.682	.853	1.053	1.308	1.692	2.035	2.445	2.733
34	.682	.852	1.053	1.307	1.691	2.032	2.441	2.728
35	.682	.852	1.052	1.306	1.690	2.030	2.438	2.724
36	.681	.852	1.052	1.306	1.688	2.028	2.434	2.720
37	.681	.852	1.051	1.305	1.687	2.026	2.431	2.716
38	.681	.851	1.051	1.304	1.686	2.024	2.428	2.712
39	.681	.851	1.050	1.304	1.685	2.023	2.426	2.708
40	.681	.851	1.050	1.303	1.684	2.021	2.423	2.705
50	.679	.849	1.047	1.299	1.676	2.009	2.403	2.678
60	.679	.848	1.046	1.296	1.671	2.000	2.390	2.660
70	.678	.847	1.044	1.294	1.667	1.995	2.381	2.648
80	.678	.846	1.043	1.292	1.664	1.990	2.374	2.639
90	.677	.846	1.043	1.291	1.662	1.987	2.368	2.632
100	.677	.845	1.042	1.290	1.660	1.984	2.364	2.626
∞	.674	.842	1.036	1.282	1.645	1.960	2.326	2.576

Table 8–2 The t Distribution.
(Adapted from Table A6 (p. 681) in Goldman and Weinberg, 1985.)

levels listed along the top row. For example, if we wanted to limit our Type I error to 5 percent, we would choose the column headed by the t associated with .05. The intersection of the .05 alpha column and the 25 degrees of freedom row is the critical value of 1.708. We infer that the difference in our samples represents a real difference in the population since getting such a large t as 4.66 by chance has a probability of less than 5 percent. We could be even more demanding and insist on an alpha level of .005. Our table shows that the critical value for t_{25} at the .005 level is 2.787. Since our finding of $t = 4.66$ exceeds even this critical value, we decide with some confidence not to accept the null hypothesis and instead say that the result is statistically significant. Note that we do not say that our conclusion is certain since there remains about 5 chances in 1,000 that we obtained our result through sample error.

PROBLEMS OF INFERENTIAL STATISTICS

Math Avoidance

An Obstacle to Learning.   When you were reading the foregoing material on statistics, how did you feel? Many students feel anxious when working with statistical or mathematical concepts. Some believe that they cannot possibly grasp statistical concepts and are defeated before even trying to learn. In extreme cases, students seem to switch off their minds and freeze up in the presence of mathematical symbols. If you are completely comfortable and confident with statistics, you can skip ahead to the next section. But if you are one of the many "math-anxious" or "math-phobic" students, you should read this section.

Math anxiety is a continuum, with different people having different levels of the symptoms. Perhaps the most damaging symptom is math avoidance, which is the flight from or avoidance of situations that involve learning or exhibiting math skills. Such avoidance serves the short-run purpose of getting away from classroom situations in which teachers ask questions that are hard to understand and answer. Unfortunately, the long-run costs of math avoidance are very high. The term **vocational filter** has been applied to the phenomenon of people taking themselves out of contention for certain careers or advancement to upper-level positions by avoiding the mathematical and statistical skills required for the most desirable jobs.

See if some of the following statements describe you:

I have avoided or postponed taking courses that involve math or statistics.
Because I know I cannot do math, I am trying to find a major or a career that does not require math skills.
When I read assigned materials that have statistics in them, I get bogged down and have to skip to the nonstatistical sections where the authors tell me what the statistics meant.

If these statements describe you, you are probably not looking forward to the parts of this text that involve math or statistical material. This book's sections on statistics are written with the math-anxious student in mind. The minimum statistics necessary to understand reports of research are included, but the derivation and computation of sophisticated statistics are omitted from this text.

Coping. For a discussion of the origins of math anxiety and for more detail on math avoidance, you may want to see a popular reference on these topics (Tobias, 1978). For purposes of this text, you should keep four points in mind. First, this is not a statistics text. The emphasis is on intuitive understanding of concepts and on the commonsense meaning of statistics presented in research reports. The goal of this chapter is to enable you to read (rather than skipping) the results sections of standard research reports, not to prepare you to calculate sophisticated statistics.

Second, you should beware of telling yourself that you cannot learn this material. Math-avoidant people often give themselves silent self-statements such as "I'll never understand that concept." This kind of message is self-fulfilling and self-defeating. It is an excuse for not figuring out how to learn the material. You have the right to flounder, to fail initially, and to try again.

Third, you can learn the limited statistical material presented here if you take it in small steps. A statistical expression such as the mean, the standard deviation, or the Student's *t* is the result of a sequence of simple operations, no more difficult than following the directions of a recipe. Sometimes the difficulty in understanding statistical expressions comes from the use of symbols or graphic conventions. If you translate the symbols into their word equivalents, you will be able to decode even the most complicated expression.

Finally, the best way to become comfortable with statistical expressions is to work with them. Later in this chapter, you will see some examples of the translation of statistical results into ordinary language. You should practice doing this same kind of exercise with the results sections of various types of research reports.

Inferential Problems

Although inferential statistics are reported in virtually all quantitative studies, they have several problems. As with most tools, inferential statistics can be misused, as the following criticisms reveal.

Sample Size and Social Significance. The number of subjects used in a study can help determine whether the calculated statistic reaches significance. Relatively small effects can reach significance if data are collected from enough respondents. As an example, consider the anxiety study described earlier in this chapter. When the biofeedback group (BF) was compared with the progressive relaxation group (PR), the BF mean (90.3) was better than the PR mean (87.5), but not significantly (n.s.) better ($t = 1.31$, n.s.). Now suppose the study were conducted on ten times the number of students. Replacing the BF sample size of 15 with 150 and the PR sample size of 14 with 140 (assuming the same means and standard deviations) has the effect of raising the t value ($t = 4.3$). In addition, increased sample sizes lead to increased degrees of freedom (288 versus 27), which means that smaller t values are required for the same level of statistical significance. As a result, an increase in the number of subjects (when everything else remains the same) increases the likelihood that a finding will be judged statistically significant ($t = 4.3$, $p < .01$).

Because statistical significance can sometimes be purchased by an increase in the number of subjects, it is important to assess the magnitude of the effect and not just whether it exists. We need to discriminate between trivial but statistically significant findings and socially significant findings. The **social significance** of a finding will depend on the importance of the variables and the practical size of the effect. The relative strength of an effect or relationship can often be determined from the data and should be sought when reading the report of the study.[2] The social importance of the variables is a subjective matter which depends on personal and social values.

Type II Error and Power. The preceding paragraphs have warned against a special problem having to do with Type I error—research giving socially insignificant results despite their being statistically significant. However, there is another side to this problem, which involves the risk of Type II error—failing to reject the null hypothesis when it is incorrect. This failure often occurs when the statistical test has low **power**. The error of accepting the null hypothesis when it is wrong has been called **beta** error (to distinguish it from alpha, the error of wrongly rejecting the null hypothesis). The power of a test is defined as 1 minus beta. Ideally, the power of a test will be as large as possible (or equivalently, beta error will be as small as possible). Some statistical tests inherently have more power than others. However, researchers are limited in their choice of tests because the statistical test is often determined by the type of data being analyzed and the assumptions made about them (see the next section, Inappropriate Statistics). Consequently, the researcher's main option for increasing the power of the test may be to increase the sample size.

The researcher will be interested in estimating the sample size needed to give his or her hypothesis a fair chance. Procedures for estimating needed sample sizes have been based on the inherent power of the statistical procedure being used and the expected magnitude of the experimental effect (Kraemer & Thiemann, 1987). If a researcher reports negative findings (that is, no support for the hypothesis of interest), his or her research may be dismissed as unconvincing if the test was of low power. On the other hand, if the statistic used was powerful and the sample size was large, the failure to reject the null hypothesis will be taken more seriously.

Inappropriate Statistics. Different inferential statistics are designed for different purposes or types of data. Detailed discussions of such statistics are found in standard texts, but a brief guide to selecting appropriate statistics is given by Andrews, Klem, Davidson, O'Malley, & Rodgers (1981). The improper use of statistical tests or the selection of a poor test (for example, one with low power) can produce misleading results. All inferential statistics are based on certain assumptions about the nature of the data. Some of these assumptions are easy to check. For example, nominal data (which categorize, for example, by religious preference) may not necessarily be appropriately analyzed by statistics designed for interval data (which assign numbers with equal intervals, for example, the number of symptoms on a checklist).

Other assumptions require some checks of the data by the analyst that may or may not be reported to the reader. For example, the *t* test assumes that the two samples being compared come from normally distributed (that is, bell-shaped curve of frequency of each score) populations. In practice, it is not known whether the population distributions are normal since data are not collected on whole populations. Instead, the sample distributions may be checked for normality. Whether the distributions are "close enough" to normal is a subjective judgment made by the investigator. Reports of such assumption checks are often omitted in published research. The authors may have selected the appropriate statistic for the problem and applied it conscientiously, with checks on all the relevant assumptions. The reader cannot know that this is the case but must take it on faith.

Sometimes, a violation of statistical protocol is done consciously, based on evidence that the statistic is **robust** (that is, relatively immune to distortion by the violation of assumptions or relatively free of assumptions). Other times, the author simply overlooks the need to check the appropriateness of the statistic. Editors review papers submitted to their journals to make sure, among other things, that the statistical analyses were done correctly. However, there are significant quality differences among journals and, sometimes, between reviewers for a single journal. Thus published research occasionally reports statistical analyses that are inappropriate to the data.

The Alpha and File Drawer Problems. Alpha was defined earlier as the level of risk that the null hypothesis would be falsely rejected. A researcher sets up the statistical tests such that she or he will incorrectly accept the hypothesis (that is, reject the null hypothesis of no effect) a predetermined part of the time—usually 5 percent or less. If a test is run just once, 5 percent seems a reasonable standard. However, a problem arises if the statistical test is conducted not one time but 100 times. By definition, 5 of these 100 tests should be in error, that is, statistically significant by accident of sampling. The **alpha problem** appears when the research is reporting dozens or hundreds of statistical tests. Computer technology has made it fast and economical to generate exhaustive statistical analyses. If there are numerous groups and many variables in a study, all possible pairwise comparisons of groups on each variable will produce tests of a great number of null hypotheses. If a few such null hypotheses are rejected at the alpha level of .05, we are left in a quandary. Should we consider these few statistically significant results as good evidence for the relationship that was hypothesized? Or should we view them as the result of chance? In sum, the alpha problem is how to interpret statistically significant results when many tests have been conducted.

There are several approaches to this problem. One is to estimate the number of "significant" findings expectable by chance as a gauge for evaluating the number observed. If the number of significant findings does not exceed that expectable by chance, the null hypotheses would be accepted even for the tests that were significant. Another approach is to set alpha at a more stringent level (for example, .01 or .001). A third is to utilize multivariate statistics, which can combine many tests into a single overall test. Only if that single test proves significant is further analysis of the many subtests warranted. With proper care, the alpha problem can be overcome in the interpretation of many tests in a single study.

The **file drawer problem** is related to the alpha problem. If a single study reports 100 statistical tests, we can still safely interpret a few significant findings. But what if each of 100 different researchers calculates one statistical test on the same question? It is unlikely that we will see more than a few of these tests in the published literature because nonsignificant or negative findings are much less likely to be published than significant or positive results. In one study, three versions of the same manuscript differed only in the statistical significance of the outcome. The "nonsignificant" and "approach significance" versions were three times as likely to be rejected by the 101 consulting journal editors used as subjects (Atkinson, Furlong, & Wampold, 1982). Thus, many of the negative findings will wind up in file drawers.

The significant findings that we read in the literature represent an unknown proportion of all studies conducted on the issue. Because we do not know about all the negative findings, we cannot judge whether the significant findings are more or less numerous than would be expected by chance. It is possible "that journals are filled with the 5 % of the studies that show Type I errors, while the file drawers are filled with the 95 % of the studies that show nonsignificant results" (Rosenthal, 1979, p. 636). This file drawer problem is the unknown risk that our publications report those studies that capitalize on chance in rejecting the null hypothesis. There is no way to solve this problem in the context of one research report. However, Rosenthal has suggested a way to estimate the tolerance of the published literature to filed null results.

Misinterpretation and Replication. Occasionally, a statistically significant finding is presented as proof that a replication would yield the same results. In fact, significant findings give confidence but never certainty about the hypothesized relationship in unmeasured samples. Significant findings do not eliminate the need for replication. Rather, the initial findings in favor of a relationship should, and typically do, elicit replications. Ideally, different investigators with different biases working with different samples in different times and places will converge on the same relationship. Such replications test hypotheses under heterogeneous combinations of researcher, subject type, and situation. This testing reduces the chance that the finding is the coincidental result of a special combination of investigator, sample, and environment. Statistically significant results cannot substitute for such independent replications. The misinterpretation and overemphasis of inferential statistics have so distressed some researchers that they have called for the abandonment of inferential statistics altogether. For examples of this point of view, see Carver (1978) and Morrison and Henkel (1970).

Finally, inferential statistics are sometimes misunderstood as providing proof for or against a causal explanation of a relationship. Statistics are often given more weight in the overall interpretation of research than they deserve. Statistics appear precise, sophisticated, and decisive. Readers who are unfamiliar with statistics struggle or skip to the end of the mysterious results section, where the author concludes that his or her hypothesis is supported by the statistical analysis. Not surprisingly, some overawed readers will conclude that the unfathomable statistics must have demonstrated the truth of the causal assertion that A leads to B. Unfortunately, A and B may be associated at a statistically significant level without A causing B. Only by careful analysis of the method section can the other numerous rivals to the A-causes-B explanation be supported or disconfirmed. In sum, inferential statistics cannot demonstrate a causal linkage by themselves. Of the many plausible counterexplanations of the observed results, statistics can address just one—that the observation is an accident of sampling. Although not trivial, this counterexplanation is seldom the only or even the most important rival.

USING INFERENTIAL STATISTICS

All inferential statistics share the same purpose and can be read even if particular symbols and the statistics they represent are unfamiliar. The key to understanding unfamiliar inferential statistics is to avoid distraction by nonessential aspects of the presentation. By skipping over those parts of the statistical presentation that are not crucial and that assume considerable statistical training to understand, you can grasp the important part of the report with less frustration.

To understand research reports, the descriptive statistics will usually be more helpful than the inferential statistics. The latter must be consulted to check one rival hypothesis—whether the findings reported in the descriptive statistics are accidental. Usually, the information carried in inferential statistics about the rival hypothesis (null hypothesis) could be presented in plain words, and, occasionally, it is so presented. When inferential statistics are presented in symbolic form or numerical detail, you can make your own translation into simple language.

Steps for Translating Inferential Statistics

1. *Identify the relationship at issue*. Typically, the inferential statistic pertains to an association of two or more variables or the difference between two or more groups on some variable. Remind yourself which are the independent and dependent variables under study. In the earlier example on biofeedback and grades, the inferential statistic t deals with the difference between two groups. The independent variable is the treatment by biofeedback versus no treatment. The dependent variable is the academic performance of each group.

2. *Identify the descriptive statistics that summarize the relationship*. For an association of two or more variables, you could look for a correlation coefficient such as the Pearson r. You would determine if the association was positive or negative and whether it appeared large or small in magnitude. For a difference between groups, you would look for the means or other measures of central tendency that describe the two groups. You would then determine which group is higher on the variable and by what magnitude. In the case of the biofeedback example, the appropriate descriptive statistic is the mean of each group (BF mean = 90.33 versus NT mean = 79.83).

3. *Identify the probability level of the inferential statistic used to test the relationship*. Is it significant at the level set by the author (usually understood to be .05)? In general, this information is transmitted by an expression such as $p < .05$ immediately after the inferential statistic or by a footnote symbol such as * which refers the reader to the significance level at the bottom of a table.

4. *Translate this information about probability into simple language about the likelihood that the observed difference (or association) occurred by chance*. For example, if $p < .01$, one might say that "the risk of obtaining the observed effect by chance was less than 1 percent." Note that to arrive at this translation, you need not make reference to the value of t, its formula, or its degrees of freedom. The information $t(25) = 4.66$ is unnecessary for the translation.

Examples of Common Statistics

This chapter has illustrated the concept of inferential statistics primarily through an example based on the t statistic. Although a commonly used statistic, it is not the only one you are likely to encounter. Two other commonly seen inferential statistics are the chi square and F. Each can be understood in the same simple terms without memorizing their computational formulas.

Chi Square (χ^2). Table 8-3 is an example of a cross-tabulation of two variables—depression by undesirable life events. The values in each cell of the table represent the number of persons categorized at the corresponding levels of life events and depression. In this example, there is no indication of which is the independent and which the dependent variable, although researchers in this area typically treat life events as a cause of increased depression. Whatever the pre-

Table 8–3 Cross-Tabulation of Depression and Undesirable Life Events

		DEPRESSION		
		Low	Medium	High
Undesirable Life Events	Low	55	62	57
	Medium	22	22	36
	High	19	33	123

$\chi^2 = 51.91$
$df = 4$
$p < .01$

sumed causal direction, it is apparent that the association of these two variables is being studied rather than a comparison of different groups.

In Table 8–3 there is no statistic describing association such as the Pearson correlation coefficient. The inferential statistic is the $\chi 2$, which tells us whether the two variables are related or independent. The reader must inspect the table to determine the direction and magnitude of the association. A glance at the table indicates that the largest cell count is 123 in the cell for high life events and high depression. There is also a relatively high count of 55 for those with low life events and low depression. These observations suggest that greater depression is associated with greater life events. Could this association be an accident of sampling? The notation $p < .01$ can be interpreted, as before with the t statistic, as less than one chance in a hundred that such a large value of this inferential statistic would be found by chance. Note that the facts that chi square was 51.91 and that it had 4 degrees of freedom were not necessary for this interpretation, although they would be needed to look up the significance level of the finding in a table of critical chi square values.

F in Regression Analysis. Table 8–4 is an example of a regression table, that is, the results of a procedure called multiple regression. The dependent variable (grade point average in this case) is typically named in the heading of the regression table and is the variable to be explained as a function of other variables. The explanatory or independent variables are listed in the Predictors column. Regression analysis is a procedure for analyzing the association of two variables while controlling or statistically adjusting for the effects of one or more other variables.

The descriptive statistics measuring association in regression analysis are the b and the beta values. The b value tells how many units of change in GPA would be expected from one unit of change in each predictor. For example, since $b = .106$ for hours of study per week, there will be a little over a tenth of a grade point gain for each additional hour of study each week. The beta value gives the same kind of information after the variables are standardized and thus permits a better basis

Table 8–4   Prediction of Grade Point Average by Multiple Regression

Predictors	b	Beta	F	p
Hours of study per week	106	.31	4.75	.03
Verbal aptitude	.003	.23	3.75	.08
Math aptitude	.001	.09	1.85	.38
(Constant = - 1.02)				
R^2 = .27				

for comparison of associations within the study (by adjusting for the fact that the different predictors are measured on different scales). The beta for hours of study (.31) is greater than that of math aptitude (.09), suggesting that study contributes more than math aptitude to grades. However, such descriptive information does not tell us how much confidence we can place in generalizing from the findings in the studied sample to the larger population.

The *F* test is used as the inferential statistic to test the significance of effects in regression analysis (although the *t* test may also be used). Are any of the associations statistically significant? If alpha is set at .05, then hours of study per week is statistically significant, as indicated by the probability values in the column labeled *p*. The *F* for hours of study per week (4.75) is significant at a probability of .03, which is less than .05, indicating that the chance of getting such a strong association by sampling error when there is no true effect is less than 3 percent. The other two variables have *F* values, which would be expected by chance more than 5 percent of the time (8 percent and 38 percent respectively) and would, therefore, usually be considered not significant. In summary, this analysis could be interpreted as follows: *As hours of study per week increase, GPA increases, and this association would be expected by chance less than 5 percent of the time.* Note that the other information in Table 8–2, such as the constant and R^2 were not required to assess the statistical inference validity of these findings.

Using Computers to Calculate Statistics

Computers are labor-saving electronic devices that can perform large numbers of simple calculations very quickly. Because complex statistics consist of many simpler arithmetic components, computers have become essential not only for calculating large numbers of simple statistics but also for complex statistics involving many variables.

A computer program for calculating statistics consists of a series of commands organized to produce the desired computation. These commands are stored so that they can be called into action on request. A program can be written so that it applies to any set of input data. All the user needs to remember or learn is how to input the data, request the desired program, and read the output.

Programs designed to calculate different kinds of statistics are sometimes packaged together for ease in applying different analyses to the same data set. There are several comprehensive statistical packages and many specialized ones. One of the most widely used and easy to operate of the comprehensive packages is the Statistical Package for the Social Sciences (SPSS). Others that you may encounter, such as BMDP, SYSTAT, and SAS, are designed along similar lines. Once data files are defined and labeled in the format required by the package, it is easy to apply any of the package's various statistical routines to the data. The computation of even very elaborate statistics may require no more commands than naming the desired analyses. Most of these statistical packages are available for personal as well as mainframe computers (Cozby, 1984).

SUMMARY

In this chapter, the important but narrow function of inferential statistics has been discussed. Whether two variables (for example, independent and dependent) are related to each other in a sample is indicated in the appropriate descriptive statistics (for example, the difference between experimental and control group means). Whether a relationship in a population can be inferred from an effect observed in a sample is the task of inferential statistics. Intuitively, we are inclined to make this inference if the observed effect is large compared to the variability among the subjects.

Inferential statistics both summarize the ratio of effect to variability and have known probability distributions. Thus the probability of any given value of an inferential statistic can be determined. The risk of making a Type I error (falsely rejecting the null hypothesis of no relationship) can be limited to some arbitrary, small level called alpha—usually set at 5 percent. If the probability of the observed value of the inferential statistic is less than alpha, the relationship is said to be statistically significant.

There are numerous problems with inferential statistics. One problem is that relatively weak, socially insignificant results can reach statistical significance if the sample is large enough. The risk of Type II error (falsely accepting the null hypothesis) also exists and must be dealt with by attention to the power of the statistical test. Inferential statistics depend on certain assumptions, which when violated, cast doubt on the results, although some tests appear to be relatively robust or immune to such violations. The risk of Type I errors is increased when many statistical tests are run (alpha problem) and when negative findings are systematically disregarded (file drawer problem). Ultimately, only replication can confirm that sample results generalize to other samples in the population.

EXERCISES

Many students miss important information in research reports when they skip the results sections because of their statistics. Fortunately, it is possible to make common sense out of apparently complicated statistics. Following the brief step-by-step guide presented in this chapter, try your hand at interpreting some inferential statistics.

1. Find a popular media report (for example, from a newspaper) of research based on a sample. Determine whether an inferential statistic is reported (typically not). If not, state the rival hypotheses (null hypotheses) that an inferential statistic would be needed to check.

2. Find a scientific research report in a professional journal that utilizes an inferential statistic with which you are acquainted (such as the t, chi square, or F from this chapter). It should be accompanied by a p value. Translate the p value into ordinary language, as illustrated in this chapter.

GLOSSARY

Alpha: Probability of wrongly rejecting a correct null hypothesis; usually set by researcher before the study (by consensus .05 unless otherwise indicated).

Alpha problem: Difficulty of deciding whether to reject the null hypothesis when a few statistically significant results are produced by many inferential statistical tests.

Beta: Probability of wrongly failing to reject a false null hypothesis.

Central tendency: In descriptive statistics, the value or score best representing a group of scores (for example, the mean).

Critical values: Values derived from the probability distribution of an inferential statistic used to determine the statistical significance of an observed value of the statistic at any given alpha level.

Degrees of freedom: In inferential statistics, amount of free information left in the data after calculating the inferential statistic.

Descriptive statistics: Statistics used to characterize a group of observations (for example, its central tendency or variability) or an association of two or more variables.

Effect-to-variability ratio: Magnitude of an effect, such as the effect of an experimental treatment compared to a control condition, that takes into account the dispersion of scores in the groups.

File drawer problem: Risk that statistically significant published findings are really Type I errors after many statistically nonsignificant but valid research reports are left in file drawers because of the publishing bias against negative findings.

Frequency distribution: Summary of a group of scores that shows the number or frequency of persons obtaining each score.

Inferential statistics: Statistics with a known probability distribution that can be computed to determine whether an effect observed in a sample or samples is due to chance.

Math anxiety: Fear of math and statistics, which can result in avoidance of math-based courses or careers.

Null hypothesis: Prediction of an outcome contrary to what is expected that serves as the rival hypothesis tested by inferential statistics; often symbolized by H_0.

p: Symbol for probability that an observed inferential statistic occurred by chance (for example, $p < .05$).

Power: Probability of a statistical test of correctly rejecting a false null hypothesis (or 1 - beta).

Probability distribution: In inferential statistics, the likelihood of occurrence (or probability) of each level of the inferential statistic for any number of degrees of freedom.

Robust: Relative immunity of an inferential statistic to violation of its assumptions.

Social significance: In contrast to statistical significance, the societal value or importance placed on a study or its outcome.

Statistical inference validity: Type of validity tested by inferential statistics, namely, the confidence that a sample finding is not due to chance.

Statistical significance: Finding said to have statistical significance when it is unlikely (usually less likely than 5 percent) to be due to chance.

Type I error: Error of rejecting the null hypothesis when it is true.

Type II error: Error of not rejecting the null hypothesis when it is false.

Variability: In descriptive statistics, the dispersion of individuals' scores from each other (for example, standard deviation).

Vocational filter: Phenomenon of people removing themselves from desirable career paths because of math avoidance.

NOTES

1.

$$\text{variability of two groups} = \sqrt{\frac{SD^2 \text{ group BF}}{N \text{ group BF}} + \frac{SD^2 \text{ group NT}}{N \text{ group NT}}} \qquad t = \frac{90.3 - 79.8}{\sqrt{5^2/15 + 6.3^2/12}} = \frac{10.5}{\sqrt{5}}$$

= 4.7. The difference between 4.7 and 4.66 is due to rounding.

2. For example, in correlational research, the strength of relationships can be described by squaring the correlation coefficient. If two variables are correlated (for example, r = .5), the square of this value, $.5^2 = .5 \times .5 = .25$, says that 25 percent of the variability in one variable is accounted for by the other. This statement also means that 75 percent (100% - 25%) of the variability is left unexplained. A correlation such a r = .1 could be significant if there were sufficient subjects (at least 400), but such a small correlation is not very informative. When .1 is squared($.1^2 = .1 \times .1 = .01$), we discover that one variable accounts for just 1 percent of the variation in the other. Obviously, further research is needed to understand the other 99 percent. If the variable in question were critically important (for example, the incidence of cancer or suicide), explaining even 1 percent of the variation might justify the effort involved. (For alternative ways of displaying effect magnitude, see Rosenthal & Rubin, 1982).

9

Designing Research for Internal Validity

INTRODUCTION TO DESIGN
A Natural Experiment
Types of Designs and Internal Validity

DESIGN CONTROLS FOR INTERNAL VALIDITY THREATS
Reverse Causation
Time, Group, and Mortality Threats

DIAGRAMMING DESIGNS
Rationale
Diagramming Different Types of Designs

APPLIED ISSUES IN EXPERIMENTAL DESIGN
Ethical Issues
Computers in Experimentation

SUMMARY

EXERCISES

GLOSSARY

INTRODUCTION TO DESIGN

A Natural Experiment

Three Mile Island. "On Wednesday, March 28, 1979, 36 seconds after the hour of 4 a.m., several water pumps stopped working in the Unit 2 nuclear power plant on Three Mile Island (TMI). [This event] escalated into the worst crisis yet experienced by the nation's nuclear power industry" (Kasl, Chisholm, & Eskenazi, 1981a, p. 472, quoting the Report of the President's Commission on the Accident at Three Mile Island).

Thus begins the report of a study of the effect of the TMI incident on the well-being of nuclear workers. As no one could foresee this particular incident, Kasl and his colleagues had to design and implement their study after the fact. Since pretest data were unavailable, there was no way to assess behavioral changes in nuclear workers assigned to the TMI plant.

To provide a standard against which the TMI workers could be compared, another group of workers was identified at a safely distant nuclear plant called Peach Bottom (PB). Attempts were made to contact all of the workers at both plants. About 61 percent of the workers from each plant participated in the study. Data consisted of the responses of the participants on a questionnaire that measured perceptions, behavioral reactions, and work-related attitudes (Kasl, Chisholm, & Eskenazi, 1981a), and job tension, psychophysiological symptoms, and stress (Kasl, Chisholm, & Eskenazi, 1981b).

The Design. The authors describe their design as a "static-group comparison" (following Campbell & Stanley, 1963) or a "one-shot survey" and note that it is a relatively weak design. They report that the TMI respondents had more periods of anger, worry, and physiological symptoms than their PB counterparts. Is this difference due to the impact of the TMI incident? A rival explanation, not ruled out in this design, is that the TMI and PB workers were different before the March 1979 incident. In the absence of pretest measures such as a survey before the TMI incident, there is no evidence concerning the equivalence of the two groups. One must make a judgment about the likelihood that the TMI and PB workers were somehow selected differently. In the judgment of the authors, "it is difficult to think of processes or variables (other than residential distance) which could select one type of worker into the TMI ranks and another type into PB ranks" (Kasl, Chisholm, & Eskenazi 1981a, p. 475).

However, the authors do report some significant differences between the two groups that must have existed before the accident. The plant at Peach Bottom was older than the one at Three Mile Island. Thus, the PB supervisory staff was older and, having more seniority, enjoyed higher incomes than the TMI supervisory staff. Moreover, there was a higher percentage of females in the TMI group than in the PB group.

Known differences between the two groups (such as the percentage of females) can be handled by analyzing the sexes separately, and the authors report few changes from the overall results when this step is taken. For example, females report more symptoms than males generally, and this sex bias would tend to exaggerate the difference between the PB and TMI groups. That is, greater TMI symptom scores may be due to the greater proportion of high-symptom-reporting females. When analyzed by sex, however, the TMI women reported more symptoms than the PB women. Thus the difference between TMI and PB on sex composition does not provide a plausible rival explanation for the overall findings. What cannot be known is whether some other unmeasured difference between the groups might provide such a rival explanation.

In summary this design consists of two groups (TMI and PB). One group differs from the other in that it worked at and lived near the site of a near nuclear calamity (TMI). The measures of possible effects were collected at the same time from both groups, and this collection took place about six months after the incident. The two groups may or may not have been equivalent on the measured variables before the incident. These elements are the essence of any research design: number of differently treated groups, number and timing of the interventions or experiences (such as the TMI incident), number and timing of the observations or measures, and information on the equivalence of the groups before the intervention. Together, they determine the vulnerability of the study to counterexplanations called rival hypotheses. In the case of the TMI study, the major difficulty stems from the possible nonequivalence of the groups.

Types of Designs and Internal Validity

Correlational Versus Experimental Designs. Two of the requirements for deciding that A causes B are (1) that A and B are associated and (2) that A happens before B. These two conditions are satisfied by the design used to evaluate the impact of the TMI incident. Association was established by the measurement of more symptoms in the TMI than the PB respondents. Temporal precedence of the causal variable was established by measuring symptoms after the TMI incident.

The first condition of association can be met simply by measurement. That is, one can find whether two variables co-vary simply by measuring them both at the same time. For example, we could find out whether time spent studying co-varies with grades by asking each student in a class to report estimated average weekly hours in study and grade point average. If this sort of measurement were all that we did, our study would be an example of **correlational design** (that is, one in which the independent variable is measured rather than manipulated). In this text, correlational designs are assumed to be based on quantitatively measured variables and are discussed in more detail in Chapter 12. Purely observational research (that is, without any interventions by the researcher) can also be conducted by using nonquantitative methods, as will be discussed in Chapter 13.

The second condition for establishing causality can be checked by timing the observations so that they occur after the presumed cause. We can do so either by making our observation after an event such as a nuclear plant mishap or by intentionally manipulating the presumed cause before making the observation. The presence of a distinct change or intervention followed by a measure constitutes **experimental design.** The unique benefit of experimentation is that it removes any doubt about the temporal order of "cause" and "effect."

Quasi-experimentation and Preexperimentation. Although the TMI study's design established association and temporal order, it did not satisfy the third requirement for inferring causation, namely, that no plausible rival explanation of the observation is left. The TMI design belongs to a family of experimental designs called **quasi-experimental design,** the essence of which is that the experimenter can control the scheduling of measures but not the scheduling of the experimental intervention. This research approach and the most common threats to it are treated in more detail in Chapter 11.

The weakest quasi-experimental designs have been labeled **preexperiments** to emphasize that they are primitive and generally to be avoided (Campbell & Stanley, 1963). These designs will help illustrate the kinds of alternative explanations to which weaker quasi-experiments are vulnerable.

One such design is the single-group, pretest-posttest preexperiment. This design measures just one group on two occasions, once before and once after the intervention. Because the effect is observed within the subjects or group, this is the simplest example of a broad research class called **within-subjects design.** This single group design is vulnerable to the threat of passing time. For example, naturally occurring maturation may account for any observed change. The members of the group are also subject to any historical events occurring between pretest and posttest that are unrelated to the event under study. Observed change may also be due to differences in the way pretests and posttests are conducted rather than to the event or intervention under study.

One solution that suggests itself is the static-group comparison, or post-only control group preexperimental design used in the TMI study. Besides having a group with an intervention, this design includes a comparison group without the intervention but with a measure at the same time. Instead of comparing the pretest with the posttest, we compare the posttest of the treated group with the measure taken at the same time from the comparison group. This is the simplest example of the **between-subjects design** since the effect is observed in the difference between groups or subjects. Since both groups would, presumably, have experienced the same time-related influences, this design is immune to such counterexplanations. Although some designs manipulate the causal variable either within subjects or between subjects, a design could employ both approaches, and the effect of the independent variable may differ depending on whether the within-subjects or between-subjects outcome is studied (Erlebacher, 1977).

Although it avoids some threats, the two-group, post-only approach is vulnerable, as we saw in the TMI example, to threats due to the possible differences between the two groups. Unless the experimental intervention is the only prior difference between the groups, we cannot be sure that it alone explains all of the differences observed later. Thus, the "control" group in this post-only preexperiment controls for time-related threats but introduces new threats having to do with group nonequivalence.

The Continuum of Internal Validity.   Validity refers to the truth of propositions. One such proposition is that one variable, *A*, causes another, as suggested by the observed association between them. **Internal validity** refers to the truthfulness of this claim of causation between variables. This kind of validity is called internal because it pertains to the causal linkage of variables internal to or included in the design.

Some research designs are rather good at supporting the truthfulness of causal inferences within the framework of the particular study. Other research designs, such as preexperiments, are quite poor at supporting such causal inferences. Thus research designs can be said to range along a continuum of internal validity. Designs that permit high confidence in causal inference are said to possess high internal validity, but those that allow many plausible counterexplanations of observed associations are said to be low in internal validity.

Perhaps a metaphor will make this clear. You may hear a design referred to as "tight" as opposed to "leaky." A tight bucket has few or no holes in it, and the water cannot leak out. A tight research design is one of high internal validity, which is to say that it has few holes or rival explanations. The relationship between internal validity and "unplugged" rival explanations is illustrated in Figure 9–1.

As suggested by the illustration, experimental designs vary in their ability to eliminate or control threats to internal validity. We will review these threats momentarily. First, let us be clear about the distinctions between the two major kinds of experimental designs.

Strong Quasi-experiments and True Experiments.   As Figure 9–1 indicates, there are two classes of experimental designs that provide better internal

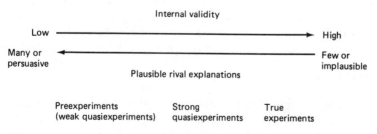

Figure 9–1   Continuum of internal validity as a function of plausible rival explanation.

validity than preexperimental designs: true experiments and strong quasi-experiments. Quasi-experimental designs include a great variety of arrangements of groups, interventions, and observations. Interrupted time-series designs improve on the one-group, pretest-posttest preexperimental design by including more measuring points. The nonequivalent control group design improves on its preexperimental, post-only counterpart by including pretests in both groups.

Despite these improvements, most quasi-experimental designs remain vulnerable to some threats to internal validity. True experiments provide a greater degree of internal validity than most quasi-experimental designs. A **true experiment** controls for time-related rival hypotheses by using two or more groups during the same period. At least one of these groups serves as a **control group** in that it reflects extraneous changes occurring during the time of the study. Such changes include effects due to historical occurrences, maturational changes in the subjects, changes in measures, and reactivity to any pretests.

The term *control* may be misleading if it is taken to mean that such changes are prevented from happening. A control group cannot stop such changes but rather serves to detect them. By analogy, earlier generations of coal miners used caged birds to protect them from odorless poison gas. If the sensitive birds died, the miners knew that they were threatened. Similarly, a control group can show the effects of some unknown influence that might serve as a rival explanation for the change observed in the treated group.

True experiments also control **group threats** by making the groups equivalent by random assignment. Although one might also attempt to equalize experimental groups by matching, random assignment is an essential ingredient for true experimentation. The importance of randomization in group composition will be emphasized in the next section on the main threats to internal validity and the main ways of "plugging" them.

DESIGN CONTROLS FOR INTERNAL VALIDITY THREATS

A primary goal of research design is to maximize internal validity—that is, to maximize the confidence we can place in the proposition that the independent variable, rather than some other factor, causes the observed change in the dependent variable. If there is no association of the independent and dependent variables, we have failed the first criterion of causal inference (that the two variables co-vary) and we need not pursue the question of internal validity. Assuming that the independent and dependent variables are associated, we can turn our attention to the most likely rival explanations of reverse causation and the several threats of time, group, and mortality.

Reverse Causation

By employing any of the experimental designs we have assured ourselves of passing one internal validity criterion, namely, that the presumed causal variable comes before the presumed effect. This design feature protects against a most basic threat to internal validity—**reverse causation**. In contrast, correlational designs that passively measure independent and dependent variables at the same time will be vulnerable to the threat of reverse causation because we cannot know from the design which variable comes first.

Time, Group, and Mortality Threats

A major concern of experimental design is with the last requirement for causal inference, namely, that no other explanation is left plausible by the design. Two classes of rival explanations, group and time threats, were identified earlier. Each can be controlled by the inclusion of one or more protective features in the research design. A third potential problem is mortality, which unfortunately cannot be so easily protected by design.

Time Threats. **Time threats** are those rival explanations that involve changes in the outcome measured within subjects because of factors other than the independent variable. Four time threats—history, reactivity, maturation, and instrumentation—can be controlled by inclusion of a control group that is subject to the same time-related factors. Each of these time threats can also be controlled by one or more other actions.

The four time threats are briefly defined here and more extensively in the chapter on quasi-experimental design, which is the research approach most vulnerable to these threats. (1) History is the threat that some event unrelated and external to the study caused the observed change. (2) Test reactivity is the threat that the observed change in the dependent variable is due to a reaction to the pretest in a pretest-posttest design. As discussed in Chapter 6, some measures are less reactive than others. (3) Maturation is the threat that the subjects in the study grow or change because of normal developmental processes, in a way that causes the observed changes in the dependent variable. (4) Instrumentation is the threat that changes in the way measures are collected account for observed changes in the dependent variable. Each of the three previous threats involve real changes in the dependent variable, which might be attributed to causes other than the experimental manipulation. In contrast, instrumentation refers to variations in the measuring instruments or procedures that can lead to apparent rather than real changes in the dependent variable.

All four of these time threats can be controlled by a control group. However, each of them can also be controlled in other ways. The threats of history and maturation can be reduced by shortening the time between sessions or eliminated by having the measures and the experimental intervention together in one session. The instrumentation threat can be reduced by standardizing and carefully monitoring the measurement procedures. Pretest reactivity can be reduced by disguising the purpose of the pretest or its relation to the study and eliminated by dropping the pretest altogether.

Two other time-related threats are not controlled simply by employment of a comparison group. One of these threats is regression to the mean, which is the tendency of scores from unreliable measures to move toward the mean (of the population from which the sample is drawn) on their second administration. This problem can affect one-group studies if the subjects are chosen for their extreme scores on the measure that is used as the dependent variable. In this case, change from pretest to posttest might be due either to regression or to the intervention. Unfortunately, the inclusion of a comparison group may not be sufficient to solve this problem. Because it is crucial that the comparison group be equivalent to the experimental group (that is, just as likely or unlikely to regress toward the mean on the posttest), regression will be considered later in the set of group threats to internal validity. Alternatively, the regression threat can be reduced by employing highly reliable measures (see the discussion of measurement theory in Chapter 5). The problem is eliminated entirely by avoiding the selection of subjects with extreme scores. The second time-related variable that is not controlled by inclusion of a comparison group is mortality, which will be discussed separately later in this chapter.

Group Threats. Group threats are rival explanations that involve differences between groups other than the experimentally manipulated differences created by the researcher. Three such group threats—regression, selection, and selection-by-time interactions—can be controlled by ensuring that groups are equivalent in all respects before the experimental manipulation begins. Each of these threats can also be reduced or assessed by procedures other than equalization. As will be discussed later, the best way of establishing equivalence of two or more groups on all variables is by random assignment of subjects to groups.

Regression to the mean can appear in multigroup studies if the subjects with extreme scores are systematically assigned to different groups, for example, highs in one group and lows in another. By random assignment, experimental and control groups can be made up so that any regression to the mean should be equal in the two groups. Suppose a group of patients is selected for having extremely high scores on whatever test measures their particular problem. They are candidates as a group to regress toward the mean, that is, toward a more healthful score to the extent that their testing is unreliable. If this group is divided randomly into treated and untreated groups, their scores should move toward health by regression at about the same rate. Any difference observed between the groups would then more likely be the result of the treatment given to the experimental group.

Selection is the threat that posttest differences between groups are due to pretest differences, that is, that subjects were selected to be different before the experimental intervention. Again, random assignment reduces the chance that groups would be different on any dimension before the experiment. The selection-by-time interaction threat is the possibility that observed differences in change between pretests and posttests are due to the combination of prior group differences and time. For example, two groups may differ in age such that one is about to embark on a growth spurt whereas the other has already experienced that growth phase or will not enter that phase for some time. If the experimental treatment is given to the growth spurt group, any differences in pretest-posttest changes between the groups may be mistakenly attributed to the treatment when it could be due to the natural maturation.

In general, group threats can be minimized by **random assignment**, that is, placing subjects in groups in such a way that the subjects all have an equal chance of being assigned to each group. Random assignment, in the context of experimental design, should not be confused with **random sampling,** in the context of survey research. Sampling refers to the process of picking a subset of individuals from a larger group or population, whereas assignment refers to dividing an already selected sample into two or more groups (for example, experimental versus control). The term *random,* however, has the same meaning in both cases; that is, each individual has an equal chance of being assigned or of being sampled.

Random assignment usually avoids systematic differences between groups but may sometimes fail. Another approach to equalization is **matching,** in which two subjects are selected to be similar on a number of criteria such as sex, age, status, and pretest scores. Then, one subject of each pair is assigned to each group. If all subjects are assigned by matching, we can be sure that the groups will be approximately equal on all the criteria used in the matching (that is, the same proportions of males and females, young and old, and so on). At first glance, it would seem that matching offers a more certain method of equalizing groups than does random assignment. Unfortunately, matching guarantees equivalence only on the criteria used in matching. The subsequent decision to assign one member of a matched pair to the experimental group rather than to the control group could introduce a systematic selection factor not controlled by matching. For example, after matching on sex, age, height, and weight, a nutrition researcher might unconsciously assign the more sickly-looking child of each pair to an experimental vitamin diet in the interest of helping the sick children. No matter how many criteria are taken into account, it is always possible that matching will fail to equalize on some important variable not considered by the experimenter. Random assignment has the advantage of avoiding systematic groupings on all criteria, including those neither measured nor thought of. One can get the benefit of both random assignment and matching by combining them. First, one would create matched pairs, as in the matching procedure. Then one would make the assignment to groups by some random process (for example, flipping a fair coin).

Mortality and Construct Validity. **Mortality** refers to the loss of subjects from a study because of death (literal mortality) or any other reason (for example, refusal to cooperate or change of residence). Such subject attrition can affect a single group study if dropping out of the study is related to the dependent measure. In that case, the comparison of the average pretest score for the whole group with the posttest average for survivors may give the false appearance of change. For example, if a drug rehabilitation program has a high dropout rate, it may appear that the average continuing patient at posttest looks better than the average incoming patient at pretest. The reason is not necessarily that the drug program rehabilitates a high proportion of admitted patients. It may only select or "cream" the easiest, most motivated patients while letting go of the more difficult problem cases.

Adding a comparison group does not automatically solve the mortality problem. If dropping out is related to the treatment, the treatment will appear effective when compared to the control group because the treatment may drive out more of the problem cases than does nontreatment. If the dropout rate is higher in the experimental group and if the "leavers" are different on the pretest measure from the "stayers," any between-group differences are suspect. This mortality threat is present in any design that lasts long enough to have dropouts. Consequently, one solution is to keep the study short enough to avoid having subjects move away, get sick, or lose interest. Failing this control (and many of the most interesting research and evaluation questions require more than such brief or one-shot designs), you will have to monitor mortality carefully. Because mortality cannot be prevented either by control groups or random assignment, it is a validity problem of a different type from group and time threats to internal validity.

Mortality can be better understood as a threat to measurement construct validity. Consider the previous example of "creaming" the best patients in the evaluation of a drug program. The posttest average score for the remaining patients fails to reflect the true posttest score of all entering patients. If the measurement of the construct of improvement were made more valid (for example, by following up and examining the dropouts as well as the participants still in the program), we would have more confidence in any resulting inferences about the program's effectiveness. Thus, although mortality is often presented as a problem in internal validity, it can be better handled as a problem in measurement.

The major problems in internal validity of reverse causation, time, and group threats are summarized in Table 9–1. Also noted are alternative control procedures for each threat.

DIAGRAMMING DESIGNS

Rationale

Why Diagrams? Whether reading others' research reports or planning your own studies, you will be characterizing designs. That is, you will be categorizing designs as being of one type or another: correlational, true experimental, preexperimental, or quasi-experimental. Beyond applying these family names for large groups of designs, you will be identifying designs as belonging to certain subtypes within the larger groupings. For example, it makes a considerable difference whether a preexperimental design is of the single-group or multigroup type. One type is vulnerable to time threats, and the other is vulnerable to group threats.

Table 9–1   Threats to Internal Validity and Their Control

Threats	Design Control	Other Control
Reverse Causation	Intervention prior to posttest	
Time Threats to Within Designs		
History	Control group	Limit intersession period
Maturation	Control group	Limit intersession period; avoid rapidly maturing samples
Instrumentation	Control group	Standardize
Reactivity	Control group, omission of pretest	Disguise pretest; use unobtrusive pretest
Group Threats to Between Designs		
Selection (confound-ing)	Random assignment	Check pretest equivalence
Regression	Random assignment	Use reliable measures; avoid grouping on extreme scores
Selection-by-time	Random assignment	Check pretest equivalence; apply controls for time threats

Different subtypes of designs are more or less internally valid. Identifying a design's type gives you more than just a handy name to call it. It also provides a diagnosis of what to be on guard for in the study. Arriving at an identification of a research design and from that identification to its chief strengths and weaknesses is made easier by diagramming.

Symbols and Meanings.   Diagramming is no more than boiling down a description of a study into its essential elements. To simplify this process, design diagrams use just three symbols. The three elements could be symbolized in different ways, but these symbols follow the virtually standard approach of Campbell and Stanley (1963).

0   stands for observation or measure.
X   stands for experimental intervention or manipulation.
R   stands for random assignment to groups.

These three symbols provide the following information, which in turn tells us the type and vulnerability of the study.

How many differently treated groups or treatment conditions are there? For diagramming, each differently treated group is given a separate line of symbols, that is, *X*s and *O*s, representing different treatment and measurement points.

Subjects may be exposed to conditions of the experiment individually or in one or more collections. What matters is how many different types of experiences are being studied. For example, in a group dynamics study, one could have ten sets of eight subjects. If five sets received one kind of problem-solving instructions and the other five received no instructions, how many design groups would you have? You might be tempted to say ten, in the sense that the subjects worked in ten sets. But from the design perspective, there are just two different conditions (that is, with or without the problem-solving instructions) and therefore two different lines of symbols. You would consider each eight-person set a design group only if you thought there was something unique that would warrant treating it as an experimentally different condition (for example, different group leaders).

When are measures (O) taken? This step does not refer to how many tests or items are collected at any time. Rather, it refers to when, in relation to the experimental manipulation (X), the measures or batteries of measures are administered. There may be a study in which 10 scales are administered at the first session, the intervention takes place in the second session, and 20 scales are administered at the third session. You would not put 10 Os at time 1 and 20 Os at time 3. What is important is how many time points have measures and how the measures are sequenced. Thus you would put one O at time 1 (representing 10 scales) and one O at time 3 (representing 20 scales), each O standing for all the measures at that time point.

What groups have interventions and what groups do not? The presence of an X indicates that the group has been treated with an experimental manipulation. A single X might represent a complex series of interventions lasting weeks. The absence of an X indicates that the group has not been so treated and can be regarded as a no-treatment control group. If there is more than one kind of intervention, the differently treated groups can be identified by Xs with different subscripts. For example, X_1 might indicate treatment with a vitamin pill containing a minimum dosage, and X_2 might indicate treatment with a vitamin pill containing a larger dosage of the same active ingredients. It is appropriate to use multiple Xs with subscripts if timing is essential, for example, $X_1 X_{10}$ for two consecutive treatments, the first with a single dose and the second with ten times the single dose.

Were the groups made up by random assignment? This fact is indicated by an R placed before the groups so assigned. It indicates that members of all groups preceded by the same R were formerly part of some larger pool of subjects who were available for this study. This larger pool of subjects may or may not have been drawn in some representative way from the population of all people. That is, the presence of the R does not imply that this pool was drawn by random sampling. Rather, the R implies that however biased a sample this pool may be, it was divided randomly, with each member having an equal chance of being assigned to each design group or condition. Typically, laboratory experiments draw on unrepresentative (that is, not randomly sampled) groups such as college student volunteers. Once such a pool of people has been identified, random assignment helps ensure that each group is similar on the average to every other group in the study.

The absence of an R indicates that the groups were not made up by random assignment. The groups may have been equalized by some other method such as matching, or they may have been intentionally selected for their differences. For clarity, a diagram might have lines drawn from the R to each group to indicate all of the groups randomly composed or a dotted line separating those groups that are randomly assigned from other groups drawn from a different sample.

In sum, the three symbols, O, X, and R can be used to communicate the number of design groups, the number and timing of measurement points, the number and group assignment of different interventions, and the composition of groups by random assignment. This notation does not tell how many subjects were used, whether they were studied individually or in clusters, how many tests or measures were collected at each observation point, what exactly the manipulation was, or how representative the subjects were. All of these pieces of information are important, but they are omitted for the sake of getting down to the essentials of the research design.

Diagramming Different Types of Designs

Independent and Dependent Variables in Correlational Designs. The minimal number of variables in a causal research design is two. By hypothesis from some theory, one of these variables is presumed to cause the other variable. The variable that is assumed to be the effect is called the dependent variable because its value is thought to depend on the value of the causal variable and is always observed, that is, represented by some measure symbolized with an O. The causal variable is called the independent variable because its value is believed to be independent of the value of the other variable and may be either observed (O) or manipulated (X).

In correlational research designs, there is no manipulation or intervention of any kind. Thus there is no X in a correlational design diagram. Since there is no manipulation, there is no control group from which the manipulation can be intentionally excluded. Both independent and dependent variables are measured at one or more times. Thus the simplest design is the cross-sectional correlational design, in which the subjects are all measured at one time, as symbolized by a single O.

Sometimes correlational designs are described in terms of multiple groups. For example, a group of subjects may be divided on some individual difference variable such as sex, and the "effect" of sex may be presented as the difference between the group of males and the group of females on some measured variable that is considered dependent. Such a correlational approach could be diagrammed by using two Os, each representing one group, but since there is no difference between the groups in their treatment, it is simpler to diagram this study with a single O. It would not be appropriate to put an X in such a diagram since the two groups are not different by virtue of an experimental event. It must be remembered that it is the presence of an experimental treatment, natural or contrived, not the presence of multiple groups or the form of statistical analysis, that separates experimental and correlational designs.

If the same group is measured at two or more times, it becomes a panel design and the group is said to be a **panel**. The panel design is also commonly used in noncausal, test-retest reliability studies in which respondents are given the same test(s) twice in succession. It is diagrammed simply by two Os: O O.

Independent and Dependent Variables in Experimental Designs. In experimental research, the presumed causal variable is an event that may or may not be manipulated. Typically, in experimental research, levels of the independent variable are fixed at just two or three levels. For example, the independent variable may be a treatment that is either present or not present. In this case, the variable has just two levels. Experimental treatments might be drugs or learning procedures. Each of these treatments could be set at an infinite number of dosage levels. But commonly, just a few are selected (for example, 0, 1, and 2 milligrams of a drug or 0, 2, and 5 hours of exposure to a training procedure). In such cases, the independent variable is said to be fixed at the selected levels.

An experimental independent variable, as distinct from a passively measured variable labeled "independent," has the special property of being clearly independent of the measured dependent variable. That is, the experimental variable is certainly not caused by the outcome variable since it is administered at the whim of the experimenter or at least occurs prior to the measurement of the dependent variable. Thus the experimental variable is more convincingly independent than is the "causal" variable in correlational research. In correlational studies, the independent variable is "independent" only by hypothesis or assumption.

Because of the special nature of the experimental independent variable, it is given its own symbol—X. Thus the one-group, pretest-posttest preexperimental design can be diagrammed as follows: O X O. If there are two groups, as in the posttest-only, two-group preexperiment (for example, the TMI study), the design requires two lines, one for each group:

$$X \quad O$$
$$O$$

For any meaningful statement to be made about the impact of X, there must be at least two measures, one representing the state of affairs after the X and one representing the state of affairs prior to or in the absence of the X. The two preexperimental designs accomplish this requirement by the contrast of the pretests and the posttests or by the contrast of the two group posttests. Such a contrast is impossible in a single measure design: X O.

True Experiments and Group Equalization. The designs offering the highest internal validity are true experiments. By definition, these designs offer both multiple groups (control for time threats) and group equivalence (control for group threats). One simple true experiment is the pretest-posttest, control group design:

$$R \begin{cases} O & X & O \\ O & & O \end{cases}$$

The R symbolizes that the two groups were randomly assigned from the same pool of subjects, presumably making the groups comparable before the manipulation. Any difference between the groups in the posttest measures should be due to the differential treatment X. This design permits the comparison not only of the two groups on posttest (between-subjects test) but also within each group between pretest and posttest (within-subjects test). Thus, one can assess the amount of change due to the manipulation within and between groups.

True experiments are necessarily "between" designs since they must have multiple groups, but they do not necessarily provide the possibility of "within" tests. Because random assignment is assumed to make groups comparable, pretests are not required in true experiments. The post-only control group design thus provides no opportunity to assess change within subjects:

$$R \begin{cases} X & O \\ & O \end{cases}$$

Mixed Correlational and Experimental Designs. Correlational and experimental approaches can be used together. A mixture of these two methods involves dividing a pool of subjects at least twice: at least once on a measured variable (the correlational component) and at least once on an experimental variable (the experimental component).

An example of a mixed design is found in a study of a relaxation treatment to reduce students' anxiety in a statistics course (Bartz, Amato, Rasor, & Rasor, 1981). First the students were divided into low- and high-anxiety groups by means of a pretest. Then the high-anxiety group was further divided by random assignment into a treatment and a control group. The experimental treatment consisted of a "do-it-yourself desensitization" procedure. The result was a three-group design with a pretest, a posttest (midterm exam), and a follow-up test (final exam).

$$R \begin{cases} O & X & O & O & (1) \\ O & & O & O & (2) \end{cases}$$
$$\phantom{R \{} O O O (3)$$

Groups 1 and 2 alone would constitute a simple true experiment based on just the high-anxiety subjects. Groups 2 and 3 alone would constitute a correlational study assessing the consequences of low versus high anxiety over time in the absence of an experimental treatment. Combining all three groups in a single study allows the additional comparison of groups 1 and 3, asking whether high-anxiety students with the treatment fare as well as untreated low-anxiety students.

This example illustrates how subjects grouped, or "blocked," on a measured independent variable can then be further assigned to different levels of an experimental independent variable. Complex designs can involve **blocking** on more than one measured variable and the assignment of subjects to levels of more than one experimental variable. An experimental design that assigns each subject to just one or another combination of two or more different independent variables is called a **factorial design**. It is appropriate to use multiple subscripts when there are multiple factors, for example, a two-factor design with treatment A, treatment B, both, or no treatment:

$$
\begin{array}{ccc}
O & X_A & O \\
O & X_B & O \\
O & X_{AB} & O \\
O & & O
\end{array}
$$

APPLIED ISSUES IN EXPERIMENTAL DESIGN

Ethical Issues

A Case in Point: An Experimental Prison.   One of the best known social experiments is the Stanford mock prison study (Zimbardo, 1975). A psychology department laboratory was converted into a "prison," and young, healthy men were selected for their stability as volunteer subjects and randomly assigned either a prisoner or a guard role. To make the results more useful, great efforts were made to achieve realism through behavioral rules, uniform clothing, and nonviolent punishment such as exercise and isolation. The study began on a Sunday night when the subjects were "arrested" by the Palo Alto police, but it was terminated just six days later because of stress. All of the ten "prisoners" reported mental anguish, and half of them had to be released early because of depression, anxiety, or psychosomatic illness. That this study was allowed to become so intense was attributed by the principal investigator to the research team's "'group think' consensus which had isolated us from external normative standards and from our own moral and human values" (p. 44). Although the results were useful in influencing the prison systems of various states, the study illustrates the danger in experimental research for human subjects. As indicated in Chapter 2, stringent safeguards have been developed in the last decade to prevent such harm.

Effect of Giving Consent. The main safeguard for subjects is the requirement that their informed consent be obtained. There remains some dispute, however, about this requirement. Some researchers feel that certain hypotheses cannot be tested if the subjects are fully informed, and they therefore support the occasional use of deception. Other researchers argue that deception cannot be justified and that nondeceptive research strategies can and should be employed (Baumrind, 1985).

It does appear that procedures for ethical safeguards can have measurable effects on the results of studies. One example appears in studies of the distracting effects of uncontrollable noise on performance in a proofreading task. A researcher studied the effects of the timing of the information to the subjects that they had the right to withdraw from the study (given either ten weeks or just before the study) in combination with the controllability of the noise (whether they had the right to turn down the volume but stay in the study). He reports that "having subjects sign the withdrawal option close to the time of the experiment has a similar effect to providing an experimental manipulation giving subjects potential control over the aversive event. . . " (Trice, 1987, p. 127).

Ethical considerations can be particularly important in the random assignment of subjects to different conditions. The comparison of two surgical treatments for breast cancer illustrates this problem. In a conventional design, a woman with breast cancer would be invited to participate in a study but would be assigned to one of the treatment conditions only after giving informed consent (Marquis, 1986). In one such study, not enough patients agreed to participate, apparently because of a reluctance to allow their surgical treatment to depend on chance (random assignment). To accrue enough subjects to complete the study, a different procedure called **prerandomization** was employed. In prerandomization, potential candidates for the study are assigned to treatment conditions *before* consent and thus know which treatment they will receive if they agree to participate. This procedure appears to accrue subjects more rapidly than the conventional procedure because only the assigned condition is described to the subjects. However, this procedure has been attacked on the grounds that the patients are receiving inadequate information about the alternative treatments on which to base consent (Marquis, 1986).

Another response to the ethical problems of socially sensitive research is to consult with the community in question. This approach has been recommended in the case of clinical trials for the treatment of AIDS (Melton, Levine,

Koocher, Rosenthal, & Thompson, 1988). When the drug AZT was the only one approved for experimentation, questions were raised about whether it was ethically correct to deny AIDS patients access to a possible cure according to the double-blind, placebo-control design. Because of the life-or-death nature of the problem, this line of research became intensely politicized. In response, it has been proposed that researchers seek a partnership with the relevant community and even to "overdisclose" the nature and risks of the research in the service of both empowering the community and protecting the validity of the research design.

Computers in Experimentation

Subject Assignment. Computers are playing an increasingly important role in all phases of social research. In experimental research, they may be used in three different phases: assigning subjects to groups, controlling the experimental procedure, and gathering the resulting data. Of course, once the data are gathered, computers almost certainly will be used in the statistical analysis and preparation of the report. Computers are convenient tools for generating random numbers for assigning subjects in a true experiment. In the absence of an appropriate computer, the researcher could use a random number table available in the back of most statistics texts. If the researcher wishes to match subjects (whether or not randomly assigning them), a computer may be helpful in sorting subjects according to predetermined characteristics (for example, grouping by gender and age).

Sequencing the Interventions. In some studies, numerous experimental manipulations are presented to each subject, and the sequence of these stimuli must be controlled precisely. In such projects, a computer may be programmed to time the stimuli, starting and stopping them in the planned order. The computer may even provide the experimental tasks. For example, a subject may be asked to proofread a manuscript presented on the screen of a computer (for further examples, see Cozby, 1984, 147–148).

Collecting the Data. It is sometimes possible to use computers to collect the research data directly during the experimental procedure rather than inputting the data after the experiment. The former procedure is called **online data collection** because the computer is connected electronically to the sensory apparatus that is monitoring the studied behavior. To take the proofreading example, the subject could indicate any errors in the manuscript by correcting them or noting them from the computer keyboard. At the end of the session, the computer could store the number of errors found, the number of missed errors, and the amount of time expended by the subject. Such online data collection saves the time of the researcher (who otherwise might have to monitor the subject's performance) and helps prevent errors both in the data collection phase and in the data entry phase.

SUMMARY

In this chapter, we have presented a shorthand method for diagramming research designs and diagnosing threats to those designs. Design groups or conditions (sets of subjects given different treatments) are indicated by different lines. A measure is symbolized by O, an independent variable manipulation by X, and group composition by random assignment by R.

The substantive focus was on identifying different types of threats to internal validity. Some of these threats are controlled or prevented by such design features as control groups or group equalization by random assignment, both of which are characteristics of true experiments. Threats to other kinds of validity are handled only in the implementation of research rather than in the diagrammable design components.

EXERCISES

The best way to build confidence in identifying and diagnosing uncontrolled validity threats is practice. There are at least four kinds of practice you should try; an example of each follows.

1. Diagram studies. Make a diagram using Os, Xs, and Rs as appropriate for a study. Try the following study as a starter:

A class of 90 students was divided into three groups by class standing: freshmen, sophomores, and upperclassmen (juniors plus seniors). The freshmen were given a special tutorial on study methods by the learning skills center that lasted a total of six hours. The sophomores were given a short version of this study-methods course in one two-hour session. The upperclassmen were given neither treatment. This was not originally planned as a study, but later it was decided to evaluate the intervention by comparing the final course grades of the three groups. Diagram this study and then repeat this exercise for research reports in professional journals.

2. Make up a study to fit a design diagram. Imagine and name the variables and procedures that would fit the following diagram:

$$
R \left< \begin{array}{ccccc} O & X & O & O & \\ O & & O & O & \\ & & O & O & \\ & & & O & \end{array} \right.
$$

Repeat this exercise by making up arbitrary diagrams and then fitting studies to them.

3. Diagnose a study. Name threats to design validity that are controlled and tell how they are controlled by the study. Name threats that are not controlled and tell how they might have been controlled by a change in design. Do this step for the designs in exercises 1 and 2.

4. Make up a scenario (story or explanation with particulars) about each uncontrolled threat you find in the previous exercise. That is, tell how it might come about by identifying a particular extraneous cause that could lead to a false inference of causation. Tell what direction this misleading effect would take. That is, would the dependent variable be expected to move up or down because of this cause? For example, if maturation were the threat, we would expect cognitive ability increases in young people over time.

GLOSSARY

Between-subjects design: Experimental design in which the treatment effect is measured by the contrast between differently treated groups.

Blocking: Dividing subjects into groups based on a measured independent variable.

Control group: Condition in which the experimental treatment is withheld to provide a comparison with the treated group.

Correlational design: Research approach in which the independent variable is measured rather than fixed by an intervention.

Experimental design: Research approach in which the independent variable is fixed by a manipulation or natural occurrence.

Factorial design: Experimental design in which each subject is assigned to one or another combination of the levels of two or more independent variables.

Group threats: Class of threats to internal validity to which between designs are especially vulnerable. Protection against such threats is provided by random assignment to groups. (See Table 9–1 for treatments of selection, regression to the mean, and selection-by-time threat interactions.)

Internal validity: Truthfulness of the assertion that the observed effect is due to the independent variable(s) in the study.

Matching: Assigning subjects to experimental and control conditions to equalize the groups on selected characteristics; can be combined with random assignment but when used alone cannot guarantee group equivalence on variables not used in the matching.

Mortality: Subject attrition from pretest to posttest, which casts doubt on the validity of the study; here conceptualized as a threat to measurement construct validity. Protection against this threat is not provided by a control group or random assignment but rather by care in defining the subjects to be measured in evaluating the experimental impact.

O: Symbol used in design diagrams to represent the collection of one or more observations.

Online data collection: Using a computer to receive and store data directly from an experiment in progress.

Panel: Correlational design in which a group of subjects is surveyed or measured at more than one time; the group itself is called a panel.

Preexperiments: Class of quasi-experimental designs that are very vulnerable to threats to internal validity.

Prerandomization: Random assignment of subjects to treatment conditions that occurs prior to informed consent.

Quasi-experimental design: Experimental approach in which the researcher does not assign subjects randomly to treatment and control conditions.

R: Symbol used in design diagrams to represent random assignment to groups.

Random assignment: Method of placing subjects in different conditions so that each subject has an equal chance of being in any group. Its aim is to avoid systematic subject differences between the experimental and control groups.

Random sampling: Drawing a representative group from a population by a method that gives every member of the population an equal chance of being drawn. Note that it differs from random assignment, which involves the placement of subjects in study groups from an already selected sample that may or may not be representative or randomly drawn.

Reverse causation: Threat to internal validity that an observed relationship is the result of causation of opposite direction from that hypothesized. Protection against this threat is provided by arrang-ing to have the independent variable occur before the dependent variable.

Time threats: Class of threats to internal validity to which within designs are especially vulnerable. Protection against such threats is provided by control groups. (See Table 9–1 for treatments of history, maturation, instrumentation, and test reactivity.)

True experiments: Experimental designs in which subjects are randomly assigned to multiple experimental and control conditions.

Within-subjects design: Experimental design in which the treatment effect is measured by the change in subjects from before to after the manipulation.

X: Symbol used in design diagrams to represent the presence of an experimental manipulation.

10

True Experimentation
Experimental Construct
and
External Validity

PROBLEMS IN TRUE EXPERIMENTAL DESIGNS

An Example of True Experimentation

Drug and Placebo Effects. As the elderly proportion of our population increases, we will all have to become more concerned with the consequences of aging. One possible intervention is the administration of medication that lifts mood or improves physical performance—a chemical compensation for the effects of aging. Consider the following true experiment that tested the impact of the drug amphetamine on the mood and psychomotor performance of 80 hospitalized elderly patients (average age was 66, range 60 to 81) by Ross, Krugman, Lyerly, and Clyde (1962).

The authors wanted to assess the "pure" effects of 10 milligrams of d-amphetamine. That is, they wanted to separate the effects of the chemical from any **placebo** effects caused by the administration of the chemical (for example, by pill or injection). Placebo effects might result from the patients' expectations, which could be raised by the appearance of medical paraphernalia associated in the past with healing. Such raised expectations might translate into a better mood or more energetic physical performance independent of the chemical effects. To separate the placebo and chemical effects, the 80 subjects were randomly assigned to four different groups:

1. Pill with amphetamine
2. Pill without amphetamine—the placebo
3. Amphetamine disguised—no pill
4. No pill, no amphetamine

Each group received orange juice. In groups 1 and 2, the orange juice was taken after the pills. In group 3, the orange juice contained dissolved amphetamine. All four groups were told that their preferences in orange juice were being solicited to guide the hospital's kitchen staff. This was a "cover story" to get the groups, especially group 3, to swallow the orange juice without creating suspicion about the study, which might have affected their behavior. To make this cover story believable, all groups answered a brief official-looking questionnaire about the flavor of the orange juice. This questionnaire served the additional purpose of testing whether the amphetamine made the orange juice given to group 3 taste any different from that given to group 4. It did not.

The instructions given to the two "pill" groups (groups 1 and 2) were neutral: "This is a study from which we hope to gain information about the effects of this drug upon mood, the way that you feel, and your eye-hand coordination" (Ross, Krugman, Lyerly, & Clyde, 1962, p. 384). Nevertheless, these subjects were in a hospital and received the drug in the same context as that in which they received their own medications. We can reasonably assume that they expected the experimental drug to be beneficial, perhaps even more beneficial than older, less scientifically advanced drugs. A variety of measures were collected from these subjects, including a six-factor mood scale. Figure 10–1 presents the mean comfort index scores based on the mood measures for each group. A high score indicates feeling friendly, energetic, and clear thinking.

There were two different and opposite effects—one from the drug and the other from the pills. The drug effect is seen in a comparison of the scores of those with the drug versus those without the drug. In the case of the two pill groups, those with the drug averaged 12.6 points less on the combined comfort index (327 – 314.4). In the case of the two no-pill groups, the drug group averaged 11.6 points less than the no-drug group (312 – 300.4). In both comparisons, the drug effect was to *lower* reported comfort.

In contrast, the effect of the pill was to *improve* mood. The pill effect can be seen in the comparison of the scores of those with the pill and without the pill controlling for drug administration. When there was no drug involved (placebo versus nothing), the pill raised the comfort index 15 points (327 – 312). Similarly, when the drug was administered, the pill raised the comfort index 14 points (314.4 – 300.4). In both comparisons, the pill effect was beneficial.

We do not usually get to isolate the drug or experimental effect from the pill or placebo effect in evaluations of treatments. Only the presence of all four groups in this design allowed us to measure these two different effects in such a convincing way. More commonly, studies provide just two groups. For example, a naive researcher might have conducted this study with just groups 1 and 4. The experimental group would have received the drug in pill form. The outcome of this pill-plus drug group would then be compared with that of a "control" group receiving nothing—neither the drug nor the pill. What might we have concluded from that study? Figure 10–1 gives the comfort index for these two conditions. The pill-plus-drug group (314.4) would have looked better than the no-pill and no-drug group (312). The difference is modest (just 2.4 points) but might have led to the conclusion that amphetamine was beneficial to the elderly.

As the full study indicated, however, such a conclusion would be incorrect. The observed improvement in mood in the drug-plus-pill group over the no-drug,

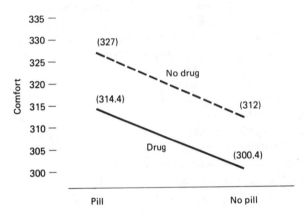

Figure 10–1   Comfort index for four experimental groups. (From Ross, S., Krugman, A.D., Lyerly, S.B., & Clyde, D.J. "Drugs and placebos: A model design." *Psychological Reports*, 1962, *10*, 383-392. Reprinted with permission of the author and publisher.)

no-pill group is entirely due to the positive effect of the pill (approximately 14.5 on the average), which exceeds the negative effect of the drug (about −12).

Experimental Construct Validity. Although the true experimental designs rule out time and group threats to internal validity, they do not assure us of **experimental construct validity**. Experimental construct validity is the extent to which the contrast of experimental and control conditions accurately reflects the supposed causal construct under study. That is, how confident can we be that the experimental and control groups differ only on the independent variable reflecting the causal construct of our theory? In the naive two-group, drug-plus-pill versus no-drug, no-pill design, we saw that the two groups differed on two different variables, both of which had substantial effects. One of those variables reflected the construct of central concern—the dosage of amphetamine—but this drug variable was confounded with (that is, inseparable from) the effect of the pill. Indeed, the pill effect, in this case, was seen to be opposite in direction from the drug effect. All this two-group design can tell us is the net or combined effect of those two different experimental interventions. If we were to diagram this study, we might want to represent both of these interventions as separately labeled Xs—one for the drug X_d and one for the pill X_p, as in Figure 10–2 (a).

The problem of having more than one intervention or event at a time is sometimes referred to as the threat of **intrasession history**, or the events internal to the research procedure. One example is the experimental intervention itself, that is, the event the effect of which is to be observed. Obviously, many other events occur within the research session that might have an effect on the dependent variable. Our imaginary two-group drug experiment is not satisfactory because it fails to control for one influential bit of intrasession history—the pill. We are interested in finding out the pure effect of the drug after sorting out the effect of the pill. This goal leads to either of two alternative experimental designs. One is to administer the drug in a concealed form so that there is no pill to produce a psychological effect. This design, which could be diagrammed as in Figure 10–2(b), is equivalent to comparing groups 3 and 4 in the original four-group study by Ross and others. Here the threat of intrasession history has been reduced by removing one extraneous event, the administration of a pill. Unfortunately, such a design

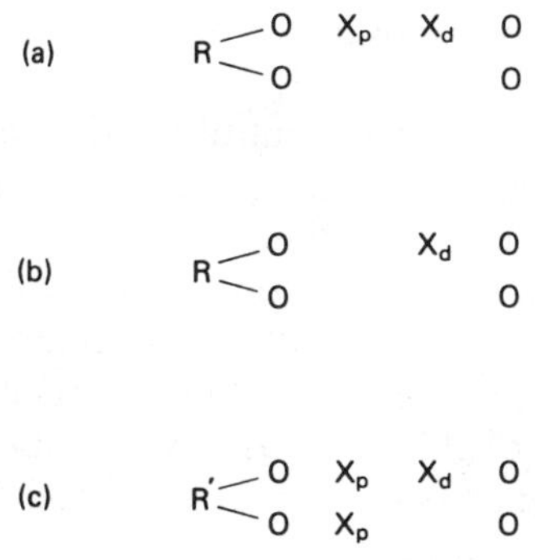

(a) $R \Big\langle \begin{array}{c} O \quad X_p \quad X_d \quad O \\ O \qquad\qquad\qquad O \end{array}$

(b) $R \Big\langle \begin{array}{c} O \quad\quad X_d \quad O \\ O \qquad\qquad O \end{array}$

(c) $R' \Big\langle \begin{array}{c} O \quad X_p \quad X_d \quad O \\ O \quad X_p \qquad\quad O \end{array}$

Figure 10–2 Alternative designs for the study of drug effects (X_d) with or without pill effects (placebo X_p).

would in many cases be unethical. It is based on denying the subject knowledge about the study and therefore the right to give informed consent.

Because of the ethical problems associated with this design, a more common two-group solution is the use of the placebo control group, diagrammed in Figure 10–2(c). This is equivalent to comparing groups 1 and 2 in the original four-group study. Here the intrasession history problem is solved by including the pill-taking event in both the experimental and the control groups. Now the two groups differ only by the presence of the drug in the experimental group.

Experimental construct validity is ensured not by random assignment but by careful operationalization of the experimental variables and inclusion of specialized control groups (such as the placebo control). There are two principal types of experimental construct threats to be considered in more detail later: control group contamination and experimental group contamination. As will be seen, both of these types of threats involve events occurring within the experimental process and can therefore be thought of as cases of intrasession history.

In the next section, we will briefly review the most common true experimental designs. In later sections, we will consider in more detail the ways in which even true experiments can go awry because of such problems as the placebo effect. Finally, we will turn to a concern that pertains to all research, not just experimental designs. This concern is external validity, which is the extent to which the findings of a study can be generalized or extended.

Variety of True Experimental Designs

Basic Designs and Their Variants. There are potentially many designs that satisfy the criteria for true experimentation, namely, random assignment to multiple, differently treated groups. The three to be discussed next illustrate the different ways in which one internal validity threat can be handled—that of pretest reactivity. These approaches to controlling pretest reactivity also serve as models for protecting experimental construct validity. The three basic true experimental designs are diagrammed in Figure 10–3.

These designs represent only the simplest versions of their types. Obviously, each could be complicated by the addition of one or more follow-up measures, as in Figure 10–4(a), or one or more prior pretests as in Figure 10–4(b). Finally, these designs could be extended by adding one or more additional experimental groups, as in Figure 10–4(c).

All three of the basic designs control for the common threats to internal validity. Each has a comparison group that is tested at the same time(s) as the experimental group to control for such time threats as history and maturation. Each has random assignment to groups, which if successful, will ensure the equivalence of the groups prior to the intervention and rule out such threats as selection.

As discussed earlier, random assignment is usually successful in equating groups but does occasionally fail its purpose. When failure occurs, the true experimental design must be analyzed as a quasi-experimental design. Because of this risk

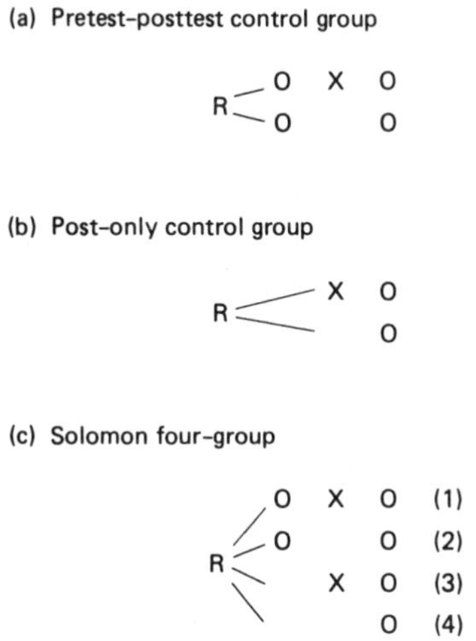

(a) Pretest–posttest control group

$$R \s<\begin{array}{ccc} O & X & O \\ O & & O \end{array}$$

(b) Post–only control group

$$R \<\begin{array}{cc} X & O \\ & O \end{array}$$

(c) Solomon four–group

$$R \<\begin{array}{cccc} O & X & O & (1) \\ O & & O & (2) \\ X & O & & (3) \\ & O & & (4) \end{array}$$

FIGURE 10–3 Three basic types of true experimental design.

(a)

$$R \<\begin{array}{cccc} O & X & O & O \\ O & & O & O \end{array}$$

(b)

$$R \<\begin{array}{cccc} O & O & X & O \\ O & O & & O \end{array}$$

(c)

$$R \<\begin{array}{ccc} O & X_1 & O \\ O & X_2 & O \\ O & & O \end{array}$$

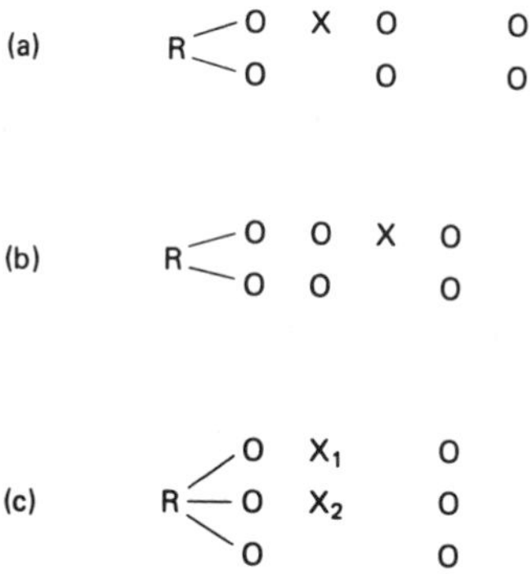

FIGURE 10–4 Some variations on a simple, true experimental design.

of failure to achieve group equivalence, true experimental designs with pretests may be preferred over designs without pretests. The pretests permit a check on equivalence before the intervention X is introduced. If the groups prove not to be equivalent on pretest, the pretest scores can be used to adjust statistically for the nonequivalence.

Test Reactivity as Intrasession History. One rationale for having these three different types of true experimental designs has to do with a particular kind of intrasession history—test reactivity. The pretest may be thought of as an unwanted "active ingredient" similar to the placebo effect. The pretest can add to or subtract from whatever effect is caused by the experimental intervention X.

A good example of the effect of testing and its similarity to the placebo effect comes from a study of psychiatric interventions by Frank, Nash, Stone, and Imber (1963). These researchers were interested in the short-term and long-term effects of a placebo on patients' psychological discomfort. Adults with a psychoneurotic diagnosis were initially tested (for about 90 minutes) by a psychologist using paper-and-pencil measures, including symptom checklists. The patients were then seen by a psychiatrist who took physiological measures of autonomic functions and readministered the outcome measures of discomfort before offering the patient a placebo pill (the treatment).

While the pill was "working," the patients were given some more paper-and-pencil and autonomic tests. They then returned to the psychologist, who administered the test for the third time that day. The patients returned after a week on the placebo for a fourth round of testing. This design is summarized in the following diagram, where X represents the placebo administration and the Os represent the repeated measures of discomfort:

$$O \; O \; X \; O \qquad\qquad O$$
Day 1   1 Week Later

The results of this study are consistent with the previous research on the placebo. On different measures and for two different groups, the average discomfort level was lower one week later than on the first test. But an analysis of the scores for the three tests on day 1 indicates that the gain was achieved before the placebo was administered (that is, by the second measure on day 1). These patients showed a further improvement in comfort immediately after the placebo (that is, between the second and third measures on the first day). Over the course of the week following the first day's measures, the average discomfort level increased somewhat but was still significantly better than initially.

Without a comparison group, it is difficult to interpret the relative effects of placebo pills and test reactivity. However, it appears that patients reacted favorably to being tested. We can speculate about how this therapeutic testing effect came about. Possibly some of the initial discomfort was due to stage fright at being confronted by strange psychologists and psychiatrists in a clinical setting. By interacting with these clinicians in the initial testing, the patients would be expected to become more at ease. These patients may also have felt that the impressive array of tests was going to help diagnose their problem and lead to a solution, thus encouraging their optimism that they would be helped. Finally, the tests involved noncritical attention from high-status professionals who patiently allowed the subjects to express themselves in repeated tests. By more than one theory (for example, systematic desensitization, client-centered counseling, and psychoanalysis), this kind of interchange is thought to have therapeutic value. By any or all of these different mechanisms, the experience of being tested may have caused a real change in the dependent variable.

In sum, testing is a potentially powerful event that may offer an explanation for the observed effect to rival that of the main treatment. For that reason, true experiments attempt to control for the effects of pretests, control that indicates ways in which other intrasession history threats may also be controlled.

The pretest-posttest control group design includes the pretest in both the experimental group and the control group. If there is a simple or main effect of the pretest, it should show up in the posttests of both groups, just as would any other extraneous influences (such as history or maturation). The difference between the posttests of the two groups should be due only to the contribution of the intervention. The posttest-only control group design controls for pretest reactivity by eliminating the pretest entirely. Assuming that randomization made the two groups equivalent, the difference between the posttests of the two groups should be due solely to the intervention.

These two designs illustrate the two fundamental ways of controlling for intrasession history—excluding the intrasession event from both groups, as in the posttest-only design, or making sure that the intrasession event appears in both groups. Will it not be the case that both of these designs yield the same estimates of the effect of the intervention? The answer is yes if the pretest reactivity effect operates independently of the intervention. However, if test reactivity has a different effect when the intervention is present than when it is absent, these two designs will yield different posttest effects.

How can one tell if the reactivity effect operates differently depending on whether the intervention is present? Quite simply, both kinds of designs can be used simultaneously. This combination design requires four groups and is called the Solomon Four-Group design, diagrammed in Figure 10–3(c). The posttests of groups 2 and 4 can be compared to reveal the impact of the pretest alone. Groups 1 and 3 can be compared to show the effect of the pretest when the intervention is present. The results of these two comparisons will reveal whether the effect of the pretest is different depending on whether the intervention is present.

EXPERIMENTAL CONSTRUCT VALIDITY

Contamination as Confounding Intrasession History

Experimental construct validity is threatened when experiments are operationalized in ways that permit contamination of the experimental variable. **Contamination** here means the presence of some intrasession events, which cause doubt that the experimental and control groups differ in only one respect—the causal variable. Unlike the pretest, which is typically distinct from the intervention and which threatens internal rather than experimental construct validity, some other kinds of intrasession history can be difficult to separate from the theoretical causal variable. There are two major categories of intrasession history threats to experimental construct validity. One type affects the experimental condition. In this case, doubt is raised about whether the experimental group received only the intervention intended by the experimenter. Graphically, this situation is illustrated by the difference between the effect of the drug (X_d) and the effect of the drug plus the effect of the placebo pill ($X_d + X_p$) in the study by Ross and others. The pill casing, X_p, contaminates the experimental condition in that it occurs with and adds something to the treatment beyond the variable under study, namely, the drug itself.

The other type of intrasession history threat is contamination of the control condition. If the control group's experience is contaminated by the presence of some experimental treatment, the no-treatment control group cannot live up to its name. In the next sections, we will first consider experimental group contamination and then control group contamination, along with their common sources of contamination and their controls.

Experimental Group Contamination

The placebo effect illustrates one prominent type of experimental group contamination, that of **demand characteristics**. The other major category is **experimenter expectancy**. Orne (1962) defined demand characteristics of an experimental situation as the cues that determine a subject's perception of the goal of the study. Demand characteristics affect research outcomes by guiding the beliefs and, in turn, the behaviors of the human subjects. In contrast, experimenter expectancy is the sum of the ways, other than the intervention itself, in which an experimenter affects or biases the behavior of the subjects to get results consistent with his or her hypothesis. Not included in experimenter expectancy bias are those behaviors that involve intentional fraud. Experimenter expectancy and demand characteristics are related to each other. One way experimenter bias can operate is through subtle experimenter behaviors, which are interpreted by the subjects as clues to what behavior they should provide. That is, the experimenter's expectancy can lead the experimenter to provide demand characteristics or cues for the subjects. However, experimenter expectancy may operate through mechanisms other than demand characteristics and so will be treated separately.

Experimenter Expectancy.   This effect has also been termed the self-fulfilling prophecy and the Pygmalion effect and has been treated most extensively by Rosenthal (see Rosenthal, 1976, and Rosenthal & Rubin, 1978, for reviews). It comes as no surprise that investigators have personal beliefs about their hypotheses and that they might have an emotional investment in whether their research supports or contradicts their beliefs. Given the reward system for scholars, we should expect that researchers would want to get the results that they expect. However, ethical guidelines usually restrain researchers from creating their results self-consciously or fraudulently. Until the evidence for experimenter expectancy effects became convincing and well known, scholars operated on the assumption that researchers would also prevent their beliefs from affecting their results unconsciously. Now it is clear that even ethical scholars could, without awareness, modify the behavior of their subjects to get the expected results. Indeed, this effect could be demonstrated with animal as well as human subjects.

Cordaro and Ison (1963) studied the outcomes of research conducted by 17 college students. These student experimenters were randomly assigned to three conditions. In each condition, their subjects were two primitive organisms called planaria. Each planarian was placed in a small V-shaped trough filled with water and fitted with electrodes and exposed to an overhead lamp. The five high-expectancy (HE) student experimenters were told that their planaria had already been conditioned to show a high response rate to exposure to the light stimulus that preceded the electrical shock. That is, these planaria could be expected to show marked anticipatory contractions or head turns when the light but not the electrical current was on. The five low-expectancy (LE) group members were told that their planaria had not yet been conditioned and not to expect much activity from them. The remaining seven experimenters were given high expectations for one planarian and low expectations for the other (called the high-and-low-expectation, or HLE, group). Actually, all 34 planaria had received the same amount of conditioning—50 training trials, each consisting of three seconds of light alone followed by one second of light plus electrical shock.

The experimenters conducted 100 trials (three seconds of light alone followed by one second of light accompanied by shock) with each of their planaria. Each experimenter served as his or her own observer by recording the occurrence of head turns, contractions, or no response on the part of the planaria. The results are summarized in Table 10–1.

One way to explain these results is to say that the experimenters were influenced in their role of observer. In the somewhat ambiguous perceptual situation of detecting a slight head or body motion in a small organism during a three-second period, the observers may have employed different criteria, depending on their expectations. Rosenthal (1976) argues that such differential measurement bias is not the same as experimenter expectancy and that such measurement bias cannot satisfactorily account for all of the animal studies of this type. Within the Cordaro and Ison (1963) study, the HLE group partially controls for this explanation of measurement bias. The HLE experimenters observed both "trained" and "untrained" planaria, and thus would be expected to apply similar observational criteria. Although the difference between the high- and low-expectation subjects is smaller in the HLE group than between the HE and the LE groups, it still strongly favors the high-expectation subjects.

In similar research with rats labeled "bright" or "dull," similar expectancy results are found even though such experiments offer less ambiguity in the

Table 10–1   Results of Expectancy Manipulation on Planaria Behavior

| | GROUP EXPECTANCY | | | |
| | HE | LE | HLE | |
Dependent Variable	High Expectancy	Low Expectancy	High	Low
Contraction as % of trials	18%	.9%	15.4%	4.9%
Head turns as % of trials	47.4%	9.9%	30%	14.5%

Reprinted with permission of authors and publisher from L. Cordaro & J. R. Ison, Psychology of the scientist: X. Observer bias in classical conditioning of the planarian, *Psychological Reports*, 1963, *13*, 787–789.

response criterion. Rosenthal (1976) concludes that the experimenters must be modifying the behaviors of their subjects to produce performances compatible with expectations. With animals, such manipulations might operate through differential physical treatment of the animals (for example, more handling or petting of "smart" than of "dumb" rats or closer attention and thus greater physical proximity to "trained" than to "untrained" planaria). Such differential experimenter behaviors are examples of intrasession history or events which might affect the outcome but which are not a part of the causal construct under study.

If such experimenter effects were found only in animal studies, social researchers might be less concerned about this problem. Unfortunately, experimenter expectancy has been reported in human research as well. Probably the most dramatic and controversial test of the self-fulfilling prophecy is reported in Rosenthal and Jacobson's *Pygmalion in the Classroom* (1968). The researchers told teachers that certain children, based on psychological testing, were late bloomers. This claim was a fiction created to mislead the teachers. Although these "late bloomers" were not different from other children in the beginning, they appeared to make significantly greater intellectual progress than their peers. Rosenthal and Jacobson argued that the teachers' expectations led them to behave differently toward their students. In particular, teachers were led to provide more educational attention to the "late bloomers" and to hold relatively lower expectations for the progress of similar children not blessed with the same label. The Pygmalion study aroused criticism (for example, Elashoff & Snow, 1971, and A. R. Jensen, 1969), which has been rebutted, and new research has been provided in support of the Pygmalion effect (see Rosenthal 1976, pp. 437–471, and Rosenthal & Rubin, 1971).

Just how teachers' expectations may be created under natural conditions and translated into differential educational treatment has been addressed elsewhere. For an example, see Rist's (1970) longitudinal observations of primary grade teachers and students and the studies of teacher bias by Babad, Inbar, and Rosenthal (1982a, 1982b). One means by which interpersonal expectancy may be transmitted is the voice tone of the camp counselor (Blanck & Rosenthal, 1984) or therapist (Rosenthal, Blanck, & Vannicelli, 1984).

Preventing Experimenter Expectancy Effects. There are at least four procedures for keeping experimenters from fulfilling their own prophecies by influencing the behavior of their subjects. One technique is to keep the hypothesis from the experimenter. This approach is called the **naive experimenter** method. It requires the availability of a person or persons who can direct the subjects in the experimental and measuring procedures but who is ignorant of the literature and theory generating these procedures. Unfortunately, the naive experimenter may, after seeing the first subjects respond to the experiment, cease being naive. He or she will probably begin to expect certain responses, and this expectation, whether consistent with theory or not, can contaminate the study.

The second approach requires the experimenter to be ignorant not of the hypotheses but only of the subject assignments. Such an experimenter is said to be

blind in that she or he cannot tell whether a given subject is receiving the experimental treatment or the control experience. This technique is typically applied in studies of drug effects, where drug and placebo pills can be prepared to look identical. Unfortunately, many treatment procedures cannot be so packaged. Also, the drug may cause noticeable side effects, which identify the subjects who are the experimental group, thus spoiling the effort to keep the experimenter from knowing the subjects' group assignment.

A third technique applies to experimenter **standardization**. In this approach, all of the experimenter's words and behaviors are strictly limited by a script, which must be followed with all subjects. This approach can also be monitored by an observer. Unfortunately such standardization may not extend to subtle nuances of voice tone and nonverbal expression, which may communicate the experimenter's expectancy as powerfully as words.

Fourth, the experimenter could be removed entirely from the experimental situation. Instructions to the subjects could be communicated by audiotape and mimeographed handouts. This approach is called the **canned experimenter** and is an extension of the standardization method. This procedure is limited to experiments that can be conducted in the highly controlled environment of laboratories. It is crucial that the same canned instructions be used in all conditions. This latter point is made in a study of two kinds of canned therapist, one speaking in a cold voice tone and the other in a warm voice tone. The warm tape condition produced better results than the cold tape using the same script (Morris & Suckerman, 1974). Where none of these four remedies can be used, the threat of experimenter expectation must be considered serious.

Demand Characteristics. Experimenter expectancy focuses on the researcher's behaviors that influence subjects to behave in a way consistent with the experimenter's hypothesis. In contrast, demand characteristics include all signals in the experimental setting that guide human subject behaviors. Demand characteristics can include interpersonal influence by the experimenter acting on his or her expectancy and also experimental cues of a physical nature, such as pills containing the active ingredient in drug studies. Any such cue present in the experimental condition but absent in the control condition is a potential rival explanation of the outcome.

Demand characteristics guide subjects by providing hints about what the study is about and what the experimenter expects to find. Two assumptions underpin the demand characteristics mechanism. First, the subjects must be curious about their experiment and must attempt to figure out what is wanted of them. Second, having guessed the study's purpose, the subjects must be motivated to change their behavior to accord with (or under some circumstances diverge from) the research hypothesis.

Demand characteristics may tend to cause the subjects to behave differently than expected by theory. For example, Turner and Simons (1974) predicted that the presence of weapons would increase the number of shocks given by subjects to a provoking partner. Interestingly, the more the subjects knew about the study (that is, awareness that the study was about their reactions to the weapons), the fewer shocks they gave. This example emphasizes how independent subjects can be in using demand characteristics to form conclusions about how to act.

There have been frequent reports of subjects' curiosity about and motivation to respond to cues in experimental conditions. Perhaps the most famous is the research that gave social science the term **Hawthorne effect**. This effect was named for the Hawthorne plant of the Western Electric Company in Chicago, which was the site of an extensive study, conducted from 1924 to 1933, of the effects of physical and social conditions on productivity (Roethlisberger & Dickson, 1939). The Hawthorne study was a collection of several quasi-experiments using different sets of workers in different settings on different tasks and different experimental interventions. This study is best remembered outside of industrial psychology for the incidental observation of what was believed to be the research artifact called the Hawthorne effect.

The Hawthorne effect is best regarded as a myth, which has been neither well defined nor well demonstrated empirically. In one specific form, it holds that the workers increased productivity because of the attention they received from the researchers. According to this view, the workers were observed to increase their output in the illumination experiment (one of the several Hawthorne experiments) after each manipulation, whether the lighting was increased or decreased. The implication was that the workers were not responding to the presumed experimental variable (that is, the lighting) but were showing the energizing effects of being observed by high-status strangers.

Close analyses of the Hawthorne data in recent decades have cast doubt on the Hawthorne effect. For example, productivity did not increase, regardless of the nature of the manipulation of experimental variables and regardless of other external events. Careful statistical analyses of the data have attributed variation in outcomes over time to such causes as personnel changes and external events like the Great Depression (Franke & Kaul, 1978), although these findings have been challenged (Bloombaum, 1983). Moreover subsequent studies have attempted unsuccessfully to replicate the Hawthorne effect (see Cook & Campbell, 1979, p. 66).

The Hawthorne effect may have endured because it is intuitively appealing. The Hawthorne investigator, Roethlisberger, observed that, unlike inanimate objects, human subjects are likely to notice that they are being studied and to form feelings and attitudes about being studied, which may in turn influence the outcome of the research. What is crucial is how the subject interprets the experience.

For example, in placebo studies, the essential factor is the belief that the chemical will make one feel better or feel worse. This point was made empirically by Johnson and Foley (1969), who compared three groups of students who received the same structured discussion of the same subject matter. The group that was told that it was in an experiment and that the treatment would be helpful (experiment-expectation) did best on the outcome measures. The other group that was told that it was experimental but that there was no basis for predicting whether the procedure would be helpful (experiment-no expectation) did no better than the group kept unaware of being in an experiment (no experiment).

Even if the Hawthorne effect had not alerted us, other kinds of experiment-caused behaviors have been observed that point to demand characteristics. One such observation is that of **evaluation apprehension,** which refers to the anxiety generated by being tested (Rosenberg, 1969). As one would expect, subjects experiencing evaluation apprehension are motivated to try to look good, intelligent, normal, or well. Under some circumstances, research produces suspiciousness in subjects (McGuire, 1969). The well-known fact that some studies have been conducted with deception or have involved unpleasant stimuli such as mild electric shock motivates subjects to avoid being "fooled" or hurt. Such subjects are likely to be on their guard in experimental settings and resistant to such procedures. Both evaluation apprehension and suspiciousness originate in the subjects (as opposed to experimenter expectancy) and serve to motivate them to react to the cues provided in the experimental setting.

In some cases the subject may believe that he or she can look best by behaving in a way that supports the researcher's theory (as guessed from demand characteristics). In this case, evaluation apprehension should bias the results in favor of the theory. On other occasions, looking good (for example, not being overly aggressive or vengeful) may conflict with the experimenter's hypothesis (that weapons will promote more shocks, as in the Turner and Simons, 1974, study). The research indicates that subjects given cues about a study would rather look good (evaluation apprehension) than meet the researcher's expectations if the theory requires looking bad (Silverman, 1977).

Despite these negative motivations of apprehension and suspiciousness, experimenters continue to recruit volunteers prepared to serve the cause of science. Such volunteer subjects are likely to respect science and trust in the wisdom and authority of scientists (Rosenthal & Rosnow, 1969). Such attitudes are likely to lead to the subject's compliance not only with actual experimental procedures but also with demand characteristics (Orne, 1969).

Preventing Demand Characteristic Effects.   Perhaps the best defense against demand characteristics is the one illustrated by the placebo study at the beginning of the chapter—the use of a placebo control group. The crucial difference between a nontreatment control and a placebo control is that the latter group receives something that looks like a treatment. For example, if the experimental manipulation is an argument for an attitude change presented in written form, the placebo control subjects could be given some equally interesting and equally long reading material on another topic. One effect of such an "attention placebo" is to prevent the controls from perceiving that they are controls. In a sense, the subjects are kept "blind" to which condition they are in, even though they all know they are in an experiment. When both the subject and the experimenter are blind to the condition to which the subjects are assigned, the study is said to be *double blind,* and both experimenter expectancy and demand characteristic threats are minimized.

A second approach is to keep the subjects from knowing that they are in a study at all, which is possible only if the subjects are studied in a naturalistic context.

If the subjects do not know that they are subjects, they will not experience evaluation apprehension, suspiciousness, or a desire for compliance with any experimental demand characteristics. For ethical reasons, this type of research design is limited to the observation of responses to mild interventions (for example, noting whether passers-by will return an intentionally dropped letter or wallet).

In a third approach, instead of keeping subjects from knowing that they are in an experiment, they are kept from knowing when and how they will be observed by using unobtrusive measures. This approach is useful when the outcome of a study is a voluntary behavior. If the subject produces this behavior only to conform to the demand characteristics of the study, she or he is less likely to produce it "off stage." An example comes from the experimental study of hypnosis, a phenomenon that is notoriously hard to pin down. Both hypnotists and subjects can have difficulty being sure when the hypnotic state has been accomplished. In a study by Orne, Sheehan, and Evans (1968), each subject was hypnotized and given the posthypnotic suggestion to touch his or her forehead upon hearing the word *experiment*. Unknown to the hypnotist, one group of subjects was selected to be easy to hypnotize and another was selected to be hard to hypnotize. This latter group was asked to act hypnotized and to try to fool the hypnotist into thinking that he had succeeded (in effect, the demand characteristics to "go along" with the hypnotist were made overt). Unknown to the subjects, the hypnotist's receptionist was an unobtrusive observer. She said the word *experiment* casually three times over two occasions and counted the number of correct posthypnotic responses. As expected, only the good hypnotic subjects consistently touched their foreheads when the receptionist said *experiment*, although subjects from both groups touched their foreheads when the hypnotist said *experiment*.

In a fourth approach, the experimenter can try to deceive the subjects about the nature of the study. The subjects can be expected to try to understand what the study is about, but telling them what the study's hypothesis really is might bias their behavior. Thus some researchers try to distract the subjects from figuring out the purpose of the study by giving them a false **cover story**. An example comes from the placebo study (at the beginning of this chapter) when subjects were told that the study was about consumer preferences in orange juice. A major drawback of deception studies is their violation of the subject's right to informed consent. Another potential drawback is that the deception may fail. To check the effectiveness of the deception, such studies often end with a questionnaire or debriefing interview about the subject's beliefs about the study.

The fifth option enlists the aid of the subjects and is called the **faithful subject** method. Subjects are told that telling them the real hypothesis would destroy the value of the study. They are then asked, for the good of the study, to comply with the experimental procedures and to suspend or avoid any hunches they may have about the study's purposes. Unfortunately, we cannot be sure that such subjects will permit themselves to look abnormal, unhealthy, or incompetent (should that be the outcome of the experimental manipulation) for the sake of science. Thus this approach may work best when evaluation apprehension is minimal.

Control Group Contamination

Control group contamination consists of unplanned or extraneous experiences in the control group that spoil the experimental contrast. If contaminated, the control group's experience represents something other than the absence of the studied intervention. An observed difference between the groups may not be due to the intervention. Similarly, if the experimental and control groups do not differ on the posttest, it cannot be concluded that the experimental intervention had no impact. The intervention's impact may not have been measured clearly.

Control group contamination can lead either to overestimation or underestimation of the impact of the experimental intervention. Contamination that leads to underestimation will be referred to as **compensatory contamination**. Contamination that leads to overestimation will be referred to as **exaggerating contamination**.

Compensatory Contamination. In the typical experimental versus control group design, the experimental subjects receive the treatment and the control subjects do not. The planned withholding of a treatment from a control group does not guarantee that the group receives no treatment. There are several ways in which "no-treatment" control groups can obtain the experimental treatment.

Control subjects will be motivated to acquire the withheld treatment when it is perceived as desirable or needed, as is often the case in experimentation on medical treatments. In mental health delivery research, this problem is termed **spontaneous remission**. Suppose a pool of subjects consists of 100 consecutive clients seeking help for depression at a mental health center. One experimental approach is to randomly assign half of these clients to the experimental treatment and half to the control condition. For ethical reasons, this procedure is usually feasible only when the number of clients exceeds the supply of service. The experimental group would receive the new treatment for depression at once, and the control group would be placed on the waiting list to receive treatment when counselors become available at the end of the experiment. Typically such studies find that the waiting list clients show substantial improvement at the end of the experiment but before they have received the intervention. Research on spontaneous remission suggests that this remission may not be spontaneous at all but rather due to treatment received outside of the experiment (Bergin & Lambert, 1978).

People in anguish are not likely to sit idly by for months while they wait their turn on the waiting list. More likely, such highly motivated help-seekers will find assistance from either professional mental health service providers or friends and family. Typically, neither the amount nor the quality of this therapeutic intervention is known to the experimenter. As a result, the experiment is compromised to the extent that a group receiving known treatment is contrasted with a group receiving unknown treatment.

If the control subjects are aware that they are being denied treatment while others are receiving a desirable experimental intervention, they may well take a competitive or vengeful interest in compensating for the denial of treatment. Even if there is no intrinsic motivation to acquire treatment, intergroup rivalry may provide the control group with the incentive to match the performance of the experimental subjects. This rivalry is particularly likely when naturally competitive production units are assigned to different experimental conditions.

Another form of individual subject contamination occurs through diffusion. If the treatment is easily transferable (for example, by information), experimentals and controls who know each other are likely to contaminate the study by exchanging their experiences.

Compensatory contamination can be brought about not only by the control subjects but also by the managers of the study. When the withheld experimental intervention is a publicly provided good or service, political pressure can be brought to terminate the experiment. The control subjects and their allies can argue on equity grounds that a perceived benefit (for example, an innovative educational program) should be offered to all. Program managers or sponsors have been known to bow to such pressures and to sacrifice the experimental distinction between groups. The anticipation of such pressures often accounts for the resistance of program managers to random assignment of subjects. The effect of this managerial compensation is usually less misleading than the effect of individual subject compensation of an unknown nature. When it is apparent that the planned difference between treatment and control subjects has failed, the study can be ignored or interpreted with appropriate caution.

Preventing Compensatory Contamination. There are several options available for minimizing compensatory contamination. Perhaps the first concern in the evaluation of a public program delivering goods and services is to determine the feasibility of denying the intervention to the control group. To avoid the eventual collapse of the study, the experimenter needs to establish the commitment of the project manager to the design in anticipation of the likely pressures to extend the treatment to the control subjects.

If control subjects can be expected to contaminate the study by replacing the denied treatment with one found outside of the study, different strategies are possible. First, the control group can be offered an alternative treatment such as a placebo. To be effective, the placebo must satisfy the subjects' desire to get some kind of help for their problem. It may serve the additional purpose of keeping the subjects blind to their condition. This alternative obviously risks ethical problems for informed consent and subjects' welfare.

Another alternative for preventing contamination is to collect measures of the help sought and received outside of the experiment. Such data could usefully be obtained from experimental subjects as well and would help in assessing and statistically adjusting for the degree of compensatory contamination.

If the intervention is easily transferable and therefore at risk for diffusion, it may be necessary to use subjects who are unknown to each other or who can be kept apart from each other during the experiment. If none of these remedies is feasible, alternate designs may have to be considered, such as within-subject time-series designs rather than between-group designs.

Exaggerating Contamination. Exaggerating contamination makes the control group's experience even more different from the treated group's experience than it was designed to be. Whereas compensatory contamination can disguise genuine experimental effects, exaggerating contamination can produce spurious effects or effects that look stronger than they actually are. A treatment may be made to look effective not because of the changes in the experimental group but because of changes in the control group. If, for example, the control condition is perceived as less desirable than the experimental condition, the control subjects may feel a "resentful demoralization" (Cook & Campbell, 1979, p. 55). Instead of overachieving to show up the experimental group, the demoralized control subjects apathetically surrender and perform less well than they otherwise would. Whether subjects will react to a situation in a spirited or an apathetic way would seem to depend on the particular subjects and the circumstances of the study.

Much the same kind of preventive arrangements can be made for this threat as for compensatory contamination. Subjects who do not know whether they are in the control or experimental condition (because of the use of placebo control or other blind techniques) are not likely to feel underprivileged. If such blind arrangements are impossible, it will be important to monitor the reactions of the control subjects—both their feelings and their actions. If preliminary research indicates that the subjects will react either competitively or apathetically, it may be useful to take them into the confidence of the experimenter to point out the rationale of the design. If the subjects understand that they were assigned by a random procedure, perhaps one that they participated in, they may take their assignment less personally. If feasible, the control subjects can be assured that if the treatment is found effective, it will be made available to them in due course.

The problem of control group contamination can be summarized diagrammatically. The control group subjects might manage to get access to the X_d treatment intended just for the experimental subjects. This case is diagrammed in Figure 10–5(a). The experimental treatment X_d (indicated in parentheses) is unintentionally present in the control group, which reduces the difference between the two groups. If the contamination leads the control subjects to behave in ways opposite to those produced in the experimental group, the apparent effect of the intervention will be exaggerated.

(a) Compensatory contamination of the control group

$$R \begin{cases} O & X_d & O \\ O & (X_d) & O \end{cases}$$

(b) Exaggerating contamination of the control group

$$R \begin{cases} O & X_d & O \\ O & (-X_d) & O \end{cases}$$

Figure 10–5

The presence of an exaggerating contaminant (indicated by $-X_d$ in parentheses) in the control group is diagrammed in Figure 10–5(b).

Experimental Group Failure

When the Manipulation Fails.   Until now, the discussion of experimental construct validity has concentrated on the threat of contamination. Another threat is the failure of the manipulation adequately to reflect the intended causal construct. Suppose a researcher predicts that decreased anxiety will produce better test scores in a statistics class. Relaxation training intended to reduce anxiety is given to the experimental group. On the final exam, the researcher is surprised to learn that the experimental group did no better than the control group. The theory that anxiety disrupts test taking may be wrong, or the relaxation treatment may have failed to reduce student anxiety. In the latter case, the theory was not tested.

Checking the Manipulation.   To assure that the manipulation has good experimental construct validity, researchers follow two procedures: pilot testing and manipulation checks. **Pilot testing** means to try the experimental treatment out on small samples before the actual experiment. If it does not seem to work correctly, it can be modified and retested until it is judged ready.

Since pilot testing and actual experimental conditions may differ, there is no guarantee that a manipulation will function the same way in both. To make sure that the treatment operated as desired in the actual study, researchers often include **manipulation checks** in the measures or **debriefing** after the intervention. In our relaxation-test performance example, the researcher might include a measure of anxiety to make sure that the treatment really worked or might interview each of the subjects after the study to hear how they perceived the intervention. Such manipulation checks are also useful in identifying the kinds of subjects on which the treatment has greater impact.

EXTERNAL VALIDITY

Generalizability and Interactions

Generalizability.   **External validity** can be defined as the extent to which research findings generalize to other populations, other times, and other settings. Whereas internal validity pertains to the truthfulness of the causal inference within a particular study, external validity pertains to the truthfulness of the causal inference in another situation or population. Thus a true experimental design could have high internal validity, but its results may apply only to the subjects, setting, and particular events of the study and thus have low external validity.

Interactions.   One way of understanding external validity is by understanding the idea of an **interaction**. Two independent variables interact if the effect (on a third or dependent variable) of one depends on the level of the other.

Recall the discussion of pretest reactivity earlier in this chapter. It was argued that in a group that experienced both a pretest and an experimental intervention, either or both could influence the outcome. The Solomon Four-Group design in Figure 10–3(c) was described as a technique for separating the pretest effect from the intervention effect. The pure pretest or reactivity effect could be measured by comparing the posttests of the two groups without the experimental intervention, one of which had a pretest and one of which did not; see groups 2 and 4 in Figure 10–3(c). The pure intervention effect could similarly be measured by contrasting the posttests of the two groups without pretests, one of which had the intervention and one of which did not (groups 3 and 4). In each case, we would be measuring the isolated or *main* effect of just one independent variable, either the pretest or the intervention.

It is possible that the only effects are main effects and that the effect of the intervention is the same regardless of whether there is a pretest. If so, the posttest difference between the experimental and control groups without a pretest (group 3—group 4) should be the same as the difference with pretests (group 1—group 2). However, these two differences can turn out to be unequal. The effect of the intervention (X) can be larger or smaller depending on whether there is a pretest. In such a case, we would say that the intervention and the pretest interact or that there is an intervention-by-pretest interaction.

When might such an interaction take place? Suppose you are evaluating a pilot test of a solar energy campaign with a power company's customers. Each is asked at pretest to assess his or her electrical and gas consumption in light of increasing energy costs. The researchers then randomly identify some of these subjects as experimentals, who are offered an incentive to retrofit their homes to utilize solar energy. The control subjects, of course, are at liberty to retrofit their homes at their own expense as well, but they are offered no incentive. At posttest, you will find out from county archives how many experimental and control subjects acquired building permits for solar retrofitting. If you observed that many more experimental than control subjects solarized their houses, you might conclude that the offer of a subsidy was effective.

Now suppose that, based on your report, the power company expands its offer of a financial incentive for solar retrofitting through a mass mailing to all customers. To your embarrassment, the rate of solar retrofitting in this second round of incentive offers might be much lower than you reported in the first round. What was the difference? The difference was that your pilot evaluation included a pretest that forced the subjects to think seriously about their fuel costs. This pretest had the effect of sensitizing the subjects to the need for solar retrofitting. The offer of a financial incentive was more likely to be accepted after the motivational experience of the pretest than if there had been no pretest (as in the second round). Thus the intervention (the incentive offer) interacted with (was more effective in the presence of) the pretest.

What has the concept of interaction got to do with external validity? In the example just described, the original research results had low external validity because of the presence of the interaction. The apparent incentive effect, thought of as an independent or main effect, did not generalize. The incentive effect on solar retrofitting did not work in just any situation; it seemed to hold only for the situations in which subjects were primed and motivated by something like the pretest.

External validity threats always include an interaction of the intervention or treatment with some other factor. Threats to external validity can be sorted into three main categories depending on the factor interacting with the treatment: setting, population, and history. In each case, the researcher's problem is to judge whether a finding is true only for the specific setting, sample of subjects, or period of time or is generally applicable.

Setting-by-Intervention Interactions

The **setting** can be narrowly understood as the experimental arrangements in the study or more broadly interpreted as the physical and social context. Both senses of the term apply to the threat of interactions with the treatment.

Experimental Setting.[1]   The experimental setting includes all experiences of the subjects due to the experiment, whether planned or unplanned. The pretest-by-treatment interaction illustrated in the solar campaign example is one such example.

Another such experience is that of the experimental manipulation. Of course, if there is only one manipulation, it makes no sense to consider one treatment interacting with itself. Sometimes, however, what is intended as a single intervention can be conceptualized as more than one treatment. For example, the delivery of an experimental drug includes both the active ingredient of the drug and the method of drug delivery such as a pill or a hypodermic. As shown by the placebo research example at the beginning of this chapter, the chemical ingredients and the pill casing can have opposite effects. In the example, these two effects were independent, but such variables could have interacted. Some research designs intentionally include more than one intervention. That is, the experimental group receives a series of different Xs, and the presence of different treatments raises the possibility of multiple-X interactions.

The control group is crucial in interpreting the effect of such combinations of interventions. Suppose the treatment or experimental group is given two interventions, X_1 and X_2. If the control group is given neither intervention, the difference between the two groups could be due to the main effect of X_1, the main effect of X_2, and/or the interaction of X_1 with X_2. Suppose the control group was given one of the interventions, X_1, perhaps a placebo control group such as that diagrammed in Figure 10–2(c). Now any difference at posttest between the experimental and control group cannot be due to the main effect of X_1 since both groups are subject to this effect. But the difference between the two groups still has two possible explanations: the main effect of X_2 and the interaction of X_1 with X_2. Which of these explanations is correct can only be determined by designing the experiment to include all the different combinations of Xs. To further complicate this picture, one may even have to consider the order in which the different Xs are experienced. It is possible that drugs X_1 and X_2 interact when X_1 is ingested first but not when X_2 is ingested first. Controlling for and measuring the differential effects of different orders of multiple Xs is treated under the heading of within-subject designs in the next chapter on quasi- experimentation.

Context. Just as an intervention may interact with another aspect of the experiment, so may an intervention interact with its environment. Any study must take place in some context, whether a university-based laboratory or a field location such as a street corner, factory, grade school, or home. Subjects will necessarily look at and react to the experimental intervention in terms of its surround. For example, a study that tape records family communication patterns in response to different manipulations by the experimenter may get different results if the recording is done in the family's home than if it is done in a university laboratory. The experimenter runs the risk that the research results will apply only to the chosen setting and not elsewhere.

A major challenge to highly controlled laboratory research is that its external validity is weakened by the artificiality of its context (all the cues that remind the subject that he or she is in a research rather than a natural situation). Insofar as laboratory circumstances are unrepresentative of the everyday or "real" world, lab-based results may not generalize to the real world. For this reason, it has been proposed that social research be conducted with more **ecological validity**. A study with high ecological validity is one conducted in a research situation representative of the natural social environment.

A closely related concept is **mundane realism**. This term refers to the resemblance of the research setting to a natural setting. The underlying assumption is that research conducted under conditions of mundane realism will promote ecological or external validity. In rebuttal, it can be argued that ecological validity may be gained at the cost of precision in identifying subtle causal mechanics. Moreover, it has been argued, the experimenter's goal ought not to be superficial mundane realism but rather **experimental realism,** that is, the arrangement of procedures in such a way that the subjects are fully engaged in the experience. Whether such engagement requires physical similarity to natural situations (that is, mundane realism) is an empirical question that cannot be taken for granted (Berkowitz & Donnerstein, 1982).

Identifying Setting-by-Intervention Interactions. The danger posed by external validity threats is that results from one study can be applied incorrectly to other cases. The general solution for preventing such wrong generalizations is to identify those settings, populations, and eras to which the findings apply and those to which the findings do not apply. In principle, this step requires replication of the research in all combinations of populations, places, and times although so many replications are not feasible in practice.

In the case of interactions of interventions with experimental setting factors, such replications can be fairly easily managed by the inclusion of additional groups or conditions. The Solomon Four-Group design illustrates such a test for the interaction of the intervention with the pretest. Similarly, multiple groups could be included in a study involving multiple interventions to test for their interaction.

The problem of intervention-by-context interactions cannot be solved merely by including additional groups in a single study. For such interactions, it is necessary to replicate the study over examples of different locations in which the theory says the cause-effect relationship should hold. In the absence of such replications, the generalization from a study should be limited to similar contexts.

History- and Selection-by-Intervention Interactions

An intervention can interact with the type of subjects or with the time period in which the study is conducted. Obviously, a study conducted on 18-year-old, middle-class, male college students may not generalize to young children or elderly adults, to young people raised in the culture of poverty, to females, or to nonacademically oriented people. Perhaps less obviously, such a study may be influenced by the way subjects are chosen or self-selected for inclusion in the study. For example, not all male college students are enrolled as social science majors and not all social science majors volunteer to participate in social science research. Perhaps some unmeasured personality characteristic of the self-selected subjects makes it possible for the intervention to have its observed effect, and the result may not hold for differently selected subjects on replication.

Just as a cause-effect relationship may appear in one type of subject but not others, so it may be observed in one time period but not another. If the experiment is conducted when a major public event is occurring, might the experimental results depend in part on these unusual external events? For example, a study of depressed mood might produce different results on the day after a popular public figure is assassinated.

Identifying History and Selection Interactions. Conservatively, a researcher should not generalize beyond his or her particular sample of subjects and period of study. Thus it is desirable to replicate studies in samples from different populations and in different time periods. One way of spotting selection-by-intervention interactions without replication is to include a variety of subjects in a single study. Theory and past research might help identify the dimensions on which to diversify the sample. Each subgroup (for example, young males, young females, old males, old females) represents a built-in replication.

Similarly, long-term longitudinal studies allow replication over occasions or eras. Many true experiments involve interventions that are relatively brief and must necessarily be located at particular times. To represent many different times, the experiment must be replicated in later months or years.

Fortunately, science is a cooperative and cumulative enterprise. Often a researcher has colleagues working on the same or similar problems in other locations, at other times, or with different kinds of subjects. When different studies vary with respect to setting, sample, and time, systematic differences in the literature may emerge and point to improved theory.

SUMMARY

Although true experimental design provides a high degree of internal validity, it is vulnerable to other validity threats. Threats to experimental construct validity and to external validity were discussed. Some of the more common threats and methods for dealing with them are summarized in Table 10–2.

EXERCISES

Unlike the threats to internal validity discussed in the previous chapter, one cannot automatically identify all experimental construct and external validity threats

Table 10–2   Threats to Experimental Construct and External Validity

Type	Threat	Possible Remedies
I. Experimental construct validity threats		
A. Experimental group contamination		
1. Experimenter expectancy	Observed effect is due to self-fulfilling prophecy—experimenter affects subject behavior.	Naive, "blind," standardized or "canned" experimenter, debriefing to check subject awareness of hypothesis.
2. Demand characteristics	Observed effect is due to motivated subjects reacting to their interpretation of cues about the study's meaning.	Placebo control, "blind" subject, naturalistic context, unobtrusive measures, false cover story, "faithful" subject, debriefing to check subject awareness of hypothesis.
B. Control group contamination		
1. Compensatory contamination	Observed absence of effect is due to acquisition of experimental treatment or its equivalent by control group.	"Blind" subjects, administrative adherence to no-treatment control design, "satisfying" placebo control, monitoring control group's behavior outside of experiment, minimum contact between experimentals and controls.
2. Exaggerating contamination	Observed effect is due to harmful awareness of denial of experimental treatment.	"Blind" subjects, explanation of assignment procedures, promise of experimental treatment later, monitoring of reactions of controls for resentful demoralization.

Table 10–2   (Cont.)

Type	Threat	Possible Remedies
II. External validity threats		
A. Setting-by-intervention interactions		
1. Experimental settings	Observed effect of X is due to its combination with some aspect of the experimental arrangements.	Identify by inclusion of multiple groups to test for interaction (e.g., with pretest, other X).
2. Context	Observed effect of X is due to its combination with some aspect of the social or physical environment.	Identify by replication in different types of settings. Increase realism of setting.
B. History-by-intervention interaction	Observed effect of X is due to its combination with some recent event or with the particular era.	Identify by replication at different times.
C. Selection-by-intervention interaction	Observed effect of X is due to its combination with some aspect of the particular subject sample.	Identify by replication in samples from different populations or by inclusion of population "blocking" variable, i.e., grouping by age or sex. Use representative subjects.

from a study's design. Using Table 10–2 as a checklist, you should critically review some true experiment for each listed threat to experimental construct validity and external validity. Repeat this review for several true experiments, until you can do it quickly and routinely.

GLOSSARY

Blind: Technique of avoiding experimenter expectancy by concealing the assignment of the subject from the researcher or of avoiding demand characteristic by concealing the assignment of the subject from the subject. When both the subject and the experimenter are blind to the assignment, the study is called "double blind."

Canned experimenter: Ultimate standardization of experimental procedure by use of tape-recorded instructions.

Compensatory contamination: Problem of control subjects acquiring the experimental treatment through rivalry or dif-

fusion; has the effect of reducing the difference between experimental and control conditions.

Contamination: Intrasession events that cause doubt that the experimental and control groups differ only on the variable to be studied.

Cover story: False explanation for the experiment used to distract the subject from guessing the true nature of the study.

Debriefing: Researcher's interview with the subject after the experiment in which the subject's beliefs about the study are checked and the subject is informed about the purpose of the study.

Demand characteristics: Cues in the experimental situation that guide a subject's view of the study.

Ecological validity: Extent to which a research situation is representative of the natural social environment.

Evaluation apprehension: Subject's anxiety generated by being tested.

Exaggerating contamination: Problem of control subjects moving in a direction opposite to that of the experimental subjects (for example, by resentful demoralization); has the effect of increasing the difference between experimental and control conditions.

Experimental construct validity: Extent to which a manipulated independent variable reflects the intended construct.

Experimental realism: Extent to which experimental procedures produce a high level of psychological involvement and, presumably, natural behavior regardless of the degree of mundane realism.

Experimenter expectancy: Mechanism(s) by which the researcher biases the behavior of the subject to get the hypothesized results; also called self-fulfilling prophesy and Pygmalion effect.

External validity: Generalizability of the study's finding to other populations, places, or times.

Faithful subject: Method for avoiding deception by asking subjects to comply with the experimental procedure and to suspend their suspicions.

Hawthorne effect: Type of demand characteristic in which the researcher's attention was supposed to increase the subject's effort; not supported by recent research.

Interaction: Two independent variables interacting in their effect on a dependent variable if the effect of one depends on the value of the other.

Intrasession history: Events internal to the research procedure as distinct from events impinging on the subjects from outside of the research situation.

Manipulation checks: Measures used to assess the effectiveness of the manipulation.

Mundane realism: In attempting to achieve high ecological validity, the extent to which a research setting resembles in physical detail a real social setting.

Naive experimenter: Method of avoiding experimenter expectancy by concealing the hypothesis from the researcher handling the subjects.

Pilot testing: Small-scale research with the experimental manipulation to determine its effectiveness before using it in the main study.

Placebo: Intervention that simulates an authentic treatment but with no active ingredient.

Setting: Experimental arrangements of the study or more broadly, the larger social context in which the study takes place.

Spontaneous remission: The apparent natural improvement of control subjects that may be due in part to compensatory contamination, that is, their acquisition of unreported therapy.

Standardization: In experimentation, the reduction of human experimenter variability in treatment of subjects by use of a fixed script.

NOTE

1. Interactions of the experimental variable X with other experimental setting factors such as the pretest or other Xs (experimental manipulations) are treated here as threats to external validity in order to keep all of the X-by-other factor interactions together under one rubric. This assignment is arbitrary, and such interactions could also be considered as threats to experimental construct validity (as done by Cook & Campbell, 1979).

11

Quasi-Experimentation

When Multiple Groups and Random Assignment Are Not Possible

INTRODUCTION TO QUASI-EXPERIMENTAL DESIGNS

An Example of Quasi-experimentation

Head Start. The Head Start program was launched full scale with an enrollment of a half million children in the summer of 1965. By 1967, Head Start was called "the country's biggest peacetime mobilization of human resources and effort" (Brazziel, quoted in Payne, Mercer, Payne, & Davison, 1973, p. 55). This program was designed to increase the learning readiness of underprivileged children entering the earliest school grades and was widely regarded as the centerpiece of the war on poverty in the 1960s.

In the mid-1960s, the Bureau of the Budget established the Planning, Programming, and Budgeting System (PPBS) to ensure the critical and quantitative analysis of all federal programs (Williams & Evans, 1972, p. 252). To provide a timely, independent analysis of Head Start, a contract was given in 1968 to Westinghouse Corporation and Ohio University, which resulted in the most influential evaluation of Head Start. This evaluation was conducted by Cicirelli and colleagues (Westinghouse Learning Corporation and Ohio University, 1969) and will be referred to as the Westinghouse Study. Preliminary results of the Westinghouse Study were alluded to by President Nixon in his Economic Opportunity Message to Congress in early 1969, when he drew the conclusion that "the long-term effect of Head Start appears to be extremely weak" (quoted by Williams & Evans, 1972, p. 255). Since President Nixon's allusion to the Westinghouse Study, this evaluation of Head Start has been debated in both the political and social science arenas (see, for example, Campbell & Erlebacher, 1970, versus Cicirelli, 1970; Magidson, 1977, versus Bentler & Woodward, 1978; Smith & Bissell, 1970, versus Cicirelli, Evans, & Schiller, 1970).

How did a social science study stimulate such a heated and enduring discussion? Part of the answer is that the program is so politically and economically important. Another part lies in the nature of quasi-experimental research design. Because of the urgency to provide an evaluation, an after-the-fact or **ex post facto design** was used. There was no time for children to be randomly assigned to Head Start and to non-Head Start conditions and followed for several years. Instead, the researchers had to gather test data on children who had experienced Head Start several years previously. This design, despite its being professionally and conscientiously applied, permits counterexplanations that have cast doubts on the conclusions of the study.

Suppose you were in the position of evaluating Head Start soon after its beginning. You have access to thousands of current first-, second-, and third-graders who experienced Head Start sessions when they were four years old. Your task is to determine how much, if anything, has been gained by these early Head Start students. You can administer tests to these treated children and to their untreated counterparts. The crucial issue is that of comparison. You expect all children, whether in Head Start or not, to show some gains over time by maturation. That is, normal development should produce some cognitive gains in all children. Your problem is to determine how much *more* the Head Start children gained than they would have gained without Head Start.

The commonsense solution to this problem is to use as controls the children who did not receive Head Start. One could simply compare the posttreatment test scores of the Head Start and non-Head Start groups of children. This simple solution would certainly be wrong for Head Start and for most other compensatory interventions (that is, programs aimed at compensating or making up the deficit of one group relative to another group). The Head Start children are, by definition, disadvantaged when compared to the untreated children. Head Start children started out at a lower level than their controls and would have to gain much more than the controls to reach parity on posttest.

How about using gain scores? Instead of comparing the posttest scores, you might compare the gains from pretest to posttest of the Head Start and control groups. In effect, you would compare the Head Start gains with the gains due only to natural maturation without Head Start. Although this approach is commonly used, it requires the assumption that the normal maturation rates of the Head Start and control children are the same in the studied period. But this assumption is almost certainly not true in this case. Given that the Head Start and control children are different at pretest, they must have been gaining at different rates prior to pretest and can be expected to continue these different maturation rates. Thus the natural gains of the non-Head Start control children would be greater than the natural gains of the Head Start children (see Figure 11–1).

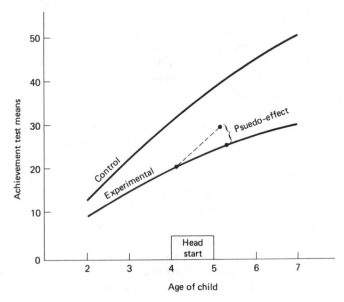

Figure 11–1 Pseudoeffect due to assuming equal growth rates. (Reprinted with permission from J. Hellmuth, ed., *Disadvantaged Child, Vol. 3: Compensatory Education: A National Debate* New York: Brunner/ Mazel, 1970), p. 198.

If there is an effect of Head Start, it should appear as a gain over and above that expected for children who are similar to Head Start children except that they did not receive the Head Start experience. Unfortunately, we do not know what the natural maturation gain is for this subgroup of disadvantaged children. If we use the control children's gains as an estimate of the expected gains for disadvantaged children who did not receive Head Start, we will expect too much. If Head Start has no effect whatsoever, and the Head Start children make normal gains because of maturation, their achievement will be less than that expected from the maturation rate of the control children. The difference is labeled the **pseudoeffect** of Head Start in Figure 11–1. That is, the *apparent* effect of Head Start in this case is to make treated children *worse* off than if they had not been treated in Head Start at all. It is a pseudoeffect rather than a real effect because it is due to our mistake in using the maturation rate of the controls to estimate the untreated maturation of the Head Start children. If Head Start genuinely had a beneficial effect on children, we would not notice or credit it unless it was large enough to make up for the pseudoeffect that makes Head Start look bad. Whether Head Start is judged to have a negative or positive effect depends on the assumption made about the natural maturation of disadvantaged children.

A Statistical Adjustment. The original evaluation of Head Start by Cicirelli and colleagues avoided both of these methods (comparing posttest scores or comparing change scores). The Westinghouse Study used a statistical adjustment technique that was intended to solve the problems raised by the nonequivalence of the Head Start and non-Head Start groups. After matching on age, sex, race, and kindergarten attendance, they used a method called **analysis of covariance**, which uses pretest information to adjust the posttest scores for parent's occupation, education, and per capita income. The idea was to equate the two groups as much as possible by matching and by statistical adjustment since the groups had not originally been equated by randomization.

Unfortunately, this technique may not have adjusted sufficiently for social class (parent's occupation, education, and income), as illustrated in a simulation by Campbell and Erlebacher (1970). The reason has to do with one of the threats to internal validity that is most troubling in quasi-experimentation—**regression to the mean**. As discussed later, regression to the mean is the tendency of extreme scores on imperfectly reliable measures to move toward the mean on subsequent tests. Campbell and Erlebacher argue that Head Start children were selected from an entirely different population from that of the control group children. The regression in their test scores will thus be toward a different mean than that to which the control group children's scores will regress. The analysis of covariance technique used in the Westinghouse Study did not take into account the unreliability of the measures. Recent research using the newest techniques for handling unreliable measures has disagreed on whether Head Start's effect was significant (Bentler & Woodward, 1978; Magidson, 1977).

The debates about the proper statistical procedure for adjusting for non-equivalence and the value of Head Start are both beyond the scope of this presentation (see McKey, Condelli, Ganson, Barrett, McConkey, & Plantz, 1985, for a review of hundreds of Head Start studies). The point is that the failure to assign subjects randomly to experimental and control conditions makes the interpretation of such evaluations more difficult and can invite lengthy arguments about the results. The goal of this chapter is to explore the major threats to the internal validity of the most commonly seen quasi-experimental designs.

Quasi-experiments and True Experiments

Random Assignment to Groups. Quasi-experiments differ from true experiments by the omission of random assignment of subjects to different conditions. Quasi-experiments have in common with true experiments that some intervention occurs to subjects who are then measured at a time likely to reflect any impact of the intervention.

Quasi-experiments appear similar to their true experimental counterparts when diagrammed. For example, in Figure 11–2(a) the diagram of a true experiment indicates that two groups were composed by random assignment of subjects (R), that each group had measurements or tests at two times (O), and that the groups differed by the intervention (X).

The quasi-experimental counterpart appears in Figure 11–2(b). Again two groups, each with pre- and postobservations, apparently differ only in their experience of the intervention or change. The crucial difference between these two designs is random assignment, which helps assure the equivalence of the groups in the true experiment.

If random assignment is so simple and so important, why are not all such studies converted into true experiments by random assignment? There are two general reasons. The first is feasibility. The evaluation of Head Start illustrates this problem. Because the evaluation of Head Start was considered urgent, its evaluators could not wait several years to retest the students. The researchers were forced to use an ex post facto design to compare groups created after the treatment.

There are reasons besides haste that sometimes make true experimental designs difficult or impossible. Some variables cannot be manipulated by investigators (for example, earthquakes, economic cycles, and passage of legislation). As a result, individuals cannot be randomly assigned in advance. Even when the

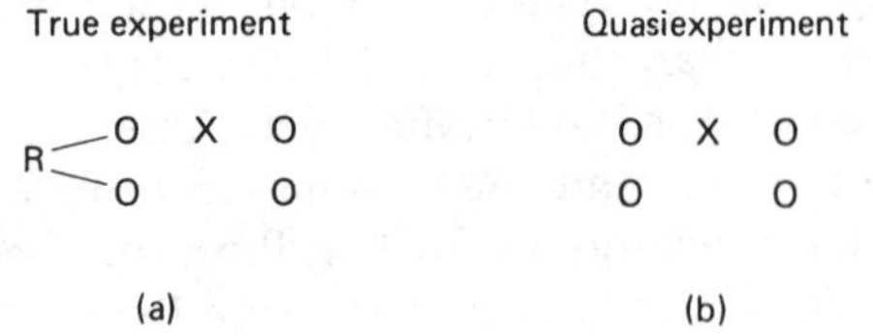

```
        True experiment              Quasiexperiment

       ___O   X   O                    O   X   O
     R
       ‾‾‾O       O                    O       O

            (a)                            (b)
```

Figure 11–2   Absence of random assignment in quasi-experiment.

intervention can be manipulated in principle, it sometimes is not feasible politically. For example, court-ordered school desegregation could, in principle, have been staged so that half of the school districts were randomly desegregated in the first year for comparison with the remaining half, which could be desegregated later. As you can imagine, such a proposal would be stymied by the conflict between the forces opposed to each other on this emotional issue. In summary, there are numerous variables of interest to social scientists that for technical, economic, or political reasons are not subject to true experimentation.

A second general reason preventing true experimentation is ethical prohibition of certain studies. For example, it may be important to know the aftereffects of trauma—either psychological (such as terror) or biological (such as starvation). Because it is unethical to inflict terror or life-threatening starvation on human beings, the study of these phenomena can proceed only with individuals not randomly chosen (for example, concentration camp survivors or disaster victims). Not only is it unethical to inflict harm on subjects, it is also unethical knowingly to allow the continuation of harm. Thus it would be unethical to deny a treatment known to be helpful to someone who has a disease in order to study the course of the disease.

Advantages and Disadvantages. This discussion suggests that true experiments are sometimes disadvantageous compared to quasi-experiments. In such circumstances, true experiments could proceed, if at all, only by selecting stand-in variables that could be studied in a more controlled way (as in simulation studies). For example, we cannot ethically assign humans randomly to conditions of prisoners or guards in real penitentiaries. However, it may be possible to simulate or role-play some of the conditions of a prison for a short time with volunteers. To the extent that simulations of dangerous conditions successfully produce the experience of harm or the threat of harm, they must, for ethical reasons, be avoided or terminated. Zimbardo, Haney, Banks, and Jaffe (1975) reported that they had to terminate such a mock prison study after one week instead of the planned two weeks because the experience was becoming dangerously real. To the extent that such simulations are harmless, they may not capture the phenomena of interest. Thus quasi-experiments may have the advantage of experimental construct validity in providing information about real situations.

On the other hand, there is no guarantee that quasi-experiments will be more advantageous than true experiments. Both are vulnerable to some of the same threats. If the dependent measure used is unreliable or is an invalid representation of the construct of interest, neither design will provide meaningful results. If the independent variable is manipulated in a transparent or intrusive way so that the subjects become self-conscious, both types of study will be suspect. Changes resulting from such a study may be attributable to the reaction of the subjects to some aspect of the experimenter's behavior other than the intended independent variable. Another threat common to true experimental and quasi-experimental designs is the possibility that observed differences between the experimental and control subjects are due to chance rather than dependable differences, a threat checked by inferential statistics.

Although quasi-experiments have some advantages over and share some of the same potential problems with true experiments, they are subject to a set of threats to internal validity from which true experiments are generally immune. These threats can be organized into two clusters called time and group.

Time threats include history, maturation, instrumentation, and pretest reactivity. In these threats something changes over time in the experience or behavior of the subjects or in the measuring process. Because the comparison group feature of true experiments protects against these threats, they primarily concern single-group quasi-experiments such as interrupted time series. Each of the time threats will be discussed in a later section, and an example of an interrupted time series study will be reviewed.

The group threats to internal validity include selection, regression to the mean, and interactions of selection with time threats such as maturation. These threats are of concern for designs in which two or more groups are composed in ways that fail to ensure their equivalence (whenever random assignment is omitted from the design). Such designs are called nonequivalent control group designs. In the following section, each of these threats will be discussed briefly, and an example of the nonequivalent control group design will be presented.

TYPES OF QUASI-EXPERIMENTS

Nonequivalent Control Group Designs

Threats. In true experiments, the equivalence of the groups is supposed to be ensured by random assignment. Unfortunately, random assignment cannot guarantee equivalence. An example of this failure comes from a study of college students as group leaders working with inpatients at a mental hospital (Rappaport, Chinsky, & Cowen, 1971). The plan was to create 40 groups, each with 8 patients. Thirty-two of these groups would be randomly assigned to the experimental (E) condition and would experience group counseling by college student volunteers. The remaining 8 groups would be hypothetical groups in that they would not actually meet but would serve as controls (C). To ensure that the E and C groups would be similar even before random assignment, all groups were made up by matching patients on five variables: age, length of hospitalization, level of education, marital status, and whether diagnosed as paranoid or not. It was expected that this matching would yield 40 groups that were nearly equivalent on the pretest variables of cognitive and behavioral performance (since time did not permit matching on pretest measures of these performance variables).

The random assignment of groups to E and C conditions should have ensured that any remaining group differences on pretest performance levels would have been eliminated. The study was conducted, and data were collected from the patients and the student volunteer counselors. After the data were in, the assumption that the E and C groups were equivalent on pretest performance was routinely checked. The investigators were shocked to discover that on 15 of the 16 pretest performance measures, the C groups were better than the E groups and that 6 of these measures showed statistically significant differences favoring the C groups. In the words of the researchers,

> The failure to have achieved a satisfactory pretest matching of Es and Cs was both perplexing and embarrassing. It was damaging to the basic design of the study and necessitated a series of improvisations, none initially anticipated, and each less than fully satisfactory. Considerable thought and effort was invested in the matching procedure beforehand and the method selected seemed defensible not only at the time, but even in retrospect. Unfortunately the facts of the situation are otherwise. Despite considerable effort, it is difficult even after the fact, to identify sources of systematic error that could account for the pretest differences between Es and Cs. However unsatisfactory or unenlightening it may be to say so, the authors consider it likely that the pretest matching breakdown was essentially a chance phenomenon. Whatever the explanation, it is clear that this breakdown had serious, negative implications for all subsequent data analyses. (Rappaport, Chinsky, & Cowen, 1971, pp. 89-90)

The effect of this chance failure of random assignment to equalize the conditions was to convert a true experiment into a **nonequivalent control group design** for purposes of analysis.

The nonequivalent control group pretest-posttest design is diagrammed in Figure 11-2(b). If the two groups differ at pretest, the meaning of any posttest difference is subject to several alternative group threats or rival explanations. The first such threat to internal validity is that the posttest difference simply reflects original differences. This threat is called **selection**. That is, the subjects were, intentionally or unintentionally, selected to be different, and this difference, rather than the experimental manipulation, may account for later differences.

The second alternative is regression to the mean, which pertains to cases in which the two groups are chosen so that one is higher and one lower on a pretest reflecting the outcome. Any group differences in change scores from pretest to posttest may be due either to the differential treatment or to regression to the mean. For example, suppose a group of students is assessed for test anxiety and the students who were high on test anxiety were selected for a course in relaxation, with the low-anxiety students serving as controls. If the treated students show a greater decrease in anxiety than the control students, this "improvement" may be attributed either to the relaxation course or to regression to the mean. Regression to the mean is an automatic tendency of extreme scores to move toward the population mean on retest. The less reliable the measure, the greater will be this measurement shift.[1] Whenever treatment programs are evaluated by giving the treatment to those most needy (that is, extreme on the dimension that treatment is expected to improve), regression is a serious threat.

Regression can make programs look less effective than they are or make harmless programs look harmful. This case was illustrated by the Head Start study with which this chapter began. Instead of pretesting and sorting one sample into highs and lows, the Westinghouse Study compared children from two different populations (higher income, no Head Start versus lower income, given Head Start). These two samples presumably began with different average levels of learning readiness. On subsequent tests, each group would tend to get scores approaching their respective means. The procedure intended to adjust for their original differences in learning readiness may not have provided sufficient adjustment when applied to imperfectly reliable data. Thus Head Start may have been made to look worse than it was because of failure to control fully for regression to different means.

Finally, original group differences can interact with time-related changes such as maturation, called the **selection-by-time interaction** threat. Suppose a fifth-grade teacher tries a new way of teaching spelling to his or her class. The teacher measures the average number of new words that the class learned (change from beginning of year to end of year). As an afterthought, the teacher decides to compare these results with the results obtained in the fourth-grade class taught by another teacher, who used a different method of spelling instruction. If the fifth-graders learned more words than the fourth-graders, it could be because of the fifth-grade teacher's new spelling approach. However, the rival hypothesis exists that the fifth graders were developmentally more advanced than the fourth-graders and would have learned to spell just as well even without the new technique. Thus the maturational nonequivalence of these two classes is confounded (confused) with the treatment difference and, in this case, works in favor of making the intervention look successful. An opposite situation arose in the case of the Head Start evaluation. The higher-income, non-Head Start control students may have had a higher cognitive development rate because of their home and school experiences. In contrast, the Head Start children may have had a slower cognitive development rate. Head Start would have had to make a significant impact to overcome this maturational rate difference before it could be seen to provide any benefits. In this case, maturational nonequivalence works against the Head Start intervention.

Casa Blanca Nonequivalent Control Group Study. When none of the group threats of selection, regression, and selection-by-time threat interactions are plausible, a nonequivalent control group design can provide convincing results. Singer, Gerard, and Redfearn (1975) employed such a design as one part of a larger analysis of the effect of school desegregation. They tested the hypothesis that educationally disadvantaged minority children will make greater educational progress in an integrated school. Other effects of busing are also suspected, including beneficial effects on the racial attitudes of whites (for example, the "contact hypothesis"; Cook, 1985) and on public opinion toward schools (see, for example, Raffel, 1985), but such additional issues are not considered in this illustrative case study.

In Riverside, California, the school board ordered the desegregation of minority schools beginning in the 1966–1967 school year. An ideal true experimental study would have compared two randomly assigned groups of students—one group to be integrated and the other group to remain for a time in their unintegrated schools—but this design was not feasible. The original plan was to bus 712 minority grade school students out of three segregated schools in the fall of 1966. It so happened that half of the students of one of these schools (Casa Blanca School) could not be desegregated in 1966 but had to wait until the following year. Thus circumstances permitted a natural experiment involving the two phases of busing. This Casa Blanca experiment was not a true experiment because the two groups were not randomly assigned. On the other hand, the two "waves" of Casa Blanca students were reasonably similar in the 1965–1966 period before busing began. The two groups did not differ on IQ tests or grades. The children were similar on pre-desegregation popularity (peer sociometric ratings), socioeconomic background, and education of the heads of their households. However, on standardized achievement tests administered in 1965–1966, the group desegregated in the fall of 1967 did score significantly higher than the group desegregated in the fall of 1966.

To measure the educational performance of the children, state-mandated achievement tests were used. The students' scores were standardized, that is, expressed relative to other students within each grade level. The reading achievement scores are summarized for the two Casa Blanca groups in Table 11–1. The design of this study for the pretest year of 1965–1966 and the two following years is diagrammed in Figure 11–3, with X indicating the beginning of busing from Casa Blanca to an integrated school.

The statistical analysis indicated no significant difference between these two groups with respect to changes in reading ability. In 1966–1967, both the experimental (desegregated in 1966–1967) and the control (not desegregated until 1967) groups showed relative decreases in reading achievement. A delayed effect of desegregation might not reveal itself until later. However, the experimental group did not gain significantly more than the control group in 1967–1968, and neither regained the positions they enjoyed before busing. The authors concluded that "as is clearly evident, there was no apparent short-term effect of desegregation" (Singer, Gerard, & Redfearn, 1975, p. 78).

Table 11–1 Reading Achievement for Two Groups of Mexican-American Students Desegregated from Casa Blanca School[*]

Group	Year Desegregated	1965–66	1966–67	1967–68
Experimental	1966	92.8 (113)	90.3 (77)	91.2 (75)
Control	1967	97.4 (107)	94.6 (105)	95.2 (111)

Numbers in parentheses are the sample sizes on which the mean reading achievement scores are based.

[*] From Table 4.1 (p. 78) of Singer, Gerard, and Redfearn (1975).

	1965–66		1966–67		1967–68
Experimental	0	X	0		0
Control	0		0	X	0

Figure 11–3   Casa Blanca Research Design

Since this study was not a true experiment, might the results be due to some uncontrolled aspect of the design? Time threats were controlled by the presence of the second, or control, group. If effects because of natural development or outside historical events were present in the experimental group, they should also have been present in the control group. A more likely source of rival hypotheses was the cluster of group threats since the groups were not created by random assignment. However, the selection threat is made less plausible by the near equivalence of the groups on the pretests of 1965–1966. The regression threat is also made less plausible since the two groups were not extremely different at pretest and the group with the slightly lower pretest scores (who should have been more likely to regress upward) was the experimental group. Thus, if regression operated, it should have favored the treated group. Finally, the threat of an interaction of selection with, for example, maturation is made less plausible because the two groups were equivalent in age and should not mature at significantly different rates. The only support for threat rests on the assumption that the slight difference in pretest achievement scores between the two groups indicated a lower maturation rate for the experimental subjects. Although this selection-by-maturation interaction alternative cannot be ruled out, it is not very parsimonious or convincing.

Another threat that could occur in this (or in true experimental) research is mortality. There was a significant dropout rate in the experimental group. Attrition is to be expected in this type of study. About one in four southern California families changes residence every year. The threat is that the number or type of dropouts from one group is significantly different from the dropouts from the other group. In fact, there was a tendency for more high-status minority children to move away. The authors concluded that this tendency was probably too small to affect the outcome of the study. Moreover, the statistical analyses were rerun with just the students who were present for all the tests, and no differences were found. Again, one could imagine a very complex interaction involving the combination of the attrition and the pretest differences in achievement in the experimental subjects that could have worked to disguise a genuinely beneficial effect of busing. However, such a complex counterexplanation is farfetched and less persuasive than the simpler explanation of the results—that busing simply had little or no effect in this case.

In conclusion, this particular nonequivalent control group study appears to have escaped threats such as selection and regression. On the other hand, the generalizability of this study is limited. Only Mexican-Americans, in one southern California school system and using one form of busing (one-way busing), were studied. Integration of other minorities, in other school systems, in other parts of the country, and using other methods (for example, two-way busing) might yield different results. Moreover, the sample and design of the study might have influenced the outcome. A review of the literature on desegregation and achievement for blacks has suggested that beneficial effects of busing are more likely to appear under two conditions: (1) for students who begin in desegregated classes as opposed to students with one or two years in segregated classes before being desegregated, and (2) when the experimental and control groups are assigned randomly (Crain & Mahard, 1983). For an extended debate about the effects of school integration by busing, see Armor (1972); Miller (1980); and Pettigrew, Useem, Normand, and Smith (1973).

Interrupted Time Series Designs

Threats. In time series designs that use one group, community, or subject, the grouping threats of selection and selection-by-time interaction cannot apply because no comparison is made between different groups. Regression could be a threat to single-group designs if the group is selected for extreme scores on some test. However, time-series designs are most commonly threatened by one or more of the four time threats: history, maturation, measurement decay, and test reactivity.

History refers to events that coincide with the experimental manipulation and account for the observed change over time. **Maturation** refers to normal developmental change in the subjects. **Measurement decay** explains observed change by unintended changes in the measurement process over time. **Test reactivity** occurs when changes in measurements are due not to the experimental variable but rather to the influence of the pretest. How can the plausibility of these threats be checked or reduced in a single-group design? In a control group study, the control group is intended to reveal any maturational, historical, or other time-related changes that might be confounded with the experimental effect. In single-group designs, the studied group serves as its own control. Changes in earlier pairs of observations can be compared with the pair of measures just before and just after the experimental manipulation. Such multiple pretest changes provide a baseline against which to assess the contribution of the manipulation. Figure 11–4 illustrates the way in which multiple pretests are made to serve as surrogate (substitute) controls. The first two pretests are assumed to capture such influences as maturation, regression to the mean, or test reactivity that might also be operating between the measures just before and just after the manipulation. In general, the change from just before to just after the manipulation must exceed the

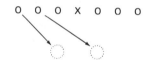

Figure 11–4 Interrupted time series—pretests as surrogate controls in single-group designs.

change between pairs of earlier pretests to be considered evidence of an effect of X over and above time effects.

The single-group, **interrupted time series design** differs from the pre-post single-group design in that it employs multiple measures before and after the experimental intervention (X). This design is based on the assumption, which is crucial to the interpretation of the results, that the time threats such as history or maturation will be reflected as regular changes in the measures prior to the intervention. This assumption appears plausible for some time threats but less persuasive for others. Test reactivity, maturation, and regression to the mean (the latter from the group threats cluster) seem the most likely processes to reveal themselves in the early tests. Suppose we witness a greater jump in scores from just before to just after X than between the first two pretests. To argue that this greater jump in scores was due to test reactivity requires a rather complicated explanation involving some delay in the test reactivity effect. In the absence of evidence supporting such a delayed test reaction, the test reactivity threat appears unconvincing. Similarly, to argue that the greater jump was due to a spurt of maturation requires us to believe that the maturation rate should suddenly spurt or decelerate just at the time X was administered. Again, this counterexplanation depends on a rather elaborate coincidence. Although it cannot be ruled out, its plausibility depends on additional evidence. The same reasoning applies to the threat of regression to the mean. The interrupted time series design controls for each of these types of threats by establishing a baseline of change before the X is administered. Of course, each of these threats can be dealt with in other ways. Highly reliable, unobtrusive measures could be applied to subjects known not to be undergoing significant developmental changes.

The two remaining time threats, history and measurement decay, are generally more serious threats to the interrupted time series designs. In contrast to the other time threats, history and measurement decay effects are more likely to include irregular, unpredictable shifts in addition to possible regular, foreseeable changes. When irregular changes and experimental interventions coincide, their effects are confounded (cannot be separated). History includes effects of environmental change (for example, decreased deaths from auto accidents because of decreased driving caused by higher gas prices) other than the intervention (for example, a new safe driving media campaign). Instrumental decay includes apparent changes in the target variable that are due to changes in the measurement procedures rather than in the phenomenon itself (for example, when a government job training program and a change in the definition of unemployment coincide with a decrease in unemployment rates).

The special advantage of time series designs (those with observations at many time points) is that regular or repeating variation can be distinguished from irregular variation that might be due to some experimental change. Regular patterns include **trends** and **cycles,** which are repeating effects that may be produced by one or more maturational, historical, or other processes. Trends are persistent increases or decreases commonly seen in long-term processes such as population growth or economic development (for example, a variable such as annual car accidents, which depends in part on the number of people who can afford to drive cars). A cyclic pattern is one of alternating rises and falls commonly seen in variables associated with seasons or business patterns (for example, monthly counts of people employed in agriculture rising in the summer and falling in the winter). As illustrated in Figure 11–5, linear trends (1), curvilinear trends (2), cycles (3), and combinations of trends and cycles (4) can be detected if there are sufficient measures. In each of these four lines, the decrease from one time point before to one time point after the intervention (X) is about the same. (The lines could equally well be drawn to show increases.) Each could be interpreted as showing an effect of X except that each is more likely the continuation of a pattern established before the intervention. We can project these patterns past the intervention to determine whether the intervention X adds any effect beyond the trend and cycles.

Figure 11–6 illustrates two time series in which there appear to be effects of the intervention X beyond the linear trend (line 1) or cycle (line 2). The dotted lines show the post-X pattern expected from the pre-X trend or cycle in the absence of X. As can be seen, these expected lines are noticeably different from the observed (solid) lines.

Researchers who work with trends or cycles often modify their variables to remove the regular changes in order to see the irregular changes that might be due to interventions. For example, instead of analyzing annual death counts, epidemiologists study annual death rates (that is, deaths per 1,000 or 100,000

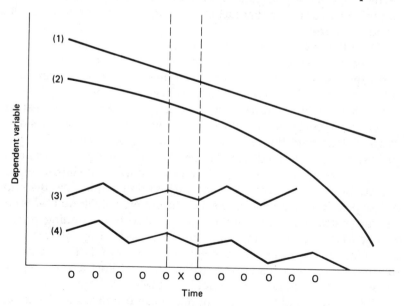

Figure 11–5   Trends and cycles.

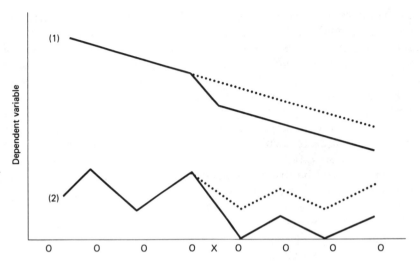

Figure 11–6   Intervention effects in trend and cyclic patterns.

population). This type of adjustment allows a researcher to detect a decrease in the death rate (for example, because of a public health education campaign) that might have been concealed by an increase in the death count simply because of an increase in population size. There are other techniques that **detrend** and **deseasonalize** (remove seasonal cycles from) time series, the details of which go beyond the scope of this presentation. However, these adjustment techniques have in common the assumption that factors causing the trend or cycle continue over the period of interest.

Once the effects of regular trends and cycles are taken into account or removed, the effect(s) of the intervention can be better understood. Figure 11–7 illustrates several different kinds of effects that interventions can have on the dependent variable. The pretest baselines are shown as straight, flat lines to emphasize that upward or downward trend and cyclic waves have been removed.

The lines in Figure 11–7 illustrate a few of the possible types of outcome patterns in interrupted time series: (1) a simple step change; (2) a permanent change in slope; (3) a delayed step change; (4) a step change followed by a return to the former baseline level; and (5) an increase followed by a larger step decrease. This variety of possible outcomes of an intervention emphasizes the importance of multiple post-X measurements. Each of the patterns in Figure 11–7 is consistent with a true effect of X. The regular changes due to continuing processes are assessed and removed by using the multiple pretests. The only plausible counterexplanation of the observed changes that follow X is that some irregular, one-time change other than X also occurred. Although such a coincidental, unique event may be judged unlikely, it cannot be entirely ruled out.

Both history and measurement decay can produce such irregular coincidental changes. Consider an evaluation of a community police department's effort

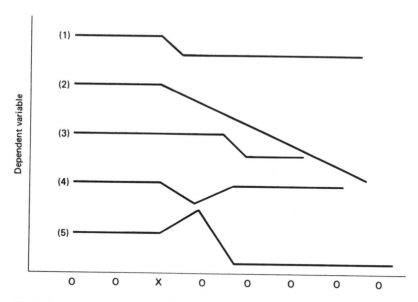

Figure 11–7 Possible intervention effects in time series.

to deter or prevent rapes. Perhaps several teams of police officers are reassigned from other details to spend full time investigating rapes or carrying out a community outreach campaign. The dependent variable for this evaluation might be the number of crimes of rape brought to trial each month starting 12 months before the new policy began. After regular trend and seasonal changes are assessed and controlled, suppose pattern 1 of Figure 11–7 is observed. That is, the number of rapes going to trial sharply decreases and levels off at a new rate. This pattern could be taken as evidence that the policy to decrease rapes is working.

On the other hand, other possible history or measurement changes must be considered. Perhaps as a result of the same public concern that led the police department to make its change, the city council also voted to install improved lighting in high-crime areas of the city. Perhaps it was the new lighting that accounted for the decrease in rape arrests and trials. This is an example of a history threat. Alternatively, a closer inspection of the district attorney's policies may reveal a change in the outcome measure. The same outcry against rape may have persuaded the elected DA to increase the conviction rate in rape cases. To get a higher rate of convictions, perhaps only the cases most likely to yield convictions are brought to trial. The remaining cases may be settled by plea bargaining to lesser assault charges. Thus the measure of rape may be shifted in a way that explains the observed change even if the actual rate of rape remains the same.

History and measurement effects can also work against the intervention. For an example, the DA might have decided to bring more rape cases to trial rather than to settle them through plea bargaining. The result would have been an apparent increase in rape (as measured by rape trials) "caused" by the police crackdown on rape. Actually, such an increase might be desirable to communicate that rape is no longer tolerable in the community as a necessary step to a long-term lowering of the rape rate (as in line 5 of Figure 11–7).

In summary, interrupted time series designs are most vulnerable to the effects of irregular history or measurement changes that coincide with interventions. In the absence of a comparison group as a control, only careful consideration of the history and measurement methods of the study can identify such threats.

Boston White Flight: An Interrupted Time Series Design. The busing of students to achieve racially integrated education has generated the controversial question of "white flight." James Coleman is the chief author of the influential study *Equality of Educational Opportunity* (Coleman, et al., 1966), which found significant educational gains for minority children who were placed in integrated schools. This report is often cited as support for busing for integration. In 1975, Coleman announced the results of his analysis of the extended effects of school desegregation on white enrollment. He concluded that desegregation in large central cities increased the loss of white students from the public schools of those cities. This finding became a prominent feature in antibusing legal actions. It is claimed that busing, whether good for minority children or not, is self-defeating because white flight will ultimately make integration difficult or impossible. The remaining whites will be too few to provide an integrated experience for the minority students, who will find themselves in the majority. This white flight thesis and its policy implications have elicited extensive research and rebuttal (see Pettigrew & Green, 1976, versus Coleman, 1976; and for a behind-the-scenes view of Coleman's project, see Hunt, 1985, chap. 2).

Interrupted time series analyses have been used to test the white flight thesis. Christine Rossell (1975–1976) concluded from her analysis that little if any white flight results from desegregation. In a subsequent critique, Diane Ravitch (1978) took exception to Rossell's method of measuring white flight. Ravitch concluded that, at least in the case of Boston, desegregation was followed by significantly increased white flight.

Rossell's measure of white flight consists of the change in the percentage of white enrollment, using the total number of students as the denominator:

$$\frac{\text{white enrollment last year}}{\text{total enrollment last year}} - \frac{\text{white enrollment this year}}{\text{total enrollment this year}}$$

Thus, using Rossell's method, if whites were 80 percent of the enrollment in 1972 and 75 percent in 1973, this figure would represent a change of 5 percent. Ravitch argues that this method

> will show small declines even in the face of large absolute movements. Consider, for example, a school district with 250,000 pupils, 200,000 whites (80% of the total) and 50,000 blacks (20% of the total). If 40,000 white pupils were to leave the district

in a single year, it would then have 160,000 whites (76.2% of the total) and 50,000 blacks (23.8% of the total). Rossell would say that the change in percentage white was -3.8%, that is, a drop of 3.8 *percentage points. But what has actually happened is that 20% of the white pupils have left the district* (since 40,000 is 20% of 200,000). (Ravitch, 1978, p. 140; italics in original)

Ravitch proposes to use a different measure, which considers absolute change in white enrollment and uses white enrollment as the denominator:

$$\frac{\text{white enrollment last year} - \text{white enrollment this year}}{\text{total enrollment last year}}$$

To illustrate the interrupted time series method, the white enrollment changes will be reported, using both the Rossell and the Ravitch methods, for the city of Boston. Figure 11–8 presents the change in white enrollment from year to year in the percentage of the total (Rossell's measure) and in the percentage of the previous year's white enrollment (Ravitch's measure) before and after the two phases of Boston's busing program.

Both measures of white flight show a pattern of white flight *before* busing, and both reach their peaks during the first two years of busing in 1974 and 1975. However, the Ravitch method indicates a much more dramatic pattern of white

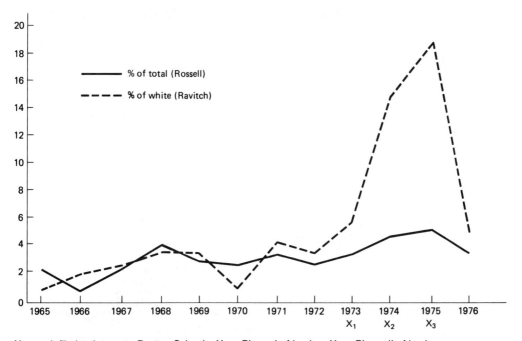

X_1 = suit filed to integrate Boston Schools; X_2 = Phase I of busing; X_3 = Phase II of busing.

Figure 11–8 "White Flight" in Boston: Two measures from 1965 to 1976. (Based on Table V, p. 143 of Ravitch, 1978. Reprinted with permission of the author from *The Public Interest, 51* (Spring, 1978), 143. Copyright © 1978 by National Affairs, Inc.)

flight than the Rossell measure, although both measures are based on the same counts. White enrollment declined from 69,400 in 1964 to 57,358 in 1972 (the year before the filing of the suit to bus) to 36,243 in 1975 (the second year of busing).

Another approach to this question uses a different variant of the interrupted time series design. Armor (1980) estimated the portion of white flight that was due to nonbusing factors (accounting for white flight before and continuing after busing) and the portion that was due to the advent of busing. Using the prebusing white flight data, he projected the loss of white enrollment assuming no busing and a continuation of the same white out-migration pattern. He then compared this projection with the actual white enrollment loss (see Figure 11–9).

Based on Armor's calculations, the loss of about 28,000 white Boston students from 1971 to 1977 consists of about 16,000 because of busing and about 12,000 because of nonbusing factors. He also notes that the actual minority enrollment stopped growing in 1975, contrary to projected growth, and suggests that this figure may represent a case of "black flight" (Armor, 1980, p. 205).

Together, these studies by Rossell, Ravitch, and Armor illustrate several points about interrupted time series analysis. First, the method can discriminate between regular preintervention patterns of change and different postintervention patterns. Thus, prebusing white flight is seen to be significant and consistent but slower than the rate of white flight during and immediately after the intervention. Whether this difference is judged to be significant in this case depends importantly

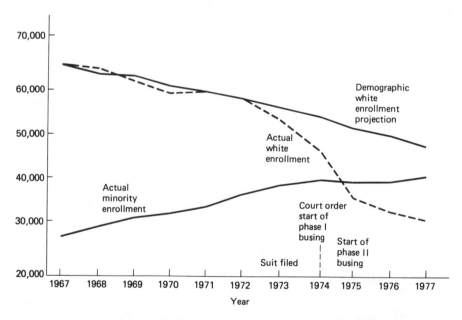

Figure 11–9 Projected and actual enrollment for Boston. (From D. J. Armor, White flight and the future of school desegregation, in W. G. Stephan & J. R. Feagin, eds., *Schools Desegregation: Past, Present, and Future.* New York: Plenum Press, 1980).

on the measure selected for interpretation. Each of these analyses is vulnerable to the threat of some irregular, unprojected cause of white flight that may have coincided with the 1974–1975 beginning phases of busing. Unless someone identifies a particular nonbusing threat (for example, a particular historical occurrence or a change in record keeping) that could plausibly account for the observed increases in white flight, such a threat remains unconvincing.

In the absence of convincing rebuttals to the evidence of white flight, the debate about the impact of desegregation on white public school enrollment no longer focuses on whether whites leave the school system. Rather, the current concern is with the timing and magnitude of the flight and its response to particular aspects of the desegregation procedure (Welch, 1987; F. D. Wilson, 1985, 1987).

Variations on the Time Series or Within-Subjects Design

The interrupted time series design is very simple, consisting of one group, one intervention, and several measures. There are several variants of this basic design that can help protect against the main threats to its validity—irregular coincidental changes, especially those of history or measurement.

Multiple Groups. One of the simplest variations is to add one or more comparison groups:

$$OOOOO \ X \ OOOOO$$
$$OOOOO \ \ \ \ \ OOOOO$$

The comparison group serves the same function as in the nonequivalent control group design; it controls for coincidental changes in such time-related threats as history. If an apparent effect of X was found in the experimental series but not in the control series, the threat of history or other time-related explanations is weakened. One would have to argue that the coincidental occurrence that caused the effect was not only irregular (not seen in the measures prior to X) but also unique to the locality or subjects of the experimental group (not seen in the control community or group). Although such a local, irregular event is possible, it is not plausible in the absence of other information. In terms of internal validity, this is the best quasi-experimental design and rivals the true experiment.

You could further expand on the logic of comparison group time series by gathering several representatives of both treated and untreated groups—in effect creating groups of treated groups and groups of control groups to "average" out any unique, coincidental factors that might occur in just one group. Just such multigroup analyses were performed by Rossell (1975–1976), Ravitch (1978), and Armor (1980) in their respective analyses of white flight. Several desegregated school districts were combined and compared with several undesegregated school districts while controlling for city size and region (North versus South). Any peculiar, irregular, local effects found in just one community should be "washed" out in the average of many similar communities in which desegregation took place over different years. The result should reveal any "pure" busing effect after canceling out random factors.

Multiple Interventions. Up to now, we have considered one or more groups, each receiving just one intervention. In some kinds of studies, it is possible to administer the same intervention more than one time or more than one kind of intervention to the same group. In experimental clinical psychology, the unit of analysis is often the individual rather than the group. The $n = 1$ or **single-subject design** in clinical research may be thought of as a special case of time series research using **multiple-intervention design** to control the time threats to internal validity. Two of the more common $n = 1$ designs are the reversal or **ABAB design** and the **multiple-baseline design**.

In the ABAB design, the manipulation (*B*) is administered twice:

$$O\ O\ O\ X\ O\ O\ O\ X\ O\ O$$
$$A\ B\qquad A\ B$$

Before each administration of the intervention (*B*), the baseline condition of no treatment (*A*) is measured. If the treatment has an effect, the evidence of the effect should appear after the first intervention. If the effect depends on the treatment, the effect should decrease or disappear when the treatment is withdrawn and appear again when the treatment is reestablished. The first appearance of the effect might be due to a coincidental occurrence of some uncontrolled variable (for example, the subject receiving some treatment elsewhere and unknown to the researchers). But the disappearance and reappearance of the effect requires a very implausible and unparsimonious set of coincidences.

Although the ABAB, or reversal, design is the most popular $n = 1$ design in clinical research (Kazdin, 1978), its principle can also be applied in group and community research. For example, Jason, Zolik, and Matese (1979) applied a reversal design in a study of behavioral community psychology that may be of interest to public health workers, city managers, and policymakers. They studied the effects of a community intervention to encourage dog owners to pick up after their pets as a way of controlling animal-carried germs and parasites in the urban environment. Actually, two interventions were employed: signs (intervention *B*) and prompting (intervention *C*). Their design was thus an ABCAC design: baseline, signs, prompting, baseline, and prompting. They reported that signs had little effect but that prompting led to an increase in owners picking up after their dogs. This picking-up behavior decreased somewhat on reversal (no prompting) and increased when prompting was reestablished.

The second most common $n = 1$ design is the multiple-baseline design (Kazdin, 1978), which uses multiple interventions aimed at different behavioral targets. Multiple measures are required in this design—at least one for each type of behavior to be studied. The first intervention (*X1*) is aimed at one behavior. Only that targeted behavior should respond significantly, and the other behavior(s) should remain unaffected. The second intervention (X2) is aimed at the second behavior and should have little effect on the first behavior if the investigator's theory is correct. The following diagram illustrates a simple multiple-baseline design:

$$O\ O\ O\ X1\ O\ O\ X2\ O\ O\ O$$

Each measuring point (O) includes at least two measures. Measure 1 should respond to X1 immediately after it is introduced, but measure 2 should remain unaffected until after X2 is applied. Again, counterexplanations of these effects must resort to complex coincidences. An example of multiple-baseline research comes from mental health work. The interventions X1 and X2 may be operant conditioning procedures aimed at shaping different aspects of behavior, such as improving the ability of a regressed psychotic patient first to dress himself (X1) and then to talk appropriately (X2). Measures of both appropriate dressing and talking would be reflected in each measurement point (for example, the nurse's daily ratings). Dressing should improve after X1, but talking should improve only after X2. At the community level, the multiple-baseline design could be applied to publicity campaigns aimed at, for example, energy conservation targeted first at bus ridership and later at car pooling.

Within-Subjects Designs. All time-series designs are within-subjects designs in the sense that they measure changes within subjects or groups of subjects. There are two major categories of within-subjects designs: complete and incomplete. In **complete within-subjects designs**, all possible orders of the various interventions are experienced by each subject, sometimes several times. Complete designs are feasible when (1) the interventions are few in number or can be applied quickly if they are numerous (for example, tests of reaction times to different pitches of sound) and (2) the impact of each intervention on the subject quickly evaporates, with little aftereffect. Thus complete designs are commonly used in studies of perceptual, physiological, or cognitive processes in which many stimuli (interventions) can be applied quickly and in all orders to each subject.

Incomplete within-subjects designs are used when only one administration of each stimulus or stimulus sequence to each subject is possible. Thus one subject may experience three conditions in the order X1, X2, X3. Since the apparent effect of X3 may be due to the preceding exposure to X1 and X2, the true effect of X3 is confounded with the order of presentation of the stimuli and cannot be determined from this single subject alone. For example, reaction time to noise (X3) may be affected by experience in reacting to visual (X1) and tactile (X2) stimuli. To control order effects in such an incomplete design, it is necessary to use more than one subject so that all possible orders of the interventions or stimuli are experienced by the group of subjects taken as a whole. Thus the effect of X3 following X1 and X2 in some subjects can be contrasted to the effect of X3 occurring first or second in other subjects. This concern with order effects will be highest in studies of interventions that are thought to produce lingering effects (for example, instructional procedures that can modify the impact of subsequent procedures). Such interventions may produce exhaustion, heightened sensitivity, practice effects, or other results that could make the subsequent intervention look more or less effective than it would have been if it had been administered in a different order. The effort to produce all possible orders of Xs over all subjects taken as a whole is called **counterbalancing** and is essential in such incomplete within-subjects designs.

SUMMARY

Quasi-experimental designs are experiments in which there is no comparison group or in which experimental and control groups are not made up by random assignment as in true experiments. Quasi-experiments are often the only feasible or ethical way to study certain kinds of phenomena. Unfortunately, most quasi-experimental designs are vulnerable to one or another of the common threats to internal validity. As a result, their interpretation is often open to debate.

Nonequivalent control group quasi-experiments are those with two or more groups that cannot be assumed to be equal on all relevant characteristics. Matching (composing groups by exchanging members until the groups are equal on measured characteristics) does not ensure equivalence on potentially important but unmeasured characteristics. Even random assignment, which usually ensures equivalence, can sometimes leave inequalities between groups. In such cases of nonequivalence, the group threats to internal validity are of special concern: selection, regression to the mean, and selection-by-time interactions. Although statistical adjustment for nonequivalence may be possible, its methods have been controversial (for example, the Head Start debate).

Interrupted time series quasi-experiments may have just one group but employ many pre- and postintervention observations to control for the time threats to internal validity: history, maturation, instrumentation, pretest reactivity, and sometimes regression to the mean. Many observations over time permit the analyst to distinguish regular and recurring change (such as trend and cycle) from the novel effects of the intervention. Unfortunately, single-group time series with a single intervention are still vulnerable to irregular occurrences (for example, history or instrumentation) that coincide with the intervention. Variations of time series designs for groups or single subjects can control for such irregular threats with comparison groups or multiple interventions (ABAB or multiple-baseline designs).

EXERCISES

Quasi-experiments are especially vulnerable to threats to internal validity. Find an example of a quasi-experimental study and determine whether it is a nonequivalent control group or an interrupted time series design. Then check its vulnerability to the most likely threats to internal validity. Repeat this exercise for a study using another type of quasi-experimental design. Continue until you can quickly and routinely scan any experiment for the common group and time threats to internal validity.

GLOSSARY

ABAB design: Also called a reversal design, a multiple-intervention design in which the experimental manipulation is administered at least twice with an intervening period in which to observe the effect of the withdrawal or termination of the initial manipulation.

Analysis of covariance: Statistical procedure for adjusting posttest scores for pretest group differences.

Complete within-subjects design: Multiple-intervention design in which all possible orders of presentation of the experimental manipulations are given to each subject.

Counterbalancing: Technique for studying all possible orders of multiple interventions in incomplete within-subjects design by the use of different subjects who, taken together, experience all possible orderings.

Cycles: Pattern in time series marked by recurring highs and lows.

Deseasonalize: Statistical treatment to remove the seasonal cycle from a time series.

Detrend: Statistical treatment to remove the trend from a time series.

Ex post facto design: Experimental design in which the control group is created after the treatment has already taken place.

History: Time threat to internal validity in which some event unrelated to the experimental intervention causes the observed change.

Incomplete within-subjects design: Multiple-intervention design in which not all possible orders of presentation of the experimental manipulations are given to each subject.

Interrupted time series design: Single-group quasi-experiment in which an experimental treatment is assessed with numerous pre- and posttests.

Maturation: Time threat to internal validity in which the observed change is due to internal developmental processes.

Measurement decay: Time threat to internal validity in which the observed change is accounted for by changes in the measurement process.

Multiple-baseline design: Multiple-intervention design in which two different treatments are applied at different times and which are assessed with measures of two different expected outcomes.

Multiple-intervention design: Within-group design in which more than one experimental manipulation is administered to the group or subject.

Nonequivalent control group design: Multiple-group quasi-experiment in which systematic differences between groups have not been ruled out by random assignment.

Pseudoeffect: Apparent treatment effect caused by contrast with noncomparable control group.

Regression to the mean: Group threat to internal validity caused by the tendency of extreme scores on unreliable measures to move toward the mean on subsequent tests.

Selection: Group threat to internal validity in which differences observed between groups at the end of the study existed prior to the intervention because of the way the members were sorted into groups.

Selection-by-time interaction: Group internal validity threat in which subjects with different likelihoods of experiencing time-related changes (for example, because of maturation or history) are placed into different groups.

Single-subject design: Also called $n = 1$ design, a multiple-intervention design applied to a single subject.

Test reactivity: Time threat to internal validity that occurs when the observed change over time is in reaction to the pretest rather than to the experimental variable.

Trends: Patterns in time series marked by long-term increases or decreases.

NOTE

1. A test score consists of the true score plus some error. As the random error component of a test becomes larger relative to the true score, the test will be more unreliable. The same person will get different scores on two different administrations of an unreliable test because of the presence of the random error factor. If someone gets an extremely high score on the first test, that high score may reflect both a genuinely high true score plus the benefit of luck in getting many favorable random errors. On retest, that person will get the same high true score but is unlikely to get the same lucky random errors that boosted the score the first time. Thus the retest score will tend to be lower, on the average, for people scoring above the mean the first time. Similarly, the people who scored low the first time will enjoy, on the average, better luck and will score higher the second time around.

12

Correlational Methods

Controlling Rival Explanations Statistically

INTRODUCTION TO CORRELATIONAL ANALYSIS

An Example of Correlation

Health, Wealth, and Age. By definition, correlational research involves the study of nonmanipulated variables. That is, variables are observed taking their naturally occurring values rather than being fixed, as in experimental designs. Some variables cannot be manipulated because we cannot make individuals take predetermined values (for example, age). Other variables could be manipulated but are seldom if ever controlled experimentally for ethical reasons (for example, health). Still other variables are manipulable in principle but seldom in practice because of the cost (for example, wealth) or because the artificiality of the manipulation would threaten external or construct validity.

If we cannot control such variables as age, health, and income, as well as many others of interest, we can at least measure such variables and try to infer causal relationships from their associations. Unfortunately, correlational designs pose some validity problems that are avoided in experimental research. To illustrate the nature of these problems, consider the following fictional example for the variables of income level, health symptoms, and age.

First, consider the relationship of income and health. If these variables are related, what causal hypothesis might explain this association? One possibility is that income causes health status. Although we might expect higher income to be associated with lower symptoms, we observe in Table 12–1 that higher income is associated with higher symptoms.

With some effort, we can manufacture theories that are consistent with our findings. One possibility is that high income is detrimental to health because of the stress of the hard work required to obtain a high income. Or we could reverse causal direction and imagine that ill health causes higher income by motivating

Table 12–1 Cross-Tabulation of Income Level and Frequency of Recent Health Symptoms

		SYMPTOMS	
		High	*Low*
Income	High	11	9
	Low	9	11
			gamma = .20

Note: The relationship of income and symptoms is summarized by the descriptive statistic called gamma. It ranges from -1 (perfect negative relationship) through 0 (no relationship) to +1 (perfect positive relationship).

people to accumulate the wealth necessary to cover their medical needs. Although these theories are implausible, they do illustrate the problem that data such as those in Table 12–1 can be consistent with several different possible explanations or theories. That is, the data do not point to a single best hypothesis or even causal direction.

Reverse and Spurious Causation. The rival explanations of the association observed in Table 12–1 fall into two major categories. These two classes of explanation are fundamental threats to the internal validity of many correlational designs: reverse causation and third-variable or spurious causation.

The two farfetched explanations illustrate the problem of **reverse causation**. One explanation has income causing health, and the second explanation has health causing income. Even if these particular explanations were plausible, we could not choose between them based on the data in the table. That is, cross-sectional correlational data (observations taken at the same time) cannot, by themselves, indicate causal direction.

Reverse causation explanations are ruled out in experimental designs by the manipulation of the independent variable. It is more difficult to eliminate reverse causation in correlational analysis. We could resort to theory to decide that a variable must be the cause rather than the effect. Alternatively, we could design correlational studies so that measurements are taken at different times to help identify the direction of causal sequence.

Although this dilemma seems bad enough, there is still another threat to the internal validity of correlational designs. The threat that an observed association is due to some third variable is called **spuriousness**. This threat is handled in true experiments by randomly assigning subjects to treatment groups. In the absence of random assignment, experimental groups may not be equivalent, and the design is vulnerable to the group threats to internal validity (for example, selection). The same problem afflicts correlational research. The presumed independent variable can be correlated with some third variable that causes both the "independent" (supposed cause) and the "dependent" (supposed effect) variable. If we could somehow remove or control the effect of the third variable, we would see that the association between such spuriously related variables disappears.

Dealing with Spuriousness

Statistical Control and Multiple Causal Paths. Look again at the data on the relationship between income and symptoms, this time controlling for a potentially important third variable—age. In correlational analysis, *control* means to hold constant. To hold constant the effect of age, it is necessary to assess the relationship of income and symptoms within different age groupings, in our example twice, once for younger and once for older subjects. These two cross-tabulations are presented in Table 12–2.

The first thing to notice is that the relationship of income and symptoms is similar in the two control tables but opposite in direction from the way it

Table 12–2   Cross-Tabulation of Income and Symptoms Controlling for Age

OLD   SYMPTOMS

		High	Low
Income	High	10	4
	Low	5	1

gamma = −.33

YOUNG   SYMPTOMS

		High	Low
Income	High	1	5
	Low	4	10

gamma = −.33

appeared in Table 12–1. The relationship was positive in Table 12–1 but is negative in the control tables, which indicates that higher income is associated with lower symptoms after controlling for age. For example, 71 percent of older, high-income respondents report high symptoms versus 83 percent of the older, low-income respondents. Similarly, 17 percent of the younger, high-income respondents report high symptoms versus 29 percent of the younger, low-income respondents. In both cases, lower-income subjects have higher symptom rates. This finding is just opposite that seen in Table 12–1, where, not controlling for age, the high symptom rate was 55 percent in high-income subjects versus only 45 percent in low-income subjects.

Controlling for a third variable does not always lead to such diametrically opposite results. It can potentially strengthen an observed relationship, reduce the relationship to zero, or as in the present case, reverse its sign. One of these effects will occur only when the third variable is correlated with both the other variables. If the third variable is unrelated to one or both of the other variables, removing it will not change the relationship. That age was correlated with income and symptoms can be seen in Table 12–3, where age is positively related both to income (a) and to symptoms (b).

We can summarize the discovered pattern of relationships among age, income, and symptoms visually. Figure 12–1 shows a set of causal paths that are consistent with the observed data. Such a set of possible relationships or hypotheses is sometimes called a **model**.

Table 12–3

(a) Cross-Tabulation of Age and Income

		INCOME	
		High	Low
Age	Old	14	6
	Young	6	14

gamma = .69

(b) Cross-Tabulation of Age and Symptoms

		SYMPTOMS	
		High	Low
Age	Old	15	5
	Young	5	15

gamma = .80

This model includes two different mechanisms by which income is related to symptoms. The first is the spurious association because of the fact that both income and symptoms are related to the third variable, age. Since age is strongly positively related to both, this variable tends to make income and symptoms appear to be positively related. This spurious association conceals the second way in which income is related to symptoms, the direct negative effect hypothesized originally.

Remember that the causal diagram in Figure 12–1 is only hypothetical, for the reasons covered earlier in the discussion of reverse causation. The negative arrow between income and symptoms might also run in the opposite direction. To develop more confidence in the causal relationships of Figure 12–1, we would need more information than is available in our simple cross-tabulations.

Partial Correlations and Path Coefficients.   Each of the arrows in Figure 12–1 could be further described by a number telling the magnitude of the association. For example, for the age-to-income relationship, we could use the associa-

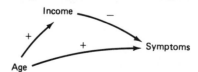

Figure 12–1   Possible causal model for age, income, and symptoms.

tion measure called gamma, which is .69 in Table 12–3. But what coefficient shall we use to describe the path from income to symptoms in Figure 12–1? We cannot use the initial correlation from Table 12–1 (gamma = .20) since we now know that this association includes the spurious association due to age as well as the direct association controlling for age.

We might use the two coefficients from Table 12–2, each of which holds for one of the two age groups. Each of these is controlled for age and reflects the direct connection of income and symptoms with the effect of age removed. Unfortunately, it is inconvenient to use two different numbers to describe a single path. If there were more than two control levels of age (young, early middle, late middle, early retired, and very old), we would have even more coefficients to deal with. Although the coefficients are the same in the two age groups in our example (–.33), there is no reason to expect such coefficients always to be equal across control groups.

The solution to our problem is to combine two or more such control correlations into a single coefficient. A single coefficient that measures an association controlling for another variable is called a **partial correlation**. In the present case, the partial gamma is –.33, the same as the two control correlations (because they were equal and based on equal numbers of respondents). Strictly speaking, the measure of partial association that is placed on a causal path is called a **path coefficient**. Although such a path coefficient is conceptually similar to a partial correlation, it is calculated differently and consists of the standardized regression coefficient generated in **multiple-regression** analysis (see the Appendix for more information on regression).

CONDUCTING CORRELATIONAL ANALYSIS

Types of Multivariate Relationships

As the preceding example illustrates, an apparently simple two-variable relationship can be radically changed by the inclusion of a third variable. The analysis of three or more variables simultaneously is called **multivariate research**. In true experimentation, even if an important causal variable is not included by manipulation, its effect on the dependent variable is controlled by the random assignment, which equalizes experimental and control groups on all the omitted causal variables. Thus the omission of such third variables in true experimentation does not endanger the internal validity of the study.

The situation is quite different in correlational research. As illustrated, the omission of such a third causal variable can lead to serious inferential errors. In multiple-regression analysis (the most common statistical approach to multivariate correlational research), the omission of important causal variables is called **specification error**. That is, the tested pattern of relationships is misspecified to the extent that any important causal variable is left out of consideration. The consequence of specification error is that we cannot place great confidence in the remaining associations. Thus multivariate research is not just desirable, it is a necessity in correlational studies. In general, the problem of correlational research is to include measures of all important causal variables in order to permit their subsequent statistical control.

Before turning to different correlational research designs, we must consider the variety of possible correlational relationships. Following are descriptions and examples of descriptive, direct causal, interactive, indirect causal, and spurious associations.

Descriptive Associations.   The observation that two or more variables are correlated does not automatically imply any particular causal connection. The interpretation of an observed association as a causal relationship is an inference that must draw on some additional information beyond the observation of correlation. Such additional information might include knowledge that the presumed cause occurred prior to the presumed effect. In the absence of such information, a causal inference must be regarded as tentative.

No one is required to draw causal inferences from observed correlations in the absence of supporting data. Often theories are developed after and, in part, from descriptive correlational research. Thus it may be adequate and useful to present the observed correlational patterns as description and avoid premature causal inference. Such an analysis is illustrated in a public health study of the social factors associated with breast self-examination (BSE). Women at high risk for breast cancer (white, married, and of high social status) were surveyed (Howe, 1981). Not surprisingly, frequency of BSE was positively associated with BSE knowledge, BSE attitude, and education. It was negatively associated with a measure of modesty. The author concludes that since the survey was cross-sectional and retrospective, these correlations cannot be interpreted causally. "BSE knowledge and a positive BSE attitude could precede, follow, or develop concomitantly with the adoption of the monthly practice of BSE" (p. 254).

Such a **descriptive association** is often represented visually by a curving, double-pointed arrow (for example, between SES and Intelligence in Figure 12–5 later in this chapter). Causal theories may have one or more noncausal correlational relationships built into them. Such descriptive relationships invite future research to establish the timing and direction of the causal sequence.

Direct, Reverse, and Reciprocal Causation.   **Direct causation** refers to the causal connection between two variables after removing or controlling other causes. Correlational evidence for direct causation going in one direction does not automatically rule out reverse causation going in the opposite direction at the same time. Indeed, for many pairs of social variables, bidirectional or **reciprocal causation** seems plausible. Reciprocal causation is the existence of both direct causal paths and is usually diagrammed by two straight, parallel, single-pointed arrows going in opposite directions.

As a particular example of reciprocal causation, consider the relationship between the violence of protesters and the violence of police at political protest rallies. Kritzer (1977) collected data from a sample of 126 protest demonstrations, with observations not only about the violence levels but also about such variables as the extent to which heavy police equipment was available and the degree of commitment of the protesters to nonviolence. One might hypothesize that the protesters provoked the police or vice versa or that each provoked the other in a cyclic way. Testing these hypotheses requires sophisticated statistical techniques. When Berry (1984) reanalyzed the Kritzer data as an example of these techniques, he found support for the reciprocity hypothesis, namely, that each side provoked the other.

Interactive Causation. Two causal variables produce **interactive causation** when the effect of one variable depends on the level of the other. Two variables may combine to produce an interaction effect even when neither variable alone has a direct effect or when direct main effects exist for either or both independent variables. Interactions are not restricted to two independent variables. Higher-order interactions have been observed for three, four, and more independent variables, although their interpretation can become quite difficult.

Interaction effects may be predicted from theory but can sometimes appear unexpectedly. Whether hypothesized or not, interactions will be discovered only if the research design includes the potentially interacting variables in the analysis. In experimental research, this is done by manipulating two or more independent variables in a factorial design. Factorial designs permit the observation and comparison of all possible combinations of the independent variables.

In correlational research, interactions can be discovered by comparing the associations of two variables at different levels of a third variable. Sometimes one of the interacting variables is thought of as a **moderating variable** in that it adjusts or affects the causal relationship between the other two variables.

An example of such a moderating or interactive effect comes from a correlational investigation of the view of oneself as a troublemaker and self-esteem in young people (G. Jensen, 1986). The results of this study are summarized in Table 12–4. One hypothesis is that young people are more likely to be low in self-esteem if they view themselves as troublemakers. Mild support for this prediction comes from the first subtable representing the entire sample (gamma = −.20). When boys and girls are analyzed separately in the next two subtables, we see that this negative association is due largely to the girls (gamma = −.37). In other words, gender moderates the association of self-esteem and troublemaking. Jensen went further and considered the effect of another variable, that of the availability of conventional status resources such as school performance or material possessions. For boys low in conventional status resources (the last subtable), high self-esteem is associated with high troublemaking (gamma = +.42); this an example of a three-way interaction.

Table 12–4 Associations between Troublemaker and Self-esteem

	TROUBLEMAKER		
	High	Low	
Entire Sample *Self-esteem*	High 44% Low 56%	55% 45%	Gamma = −.202
Boys Subsample *Self-esteem*	High 50% Low 50%	53% 47%	Gamma = −.043
Girls Subsample *Self-esteem*	High 40% Low 60%	59% 41%	Gamma = −.370
Boys Low in Conventional Status Resources *Self-esteem*	High 56% Low 44%	34% 66%	Gamma = .420

Boys high in conventional status resources, gamma = −.309
Girls low in conventional status resources, gamma = −.321
Girls high in conventional status resources, gamma = −.370

From Gary Jensen (1986), *Dis-integrating integrated theory: A critical analysis of attempts to save strain theory.* Paper presented at the Annual Convention of the American Society of Criminology, Atlanta.

In summary, an interaction effect is present when the relationship between two variables varies with the level of one or more other variables. Although the visual representation of interactions is not standardized, one approach is to symbolize an interaction as a separate variable made up of the product of its constituent variables. The statistical test of an interaction is applied to a created variable, which consists of the product of the interacting terms.

Indirect Causation. **Indirect causation** refers to the causal path from an independent variable to a dependent variable via an **intervening variable.** The link between the first or independent variable and the second or intervening variable is a simple, direct causal path. Similarly the link between the intervening variable and the dependent variable is another simple, direct causal path.

If the intervening variable were omitted from the analysis, the first variable would appear to be the direct cause of the dependent variable. The advantage of multivariate analysis in this instance is that it can show that the effect is transmitted through the intervening variable. The causal connection between two variables may be entirely direct, entirely indirect, or partly direct and partly indirect. The last case is illustrated in Figure 12–1, where age has a direct path to symptoms and an indirect path via income.

Whether two variables are related directly or indirectly concerns both theorists and interventionists. Naturally, theorists would like to understand causal mechanisms as thoroughly as possible. When scientists work with a causal association without an explanatory mechanism, they sometimes refer to the missing link as a "black box." Presumably, inside the black box are one or more intervening variables that transmit the causal influence between the observed variables. Scientists devote a good deal of their research trying to open such black boxes.

Including intervening variables in their analysis may actually help in detecting the existence of a connection between two variables. Some indirectly related variables have a simple **bivariate association** (or two-variable correlation), which can fail to reach statistical significance when the two variables are related only by their links with the intervening variable, both of which may be small in magnitude although statistically significant. In such a case, the weak direct effect from the independent variable to the intervening variable is further weakened when it is passed along the weak path from the intervening variable to the dependent variable. By including the intervening variable, we may find evidence for an indirect link even though the simple association between two variables appears close to zero.

Interest in intervening variables also comes from policymakers who want to apply scientific knowledge. You might imagine that such interventionists would not care about the black box between cause and effect. However, they may not be able to manipulate the first variable in the sequence. In that case, they will want to know the intervening variable and whether it might be manipulable. For example, suppose we observe that parental social status has a causal connection to criminal behavior (as will be discussed in the next example). Since parental status is difficult if not impossible to modify, the criminologist is interested in identifying an intervening variable that might be subject to intervention, such as educational performance.

How can we discriminate between direct and indirect effects from correlational results? The procedure is the same as the one used to detect spurious association—the method of partial correlation. The direct effect of one variable on another is measured by the association between the two after partialing out or statistically controlling the effect of the intervening variable(s). The indirect effect is a function of the two (or more) direct links passing through the intervening variable(s). If the indirect path via the intervening variable is estimated by regression analysis, the indirect effect is the product of the standardized path coefficients on the paths involving the intervening variable.

An example will illustrate the search for indirect effects. Socioeconomic status is consistently found to be associated with criminal behavior. However, it is possible that parental status does not cause criminal behavior directly but does so indirectly through an intervening variable such as education. A correlational study analyzed these variables in the longitudinal records of 3,421 Danish males

(McGarvey, Gabrielli, Bentler, & Mednick, 1981). Parental status was measured by occupational prestige, and the subject's educational performance was measured by his highest grade level and by his score on a draft board intelligence screening test. Criminality was based on the number of arrests and the severity of the crimes by the time the sample reached an average age of 26. Other measures were included, but only the relationships among these three are summarized in Figure 12–2 (using the standardized coefficients from sample A of the split-sample study).

Note that there is no direct path between parental status and criminal behavior because the coefficient for that path was not significantly different from zero. Although there is a significant negative bivariate association between parental status and criminal behavior, it is accounted for by the indirect path from parental status to educational performance to criminal behavior. The magnitude of the indirect effect of parental status on criminal behavior via educational performance is the product of the standardized coefficients on the two intervening links, that is, .46 X −.39 = −.18.

Spuriousness. The threat that a supposed causal relation is spurious (that is, not interactional, direct, or indirect) lurks behind all observations of association. One can always raise the possibility that an association interpreted as causal would disappear if some **confounding variable** were introduced into the analysis. A confounding variable causes both independent and dependent variables and accounts for their association (for example, the age confound of income and symptoms in the first example in this chapter). Such criticism should be translated into a test by an analysis that controls for the alleged confounding variable.

An example of such a criticism comes from the study of suicide and its predictors. Some research has suggested that the feeling of hopelessness is related to subsequent suicide, especially in those persons with previous suicide attempts. However, the alleged causal connection from hopelessness to suicidal thinking or ideation would be spurious if both of these variables were due to some third, or confounding, variable. Such a confounding variable has been proposed—the

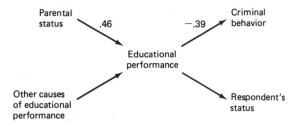

Figure 12–2   Indirect effect of parental status on criminal behavior via educational performance. (Adaptation from B. McGarvey, W. F. Gabrielli, Jr., P. M. Bentler, & S. A. Mednick, Rearing social class, education, and criminality: A multiple indicator model, *Journal of Abnormal Psychology, 90* (1981), 354–364. Copyright © 1981 by the American Psychological Association. Reprinted by permission of the publisher and author.)

tendency to answer in a socially desirable direction. That is, an association between self-reported hopelessness and suicidal thinking could be due to the differential tendency of some people to avoid saying socially undesirable things about themselves. People high in this tendency will report neither hopelessness nor suicidal thoughts, even if they have them. Those low in social desirability will tend to admit some feelings of hopelessness and suicidal thoughts, even if they are of the relatively common variety that many people tend to have from time to time. The net effect gives the appearance of a positive association between hopelessness and suicidal thinking, even if they are unrelated causally.

To test this possibility, subjects were asked to fill out the Bell Hopelessness Scale, the Suicidal Behavior Questionnaire (for past suicide attempts and for estimated likelihood of future suicide), and the Edwards Social Desirability Scale (Linehan & Nielsen, 1981). As expected from earlier research, hopelessness was positively and significantly related to the estimated chance of future suicide among those who were seriously suicidal in the past ($r = .39$). Figure 12–3 illustrates what happened to the relationship between hopelessness and future suicide when social desirability was controlled.

As illustrated, social desirability is strongly negatively correlated with both hopelessness and future suicide. The partial correlation of hopelessness with future suicide drops to .14, which is not statistically significant. These results were interpreted as casting doubt on the self-report research, which tries to link suicide to predictor measures such as hopelessness. Here the problem of spuriousness is a special case of the construct invalidity of the self-report measures. Instead of measuring the construct hopelessness, for example, this variable actually measures, at least in part, the construct social desirability.

Indirect Causation Versus Spuriousness. The threat of spuriousness can also arise even in studies from which no important third variable is omitted. This situation occurs when the theory is uncertain in identifying causal direction. Remember that in correlational analysis, the naming of variables as independent

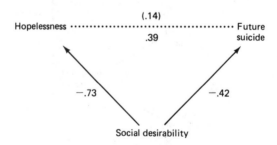

Figure 12–3 Spurious relationship of hopelessness and future suicide due to social desirability. (All coefficients are simple correlations except for the one in parentheses, which is a partial correlation that controls for social desirability.) (Adapted from M. M. Linehan, & S. L. Nielsen, Assessment of suicide ideation and parasuicide: Hopelessness and social desirability. *Journal of Consulting and Clinical Psychology, 49,* 1981, 773–775. Copyright © 1981 by the American Psychological Association. Reprinted by permission of the publisher and author.)

or dependent is often arbitrary. No experimental manipulation assures us that the independent variable is indeed causal. Similarly, the third variable in multivariate analysis is labeled "intervening" or "confounding" according to the theory. Consider the two causal diagrams in Figure 12–4.

Figure 12–4(a) describes an indirect causal path from A through B to C. For a real example of this type of pattern, see Figure 12–2. Figure 12–4(b) describes a case of spurious association between A and C, which disappears when the confounding variable B is controlled (as in Figure 12–3). These two causal diagrams differ only in the direction of the link between A and B.

How can we tell which of these two models better fits the data? If we compare the simple correlations between A and C, both models would give the same result. That is, A and C appear to be associated, and the magnitude of the associations would be the same regardless of the true causal pattern. To check for indirect causation, we test the partial correlation between A and C, controlling for B. This partial correlation is symbolized as $r_{AC.B}$. In the indirect causation case, $r_{AC.B}$ would be zero because A is connected to C via B. To check for spuriousness, we also check the partial correlation. Again if B accounts entirely for the AC relationship, $r_{AC.B}$ should be zero. Thus we get the same simple and partial correlations in both cases. In sum, our correlational analysis cannot tell us whether our data support indirect causation or spuriousness without further information.

Weak Inference.   Our decision about whether two correlated variables are causally related depends on a theory of causation. One meaning of causation is the commonsense notion of a mechanism by which a cause produces an effect (called the **generative theory** of causation). In contrast, **weak inference** of causation requires only that the cause and the effect be shown to co-vary after possibly confounding variables are controlled (also called the **regularity theory** of causation). According to generative theorists, regularity does *not* "constitute an explanation of that covariation, but merely justifies the rather weak claim that the causal event is statistically (that is, causally) relevant to the consequent event" (Baumrind, 1983, p. 1296).

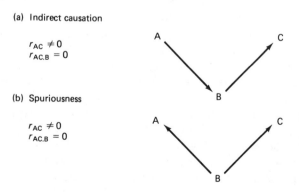

(a) Indirect causation

$r_{AC} \neq 0$
$r_{AC.B} = 0$

A   C

B

(b) Spuriousness

$r_{AC} \neq 0$
$r_{AC.B} = 0$

A   C

B

Figure 12–4   Dilemma in choosing between indirect causation and spuriousness.

According to the generative theory of causation, correlational designs can provide evidence for the fit of a given causal model to a set of data. Such a fit is necessary but not sufficient evidence for the model. It is necessary because a poor fit between a model and the data would tend to cast doubt on the model. But such a fit is not sufficient because there may be more than one plausible and well-fitting model—for example, the model in Figure 12–4(b), which fits as well as the model in Figure 12–4(a). Because you are likely to encounter path analysis, a widely used approach to model fitting, the following section introduces this technique.

Path Analysis

Approach. **Path analysis** uses statistical coefficients and graphic diagrams to express the relationships among variables along theoretical causal paths (Asher, 1976; Heise, 1975). Even if coefficients are not yet available, a theoretical model can be usefully presented in the form of a visual diagram that uses arrows to join the names of the variables. If the supposed causal variable has its causes outside the theory under investigation, it is called exogenous and has no arrows leading to it. Causal arrows lead from such exogenous variables to presumed dependent variables, called endogenous variables. Endogenous variables may also cause other endogenous variables, in which case they serve as intervening variables.

To provide estimates of the sizes of the causal relationships, multiple-regression analysis is usually performed (Schroeder, Sjoquist, & Stephan, 1986). One regression equation is formulated and solved for each endogenous variable. The resulting standardized regression coefficients are called path coefficients, and they can be placed on the corresponding arrows. Their signs tell the direction of association (does one variable increase or decrease in size as the other increases?), and their magnitude tells how strong the relationship is in comparison to coefficients on other arrows.

The overall fit of the model to the data is gauged by the extent to which the endogenous variables are explained by the causally prior exogenous and endogenous variables. The extent of the explanation is indicated in either of two equivalent ways—R^2 and the residual. The R refers to the multiple correlation coefficient, which measures the association of a dependent variable with all of its causal variables. The square of R (R^2) expresses the percentage of information in the dependent variable that is accounted for by all of the causal variables taken together. The **residual path** is represented by an arrow pointing to an endogenous variable from no variable. Such an arrow represents the contribution of all the unmeasured forces outside the model. The path coefficient placed on this residual path is a function of the difference between perfect explanation (that is, when $R^2 = 1$) and the amount of explanation found in this particular test (R^2 observed), or $1 - R^2$. The actual value placed on the residual path is the square root of this difference, or $\sqrt{(1-R^2)}$. Thus a good fit between model and data will result in a large R^2 (approaching the value 1) and a small residual path coefficient (approaching zero).

Example of Educational Attainment.   To illustrate path analysis, consider the path diagram reported by Sewell and Shah (1967). Figure 12–5 presents an analysis conducted on the females from a large sample of people who were Wisconsin high school seniors in 1957. A survey in 1957 measured the educational plans and family socioeconomic status of the seniors. A follow-up survey in 1964–1965 measured the educational and occupational attainments of one-third of the sample of these same women. Intelligence scores were obtained archivally from a standard test administered to all Wisconsin high school juniors. Educational attainment was determined from the follow-up survey and coded as follows: 0 = did not attend college; 1 = attended but did not graduate from college; and 2 = graduated from college.

A considerable debate has raged over the relative influence of parental social class versus the students' ability on later attainment in education, occupation, and adult social class. This debate touches a political nerve because we justify our economic system's differential distribution of wealth on the grounds of merit. Individuals with greater ability and effort merit larger slices of the societal pie. However, some social critics have alleged that entry to high-status careers is awarded not on the basis of individual ability but rather is inherited from parental social status.

Figure 12–5 displays results that directly address this debate. Two different regression equations were used, one with socioeconomic status (SES) and intelligence, predicting college plans; and the other with SES, intelligence, and college plans, predicting educational attainment. The first equation did not fit as well ($R^2 = .24$) as the second ($R^2 = .60$). These results indicate that both sides of the debate have some basis in fact. Both SES and intelligence influence college plans, although the SES effect seems to be larger in this particular sample. In turn, college plans strongly influence ultimate educational attainment. Both SES and intelligence affect educational attainment in two ways—directly, controlling for each other and for college plans, and indirectly via college plans. The total SES effect on attainment is the sum of the direct effect (.13)

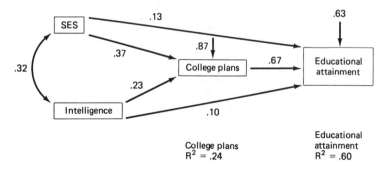

Figure 12–5   Path diagram for effects of socioeconomic status (SES), intelligence, and college plans on educational attainment in women. [From W. H. Sewell & V. P. Shah, Socioeconomic status, intelligence and the attainment of higher education, *Sociology of Education, 40,* 1967, 1-23] .

and the indirect effect (SES to college plans times college plans to educational attainment, or $.37 \times .67 = .25$). This total SES effect $(.13 + .25 = .38)$ exceeds the total intelligence effect $(.10 + .23 \times .67 = .10 + .15 = .25)$.

Notice that the two equations in Figure 12–5 did not fit equally well and that neither was close to perfect. How can we judge whether the model as a whole, including both equations, provided a good fit to the observed data? The separate R^2 for each equation in a multiple-equation model cannot tell us about the overall fit. Fortunately, there are procedures for fitting multiple-equation models that provide such overall significance tests. For example, see the study described previously on the relation of social class to criminality (McGarvey, Gabrielli, Bentler, & Mednick, 1981). This study used a procedure called maximum likelihood analysis of structural equations (for a summary of this approach, see Bentler, 1980, and Maruyama & McGarvey, 1980). Different computational procedures have been developed for structural equation modeling, the best known of which is called linear structural relations (LISREL, developed by Jöreskog & Sörbom, 1981). These statistical procedures provide single tests (based on the chi square statistic) that can be used to assess overall model fit (see Bentler & Bonett, 1980). Another advantage of this method is that it can utilize several different measures of each construct to permit analysis of the underlying construct, or **latent variable**, controlling measurement error. Other recent advances permit improved analysis of models with categorical dependent variables (such as the three-level variable educational attainment employed here). Such analytic techniques are based on log linear methods (for more information, see Fienberg, 1977).

In summary, the theorist can predict the ways in which each variable relates to each other variable in the model, including both causal paths (direct, indirect, or interactive) and noncausal paths (descriptive correlation or confounding by a third variable). Once the data are collected, they can be analyzed in a way that gives estimates of the strength of each of the hypothesized paths and the overall fit of the model to the data. Paths with very small coefficients or even whole models with poor overall fits may be abandoned in search of theories that do a better job of explaining the observations. However, if a model is found to fit the data well, the cautious researcher will remember that the design is correlational and that any causal inferences are weak.

To strengthen the inferences from a correlational study, the researcher will have to attend to the study's design. For example, in order to provide support for the inference of causality, it will be helpful to measure variables with known temporal priorities, that is, that the supposed causal variable must be causally prior to the supposed dependent variable. When such naturally ordered variables cannot be identified, the researcher may need to use a longitudinal design in order to measure the uncertain variables at different times. Another aspect of measurement that can affect the interpretation of results is the degree of aggregation of the data. The following section surveys the issues that arise in different types of designs, whether longitudinal or cross-sectional and whether individual or aggregate level.

Types of Correlational Designs

Definitions. Experimental designs are necessarily longitudinal in the sense that the independent variable is manipulated prior to the measurement of the outcome. In contrast, correlational designs are commonly applied to cross-sectional data. **Cross-sectional correlation** is based on measures taken of the "independent" and "dependent" variables at the same time. For example, the census questionnaire asks us questions about age, housing, and other personal matters at one time every ten years. However, **longitudinal correlation** could be applied to data that are collected over time. For example, a survey researcher might interview a group of subjects and then reinterview the same subjects one year later to assess changes in housing, finances, health, and so forth.

Individual-level data include measures of particular persons. That is, the individual subject is the unit of analysis. In contrast, **aggregate-level data** include measures of groupings of persons. The grouping may be spatial (for example, the average educational level by state) or temporal (the average educational level by decade). Any aggregation must specify both time and space (that is, grouping education by some spatial unit such as a nation or state and by some time unit such as a year or decade). Correlational analysis studies vary along one of these dimensions. If education in a nation is studied over time, the unit of analysis might be a year. If education in a particular year is studied over states, the state is the unit of analysis. In either case of aggregation, we cannot know about any particular person who was included in the measure. We have lost the educational attainment of each individual who was a member of the population in the state and time studied.

Typology by Longitudinality and Level of Analysis. Table 12–5 represents the division of studies simultaneously by time and level of analysis. Each of the four cells is the location for one combination of characteristics, either cross-sectional or longitudinal and either individual or aggregate level. To illustrate the differences among the designs belonging to these different cells, a similar question is asked in each cell. The differences in the way each cell's designs would operationalize this question demonstrate the differences in the kind of inferences these different designs can support.

The common question asked of all four approaches in Table 12–5 is "Does economic stress cause suicide?" Observe how this question is modified as it is asked in terms appropriate to each cell. It should be clear that depending on whether you operationalize your study cross-sectionally or longitudinally and at the individual or the aggregate level, you will be asking rather different questions. Not surprisingly, these different questions can receive quite different answers. If you are interested in the actual research that corresponds to each cell, see the reviews by Dooley and Catalano (1980, 1986).

There are two main reasons for locating correlational studies in terms of the typology of Table 12–5. The first is to avoid making wrong causal inferences

Table 12–5 Typology of Correlational Studies by Longitudinal—
Cross-Sectional, and Level of Analysis:
Illustrated by Question: "Does Economic Stress Cause Suicide?"

Individual
Level

Unit: Individuals at one time		*Unit:* Individuals measured over time	
Sample Question: Does current suicidal intention correlate with current economic status?		*Sample Question:* Does change in suicidal intention correlate with recent economic life events such as job loss?	
Cross-Sectional	1	3	Longitudinal

Unit: Spatial aggregate (e.g., state)	2	4	*Unit:* Temporal aggregate (e.g., year)
Sample Question: Does the suicide rate corre-late with unemployment rate over states?		Sample Question: Does the suicide rate corre-late with unemployment rate over years?	

Aggregate
Level

across levels of analysis. The second is to avoid making wrong inferences with respect to cross-sectional correlation (static) or longitudinal correlation (dynamic) studies. These two types of inferential problems are examined in the following sections.

Cross-level Inference and the Ecological Fallacy.

A **cross-level inference** is a generalization from research at one level of analysis to another level. Usually, such cross-level inferences are made from aggregate-level research to individual-level interpretations. Unfortunately, such inferences can be wrong. Robinson (1950) showed that the correlation between variables at the aggregate level can differ substantially from the correlation of the same variables measured on individuals. The term **ecological fallacy** was coined to describe the erroneous individual-level interpretation of aggregate-level research results.

Robinson (1950) used 1930 U.S. census data to study the relationship of race and literacy. He found that this correlation was much larger at the aggregate level (grouping by areal or spatial units) than at the individual level. Subsequently, Firebaugh (1978) reanalyzed these same data. He demonstrated that the grouping variable plays an important part in the cross-level bias. Illiteracy varied considerably across regions (higher in the South) for both blacks and whites. Moreover, there was an interaction between race and region (blacks in the South had much higher illiteracy than blacks in the North). When the main effect of region and the interaction effect of race by region were taken into account, the net relationship between race and illiteracy became quite small.

Why does aggregate-level analysis misestimate the true individual-level relationship? There may be different reasons, depending on the nature of the grouping variable (whether it is correlated with the presumed independent variable, as race is correlated with region) and the type of statistical analysis (correlations versus regression coefficients). For our purposes, it is sufficient to illustrate the possibilities with one common cause of the ecological fallacy—group effects. Data are aggregated within groups (for example, spatial units such as northern and southern regions, as in the Firebaugh reanalysis of Robinson). Such groupings may contribute their own effects over and above the effects of the individual-level variable. In the case of the illiteracy study, region was correlated with racial composition. Thus, the aggregate measure of race was actually a proxy or stand-in measure for region of the country, the grouping variable. That is, a high score on aggregate racial composition was tantamount to a high score for being southern on the dimension of region. Firebaugh (1978) speculates that this grouping effect operated indirectly on illiteracy. Through various historical processes, the direct causes of illiteracy, such as the quality of the schools, became associated with region.

Individual and aggregate correlations will differ when the aggregate version of the causal variable actually measures some important group cause over and above the individual causal variable. Individual- and aggregate-level associations will give the same results (that is, there will be no ecological fallacy or generalization error) only when the aggregated causal variable adds nothing to the individual causal variable. Robinson (1950) got a strong relationship between aggregate race and aggregate literacy because his analysis included the strong group effect of unmeasured variables. When this group effect is removed, as it is in individual-only analysis, individual race and literacy are seen to be much less strongly related.

It should be noted that cross-level interpretive errors can operate both ways. Robinson (1950) was right that it could be erroneous to generalize from the aggregate to the individual, but it is also incorrect to assume that individual-level findings describe aggregate-level relationships. We might call this interpretation error the atomistic fallacy. In the present example, if we were to generalize from individual data to groupings by region, we could fail to note the important interaction effect of race and region on literacy noticed in the aggregate-level analysis.

This discussion of cross-level inference illustrates how a research question can be operationalized in different ways at different levels of analysis. In Firebaugh's (1978) reanalysis of the 1930 census data, the question of association of individual race to individual literacy falls in cell 1 of Table 12–5 (individual, cross-sectional). In that cell, the question becomes "Does race correlate with literacy across individuals?" But at the aggregate level (cell 2—aggregate, cross-sectional), the question becomes "Does the racial composition of a region correlate with the literacy rate over regions?" The latter question, as demonstrated by Robinson and by Firebaugh, produces a different answer from that produced by the former question. Similarly, the question about economic stress and suicide in Table 12–5 can yield different answers depending on how it is operationalized. For example, aggregate characteristics that are associated with aggregate poverty (say, social disintegration) may have a strong influence on aggregate suicide rates over spatial units that group by poverty. But at the individual level, personal poverty may be much less strongly related to suicidal risk (for a discussion of the greater aggregate effect of social disintegration, see Leighton, Harding, Macklin, Macmillan, and Leighton, 1963).

Inferences from Cross-Sectional and Longitudinal Studies. Cells 1 and 2 in Table 12–5 both include cross-sectional or static studies. Observations are made at one time for both "independent" and "dependent" variables. The common problem of such static research is the dilemma of ruling out reverse and reciprocal causal connections. Unless independent information about causal priority is available, the analyst points causal arrows arbitrarily. It is desirable to collect longitudinal data to establish temporal sequence.

One might imagine that in Table 12–5, cells 2 and 4 differ only in that cell 4 improves on the static nature of cell 2 with dynamic data. Unfortunately, crossing the dividing line between cross-sectional and longitudinal research, even within the same level of analysis, can drastically transform the question that is being asked. The test of this assertion comes from attempts to analyze the same relationship with the same data organized first cross-sectionally and then longitudinally. An example of this comparison comes from Indian data on the relationship between birthrate and literacy (Firebaugh, 1980). This study compares the approach of cell 2 with the approach of cell 4 in Table 12–5. In the case of the cell 2 analysis, the units of analysis are spatial; they are districts of the Punjab measured at one time. In Firebaugh's report, this analysis was replicated 11 times, once for each of 11 years of available data. In cell 4, the units of analysis are the years over which a particular Punjabi district varies. This analysis was also replicated 11 times, once for each of the 11 districts.

We would expect these two different methods to produce similar answers. That is, increasing birthrate should be associated, if related at all, to either increasing literacy or decreasing literacy. Surprisingly, the two different approaches gave opposite answers. The ecological (measures over spatial units) relationship (cell 2) was positive, with high-literacy districts having high birthrates. This positive relationship was found in each of the 11 years studied. In contrast, the over-time relationship (cell 4) was negative. Within a district, rising literacy was associated with decreasing birthrate. This relationship was found in each of the 11 districts.

These contrary findings seem unreasonable at first glance. Assuming that literacy is the cause (this assumption is arbitrary since the relationship studied is synchronous, or "on time," and not "lagged" with one variable preceding the other), fertility should behave in the same way across methods. If the time-unit relationship is correct, increasing literacy is producing decreasing fertility. Assuming that this negative relationship between literacy and fertility has operated through time, we should observe a similar negative relationship between these variables in the ecological analysis over districts. That is, at any time, the districts that have enjoyed the greatest gains in literacy should have the lowest birthrates, and less fortunate districts with less advanced educational systems should have the greatest birthrates. Such a pattern would produce a negative correlation over spatial units similar to the negative correlation over temporal units. The fact that we do not get this harmonious result indicates that an assumption is wrong.

The false assumption is that the dynamic process operated prior to the study. In fact, in the first year of the observations, districts with high literacy also had high fertility. This pattern of differences across units is called the **unit effect**. This relationship implies that some historical process(es) led to a positive association of the variables of literacy and fertility (for example, wealth produced by favorable agricultural land may have supported both a high birthrate and investment in education). Subsequently, the pattern changed, and now the effect of increasing literacy appears to be decreasing fertility (possibly because of a new causal process having to do with the changing means of production and distribution). Since this negative relationship can operate in each district, the districts will tend to move together, that is, down in birthrate as they move up in literacy, thus preserving their relative standing. Thus even if a district decreases its fertility as a function of increased literacy, it can still retain the relatively high (or low) position on both fertility and literacy that it had in 1961.

In sum, crossing the border between cross-sectional to dynamic research designs can transform the original question, just as does changing the levels of analysis. The interpretation of research results generally and correlational results specifically must be limited to the kinds of inferences appropriate to both the level and the time design of the analysis.

SUMMARY

Correlational research can provide only weak support for causal linkages. Two variables may co-vary because either variable causes the other (reverse causation) or because both are caused by another variable (spuriousness). Reverse causation can be ruled out by theory or by additional evidence that establishes temporal priority of the "cause," as in longitudinal research. Often, however, the variables are measured at the same point in time and appear to cause each other (reciprocal causation).

Spuriousness can be checked by statistical procedures that control or remove the effect of the potentially confounding variable(s). Unfortunately, some unmeasured confounding variable may be left uncontrolled, or some other model may fit the observed data equally well (for example, the dilemma of choosing between indirect causation and spuriousness). A widely used method for comparing theory with correlational data is path analysis. Even with sophisticated statistical procedures, however, causal inferences are weak because alternative theories may also fit the data.

Two dimensions especially relevant to correlational designs are the level of analysis (aggregate versus individual) and time span (cross-sectional versus longitudinal). One cannot automatically generalize from one level to another, for example, from aggregate to individual (risking the ecological fallacy). Nor can we generalize from one time span (for example, cross-sectional) to another (longitudinal).

EXERCISES

1. Since the interpretation of correlational research depends on an understanding of the statistics that describe association, you should read the part of the Appendix dealing with correlations and the way associations are summarized graphically. Then identify several studies employing the correlational design, that is, using passively observed, nonmanipulated causal variables.

2. Select a simple correlational study on a topic of interest to you. The results might be summarized in one or more tables (or matrices) of correlations that describe the simple or partial associations of interest or in the form of a path diagram. Identify a pair of variables that are suspected of being causally related. Evaluate the correlational evidence in support of the causal relation and assess such rival possibilities as reverse causation and spuriousness.

3. Using the same sample study, determine which design type it fits into: cross-sectional or longitudinal and individual or aggregate level. Then consider whether the inferences are appropriate to these design characteristics.

GLOSSARY

Aggregate-level data: Based on spatial or temporal unit of analysis consisting of sums of individuals.

Bivariate association: Association between two variables.

Confounding variable: In a case of spuriousness, the "third" variable, which actually causes the association of the two variables of interest.

Cross-level inference: Drawing a causal conclusion at one level of analysis from data from another level.

Cross-sectional correlation: Association of variables measured at the same time; also synchronous, or on-time, correlation.

Descriptive association: Presentation of the observed relationship between variables without judgment of possible causality.

Direct causation: Impact of one variable on another not passed through another variable.

Ecological fallacy: Error that arises sometimes in cross-level inference when drawing individual-level conclusions from aggregate data.

Generative theory: Holds that the cause produces the effect. This is an understanding of causation that requires strong tests.

Indirect causation: Causation of one variable by another that passes through one or more intervening variables. The total effect of one variable on another is the sum of the direct and indirect effects.

Individual-level data: Based on the unit of analysis consisting of individuals.

Interactive causation: Direct causation of one variable by another that varies with the level of another variable.

Intervening variable: In indirect causation, the middle or go-between variable.

Latent variable: Unmeasured variable constructed statistically from several measured variables.

Longitudinal correlation: Association of variables measured at different times. One variable is said to "lead" (come before) or "lag" (come after) the other.

Model: One possible patterning of causal relationships. Usually different models are pitted against each other to see which best fits the observed data.

Moderating variable: In interactive causation, the variable that determines the extent of direct causation of one variable on another.

Multiple regression: One statistical procedure for conducting multivariate research.

Multivariate research: Analysis of three or more variables.

Partial correlation: Measure of association between two variables after statistically controlling one or more other variables. Order of correlation is the number of variables controlled (for example, 0-order is simple correlation, first-order partial controls one variable, and so on).

Path analysis: A graphic representation of a causal model that includes statistical estimates of the strength of the relationships.

Path coefficient: Standardized regression coefficient from a multiple-regression analysis that describes the magnitude of association between two variables in path analysis.

Reciprocal causation: Two variables associated because each causes the other.

Regularity theory: Holds that causation is shown by a nonspurious association between two variables, an understanding of causation that requires a weak test.

Residual path: In path analysis, the causal path representing the effect on the outcome variable of all variables not specified in the study.

Reverse causation: Rival explanation for an observed association according to which the causal direction is opposite to that hypothesized.

Specification error: In regression analysis, omission of an important causal variable. Such an error can lead to misestimation of the relationships among variables included in the analysis.

Spuriousness: Two variables associated because both are caused by another variable.

Unit effect: Pattern of preexisting differences across spatial units that accounts for the discrepancy between analysis over time and analysis over space.

Weak inference: Conclusion of causality based on the regularity theory of causation. Involves finding unconfounded covariation between variables in question that is consistent with a model; equally good-fitting alternative models are not ruled out.

13

Qualitative Research

Observing Without Quantitative Measures

INTRODUCTION

Example of Qualitative Research: *When Prophecy Fails*

Prophecy from planet. Clarion call to city: Flee that flood. It'll swamp us on Dec. 21, outer space tells suburbanite. (Festinger, Riechen, & Schachter, 1956, p. 30)

This headline appeared on September 23, during the mid-1950s, over a short article in the back pages of a midwestern city newspaper. The prophecy was based on messages received by automatic writing. Apparently superior beings from the planet Clarion were using a suburban housewife's hand to write their communiqués. Besides this warning of earthquake, flooding, and general calamity, the Clarion beings sent many messages describing a comprehensive belief system. The news story did not cause an evacuation or even very much interest in the general community.

Dissonance Theory.   The story did spark considerable interest in a small group of social researchers who were hoping to field-test a theory. These researchers were curious about a phenomenon that had appeared from time to time throughout history—the increase in recruitment (proselyting) following the failure (disconfirmation) of an important belief held by a religious group. The researchers wanted to confirm this phenomenon by direct observation and to test their explanation of it. They derived their hypothesis from the theory of cognitive dissonance, in which two inconsistent (that is, dissonant) ideas produce an uncomfortable tension. In an effort to reduce this discomfort, the person will strive to change one of the ideas to make them compatible or to reduce the importance of the inconsistency.

These researchers thought the September 23 prediction of a December 21 flood offered a good test of dissonance theory. They were confident that on or after December 21, they would witness considerable dissonance between the belief in the source of the prediction (the Clarion messages) and the recognition that the messages were wrong. On the basis of historical precedent, the response could be expected to be retention of the belief and heightened activity to recruit new members. *"If more and more people can be persuaded that the system of belief is correct, then clearly it must, after all, be correct"* (Festinger, Riechen, & Schachter, 1956, p. 28; italics in original).

What determines whether a believer responds to dissonance by giving up the belief or by seeking new converts? The researchers suspected that social support determined the outcome. In isolation, a believer cannot be expected to hold out against the facts of disconfirmation and the skepticism of the nonbelieving community. But a member of a group of believers can draw on others for support in the effort to retain faith and to recruit new members.

Cognitive dissonance and reactions to disconfirmation can and have been studied with quantitative measures and experimental designs. However, it is unlikely that those predicting an imminent end of the world would be interested in submitting their beliefs to study by skeptical social scientists armed with paper-and-pencil tests. The researchers decided to test their hypotheses by using the method of qualitative research. Since they could not bring the phenomenon into the controlled circumstances of the laboratory, they went out to the field as participant-observers. Since they could not impose the structure of quantitative tests and measures on their subjects, they gathered data by looking, listening, and recording their observations when and as the opportunity permitted. For the complete report of this study, see Festinger, Riechen, and Schachter (1956).

Observing the Faithful.   Beginning in early November, the research team began approaching the believers. Entry was gained in various ways, but usually by expressions of interest in the messages from Clarion and occasionally by the report of a fictitious dream or mystical experience of interest to the believers. These participant-observers did not tell the believers that they were conducting a systematic study of them and their reactions to disconfirmation. Altogether, 33 persons were observed, and observations yielded 1,100 pages of transcribed materials. This material was collected by the three authors and four assistants, who had contact with the believers until the group disbanded on January 9.

The observers witnessed three distinct disconfirmations surrounding the cataclysm predicted for December 21. The believers expected to be picked up by flying saucers on the afternoon of December 17, at midnight on December 17, and finally at midnight on December 20. The observers witnessed a variety of responses to these disconfirmations, including an increase in proselyting, especially among those committed believers enjoying the most social support.

Definition of Qualitative Research

Nonquantitative Observation.   The term **qualitative research** will refer here to social research based on nonquantitative observations made in the field and analyzed in nonstatistical ways. The subjects may or may not be aware that they are being observed for social research purposes. The observers may or may not participate actively in the lives of the subjects, although the term **participant observation,** which is sometimes used synonymously with qualitative research, does imply such participation. Qualitative research is invariably conducted in the field (that is, wherever the subjects normally conduct their activities). For this reason, qualitative research is sometimes referred to as **field research.** The term *field research* will be avoided here because quantitative research can be and frequently is also conducted in the field (for example, standardized interviews as part of a home survey and standardized observational measures taken on street corners as part of quasi-experiments).

The situational factors that require nonquantitative observation and the characteristics of such a methodology have implications for both research design and subject sampling. As a result, qualitative research must be explored in terms not only of measurement and inferential statistical validities but also of internal and external validities. We will return to a review of these validities as they apply to qualitative research at the end of this chapter.

Summary and Advantages of Nonquantitative Observation. The characteristics of nonquantitative observation can be summarized briefly. It entails direct observation and relatively unstructured interviewing in natural field settings. Where possible, genuine social interactions occur between the participating observers and the subjects, and pertinent documents and artifacts are collected. Typically, such observational data collection is less structured than quantitative research, being flexible, spontaneous, and open-ended.

These characteristics and the common tendency of observers to become personally involved in their field setting have been identified as threats to the reliability and validity that are the goals of quantitative observations. However, these very characteristics are potential strengths, one of which is that the observer minimally disrupts the setting and group being studied. After becoming accustomed to the observer's presence, the subjects can be expected to go back to their normal routines. Also the qualitative observer who looks, listens, and flows with the social currents of the setting can be expected to acquire perceptions from different points of view. Interviews with different subjects and observations at different times and places in the same social network are likely to defeat any effort to "fake" behavior. Comparing and contrasting different interviews and perceptions of the same subject or behavior are likely to produce clearer understanding by **triangulation** than any single perspective, such as that of a quantitative test or battery of tests.

Because of these strengths of nonreactivity (that is, the observer does not change the natural setting) and comprehensiveness of observation, it has been argued that qualitative observation is the standard by which other research methods can be judged. That is, the data of the qualitative observer may be more detailed and less distorted than those of other approaches. Thus, even though the quantitative criteria of reliability and validity cannot be applied to qualitative data, such data have an intuitive appeal as accurate and unbiased. For a more extensive debate about the relative merits of quantitative and qualitative methods, see the exchanges of Becker and Geer versus Trew in McCall and Simmons (1969). As will be seen, however, a research approach must provide more than valid observations; it must satisfy the other validity criteria that pertain to drawing causal inferences. For this reason, we will be interested in its design.

Design. That qualitative research can have a structure similar to that of quantitative studies is sometimes overlooked. For example, *When Prophecy Fails*, the study by Festinger, Riechen, and Schacter (1956), can be thought of as a single-group, interrupted time series quasi-experiment with repeated trials. Consider the experience of disconfirmation of belief as the independent variable. The believers experienced three such disconfirmations in a period of four days. Prior to, between, and following these disconfirmations, the observers attempted to note all proselytinglike behaviors of the believers (for example, calling the press with news releases, welcoming outsiders for persuasion sessions, and intensifying efforts to increase the faith of uncommitted members). This sequence of observations of proselyting (symbolized by O) and disconfirmations (symbolized by X) could be summarized in the usual diagrammatic way. The disconfirmations (Xs) occurred at 4 P.M. ($X1$) and midnight ($X2$) on December 17 and at midnight on December 20 ($X3$):

$$\dots O\ O\ O\ X1\ O\ X2\ O\ O\ O\ O\ O\ X3\ O\ O\ O\dots$$

If qualitative research can be understood as a variation of experimental or correlational designs, why treat it as a separate class? There are two main reasons. The first is that the nature of qualitative research necessarily complicates and blurs the design, as will be noted later. The second reason, which will be explored in the next section, pertains to the relation of research to theory and hypothesis formation. As will be seen, some qualitative researchers do not share the theory-testing assumptions of most quantitative researchers.

To illustrate the way experimental design is blurred in qualitative research, consider the timing and nature of the observations, or Os, in the example. Ordinarily in quantitative research, the measures are standardized tests or indicators gathered at the same time for all subjects, or at least in the same way over time. In *When Prophecy Fails*, the observations are necessarily incomplete. At the beginning of the study, several different observers gained entry at varying times to the inner circle of believers in two different locations. After entry, observations were possible only when at least one observer could be present, and not all members and activities of the group could be observed even when observers were present because sometimes, the believers met privately in pairs or small groups. At times, the observers had to leave to record their notes or to sleep. Thus the apparent completeness and regularity of the observations implied by the sequence of Os understates the gaps in the observational record.

Aside from such gaps, the observers necessarily varied over time in what their understanding, roles, and fatigue allowed them to see. As participants, their roles changed from curious strangers to full members to potential leaders. Believers sometimes asked the observers to conduct group meetings and even wondered if the observers might not be aliens from Clarion present to evaluate them. In sometimes lengthy meetings, the observers no doubt became weary and oscillated between boredom and emotional arousal.

Such variation was further compounded by the development of the observers' familiarity with and conceptualization of the people and situations under observation. For example, the principal investigators were interested in measuring increases in proselyting behavior. But what should or could be considered increased proselyting behavior? The range and classification of potential proselyting behaviors grew and crystallized with experience in participant observation in the particular setting. The regularity of the repeating *O*s in the diagram fails to reflect a necessarily disordered, dynamic, and uncontrolled measurement process. Thus, although qualitative research can be conceptualized in experimental or correlational design terms and shares similar internal validity threats, it is much less ordered and is more vulnerable to certain threats (for example, changes in instrumentation).

Differences from Other Approaches. Qualitative research can be placed in the context of the other major research approaches. On a continuum of researcher's control, true experiments would fall at the high end and qualitative research at the low end. In true experiments, researchers control the assignment of subjects to groups that are given different experiences invented by the researcher. In contrast, the qualitative researcher has only the power to visit the subjects in their natural habitat and observe them nonquantitatively, constantly adapting the observational strategy to the rhythm, style, and preferences of the subjects.

The most obvious difference between quantitative and qualitative research can be seen in the notational system used to report the findings. Numbers, figures, and inferential statistics appear in the results sections of quantitative studies. In contrast, qualitative research typically reads like a story written in everyday language. A stranger enters a group or community, gets acquainted, has experiences and relationships, and then shares the insights gained on reflection.

RATIONALE: SCIENTIFIC APPROACH AND FEASIBILITY

How does the investigator decide whether to work quantitatively or qualitatively? To some extent, investigators are limited by their training and tend to use the method that feels most comfortable and effective. But two other factors also influence the choice of method. One of these is the general scientific approach of the scholar. Different philosophies of knowledge point to different methods of gathering and presenting information. The other factor has to do with the practical limits on the way researchers can operate. As mentioned in the previous section, research strategies vary in the amount of control required of the investigator. Sometimes qualitative research is the most or only feasible method, given the nature of the subjects and their environment.

Models of Knowing

Positivism Versus Phenomenology. To this point, this text has presented an approach to knowing that characterizes most of quantitative social research. Growing out of the tradition of **positivism,** this approach seeks to understand the general principles (or laws) that apply to any set of specific events or experiences. Implicit in this positivist approach is the assumption that there is an objective reality that we can see, however dimly, and that exists independently of the perceiver. The business of science is to come to "know" this objective, underlying reality. Quantitative social research proceeds by offering tentative laws (called theories), which are then subjected to empirical verification, that is, attempts to disconfirm the tentative laws through their testable implications, called hypotheses. (For more detail on this approach, see Cook & Campbell, 1979, chap. 1, and the appreciation of Campbell's epistemology in Brewer & Collins, 1981, pt. I.)

Quantitative or numerical methods are convenient for summarizing results, assessing measurement reliability and validity, testing inferences from samples (statistical inference validity), and planning precise research designs with high internal validity. As a consequence, qualitative or nonnumerical methods will be utilized only under two circumstances. One of these conditions, given positivist assumptions and goals, is when quantitative procedures are not feasible. In such a case, the fitness of a theory may still be tested by comparing the hypotheses with qualitative data. As will be seen in the next section, the qualitative method of participant observation may have the essential advantages of minimal reactivity or even total unobtrusiveness.

The second condition occurs when the researcher does not subscribe to positivist assumptions (for example, Patton, 1980, pp. 44–46; Smart, 1976, p. 77). Some researchers do not accept that there exists, or that they have the responsibility of seeking, an objective, underlying reality. Rather, they have more interest in understanding daily life and activities from the actor's subjective point of view. The concern with understanding the point of view of the "subject" derives from different sources. One source, which has given its name to a style of research within sociology, is called **symbolic interactionism.** This perspective emphasizes

> (1) human beings act toward things on the basis of the meanings that the things have for them; (2) these meanings are a product of social interaction in human society; and (3) these meanings are modified and handled through an interpretive process that is used by each person in dealing with the things he/she encounters. (Meltzer, Petras, & Reynolds, 1975, p. 54)

If there is no objective reality or at least none that is ascertainable, the reality is what the actor thinks, feels, and says it is. One implication of this view is that there is no reason to impose an external theory on the subjective views of the actors. Preconceived hypotheses, constructs, and measures will only hinder the researcher in understanding the actor from the actor's point of view. This understanding is the essence of the philosophical perspective called **phenomenology.** When applied to the social sciences, this perspective emphasizes that social "facts," unlike physical facts, are "characterized by and only recognizable because of their meaningfulness for members in the social world" (Smart, 1976, p. 74). It follows that the researcher's primary task is to discover the meaning of things and events to the members of the social group of interest.

This phenomenological approach has had particular appeal in anthropology, where it is embodied in a methodology called **ethnography** or ethnomethodology. Although the term suggests a general method for describing (*graphy*) a cultural group (*ethno*), it has come to mean the particular method of describing a social group from the group's point of view. "The ethnographer tries to obtain the cultural knowledge of the natives" (Werner & Schoepfle, 1987a, p. 23). Such an approach would be especially relevant to anthropology because that social science is confronted with the special problem of **ethnocentrism,** that is, perceiving other cultures from the perspective of one's own cultural assumptions and biases. How far some ethnographers have distanced themselves from the positivist perspective is illustrated by the following definition: "Ethnomethodology is not a method of pursuing the truth about the world. Rather, it examines the many versions, including its own, of the way the world is assembled" (Mehan & Wood, 1975, p. 114). When carried to its extreme, this phenomenological approach implies an immersion in the studied group in which "the researcher must begin by first becoming the phenomenon . . . a full-time member of the reality to be studied" (p. 227).

The ethnographic approach is necessarily qualitative. Consider the classic study *Tally's Corner* (Liebow, 1967). Elliot Liebow, then a graduate student of anthropology, wanted to understand the nature of life among a small group of poor black men centered on a corner in an inner city. Tally was a 31-year-old man who became one of Liebow's **key informants,** that is, a source of interview information and a main link between the social scientist and the rest of Tally's social circle.

Consistent with the phenomenological approach, Liebow's goal was to describe "lower-class life of ordinary people, on their own grounds and on their terms. . . . [The data] were to be collected with the aim of gaining a clear, firsthand picture . . . rather than of testing specific hypotheses . . . [with] no firm presumptions of what was or was not relevant" (Liebow, 1967, p. 10). The avoidance of seeking objective general laws is explicit elsewhere: "The present attempt, then, is not aimed directly at developing generalizations about lower-class life from one particular segment of the lower class at a particular time and place but rather to examine this one segment in miniature . . . " (p. 16).

The emphasis on seeing the world through the eyes of the actors is exemplified in Liebow's analysis of time perspective. He notes that one theory explains lower-class behavior in terms of a defect—the absence of a sufficiently well-developed future time orientation. Liebow attempts to understand the same behavior not from the standpoint of a theory but from that of the men. He sympathetically takes the side of his subjects and tries to persuade the reader also to see through the actor's eyes: "Thus, when Richard squanders a week's pay in two days it is not because, like an animal or a child, he is present-time oriented, unaware of or unconcerned with his future. He does so precisely because he is aware of the future and the hopelessness of it" (Liebow, 1967, p. 66). Liebow quotes Richard's rationale: "'I've been scuffing for five years from morning till night. And my kids still don't have anything, and I don't have anything'" (p. 67). Liebow concludes that the "apparent present-time concerns with consumption and indulgences—material and emotional—reflect a future-time orientation. I want mine right now is ultimately a cry of despair, a direct response to the future as he sees it" (p. 68).

Hypotheses: Before, After, or Never. The preceding discussion can be summarized as follows: Qualitative research may be employed within either the positivist framework or a phenomenological approach such as ethnography. In the latter case, interviews and observation will be aimed at in-depth understanding without theoretical preconception and without the goal of formulating general laws that go beyond the particulars of the people, place, and time studied. In this case, qualitative research will not be organized around hypotheses as usually defined. The qualitative researcher may speculate, after the data have been collected and interpreted, about the implications for wider segments of the population. However, theory as a formal statement of objective laws is not claimed.

Research that attempts only to portray phenomena has been termed descriptive. Since our focus is on causal rather than descriptive research, we will be more interested in qualitative research that employs hypotheses and is based on the positivist approach to knowing.

Causal research that is structured to test prior hypotheses is called **confirmatory research.** Alternatively, the research may begin without specific hypotheses but only a general question, in which case it is called **exploratory research.** In this case, hypotheses are generated from the data. Such *post hoc* hypotheses may then be tested in the usual hypothesis-first, confirmatory way.

A clear example of the confirmatory, hypothesis-first type of qualitative research appears in our opening example from *When Prophecy Fails*. Early on, the authors state five conditions under which they expect to see increased proselyting following disconfirmation. Together, these conditions represent testable hypotheses (Festinger, Reichen, & Schachter, 1956, p. 4).

In contrast, exploratory qualitative research seeks to build theory rather than test it. In commenting on this exploratory process, one qualitative researcher noted, "Model building is an ongoing process. Because a participant-observer does not go into the field with a hypothesis, the end point of such a study is not always obvious. The construction of the model signals the end of the study, and first attempts at model building usually are made long before the researcher leaves the field" (Browne, 1976, pp. 81–82). As illustrated by *When Prophecy Fails*, the participant-observer can go into the field with hypotheses. However, there are necessarily times at the beginning of genuinely original projects when the existing theory is judged inadequate or even misleading. The researcher feels the need for exposure to the data without preconception in order to discover and formulate a fresh theory.

An example of the exploratory approach comes from another study of a cult predicting the end of the world. A graduate sociology student was curious about how cults recruit and retain members in the face of a disapproving and even hostile society (Lofland, 1966). Almost single-handedly, the researcher observed the group for about 15 hours per week for the first nine months and for four days per week as a live-in participant for another three months. The product of this research was not only a description of the formation of a particular cult but also some general principles that could be translated into testable hypotheses. For example, Lofland articulated a series of conditions for recruitment into a cult that together represent a model or theory of conversion (chap. 3).

Another example illustrates how the exploratory qualitative researcher can sometimes fill in the gaps in existing theory. Research has documented the overarching relationship between poverty and low academic achievement. One explanation for this relationship is the self-fulfilling prophecy, that is, that the low expectations for poor students help cause their low performance. However, the earliest empirical confirmations of this theory did not spell out the mechanism by which the self-fulfilling prophecy operated within particular teacher-student interactions. One researcher took as his goal "to provide an analysis both of the factors that are critical in the teacher's development of expectations for various groups of her pupils and of the process by which such expectations influence the classroom experience for the teacher and the student" (Rist, 1970, p. 413). The conceptual product of the observation of one class of children from kindergarten through second grade was five general propositions and a number of interactional processes that were detailed in stages. Such propositions and processes can be translated into testable hypotheses in quantitative terms through the operationalization of the constructs.

In summary, qualitative research may or may not entail hypotheses. Typically, qualitative research in the phenomenological tradition is descriptive rather than causal and focuses on the particular actors being observed rather than on generalizations to the larger population. On the other hand, if the researcher works in the positivist tradition, he or she will necessarily need some hypotheses. Since this researcher will be concerned with causal laws of general applicability, he or she will either test prior hypotheses (confirmation) or generate new ones (exploration).

Feasibility

Qualitative research may be the preferred method when hypotheses cannot be operationalized in quantitative terms. One instance occurs when the theory is insufficiently developed to provide well-defined hypotheses. Another occurs when the natural social situation provides the only or best laboratory but cannot be entered with the usual standardized measurement techniques, for example, when the actors under observation would change their behavior in response to being measured quantitatively.

Sometimes actors will tolerate a known observer in their midst but will not respond naturally in the presence of quantitative procedures. In such a case, qualitative measures serve well because they are less reactive, in the sense that they do not constantly remind the actors of their being observed. Other times, actors would not behave normally or speak frankly if they knew they were being observed at all. In this case, qualitative measures may be used by participants who wish to conceal their observer status. In such a case, the observation is entirely unobtrusive.

Nonreactive Data Collection. The essence of participant observation is immersion in the natural, undistorted social processes under study. To the extent that observing the social phenomenon changes it, the value of the research will have been lessened or even lost. The greatest advantage, in principle, of qualitative over many quantitative methods is that the participant-observer procedure is less reactive.

Nevertheless, there always remains the risk that the actors will change their behavior or conversation in the presence of the observer. As Becker says, the researcher "must learn how group members define him and in particular whether or not they believe that certain kinds of information and events should be kept hidden from him. He can interpret evidence more accurately when the answers to these questions are known" (Becker, 1958, pp. 655–656). If the reactivity cannot be eliminated entirely, perhaps it can be adjusted for in the final analysis.

However, participant-observers have good reason to believe that their data are relatively little distorted by their presence. Gaining admission to the field and acceptance by the key informants means that they are entrusted with a large measure of confidence. If the actors wish to conceal themselves, it will be much simpler and more effective to deny the observer entry than to sustain a charade for the potentially hundreds or thousands of hours of the observer's presence. This long duration, the multiple informants, and the many cross-comparisons of observational and interview data (or triangulation) all tend to discourage any sustained reaction on the part of the actors.

Consider Rist's (1970) two and one-half years of observing the same students in kindergarten, first grade, and second grade. However peculiar and reactive his presence may have been initially, as a nonteaching adult, he surely was accepted and ignored after a while. After the novelty wears off, such an observer's presence is not likely to have much effect on five- and six-year-olds with their own games, lessons, and friendships to pursue. Similarly, Lofland's (1966) involvement with his doomsday cult must also have passed through an early reactive stage. After months of involvement, approval of his presence by the leadership, and finally residential status in the group, his observations seem unlikely to have been tainted by reactivity. Once the observer has gained entry and established an acceptable role, unstructured interviewing and observation is probably a safely nonreactive data-gathering method.

Despite the reasons for trusting the accuracy of qualitative research, some studies have been challenged on grounds that the observer was misled by the observed. One of the most controversial of these challenges appeared in Derek Freeman's critique of Margaret Mead's research in Samoa. In 1925, Mead was a young student going to study adolescence, a developmental period known in

American and European cultures for its emotional stresses and conflicts. Mead reported, in contrast, that Samoan adolescence was more relaxed because promiscuity before marriage was permitted. This finding was consistent with her belief that adolescent turmoil was due not to biology but rather to cultural restrictions. Freeman contends that Mead's characterization of Samoan adolescence was incorrect because Samoans place a high value on female virginity. Mead was misled, Freeman argues, by her young female informants, who were simply teasing her (Freeman, 1983, pp. 288–291). Mead went on to become a world-famous anthropologist and, in death, can no longer defend her fieldwork. However, the fact that such doubts can be raised about informants points to an inherent vulnerability of this methodology.

Unobtrusive Participant Role. To minimize reactivity and to gain entry into otherwise forbidden settings, the researcher may have to be **unobtrusive,** that is, operate without informing the actors of his or her observational role. Again, as summarized by Becker (1958), if the observer works undisclosed, "participating as a fullfledged member of the group, he will be privy to knowledge that would normally be shared by such a member and might be hidden from an outsider. He could properly interpret his own experiences as that of a hypothetical typical group member" (p. 655).

Commonly, the participant-observer's role will be unknown to some actors. For example, as Liebow (1967) moved among Tally's circle of acquaintances, not all of the actors were equally informed of his observational role. He might be known as Tally's friend, with whatever that implied, but it is possible that not all of the actors knew that he was compiling extensive notes on their conversations and actions.

The ultimate potential cost of being a known or obtrusive observer is illustrated by Lofland's (1966) experience. Although initially tolerated as a self-identified observer, he was finally excluded from the group when it became clear that he was not going to convert. Apparently, he was allowed entry only in order to provide a better opportunity to recruit him.

Lofland's exclusion is pertinent as a contrast to the situation in *When Prophecy Fails* (Festinger, Reichen, & Schachter, 1956). That research team elected to enter the cult as participants not identified as observers. As a result, the observers obtained access to the final days of the group. Observation of the aftermath of the disconfirmation might otherwise have been denied them as the cult became more concerned about its public image and paranoid about its possible persecution. Such disguised or unobtrusive qualitative studies are fairly common.

Ethical Issues. However, such studies raise serious ethical problems. Genuinely unobtrusive qualitative research cannot proceed if the observed are told of the study and asked to give informed consent. Consequently, the researcher and the human subject protection committee that reviews his or her plan must assess the subjects' risks and the researchers' ability to protect their confidentiality.

Sometimes field researchers have to protect their field notes. An example is the case of a sociology student named Mario Brajuha who had been working and observing in a restaurant that subsequently burned down (Thaler, 1985). A New York State grand jury demanded to see his notes for an arson investigation. Brajuha was prepared to testify about some of his observations but felt obliged to protect some communications, which he felt were privileged and private. The state's case against Brajuha was dismissed when a compromise was worked out in which an edited version of his research journal was offered in evidence.

METHODOLOGY: TECHNIQUES AND VALIDITY THREATS

Techniques

The methodology of qualitative research includes the techniques of semi-structured interviewing and participant observation in natural field settings. This methodology can be broken down into a series of steps: (1) gaining entry; (2) category definition and data collection; (3) data recording; and (4) analysis. The following brief discussion will address each of these steps. For detailed guides to participant observation, see such treatments as Lofland (1971), Schwartz and Jacobs (1979, pt. II), and Werner and Schoepfle (1987a, 1987b). Many examples of the problems and procedures of qualitative research can be found in Glazer (1972) and Golden (1976, chap. 2).

Entry. For a social scientist to function, he or she must be present during the behavior and must occupy a role that does not cause the actors to change their natural behavior. Of course, the researcher can attempt to gather data by interview only. Sometimes, one or more key informants, actors from the setting of interest, will provide information about the setting to the interviewer. However, data drawn only from informants are usually regarded as unsatisfactory.

Although helpful in suggesting important categories of observation and subjective interpretations of data, informants have additional value as contacts linking the researcher to the informant's network. Thus the researcher typically begins the **entry** process by persuading one or more members of the setting to accept him or her. If an observer role can be defined that is satisfactory for these initial contacts, the observer will usually be accepted by other members as well. For example, Lofland (1966) and the Festinger team (1956) both found that acceptance could be accomplished by approval from the central leadership of each cult under study.

The method of gaining acceptance by key members of a setting varies with the nature of the setting. In some settings, the observer's role may be known to the key informants (for example, Tally in *Tally's Corner*). In others, acceptance may be judged possible only if the participant conceals his or her interest in observation (for example, *When Prophecy Fails*). In both cases, the participant's role must permit him or her to be curious and in need of instruction by other members. Sometimes such a "student" role is natural, as in the case of prospective recruits to a cult's belief system. In other cases, the observer may "purchase" his or her entry and continued presence in some way—for example, by conferring status or offering aid (such as Liebow offered to one of Tally's friends in a legal matter). After a while, the observer may enjoy the bond of friendship with one or more of the setting's members. Possibly one or more actors will become interested in the researcher's task and support the activity out of curiosity or a desire to produce the best possible report about his or her own setting.

Category Definition and Data Collection. In the typical quantitative study, category or variable definition precedes data collection. In contrast, participant-observers are guided by general questions, which cannot be translated into standardized measuring procedures. As a result, the participant-observer simultaneously engages both in observing and in choosing what and how to observe. For example, the Festinger team (1956) knew at the beginning that they wanted to study proselyting. But how proselyting would appear in behavioral terms had to be discovered in the process of observing. Thus, such acts as being more or less responsive to callers from the media came to be included in the category of behaviors representing proselyting.

The alternating processes of observation and of category or variable specification repeat or iterate throughout the study. This approach has the advantage of helping to avoid blinding preconceptions and rigid measurement procedures. The flexibility and sensitivity may allow profound penetration of the subject matter. The counterparts to these advantages are threats of measurement unreliability, instrumentation shift, and bias.

Recording Data. What is to be observed will vary from study to study, depending on the topics, and over time within a study, evolving with the definitions of the categories and the researcher's interests. Lofland has noted that different levels of analysis may be of interest to the observer, ranging from brief acts up to entire settings, and that recorded observations may be analyzed to provide either static cross-sectional or longitudinal descriptions (Lofland, 1971, pp. 14–15).

How does the observer make sure that the full range of categories is comprehensively covered and recorded? Comprehensive observation requires the observer to be present at the times and places of the actions of interest. Unless the observer knows in advance when these activities are going to occur, he or she must take up virtual residence in the setting. If information is to be gained by interviewing, the interviewer has more control of when and where the interview will take place. However, since the standardized questionnaires of quantitative research are not feasible, informal interviewing must be semistructured along some preset guidelines. An **interview guide** may be written or memorized and provides a checklist of topics that the interviewer wants to cover. These checklists include reminders about the categories of interest to the researcher in an order that seems likely to promote rapport (usually holding more threatening questions until later). The guide provides only a general approach. The actual questions are composed on the spot to fit the natural rhythm of the dialogue and to promote maximum, unbiased disclosure by the interviewee. The art of such interviewing requires a sensitive ear and the ability to probe gently without suggesting any desired answers.

The material elicited by the interviewer can be recorded either by tape recorder (if the interviewer is known as an observer, if the presence of the recorder is not reactive, and if the project can afford to transcribe the audiotapes) or by handwritten notes. In either case, the resulting transcripts should be labeled with pertinent information such as the interviewee's identification (name or code number), demographic characteristics, and location in the social network or setting under study along with the time and place of the interview.

In the case of unrecorded interviews and of observations of behaviors in the setting, the observer must make the notes as extensive and accurate as possible. Field notes should be recorded as soon as possible after observation. Since conspicuous note taking may spoil the observer's accepted role, the observer may have to make brief notes of key words and phrases in fleeting moments of privacy (for example, going to the bathroom, or stepping out for a walk). As soon as possible thereafter and certainly before the end of the day, full, detailed notes should be constructed from the jotted notes and recollections. Since it is easier and faster to talk than write, some researchers compose their full notes on a tape recorder. Whether taped or handwritten, these notes should then be typed with multiple copies. One copy can be kept as a permanent record of the raw data. Other copies can be cut up, rearranged, and annotated as part of the analytic process. Because qualitative research may extend for months and the researcher does not want to omit any potentially useful details, the resulting typescripts can easily run to hundreds or thousands of pages.

Analysis. The analysis of qualitative data begins with the first observation. As the observational phase winds down, analysis becomes more intense. The goal of analysis is to organize the hundreds of pages of raw observational notes into a meaningful pattern. The essence of this task is the interconnection of discrete observations within a small number of conceptual categories. It is analogous to a jigsaw puzzle. The researcher fits and refits the pieces according to a variety of preliminary models until there are no or few pieces left over and the fit seems subjectively and logically satisfying.

The resulting "jigsaw" picture must still be presented clearly and convincingly in a final report. A common method of telling the story of the qualitative research project is to relate quotations from interviews and anecdotes from the field observations as illustrations of and support for the analyst's general argument. If the analyst produces a causal model, the approximate frequency and distribution of the different categories of observation (for example, high versus low proselyting) are offered as evidence.

Validity Threats

There are numerous difficulties with the causal analysis of qualitative data (for advice in making such inferences, see Becker, 1958). In this final section, we will review qualitative methodology from the standpoint of each of the four main types of validity: construct, internal, statistical inference, and external (for a more extensive treatment see Kidder, 1981, and LeCompte & Goetz, 1982).

Construct Validity. Two different kinds of construct validity have been discussed—measurement and experimental operational. Both are vulnerable to threats in qualitative research. Measurement construct validity is particularly problematic. By definition, participant observation is unstandardized. As a result, observations are more than usually prone to random measurement error and, thus, unreliability. Measurement validity can be no greater than measurement reliability, and since the observations are nonquantitative, it is difficult to estimate the extent of unreliability. Because the observer often works alone, in varying circumstances, and with varying categories, there is good reason to expect unreliability to be a major problem.

Even if reliability were not a problem, there would still be concern for measurement construct validity. The measuring instrument in qualitative research is an individual without the support of standardized instruments. The observer intentionally uses his or her feelings, curiosity, hunches, and intuition to explore and understand the setting. Consequently, one observer may arrive at results quite different from another or from data collected by a different method. An example is the previously noted critique of Margaret Mead's analysis of Samoan culture by Freeman (1983).

The qualitative observer also runs the risk of being biased by the feelings, loyalties, or antagonisms generated by the setting and the actors in it. To achieve access to the most secret behaviors and perceptions of the actors, the observer must be or appear to be trustworthy and likable. Whether an observer can gain the necessary trust and friendship without reciprocating some genuine affection is arguable. The risk is that the observer will leave the neutral, even skeptical, role of scientist and adopt the role of committed member in the setting. Such a role shift is called **going native.** Practically speaking, it represents little threat to published research since it ordinarily terminates the study unless the observer elects to publish a propaganda piece.

Experimental construct validity is less pertinent to qualitative methodology since the researcher seldom intentionally creates experimental manipulations in the natural setting. On the other hand, the observer may welcome the opportunity to follow the consequences of naturally occurring changes. However, the entry of observers at or near the time of a natural experiment may change the meaning of the experimental change, as in *When Prophecy Fails*. Near the time that the cult was anticipating a major predicted event, the researcher introduced several new participant-observers. Some had cover stories that led the cult to increased confidence in their beliefs and social support resources. Thus, not only can the setting bias the observer but also the observer can change the setting, thereby distorting the results.

Internal Validity.   The design of qualitative research can at best approximate quasi-experimental designs, with all the threats to internal validity that implies. More commonly, qualitative studies resemble correlational designs, with no manipulation of the independent variable at all.

In correlational designs, causal inferences may be drawn, at varying risk of error, from the association of two variables. Unfortunately, qualitative research sometimes describes two characteristics, one or both of which are nonvarying. In such cases, no causal inference can be drawn because no association can be established. Descriptions of the coexistence of one level of one variable and one level of another variable say nothing about their causal linkage. For example, suppose that an observer notes that all ten members of a cult are right-handed. This information is summarized in Table 13–1.

A glance at this data might imply an association between being right-handed and cult membership. Is right-handedness a cause of cult interest or membership? It may be, but this imaginary data set does not support that inference. The problem is that there is no evidence about noncult members showing how many of them are right- *and* left-handed. The coexistence or coincidence of single levels of two variables without information about the other levels cannot support the claim of causation. Suppose we found that eight, nine, or ten out of ten noncult members were also right-handed. Such a finding would tend to indicate that most people, whether cult members or not, are right-handed.

Statistical Inference Validity.   In the last example, we saw how information collected qualitatively might be translated into quantitative terms. When such translations are done, usually by a contingency table, inferential statistics can be applied. More commonly, qualitative data are not amenable to inferential statistical analysis. As a result, the kind of validity tested by inferential statistics simply

Table 13-1. Right-Handedness and Cult Membership: An Imaginary Qualitative Data Set

	Right-Handed	Left-Handed
Cult Member	10	0
Noncult Member	Not observed	Not observed

cannot be assessed. This may or may not be a handicap, depending on the researcher's intention.

Remember that inferential statistics test how confidently we can generalize from a sample to the population from which the sample was drawn. Often, the qualitative researcher has little interest in generalizing to a larger population. If the researcher wants to describe in the deepest and most detailed possible way the characteristics of a unique setting or group, she or he may not desire a population-wide generalization.

External Validity. External validity is difficult to assess in any kind of research. There is no statistical procedure in quantitative research for estimating the confidence we can place in generalizations to other populations, places, or times. Thus qualitative research is at no disadvantage to other methodologies in this respect. Indeed, qualitative researchers typically have less interest in such generalizations since they often select cultures, subcultures, settings, or groups for their uniqueness.

SUMMARY

Qualitative research differs from quantitative research in its use of participant observation, semistructured interviewing, and nonstatistical methods of analysis and reporting. Whereas quantitative research may or may not take place in the field, qualitative research necessarily takes place in the natural setting and with a minimum of disturbance (that is, no intentional experimental manipulation).

Qualitative research is the preferred methodology of scientists who wish to describe everyday life from the point of view of the actors (phenomenological perspective). Since no objective laws are being sought, no hypotheses are stated. Qualitative research methods are also used by researchers in the positivist tradition. They may either test hypotheses that are derived from theory before the observations begin or generate hypotheses afterward. In the former case, qualitative research may be the only feasible way to gather data from subjects who would otherwise avoid known researchers or behave artificially in the face of reactive methods. In the latter case, qualitative methods are often appropriate because the theory is still too primitive to specify clear hypotheses or to suggest operational procedures for measuring constructs. The price of these advantages is a host of threats to construct, internal, and statistical inference validity.

Qualitative research begins with gaining entry into the target social setting and the establishment of a role in which the observer can acceptably make inquiries. Data collection consists of observing and interviewing, and these activities alternate continuously with reevaluation and reformulation of the variables and categories that guide observations. Because of the extensive but nonreactive nature of qualitative data collection, data recording will usually be lengthy but out of sight of the subjects, that is, brief note taking and/or later recording. These records become the pieces that, in the final analysis, are arranged into an internally consistent and logically satisfactory portrayal.

EXERCISES

1. The easiest route to understanding qualitative methods is to read and critique a report of such research. Short examples of qualitative literature can be found in readers (for example, Golden, 1976, chap. 2). For critical commentary on several qualitative studies, see Glazer's study (1972). Finally, for the deepest immersion, select one complete report (for example, any of those referred to in this chapter). While reading your selection, try to identify a pair of independent and dependent variables and the hypothetical causal connection between them. What validity threats are uncontrolled and how serious do they seem? Try to imagine and design a quantitative study that might test the same hypothesis (assuming your qualitative study has a hypothesis), while controlling for the major threats to the qualitative study. What advantage does the qualitative study have over your imaginary quantitative study (for example, feasibility or reactivity)?

2. A more demanding approach to understanding qualitative research is to attempt it yourself. Since a prolonged study is impractical as a training exercise, try to plan and execute the beginning stages of a modest qualitative study. Pick a setting or group to which you do not already belong but to which you might gain entry without risking harm to yourself or others. If you can formulate a general causal question, do so. If not, plan only to try to describe the setting and actors from their point of view. Make an attempt to gain entry, that is, visit, get acquainted with at least one actor, and observe and interview for a single session. While observing and interviewing, attempt to conceptualize one or two dimensions or characteristics of the setting or people around which you can organize your data. As soon as you leave the setting, write up your notes in as accurate and complete a form as possible. Then, sifting through your notes, write a brief report of your experience aimed at drawing a conclusion about your hypothesis, formulating a hypothesis if you had none on entry, or describing the actors' point of view. Consider in your report the ethical issue of observing others. Did you reveal yourself as an observer? If so, what was the probable effect? That is, was your observation reactive? If not, why not and at what risk to those you observed?

GLOSSARY

Confirmatory research: Data collection and analysis aimed at testing prior hypotheses.

Entry: Crucial first step in which the qualitative researcher gains access to the social setting to be studied.

Ethnocentrism: Perceptual bias because of one's own cultural beliefs.

Ethnography: Field research technique originating in anthropology that emphasizes the phenomenological approach.

Exploratory research: Data collection and analysis aimed at formulating hypotheses.

Field research: Generally, any social research taking place in a natural setting; more narrowly, equivalent to qualitative research.

Going native: Role shift in which the researcher gives up the neutral scientific perspective and becomes a committed member or proponent of the group under study.

Interview guide: Checklist of topics which the qualitative interviewer wants to cover.

Key informant: Member of a social setting who serves as a major source of information about the setting to a qualitative researcher.

Participant observation: Common qualitative research method in which the researcher enters the social setting to be studied and actively joins the subjects in their normal activities.

Phenomenology: Philosophical perspective that emphasizes the discovery of meaning from the point of view of the studied group or individual.

Positivism: Approach to knowledge based on the assumption of an objective reality that can be discovered by offering tentative theories and then testing them empirically.

Qualitative research: Social research based on nonquantitative observations made in the field and analyzed in nonstatistical ways.

Symbolic interactionism: Theoretical perspective that concerns itself with the meanings that things and events have for human beings and the production of these meanings in human interchange.

Triangulation: Method of comparing observations from different times and sources to arrive at a correct analysis.

Unobtrusive: With respect to qualitative research, unobtrusive observation involves entry and participation without the knowledge of the subjects that they are under scientific scrutiny, that is, without informing subjects of the observer's true status.

14

Interpreting Research
A Summary of Research Design and Methods of Review

ASSESSING INDIVIDUAL STUDIES

This first section will summarize the major types of validity and their threats. Since study designs differ in their vulnerability to such threats, it is useful to relate the type of threat to the type of design. After reviewing the basic designs and their common threats, we will consider a sequential strategy for assessing a research report's overall validity. The second section of this chapter discusses the evaluation of a literature, that is, reviewing many studies on the same question.

Designs and Threats

Guide to Research Designs. The major types of research designs are summarized in the decision tree of Figure 14–1. The first distinction is between

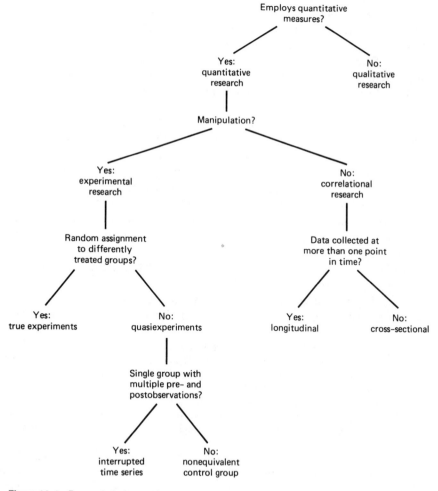

Figure 14–1   Research design typology.

qualitative and quantitative designs. In qualitative research, observations are collected and reported in everyday language, not statistically. In quantitative research, standardized measurement procedures are used to assign numbers to observations, and statistics are used to summarize the results.

Quantitative designs can be further divided into active or experimental designs and passive or correlational designs. If the causal variable is the result of a change, either an intentional manipulation by the researcher or some unplanned event such as a natural disaster, the design is an experiment. Experiments can be further divided into true experiments and quasi-experiments. True experiments are distinguished by the random assignment of subjects to differently treated groups.

Quasi-experiments are divided into two major types. Interrupted time series designs employ just one group (or subject) observed at several points before and after the manipulation(s). Nonequivalent control group designs employ two or more differently treated groups but lack random assignment. Two other types of quasi-experiments are infrequently encountered: (1) very weak preexperimental designs and (2) very strong combination designs such as interrupted time series with nonequivalent control groups.

Correlational designs can also be divided into subcategories. The most important distinction is between cross-sectional designs (or one-shot surveys) and longitudinal designs such as panel or trend surveys.

Guide to Validity Threats. Table 14–1 condenses the material in the preceding chapters on validity threats and types of research design. The basic design types are presented from left to right: true or randomized experiments, quasi-experiments, correlational studies, and qualitative studies. Arranged vertically are the four major types of validity: construct, internal, statistical inference, and external. Remember that the term *validity* refers to the probable truth of an assertion. These four types of validity represent four different types of concerns that we might have about the general assertion that "construct *A* causes construct *B*." When assessing the overall validity of such an assertion, we will proceed by considering the probable truthfulness of the assertion with respect to each of these four types of validity.

To summarize their meanings, each of the types of validity can be associated with a simple question illustrated visually in Figure 14–2 and verbally as follows:

Construct validity: Does the measured or manipulated variable reflect only or primarily the intended construct? A measure that reflects some unintended construct or nothing but random noise (that is, an unreliable measure) is said to have poor construct validity.

Internal validity: Is the observed effect due to the presumed cause or is the apparent relationship due to some other causal process? Internal validity pertains to the design of studies and involves the analysis of a variety of rival hypotheses or explanations.

Statistical inference validity: Does the observed relationship between the variables hold for the population from which the sample was drawn, or is it so

Table 14–1 Validity Threats and Research Designs

| | | DESIGN TYPES | | | | |
| | | QUASI-EXPERIMENTS | | CORRELATIONAL STUDIES | | |
Validity Types	TRUE EXPERIMENTS	Interrupted Time Series	Nonequivalent Control Groups	Longitudinal	Cross-sectional	QUALITATIVE STUDIES
1. *Construct*						
A. Measurement	√	√	√	√	√	*
B. Experimental	*	*	*	NA	NA	*
2. *Internal*						
A. Time		*		*		*
B. Group			*	*		*
C. Reverse causation					*	*
3. *Statistical inference*	√	√	√	√	√	*
4. *External*	*	*	*	*	*	*

Key: √ = threat should be checked in the data.
    * = threat difficult to check.
    NA = not applicable.
    blank = validity threat probably ruled out.

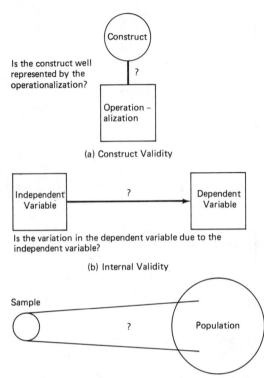

(a) Construct Validity

Is the construct well represented by the operationalization?

Is the variation in the dependent variable due to the independent variable?

(b) Internal Validity

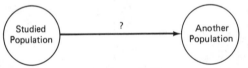

Is the sample estimate a good reflection of the population?

(c) Statistical Inference Validity

Can the findings in one population (place or time) be generalized to another population?

(d) External Validity.

Figure 14–2 Graphic summary of validity types.

small that it probably occurred by chance (that is, by sampling error)? This validity issue is judged by inferential statistics.

External validity: Does the observed relationship hold for other people, places, and times? In other words, is the sample of subjects, places, and times in the study appropriate as a basis for broader generalizations?

Two major subtypes of construct validity are noted in Table 14–1. Measurement construct validity refers to the validity of measures of passively observed phenomena. The most common threats to measurement construct validity come from poor measurement development, which leads to excessive random error (unreliability) or systematic error (measurement of the wrong construct). A different measurement problem is posed by mortality or attrition, which changes the sample on which measures are based.

In contrast, experimental construct validity refers to the validity of manipulated independent variables. Experimentally defined variables can be invalid because of contamination of either the experimental group or the control group. This problem area includes demand characteristics (for example, placebo effect), experimenter bias, and other such sources of contamination.

Internal validity threats can also be divided into subtypes, three of which are noted in Table 14–1. One type is the threat of reverse causation, which arises in cross-sectional correlational studies. Another type, time threats to single-group studies, include such rival explanations as history, maturation, instrumentation, pretest reactivity, and under certain conditions, regression to the mean (although regression to the mean can be controlled by means suitable to the group threats). These threats all represent causes, other than the independent variable, that can affect the dependent variable measured over time. The third type, group threats, includes selection, regression to the mean, and selection-by-time interactions. These threats usually involve preexisting differences between experimental and control groups, which can account for group differences or change scores. Selection also appears as a threat in correlational designs, where it is called confounding or spuriousness.

Design Strengths and Weaknesses. One validity threat that cannot be ruled out regardless of the research design type is external validity. Whether the study is a true experiment or a qualitative study, the generalizability of the results cannot be assumed. Only by careful comparison of the sample, situation, and time of the study with the population, location, and era of intended generalization can one judge external validity. For this reason, in Table 14–1 the asterisk (*) indicating "threat difficult to check" is placed in all design columns for external validity.

On all other validity dimensions (rows) in Table 14–1, different design types (columns) reveal different patterns of strengths and weaknesses. For example, statistical inference validity can be assessed with some precision in any study employing quantitatively measured variables and inferential statistics. Thus the checkmark ($\sqrt{}$) indicating "threat should be checked in the data" appears in the columns for all experimental and correlational designs. But in the column for qualitative studies, the asterisk indicates that this validity problem cannot be checked by inferential statistical methods. A similar pattern of checks and asterisks is found in the measurement construct validity row.

Experimental construct validity is not applicable in nonexperimental designs. Thus, the NA for "not applicable" appears for that row in the nonexperimental columns. In the true experimental and quasi-experimental columns, asterisks appear for experimental construct validity, indicating the difficulty with which this problem is assessed.

Finally, the internal validity threats form distinctive patterns across the design types. True experimental designs are generally considered immune to all threats to internal validity, as indicated by the blanks in the appropriate cells.

Quasi-experimental and correlational studies are protected from some internal validity threats but not others. Correlational studies are vulnerable to the threat of spuriousness, which can be checked only if the potential confounding variable is measured and controlled statistically—hence the asterisk in the group row. Depending on the temporal design, correlational studies are also vulnerable to time or reverse causation threats. Qualitative studies, with the least control, are vulnerable to all internal validity threats.

Strategy for Evaluation

Categorizing the Design.   The first task in evaluating a study is to identify the design used. As described in Figure 14–1, you might begin by determining whether the design is quantitative. Quantitative designs permit quantitative evaluation of measurement construct validity and of statistical inference validity. The checkmarks in the measurement validity and statistical inference validity rows for the quantitative design types reflect the possibility of quantitative assessment in these areas.

Quantitative designs are further divided into experimental and correlational designs by the presence or absence of an experimental manipulation. If at least one of the independent variables is created by intervention, whether naturally or by intention, the reader must assess experimental construct validity. The asterisks for experimental designs in the experimental construct validity row in Table 14–1 indicate that this assessment is often subjective and difficult. For example, one must judge whether demand characteristics (for example, a placebo effect) might have contaminated the experimental group experience and whether adequate countermeasures were taken (for example, a placebo control group).

Diagramming As an Aid to Checking Designs.   Internal validity threats in experimental designs depend on such design components as whether there is more than one group, whether groups are composed by random assignment, and whether measures are taken at more than one time before and after the experimental manipulation. Such characteristics of research designs can be conveniently diagrammed by using the notation of Xs for manipulated independent variables, Os for observations, and Rs for random assignment to groups. After diagramming the design, one can easily spot the internal validity threats of highest risk. In Table 14–2 a series of design diagrams are paired with possible threats to their internal validity.

One logical sequence for the assessment of validity concerns is the order presented in Table 14–1. After locating the specific subtype of the design, the evaluation can proceed down the appropriate column to assess each type of validity.

Construct Validity.   The first question in assessing the overall validity of an assertion from a study might be "Do the variables in the study reflect the studied constructs?" If the answer is no, the remaining validity issues are irrelevant. Even

Table 14–2 Some Design Diagrams and Internal Validity Threats

Design and Diagram	Threats
a. Single Group Preexperiment *O X O*	Time threats, e.g., maturation

b. Post-only Control Group
     Preexperiment
     X O
     O
	Group threats, e.g., selection

c. Interrupted Time Series
     Quasi-experiment
     O O O O X O O O O
	Time threats, e.g., history

d. Nonequivalent Control Group
     Quasi-experiment
     O X O
     O   O
	Group threats, e.g., selection-by-time
	interaction

e. True Experiment
     O X O
     R
        O   O
	Internal validity threats implausible

if the study has high internal validity, high external validity, and the results are not attributable to chance (statistical inference validity), the findings say nothing about the constructs of interest.

In the case of the experimental designs, present quantitative evidence about the construct validity of the measured dependent variables and any measured independent variables. In the case of the experimental designs, one or more of the independent variables will be fixed at different levels by intervention and cannot be assessed by quantitative validity coefficients. In such cases, the reader will have to inspect the experimental procedures for possible contamination.

Internal Validity. If the variables reflect the intended constructs, are the observed effects due only to the studied independent variable(s), or could they be the result of other causes? If the design is a randomized experiment or a very strong quasi-experiment (for example, an interrupted time series with control groups), we need not concern ourselves about internal validity. In such designs, the threats of time (for example, history), group (for example, selection), and reverse causation are ruled out by the design.

In the case of weak quasi-experiments, correlational designs, and qualitative studies, several internal validity threats remain uncontrolled. Only a careful inspection of the procedures and, sometimes, statistical controls (for example, partial correlation) can help check the plausibility of rival hypotheses. If the design is judged low in internal validity, our confidence in the study's results will be weakened regardless of the level of statistical significance. If we cannot determine the cause of an effect from a study because of the weak internal validity of the design, it does not make sense to generalize the results to other people, places, or times (external validity).

Statistical Inference Validity. If the study's measures and design are valid, the reader will next want to check the inferential statistics. Could the results in favor of the hypothesis be due to sampling error? Inferential statistics provide a probability estimate of the likelihood that we would obtain the observed results when in fact there is no relationship in the population. Since inferential statistics depend so heavily on the sample size, they cannot be used to gauge the magnitude of the relationship. A rather small, socially unimportant finding may reach statistical significance. Alternatively, a relatively large finding suggesting a substantial connection between the variables of interest may fail to reach statistical significance because of a small sample size or a low-power statistical test. As a consequence, the substantive interpretation of the results depends on the magnitude of the findings, not only the inferential statistics.

In the quantitative designs, inferential statistics will be routinely presented. Some readers go first to the inferential statistics to see whether the findings are sufficiently large (not due to chance) to warrant further inspection. However, stopping your analysis at this point would be a mistake because passing the inferential statistical validity test does not guarantee any of the other types of validity. Moreover, failure to reach statistical significance may, under certain circumstances (adequately large sample size, reliable measures, or sound design), be an interesting negative finding suggesting useful interpretations. Since most studies include numerous variables and hypotheses, there will be many different inferential statistics, one for each test. To interpret the pattern of findings, some significant and others not, you will need to understand the different variables (some with more construct validity than others) and the nature of the different design components (some with more internal validity than others). Thus an appreciation of the meaning of the inferential statistics will require prior consideration of the measures and design.

External Validity. If an assertion is regarded as valid on each of the three preceding types of validity, it is appropriate to consider external validity. If, however, a research finding is regarded as doubtful because it is due to chance, the product of a design with low internal validity, or based on invalid measures, its generalizability hardly warrants consideration.

The external validity question is this: "Does the finding of this particular study hold for other people, situations, or times?" One can best answer this question by repeating the study with different subjects, in different situations and places, and at later times. Such replications test the generalizability, not to all people, places, and times, but only to the subjects, situations, and time used in the replications. If the assertion from a study is generally true, it should show up in any subsequent replication. Thus any failure to replicate casts some doubt on the external validity of a previous finding.

Successful replications (however many) cannot establish absolute external validity. There is always another population-place-time combination not yet studied. However, numerous replications that test the assertion in many different combinations of population, place, and time can lend credence to an assertion. If the assertion is theoretically unaffected by population, place, and time, these variables can be regarded as irrelevant. Such varied or **heterogeneous irrelevancies** in replications ensure that the findings are not due to the coincidental combination of just one type of subject in a particular situation at a particular time. Partial replications, those that differ from the original study on such irrelevancies, are both desirable and frustrating. Very often different studies of the same question yield different answers. The next problem in evaluating research is to assess the conflicting results from multiple studies.

EVALUATING MULTIPLE STUDIES

Establishing Facts and Resolving Conflicts

Unfortunately, multiple studies of the same question rarely achieve unanimous agreement on the same answer. A research area that produces conflicting findings invites a **literature review** to accomplish one or both of two main goals: identifying any "facts" that *can* be agreed upon and suggesting new explanations that can reconcile the conflict.

Selecting Studies for Review. The first step in reviewing a literature is to define it. That is, which studies are to be included in the assessment? Typically, the reviewer specifies the hypothesis or research question that the studies are to have in common. For example, does preschool enrichment provide long-term educational benefits (for a review of this literature, see McKey, Condelli, Ganson, Barrett, McConkey, & Plantz, 1985)? Ideally, the reviewer then assembles all available studies of the specified type. If some studies are overlooked, we cannot know if the reviewer's conclusion applies to all studies or only to a biased selection of studies.

Since assembling all studies may prove impossible or impractical, reviewers often limit their analysis by time (for example, all studies published after 1975) or location (say, all studies published in English-language journals). Studies can be selected for review on other criteria as well, including some that can have major effects on the reviewer's conclusions.

One criterion for study selection involves the operationalization of constructs. For example, the construct of the impact of preschool enrichment has been measured in different ways—cognitive development, socioemotional development, and child health. One could review only those studies that measured students' educational achievement on standardized tests. Alternatively, the reviewer could choose studies with all types of outcome measures, either treated together or presented and interpreted in measure-specific clusters. The latter approach has the advantage of identifying possible differences in the effects on different outcome indicators.

Another type of selection criterion is the quality of the study. One point of view is that credence should be placed only in the best available studies—those with the most valid measures and designs. In this approach, each study would be evaluated and graded separately along the lines described in the first part of this chapter. Only the studies meeting or surpassing certain validity requirements would be reviewed. Another point of view favors including all studies on the same question but reviewing them separately by type of design or level of validity. This approach permits testing the possibility that the likelihood of results in favor of the hypothesis varies with the quality of the study.

Establishing the Facts. Perhaps the most common motivation for literature reviews is to determine what findings are most prevalent or credible. Because of the probabilistic nature of inferential statistics, we expect that some statistically significant results are found by chance. In any large sample of studies, we expect to find a few results that are accidental. By reviewing many studies together, we expect such inferential errors to stand out as exceptions to the pattern of "true" findings.

Several different studies of the same type on the same topic can provide more confidence in a finding than can any single study because virtually every study will have some uncontrolled validity threats. If all studies have the same validity threats, they are all doubtful for the same reason. But if different studies are vulnerable to different validity threats, no single threat will impinge on all studies. For all such studies to be invalid, you would have to assume a very complex and unlikely set of events or conditions. Thus a time threat to the internal validity of an interrupted time series analysis might be controlled in a nonequivalent control group analysis of the same issue. At the same time, the interrupted time series design checks on the selection threat to the nonequivalent control group design. Neither study alone would be convincing, but together they allow more confidence for the reviewer's interpretation.

An example of a review that sought and found near consensus was Durlak's (1979) study of the comparative effectiveness of professional and paraprofessional psychological helpers (therapists, counselors, advisers, and so on). Durlak identified 42 studies in which professionals and nonprofessionals were compared. In the great majority of these studies (28), no difference was found. Of the minority of studies in which there was a statistically significant difference, most favored the paraprofessional (12 of the 14). Durlak concluded from his review that paraprofessionals are equal to or better than professionals as measured by client outcomes. The studies were subcategorized by five levels of research deficiency, but design deficiency did not seem to be related to the overall conclusion (see Table 14–3).

Resolving Conflicts. In other cases, the reviewer may not find consensus in a literature. Even after controlling for quality, there will be too many sound studies on both sides of the question to settle the issue, and reviewers will suspect that some unidentified variable accounts for the discrepant findings. Suppose *A* appears to cause *B* in some studies but not in others. Is there some variable *C* that is present when *A* causes *B* but absent in those studies in which *A* does not cause *B*? If so, *C* is said to interact with *A* to cause *B*, or in other words, to condition the effect of *A* on *B*. Such an interaction is at the heart of the problem of external validity.

A good example of the search for such a **conditioning factor** is provided by Collins and Hoyt (1972). These authors began with a persistent discrepancy in the literature on attitude change under forced compliance. Researchers had noted that when obliged to engage in counterattitudinal behavior (for example, giving a speech advocating a position opposite to one's own belief), people would shift their attitude to become more consistent with their behavior. One explanation was based on dissonance reduction theory, which held that people are uncomfortable with dissonant or inconsistent cognitions such as holding one attitude while arguing in favor of the opposite view. Research found that subjects given smaller inducements to engage in the counterattitudinal behavior were more likely to change their beliefs, a finding interpreted as support for the dissonance reduction theory. Subjects who were paid less to argue against their belief should feel greater dissonance because they have less reason (that is, less pay) for suffering the conflict. However, other research cast doubt on this theory, with results showing that greater incentives were associated with greater attitude change. Both kinds of studies were well conducted, and the disagreement could not be resolved by rejecting one set of studies on validity grounds.

Collins and Hoyt (1972) reviewed this conflicting literature to find a way of reconciling its differences. They pointed out that the monetary incentive research method was confusing because other explanations (besides dissonance theory) could account for the findings. They argued that the crucial missing ingredient was whether subjects were made to feel responsible for an important consequence of their counterattitudinal behavior. They predicted that low monetary inducement would lead to more attitude change under conditions of high responsibility and consequence, consistent with dissonance theory. A new study produced from their analysis of the literature supported this revised theory. Thus a careful review of many conflicting studies led to the identification of new conditioning variables (responsibility and consequence) that are involved in the relationship of interest.

Review Methods

There are a variety of ways of reviewing or combining the results of multiple studies. One type of strategy requires the reviewer to obtain the data on which the various studies are based (for example, Cook & Gruder, 1978; Light &

Table 14–3 Characteristics, Outcome, and Experimental Quality of Comparative Studies of Paraprofessional and Professional Helpers

Study	Experimental Quality	Paraprofessional Helpers	Client and Helper Sample Size[a]	Results Significantly Favoring
Group 1: Individual or group psychotherapy or counseling				
Ellsworth (1968)	A	Psychiatric aides	327 psychiatric inpatients (?, ?)	Paraprofessionals
Jensen (1961)	B	Nurses and attendants	75 psychiatric inpatients[b] (?, 3)	Neither group
Karlsruher (1976)	B	College students	60 school children[b] (20, 6)	Neither group
Miles, McLean, & Maurice (1976)	B	Medical students	120 psychiatric inpatients (60, 27)	Neither group
O'Brien, Hamm, Ray, Pierce, Luborsky, & Mintz (1972)	B	Medical students	86 psychiatric outpatients (4, 12)	Neither group
Truax (1967)	B	Adult women	Over 300 vocational rehabilitation clients (4, 4)	Paraprofessionals
Truax & Lister (1970)	B	Adult women	168 vocational rehabilitation clients (4, 4)	Paraprofessionals
Weinman, Kleiner, Yu, & Tillson (1974)	B	Community volunteers	179 psychiatric outpatients (?, ?)	Neither group
Anker & Walsh (1961)	C	Occupational therapist	56 psychiatric inpatients (1, 1)	Paraprofessional
Appleby (1963)	C	Psychiatric aides	53 psychiatric inpatients[b] (?, ?)	Neither group
Colarelli & Siegel (1966)	C	Psychiatric aides	477 psychiatric inpatients (8, ?)	Neither group
Cole, Oetting, & Miskimins (1969)	C	Adult women	22 adolescent delinquents[b] (2, 2)	Neither group
Engelkes & Roberts (1970)	C	Adult counselors	1,502 vocational rehabilitation clients (142, 67)	Neither group
Mosher, Menn, & Matthews (1975)	C	Adult counselors	44 psychiatric inpatients (6, ?)	Paraprofessionals
Poser (1966)	C	College students	295 psychiatric inpatients[b] (11, 15)	Paraprofessionals
Sheldon (1964)	C	General physicians and nurses	83 psychiatric outpatients (?, ?)	Professionals better than physicians but equal to nurses
Mendel & Rapport (1963)	D	Psychiatric aides	166 psychiatric outpatients (?, ?)	Neither group
Covner (1969)	E	Community volunteers	Alcoholics[c] (?, ?)	Neither group
Magoon & Golann (1966)	E	Adult women	Psychiatric outpatients[c] (8, ?)	Neither group
Group 2: Academic counseling or advising for college students				
Zunker & Brown (1966)	A	College students	320 college students (8, 4)	Paraprofessionals
Brown & Myers (1975)	C	College students	303 college students (?, ?)	Neither group
Zultowski & Catron (1976)	C	College students	188 college students (10, ?)	Neither group
Murray (1972)	C	College students	166 college students (20, 9)	Neither group

Table 14–3   (Cont.)

Study	Experimental Quality	Paraprofessional Helpers	Client and Helper Sample Size[a]	Results Significantly Favoring
	Group 3: Crisis intervention for adults			
Knickerbocker & McGee (1973)	B	Community volunteers	92 adults and adolescents in crisis (65, 27)	Paraprofessionals
DeVol (1976)	E	Adult counselors	45 adults in crisis (4, 5)	Neither group
Getz, Fujita, & Allen (1975)	E	Community volunteers	104 adults in crisis (?, ?)	Neither group
	Group 4: Interventions directed at specific target problems			
Kazdin (1975)	A	College students	54 unassertive adults and college students (?, ?)[d]	Neither group
Lick & Heffler (1977)	A	College student	40 adult insomniacs[b] (1, 1)	Neither group
Moleski & Tosi (1976)	A	Speech pathologist	20 adult stutterers[b] (1, 1)	Neither group
Elliott & Denney (1975)	B	College students	45 overweight college students[b] (3, 1)	Neither group
Levenberg & Wagner (1976)	B	Public health officer	54 adult smokers (1, 1)	Neither group
Levitz & Stunkard (1974)	B	Community volunteers	234 overweight adults[b] (8, 4)	Professionals
Lindstrom, Balch, & Reese (1976)	B	College students	68 overweight college students[b] (4, 1)	Neither group
Penick, Filion, Fox, & Stunkard (1971)	B	Adult volunteers	32 overweight adults (2, 1)	Neither group
Russell & Wise (1976)	B	College students	42 speech-anxious college students[b] (3, 3)	Neither group
Ryan, Krall, & Hodges (1976)	B	College students	72 test-anxious college students[b] (1, 2)	Neither group
Werry & Cohrssen (1965)	C	Parents	70 enuretic children[b] (22, 4)	Paraprofessionals
De Leon & Mandell (1966)	D	Parents	87 enuretic children[b] (56, 4)	Paraprofessionals
Fremouw & Harmatz (1975)	D	College students	30 speech-anxious college students[b] (11, 1)	Neither group
	Group 5: Other interventions			
Lamb & Clack (1974)	B	College students	1,192 college students (?, 2)	Paraprofessionals
Schortinghuis & Frohman (1974)	C	Community volunteers	37 handicapped children (4, 3)	Paraprofessionals
Wolff (1969)	D	College students	88 college students[b] (4, 4)	Neither group

Note. A indicates that the design criteria were mainly satisfied; B, that one or two criteria were deficient; C, that three or four were deficient; D, that five were deficient; and E, that deficiencies were present in more than five criteria.
[a]Figures in parentheses are the number of paraprofessional and professional helpers, respectively; a ? indicates that the exact number of helpers was not specified.
[b]Includes no-treatment or attention-placebo control groups.
[c]Five therapists participated but a breakdown according to helper groups was not provided.
[d]Client sample size was not indicated.
From Table 1 (pp. 82–83) of Durlak, 1979.

Smith, 1971). This approach amounts to a reanalysis and goes beyond what we refer to here as literature review. However, two basic types of literature review can be accomplished with just the information typically summarized in research reports: the traditional (tabular) approach and the meta-analytical (statistical) approach.

Tabular Review. **Tabular review** is based on tables that summarize the results from numerous studies, for example, the Durlak (1979) review mentioned previously. The results of the Durlak review are presented in Table 14–3. Each study is described on one line of the table with information about the study's conclusions along with selected information about such aspects of the research as type and number of subjects. Different subtables are commonly provided to discriminate among studies with different settings, with different levels of measurement or design validity, or different variants of the main hypothesis.

Meta-analytic Review. In contrast, **meta-analytic review** combines the results of numerous studies into a single numerical value. This approach has rapidly gained favor since its appearance in the late 1970s (Bangert-Drowns, 1986; Green & Hall, 1984). Rosenthal (1978) has described various ways of combining such statistics as t values; standardized, or z, scores; and p values. Detailed treatments of the meta-analytic approach have been offered by Glass, McGaw, and Smith (1981) and by Wolf (1986). For an influential, early example of this approach, see the meta-analysis of psychotherapy outcomes by Smith and Glass (1977). In this study, 375 evaluations of psychotherapy were combined. Each study contained at least one comparison of the average difference between treated and control patients. For each such comparison, the difference was "standardized" by dividing it by the standard deviation of the studied variable from the control group of the study. The resulting statistical value, symbolized by d, is an example of an **effect size**. Effect sizes were combined across studies to arrive at an overall average effect size. The average study, using this method, found that psychotherapy clients surpassed controls by .68 standard deviation. This average effect size means that the average treated client was better off on the outcome measure than 75 percent of the control clients.

Besides the statistic d, other measures of effect size can be and have been used in the meta-analysis of groups of studies. For example, the correlation coefficient r has been used as the estimate of effect size in a review of the association of personality characteristics and selected diseases (Friedman & Booth-Kewly, 1987). Since different studies may report results using different kinds of statistics (t, F, chi square, and so on) it is necessary for the meta-analyst to convert the various results into a common metric, whether that be d, r, or some other coefficient.

One advantage of calculating an effect size is that it can be subjected to further analysis. A good example comes from the meta-analysis of professional and nonprofessional treatment outcomes by Hattie, Sharpley, and Rogers (1984).

Using 39 of the same 42 studies as Durlak, these reviewers calculated effect sizes for each of the possible 154 tests (studies could have more than one test comparing professionals and nonprofessionals if there were, for example, more than one outcome variable measured). Each effect size (d in this case) was equal to the mean of the paraprofessionals' clients' outcomes minus the mean of the professionals' clients' outcomes standardized by the standard deviation of the professionals' group. Consistent with but more emphatic than Durlak's conclusion, the nonprofessionals' clients enjoyed a substantial margin of benefit over that of professionals' clients (average effect size = .34). Table 14–4 presents a summary of the further analyses of these findings.

The studies were divided into two or more groups according to each of the questions posed by the researchers. For example, studies were divided into those judged to be valid (15 studies) and those not valid (27), and the average effect sizes of these two groups were compared. For the 57 effect sizes in the 15 "valid" studies, the average effect was .20, versus .42 for the 97 effect sizes in the other 27 studies. Should we conclude that invalid studies produce higher effect sizes than valid studies? We cannot draw this conclusion because the inferential statistical test of this difference was not significant ($F = 1.01$, $p = .32$). Contrast this analysis with that in Durlak (Table 14–3), where the validity of each study was graded (A to E). Although the intent is the same, the meta-analytic procedure permits much more precision.

Selecting a Review Method. Tabular and meta-analytic review methods both have their proponents. As illustrated, the distinctive advantage of meta-analysis is the precision and conciseness with which it can summarize a host of studies in a single coefficient. The closest equivalent in tabular analysis is the calculation of the percentage of studies with significant results in favor of one or another hypothesis. Unfortunately, statistical significance depends on sample size. Thus, this box score method may misestimate the magnitude of support for the hypothesis.

On the other hand, meta-analysis is not appropriate when there are relatively few studies, and it is not applicable to studies that fail to report results in statistical terms. There is also a fear that boiling down results into a single measure, such as average effect size, may divert attention from the important differences among studies that might explain conflicts in findings. For example, if half of the studies found that A was positively related to B and the other half of the studies found that A was negatively related to B, the average correlation coefficient for all studies taken together might be close to zero, indicating no relationship. However, if carefully evaluated study by study, a tabular reviewer might discover a conditioning variable that could explain the two different patterns of findings. Of course, meta-analytic reviewers could easily divide studies into those with positive or negative effect sizes and compare these two groups in terms of any measured characteristic of the studies.

Table 14–4 Summary Statistics and *F* Tests of Comparisons Between Professionals and Paraprofessionals

Criteria	No. of Effects	M	SD	F	p
From Durlak (1979, 1981)					
Quality of design					
Satisfactory	21	1.21	1.77		
1-2 deficiencies	61	-.08	1.14		
3-4 deficiencies	51	0.46	1.06		
5 deficiencies	19	0.43	1.00		
> 5 deficiencies	2	-.10	0.13	4.90	<.01
Assigned to groups					
Random	96	0.42	1.35		
Matched	17	0.50	1.41		
Neither random nor matched	41	0.09	0.92	1.11	.34
From Nietzel & Fisher (1981)					
Therapist state confounded by differential type of treatment					
Yes	48	0.68	1.72		
No	106	0.18	0.96	5.39	.03
Contrasted only 1 paraprofessional, 1 professional					
Yes	22	0.19	0.80		
No	132	0.36	1.32	0.35	.56
Different amounts or durations of treatment					
Yes	13	-.41	1.66		
No	141	0.41	1.20	5.08	.03
Collaboration between paraprofessional & professional					
Yes	2	2.08	3.21		
No	152	0.31	1.22	3.95	.05
Validity					
Valid (15 studies)	57	0.20	0.97		
Not valid (27 studies)	97	0.42	1.40	1.01	.32
Adequacy					
Adequate (5 studies)	23	0.40	0.47		
Not adequate (37 studies)	131	0.33	1.35	0.07	.79
Crucial flaws					
Yes (24 studies)	75	0.40	1.55		
No	79	0.28	0.91	0.38	.54

From Table 1 (p. 537) of Hattie, Sharpley, & Rogers, 1984.

Does Review Method Make a Difference? To test the possibility that different review methods yield different conclusions, a true experiment was conducted with a group of faculty and graduate students as subjects (Cooper & Rosenthal, 1980). Subjects were asked to review the same seven research articles by either the meta-analytic or the tabular method. The meta-analytic reviewers concluded that there was more support for the hypothesis and that the magnitude of the effect was greater than did the tabular reviewers. Based on this study, the authors advocated meta-analysis as a way of deriving more rigorous and objective review conclusions.

In contrast, two other researchers compared two reviews of the same subject matter by different authors, one traditional and the other meta-analytic (Cook & Leviton, 1980). This comparison of reviews indicated that the differences in their conclusions were not because of differences in review method. Rather, the different conclusions were traced to different criteria for selecting articles to review. Controlling for article selection, the different review methods would have yielded essentially the same conclusions. The implication was that some alleged weaknesses of the traditional review method are not inherent and that both methods, if well done, will converge on the same assessment.

Since meta-analysis can be applied only to certain kinds of quantitative reports, the adequacy of the original reports influences the decision to include them in the review and the conclusions that may be drawn from the review. Fields of research that rely on qualitative or case study methods will not be suitable for meta-analysis. When the literature on a question is a mixture of quantitative and qualitative reports, the meta-analysis may be biased by its inclusion of only the quantitative studies. Reporting deficiencies within studies (for example, omission of some statistics or other information about the validity of the study) may similarly influence outcomes (Orwin & Cordray, 1985).

If the effect under review is fairly well agreed upon, meta-analysis may be more convenient as a summarizing technique since it estimates a handy average effect magnitude. On the other hand, if the task is to identify an unknown conditioning variable that accounts for consistently discrepant results, neither review method will automatically succeed or replace imaginative and persistent puzzle solving on the part of the reviewer.

SUMMARY

In this chapter, the various threats to validity and the various research designs have been reviewed together. The result is a strategy by which any study can be systematically assessed for overall validity. The steps include identification of design type and assessment of threats to each of the four major types of validity. The best confirmation of a study's conclusions (and of the study's external validity) is by multiple independent replications with variations in subject type, place, time, measures, and design.

Findings from many studies can be reviewed by the tabular or traditional method or can be combined into summary statistics by the more quantitative, meta-analytic method. Evidence is mixed on the question of whether the review method influences review conclusions. Although the methods appear to have somewhat different strengths and weaknesses, they can produce similar conclusions if both are well implemented.

EXERCISES

1. As a preliminary to reviewing research, make sure that you can categorize social research by following the decision tree in Figure 14–1. First, try to summarize a made-up example of each type of design. Second, see if you can locate one example of each design type in professional research journals and then summarize each design you collect. Finally, test your understanding by exchanging your summaries of made-up and actual designs with a classmate. See if you can correctly categorize each one of these design summaries.

2. Read a critical review of a research report along with the reply of the author of the first report. You can find such reviews and rebuttals in the form of letters to the editor or commentary in many social science journals (for example, *American Sociological Review* or *American Psychologist*).

3. Try doing your own critique of a published or unpublished study. Follow the strategy outlined in this chapter. Identify the study's design and assess each of the four types of validity.

4. Find and read a critical review of a research area (for example, in *Psychological Bulletin*). Better yet, try to find two different reviews of the same research area and compare their conclusions. Identify and evaluate the type of review method(s) used (tabular or meta-analytic).

5. Try your hand at reviewing a small sample of research articles. Obtain a few articles (three to five) on the same question, and read them critically. Then try to draw an overall conclusion with the traditional tabular method. If you are comfortable with statistics and have access to more studies for review, try a meta-analysis of these same studies.

GLOSSARY

Conditioning factor: Variable, the value of which determines the nature of the relationship between two other variables; sometimes found to explain conflicts in literature reviews.

d: Commonly used effect size measure consisting of the difference between the treated and untreated groups in a study, divided by the standard deviation (usually of the control group).

Effect size: Standard numerical characterization of a relationship found in a study commonly used in meta-analysis.

Heterogeneous irrelevancies: Variations in factors such as population, place, and time in replications that, if they do not affect the outcome, support the external validity of a finding.

Literature review: Analysis of a body of research on a topic that tries to identify findings supported by the work as a whole or to resolve conflicts in the work.

Meta-analytic review: The statistical approach to literature review in which each study is reduced to one or a few summary numbers, which can then be analyzed quantitatively (for example, averaged to provide an overall numerical estimate of the relationship across all studies).

Tabular review: The traditional approach to literature review in which each study is summarized in a line in one or more tables, and commonalities or differences in the literature are assessed.

15

Applied Social Research

INTRODUCTION

Life-and-Death Decisions

A man named McCree was convicted of murder in Arkansas in 1978. In his trial, eight potential jurors were disqualified because they opposed the death penalty. Under the Sixth Amendment, defendants have a right to a fair cross section of the community on the jury. However, some jurors say they would not consider the death penalty, in effect saying they would not follow the law of states such as Arkansas, which have the death penalty. Such jurors can be excluded from the death penalty phases of capital trials. The resulting juries consist of "death-qualified" members, who may have a different disposition toward conviction than the excluded members.

McCree's prosecution, after winning the guilty verdict, decided not to seek the death penalty. McCree appealed his conviction on the basis of social science evidence and won a reversal in the district court and the court of appeals. These courts based their decision on a number of studies that found that death-qualified juries would be statistically more likely to find defendants guilty than non-death-qualified juries given the same evidence (Bersoff, 1987). The argument was that if less conviction-prone jurors had been permitted on McKee's panel, he might not have been found guilty.

The case went to the Supreme Court, whose decision was tantamount to a trial of social science, both of the credibility of social science and of its relevance to the Court. Contrary to the lower courts, the Supreme Court held in 1986, six to three, for the states and against McCree (and against social science). The majority found "flaws" in the social research evidence in that all but one of the 15 cited studies was deemed inappropriate to the issue (for example, for using simulations rather than actual juries in capital cases). Contrary to the majority's criticisms of the research, most observers (including the lower courts) considered the scientific evidence to be convincing. However the Court does not disdain social science in general and, in fact, has used social science to support opinions in the past.

In any event, the Court expressed its opinion in a way that removed the issue from social scientific analysis. Instead of inviting social scientists to come back with further evidence on the question, the Court interpreted the Sixth

Amendment as requiring a jury reflecting the composition of the community, defined in terms of immutable characteristics such as race or gender and not in terms of shared attitudes such as opposition to the death penalty. That is, even if the research had been perfect in the Court's view, the decision would have remained the same (W. C. Thompson, 1989).

This episode illustrates several points. The first is that social science can be and has been used to address very serious social problems. When scholars conduct studies to help in making such decisions, they are doing what is called applied social research. A second point is that such research must be of high quality and consistency. Such research must meet the scrutiny of not only fellow scholars but also the adversaries of the opposing view (in the McCree case, the lawyers for the states). Had the death-qualification research been of low quality or unclear in its thrust, it would not have persuaded the lower courts to rule for McCree. The final point is, to the chagrin of social scientists, that seemingly compelling findings may be disregarded because of other considerations. Observers suspect that this Court (although perhaps not some future court) intends to use social science findings as window dressing for decisions arrived at on other grounds but not as the sole basis for opinions that conflict with its preferred decision (W. C. Thompson, 1989).

Judging the Success of a Program

If applied social research includes any study that has a bearing on some real-world decision, much if not most of social research has the potential to be applied. Although the simulated death-qualified jury studies are clearly an important application of social research, the term *applied social research* is more commonly reserved for program evaluation, which is the primary focus of this chapter.

Definition of Program Evaluation.   Evaluation research has been defined in various ways (see Glass & Ellett, 1980). The working definition of **program evaluation** used here is social research applied to the judgment of a program's success.

The importance of program evaluation stems from the assumption that social programming is determined rationally. On this assumption, social institutions support projects that have demonstrated effectiveness and efficiency. In the private sector of the economy, effectiveness and efficiency are determined by supply, demand, and profits. In the public sector, there is no signal from the marketplace about the success of educational, penal, mental health, and welfare programs. Program evaluation can provide feedback on nonprofit activities that serve a variety of public purposes.

An Evaluation of Compensatory Education.   Program evaluations have been applied to a wide array of interventions including some of the most expensive federal investigations (see Hunt, 1985, for summaries of such multimillion dollar evaluations as the Survey of Income and Program Participation and the Income Maintenance Experiments). In this chapter we will focus on one illustrative program evaluation involving compensatory education, which includes a range of interventions intended to raise the level of later educational achievement of the disadvantaged. Many of the benefits of the educational success of disadvantaged children accrue to society as a whole, and the service cannot be "sold" to its impoverished clientele. Thus the return of profit does not apply as a measure of the program's effectiveness.

Early efforts to offset educational disadvantages (for example, Head Start) began in optimism but became mired in controversy about their effectiveness. Some of the controversies arose from methodological problems. For example, some early evaluators of the Head Start program arrived at different conclusions, depending on the statistical method used to control for preexisting differences between Head Start experimental and non-Head Start control subjects (see McDill, McDill, & Sprehe, 1972). Because of the importance of this program and the difficulty in evaluating it, numerous studies have appeared in the past two decades. The most comprehensive review to date found a positive effect (McKey, Condelli, Ganson, Barrett, McConkey, & Plantz, 1985).

One of the programs included in the review is the Perry Preschool Project, begun in 1962 (see Schweinhart & Weikart, 1980). This project was designed from a theory that holds that extra stimulation for preschool children from impoverished backgrounds would produce greater cognitive ability at school entry, higher expectations for academic success, higher commitment to schooling, and greater academic achievement through secondary school. These theoretical expectations were tested on 123 of the poorest black children in a small midwestern city. These children were selected from five birth cohorts from 1958 to 1962 in the same elementary school attendance area and were from families of low socioeconomic status. All of the children had IQ scores at entry in the educably retarded to low normal range of 70 to 85. These children were divided into experimental (preschool education) or control groups as their cohorts reached age 3 (for the 1959 to 1962 cohorts) or 4 (for the 1958 cohort). Both groups were studied through high school to evaluate the long-term impact of the intervention.

The need for this intervention with this sample is apparent from a description of the children's family circumstances. Less than 20 percent of the parents had high school degrees themselves. About 50 percent of the families had single heads of households. In 40 percent of the families, no one was employed, and in the rest, most jobs were of the unskilled kind.

In the preschool years of the five cohorts, the experimental subjects received 12½ hours of classroom experience and, with their mothers, 1½ hours of home visitation each week for 30 weeks per year. The classroom intervention offered a high ratio of teachers to students (4 per 20 to 25 students). The exact nature of the preschool intervention evolved as the teachers interacted with both their students and the researchers. The resulting cognitively oriented curriculum is detailed elsewhere (see Hohmann, Banet, & Weikart, 1979). With several researchers assigned continuously to the project, the instructional and home visit components were carefully monitored, both to document this learning laboratory and to provide a description of the technique for later use by others.

To avoid the controversy and ambiguity of previous evaluations of compensatory programs, the evaluation of the Perry Preschool Project was designed to have the highest possible validity. The most important element in this design was the assignment of children to produce initially equivalent groups. A quasi-random method was used to assure that the groups were equal in initial IQ, sex ratio, and average socioeconomic status. Children of equal IQ-level pairs were exchanged between groups to achieve balance on sex and status. There were two exceptions to this assignment process. First, younger children were always assigned to the same group as their older siblings to avoid having an older sibling in the preschool program sharing the experience with a younger sibling assigned to the control condition. Second, five children originally assigned to the experimental group but who were unable to attend because of working mothers were transferred to the control group. Finally, the two groups were arbitrarily assigned to the experimental ($n = 58$) or control ($n = 65$) conditions. These two groups were similar at entry except for proportion of working female heads of family because of the shift of five experimental subjects as noted.

A major problem with most longitudinal studies of the panel type is attrition. Fortunately, the Perry Preschool Project was able to maintain contact with most of the subjects through age 19 (121 of 123 completed the age-19 reinterview; Berrueta-Clement, Schweinhart, Barnett, Epstein, & Weikart, 1984). Given the similarity of the groups in the beginning and the apparent absence of an attrition problem, the impact of the Perry Preschool intervention is measured by the difference between the groups at posttest. On such measures as value placed on schooling, years spent in special education, test-measured competence in skills of everyday life, likelihood of being arrested, likelihood of being employed, median income, and job satisfaction, the experimental group did better than the control group.

The Perry Preschool Project was judged to return a "social profit" in terms of the monetary estimates of societal benefits gained by the intervention compared with its costs. This favorable conclusion was arrived at through a sequence of evaluative stages, which will be defined and detailed in the following sections.

Distinguishing Types of Evaluative Research

Basic Versus Applied Research. The terms *basic* and *applied* (or evaluative) research imply a clear distinction between two classes of research. However, this distinction cannot be determined by methodology, location, or motivation of the work. All kinds of research methodology can be found in the evaluation literature, including true experiments and qualitative research, not just quasi-experiments. Although applied research is located outside academe in the populations served by the projects being evaluated (Rossi, Wright, & Wright, 1978), university-based researchers also often test their theories in the field in an effort to achieve better validity.

Perhaps the most common meaning of the basic-versus-applied distinction is that found between the motivations to solve a problem and those to advance theory (Deutsch, 1980). Theory-oriented research is characterized as being analytic (focusing on isolated variables), interested in finding enduring truths, and in pursuit of "interesting" or surprising phenomena. In contrast, problem-centered research is supposed to be synthetic (operating within a set of interacting, real-world variables), pragmatic (what works?), and socially concerned (high ethical awareness of research implications). But such characteristics are not mutually exclusive. Some of the best research combines the theoretical and the pragmatic. For example, the Perry Preschool evaluation would qualify as problem-centered, but the project was based on a theoretical model. The data returned by the evaluation served not only to evaluate the intervention but also to test the theory. Calling a study a "program evaluation" is only to say that it has its primary motivation in problem solving, not that it is devoid of theory.

Ideally, theoretical and applied interests should interact in research. Theory can provide guidance in program design and can help identify the kinds of constructs to be operationalized in a comprehensive evaluation of the intervention. In exchange, programs offer opportunities to test causal assertions in real-world contexts. For example, psychologists and economists might want basic research to test the hypothetical relationship between the security of a person's income and the desire to work. But such a study is so expensive that it could only be conducted as part of a program aimed at solving a major problem in social welfare (as was the justification for the income maintenance experiments).

The desire to "scientize" public decision making is a common bond between basic and applied researchers. The movements for consumerism and productivity have helped reinforce the demand for scientific evaluation of both private goods and public services. These movements have in many cases been institutionalized as mandatory components in the budgets of social programs. Consequently, we can expect a continuing demand for social researchers to apply their skills to evaluation.

Social Impact Assessment Versus Program Evaluation. The role of the social scientist in public policy has been defined in various ways (see Finsterbusch & Motz, 1980). The use of social research methods to gauge the social consequences of an intervention can be divided into two types: social impact assessment and program evaluation.

Since both **social impact assessment** (SIA) and evaluation research (ER) estimate the outcome of planned change, they are often closely related activities. The following characteristics of SIA help distinguish it from ER, although in practice some intervention assessments would involve both types. Unlike ER, SIA usually (but not always) assesses the consequences of an intervention before it takes place. One of the major motivations for SIA is to provide planners with information about the future costs and benefits of each of several alternatives. Whereas ER focuses primarily on whether an intervention met its stated goals, SIA attempts to measure all possible consequences of an intervention. This distinction is blurred because good ER is designed to observe important unanticipated outcomes, and it is difficult in practice for SIA (or any research for that matter) to measure all types of possible effects. Nevertheless, SIA is typically more multidisciplinary than ER, with specialists in each area of possible impact—economic, psychological, environmental, social, and biological. Finally, SIAs can be applied to any proposed intervention, public or private, even those without explicit goals for social welfare (for example, expanding or locating an airport, a nuclear reactor, or a city). In contrast, ER is usually reserved for assessment of the consequences of more narrowly targeted interventions (for example, effects on children of a new educational project or on the mental health of the clients of a new therapy system).

The greater emphasis of SIA on future effects on the total population in all domains requires different methodologies from ER. For example, the interest in the total population suggests regular survey or archival measures of the well-being of the entire population or representative samples thereof. We currently have regular evaluations of the economic well-being of the whole population (for example, monthly unemployment and inflation rate reports) by which economic policies are assessed. A social counterpart to economic indicators has been suggested but not instituted as a routine government function. Called **social indicators,** these monthly or quarterly reports could summarize the health and social well-being of the population. Such social accounts could be used as a report card on the success of public policies. Although the Department of Commerce has issued two collections of social indicators, a proposal for an annual social report (the Full Opportunity and Social Accounting Act of 1967) has not yet been legislated (Finsterbusch & Motz, 1980).

The legislative impetus for SIA came from the National Environmental Policy Act of 1969, which mandated systematic studies of the direct and indirect effects of all federal actions affecting the human environment. Social impacts were judged by the courts to be included in the meaning of environmental impacts for the preparation of the environmental impact statements. Under this law, new projects can be delayed until the necessary **environmental impact statements** are filed and publicly aired (Meidinger & Schnaiberg, 1980).

Stages of Evaluation Research. The remainder of this chapter will focus on evaluation research, although many of the same issues appear in the closely related area of social impact assessment. Evaluation research may usefully be divided into different types, each of which is related to a different stage of the overall evaluation process. For convenience, a five-stage typology will be used here.

1. *Needs assessment.* In this stage, descriptive research methods are used to identify a set of goals around which the intervention can be planned.
2. *Program monitoring.* In this stage, the ongoing intervention is checked to see how well it conforms to the specifications of the plan.
3. *Program impact.* At this stage, it is determined whether the goals are met by the program.

4. *Efficiency.* This analysis weights the program's success by its costs.
5. *Utilization.* Studies of this type measure the extent to which the evaluation is used and the factors that influence utilization.

Each of these five types of evaluation research will be briefly illustrated and described in the following sections. Each type could warrant its own chapter, and the following presentations should be considered introductory. For more detailed treatments, see a text on evaluation (for example, Posavac & Carey, 1985; Rossi & Freeman, 1985).

NEEDS ASSESSMENT

What Are the Goals?

Definition. The **needs assessment** stage is concerned with identifying goals rather than determining whether the goals have been met. Thus, needs assessment is usually conducted in the early, formative stages of program development. Usually based on survey or archival data, needs assessment establishes that an unmet need exists and describes its size and location. This information both justifies the program (that is, helps motivate the funders to provide resources) and determines its goals (that is, what type of service is to be delivered to whom).

Usually, the needs assessment provides definitions of the target population to whom the program will provide services. These definitions typically include geographic (for example, catchment area) boundaries and social characteristics (for example, elderly above age 65). Such targets are usually set on the basis of the magnitude of need associated with the social and geographical characteristics (for example, severity of health or nutrition problems found in the elderly).

Rationale. Ideally, scarce resources will be allocated with priority given to those areas and populations with the greatest unmet need. The failure to conduct a needs assessment can lead to resource misallocation. Existing projects may expand, because of the enthusiasm of their staffs, into areas with little actual need or with needs different from the ones best served by the program. Needs assessment is also helpful in the subsequent evaluation of program impact when the outcome is compared with the original goals.

Method

Examples. Failure to match the program with the need results in scarce resources flowing away from the locations of the greatest need to populations with less or no need. Such misallocations can occur because an adequate needs assessment is not conducted, because criteria other than need guide the allocation decision, or both. For example, Chu and Trotter (1974) identified some community mental health funding decisions in which federal funds were expended on facilities catering to the well-to-do, whereas poor areas received no increased services.

The Perry Preschool Project previously described illustrates a successful matching of a new service with a population in great need. Earlier research indicated that children reared in poverty had poor academic performance. Using available archival data, the researchers were able to identify the poorest area in their city. They cited an earlier housing commission analysis that judged their target area to be "one of the worst congested slum areas in the state" (Schweinhart & Weikart, 1980, p. 17). Records of school dropouts and criminal behavior for the area corroborated that the target community was rife with the problems commonly associated with poverty and poor school performance.

Existing Records. Many programs, as illustrated by the Perry Preschool Project, employ already-collected data to assess need and to target their services. County and city planning offices have descriptive information about the community from the most recent decennial census or more recent and more specialized sample surveys. Such data can provide accurate descriptions, down to the census tract level, about the population (for example, age, sex, and ethnicity).

Additional archival records can provide supplementary information of a more specialized kind such as court and police records on criminal deviance, school records on attendance and performance, hospital and coroner records on health and mortality, and election records on voting and political behavior. Together, these data can help profile any section of the community on multiple dimensions. Such a description of a community is called a **social area analysis** and is a common first step in needs assessment.

Specialized Surveying. Such existing survey and archival data may not address the particular problem of interest to the needs assessor. For example, what is the unmet need for mental health services in a catchment area for which a community mental health center is under consideration? Existing records can only provide information on variables thought to correlate with mental disorder (for example, poverty) or on current service delivery (that is, met need). To estimate the proportion of the population in need of service requires a special survey of a representative sample. Such a survey could not only measure the **incidence** (number of new cases in some time period) and **prevalence** (number of existing cases at some point in time) but also could estimate the number of people who would seek or accept service of the kind and at the location and price to be offered by the proposed new program.

Such "market" surveys of the client population could be supplemented by surveys of other interested parties. For example, before establishing a new mental health center, the planners would want to consult the existing mental health providers and the providers of related services such as social work agencies, police, courts, and schools as well as relevant government and civic groups in the area (see, for example, Weiss, 1975).

PROGRAM MONITORING

Is the Intervention Being Conducted as Planned?

Definition.   **Program monitoring** consists of the description and assessment of the means as distinct from the ends of the project. The means include the quantity and quality of the intervention that is intended to meet the goals. For example, an educational program might be specified in terms of textbooks, audiovisual aids, teaching plans, and the intensity of the effort (number of students, teacher-to-student ratio, and number of hours per week of student contact). Such detailing of the planned, day-to-day procedure may be required in advance both to justify the program's funding and to determine its detailed budget.

Program monitoring involves recording the actual activities of the project. For example, the monitoring of an educational program could measure the number of students attending classes, the actual teacher-to-student ratio, and the number of hours of student-teacher contact each day or on the average across sampled days. The quality of the educational experience could be rated by observational procedures involving classroom visits by expert judges.

Rationale.   There are two main purposes of program monitoring: simple management and making sure that the intended intervention has been realized. The managerial purpose is to account for the flows of revenues and costs and to monitor the numbers of clients and staff that correspond to the budget. Such monitoring is customary in any business or government agency. **Management information systems** (MIS) are frequently established to provide managers continuous feedback on the program's operation. Such MIS procedures entail routines by which contacts of clients (for example, students or patients) and staff (for example, teachers or therapists) are counted. Such MIS procedures yield quantitative descriptions of the program, which translate into budgetary terms (for example, salaries for staff and revenue based on client utilization).

The second purpose of program monitoring is to make sure that the project under study is delivering the type of intervention called for in the proposal (similar to experimental construct validity). As Rossi (1978) has observed, many social service programs are designed to conform to high theoretical and laboratory standards, but in practice these programs are highly operator-dependent. The actual service may little resemble the intended service and thus provide no test of the intended intervention. Monitoring the conformity of the actual to the ideal may require a more energetic quality assessment than provided by the standard MIS.

Method

Preschool Curriculum Example.   An illustration of the evaluation of program process and quality comes from the Perry Preschool Project. Out of this project came a second study, which compared the cognitively oriented method of the Perry Preschool Project with two other compensatory educational methods—the language-training curriculum and the unit-based curriculum. These three curricula represented different theories with respect to the optimal roles of the child and the teacher (for details, see Weikart, Epstein, Schweinhart, & Bond, 1978).

To ensure that the curricula were being faithfully implemented, several observational systems were employed to describe and compare the teacher-student interactions under the different curricula. In one monitoring system, observations were recorded every 25 seconds, with 20 observations for each child in the class. Observed behavior included the child-child, child-material, and child-adult interactions. The results confirmed that the three curricula produced the expected differences in classroom process. For example, the cognitive curriculum produced lower levels of direct teaching by adults (that is, 12 percent for showing or telling) than either of the other curricula (33 percent in the language-training and 23 percent in the unit-based curriculum).

Designing Program Monitoring. No single methodology or standardized measure can be used to monitor all programs. Managers will need to adapt their MIS procedures to the budgeting requirements of the program funders. For example, if a mental health program is reimbursed for each patient-therapist session, the MIS will need to record only minimal data for every contact (for example, identity of the patient, identity of the therapist, and type of service). On the other hand, if the project is an experimental demonstration of a theoretically interesting new procedure, the measure will have to be tailored carefully to reflect the conceptually important qualities of the intervention.

Just because a program is expending funds and serving clients at the expected numerical levels does not guarantee that it is being implemented as planned. To check the more qualitative aspects of implementation, a **program audit** by an outside evaluator may be necessary. Using the program's proposal or charter as a guide, such auditors would inspect program records (including the MIS) and collect original observations. The auditors would generate a description of the clientele and the services on the dimensions pertinent to the program's mission. Areas of accountability might include coverage (who is served?), service (what is the delivered service?), finances (are expenditures proper?), and the law (is the program obeying all applicable laws?). See Rossi and Freeman (1985).

PROGRAM IMPACT

Is There an Effect?

Definition. Of the five stages of evaluation, **program impact** makes the most use of the causal research methods covered in earlier chapters. Unlike the largely descriptive methods of needs assessment and program monitoring, program impact evaluation attempts to establish that the observed outcome is caused by the program. Whereas the first two types of research determine ends and describe the means used to achieve them, neither addresses the question of whether the means actually achieve the ends.

Rationale. Program impact research is central to the purpose of program evaluation as defined here—determining the success of the program. Pursuing worthy goals by the theoretically correct intervention does not guarantee program success. The goals may well be accomplished—but not necessarily by the program. Alternatively, the program may have some effect but on other than the intended outcome variables. Thus the impact stage of evaluation resembles hypothesis testing in more basic research and is subject to all of the threats to validity covered in this volume.

Method

Perry Preschool Project. As with the previous types of evaluation research, the Perry Preschool study also had a major component addressed to impact assessment. The "hypothesis" of this project was that the cognitive curriculum would achieve the goals of improved school performance and commitment to schooling in later years.

Since preschool students might develop academic ability and commitment to schooling for a variety of reasons over the course of their education, a control group design was essential. The control group would be subject to the same developmental and historical influences experienced by the preschool group and would thus "control" for these threats to internal validity. If experimental and control group children were different to begin with, however, any subsequent differences could be due to their initial difference. To rule out these group threats to internal validity, a quasi-random assignment procedure was used. Thus any difference between groups at, for example, ages 14 and 15 should be due only to the differential treatment and not to differences at ages 3 and 4.

The hypothesis of the Perry Preschool study received support on several outcome measures. For example, on a high school reading achievement test, the experimental students passed about 37 percent of the items compared to just 30 percent for the control group. This difference would occur by chance (that is, by sampling error when there was really no difference) less than 5 percent of the time (Schweinhart & Weikart, 1980, p. 41). The measure used was highly reliable and considered a valid test of reading, and the program monitoring step showed high experimental construct validity. In sum, it seems reasonable to conclude that the Perry Preschool Project was successful. In terms of external validity, the cognitive preschool intervention would be expected to generalize to similarly disadvantaged children if the intervention is implemented with the same quality.

Research Design Problems. As the Perry Preschool Project illustrates, program impact evaluation is a special application of the general class of causal research designs. Critics of claims of program success can raise the same doubts about validity as are raised in all social research. The same methodological techniques that protect against validity threats in more basic social research can, in principle, be employed in applied research.

Implementation of valid research poses difficulties under the most favorable circumstances. The constraints under which program impact evaluation is conducted add further difficulties. Sometimes, the ideal research design for internal validity purposes (that is, the true experiment) is not feasible because of the nature of the intervention. For example, the introduction of traffic laws in some states (the experimental group) but not in others (control) cannot be assigned by the evaluator. In such cases, the evaluator must use quasi-experimentation to study the effect, for example, an interrupted time series (D. T. Campbell, 1975).

Such difficulties and the need for design flexibility are inherent in certain settings and interventions and thus common to both basic and applied research. Of special concern here are several different problems that are characteristic of impact evaluation. Although some of these problems can arise in other stages of evaluation, they will be noted here because they regularly arise in attempts to grade the success of interventions. The three problems include (1) resistance and bias on the part of program participants; (2) hindrance in using random assignment to groups; and (3) measurement of all the effects.

Resistance and Bias of Participants.   Program participants include both staff and clients. Both have good psychological and/or material reasons to be biased about the outcome of their projects. For example, although early research on Head Start found little evidence of success in standardized test scores, parent interviews consistently revealed client support for the continuation of the program (Scheirer, 1978). From cognitive consistency theory, one would predict that parents sending their children to a program with high hopes for success will be more comfortable believing the program to be successful than believing it to be a failure. Similarly, staff members are both psychologically (from the same consistency theory) and materially (income from the job) invested in the success of their program. The self-interest of the program's participants makes difficult the objective evaluation of the program's success. Program evaluators must expect such bias and be prepared to adjust for it.

There are two major consequences of this bias. One is in measurement, and the other is in gaining access to the program to conduct the evaluation. The biased opinion of the participants casts doubt on any measures of a subjective kind. A survey showing that most participants feel positively about their project has less credibility than more objective measures of the project's impact. Thus subjective measures, if taken at all, should be supplemented with measures tapping the expected outcome in less biased ways.

The second and related consequence of participant bias is resistance to evaluation, especially by the staff. Various reasons may be offered for such resistance (for example, fear that evaluation may overlook subtle but valuable effects or that it will inhibit program innovation). Ever present is the staff's fear that an impact evaluation will find no basis for continuing the program and thus lead to job loss. In either event, the staff may resist entry by the evaluators, withhold cooperation with evaluators if they gain entry (for example, declining to assist in the administration of objective measures), or even commit sabotage (for example, manipulating program records). Gaining entry and cooperation is an art that places a premium on the interpersonal skills and sensitivity of the evaluator. The evaluator, more than the basic researcher, has to remember that the research activity has emotional as well as scientific meanings to the participants and must take these emotions into account when conducting the study.

Random Assignment. Random assignment may be both desirable (for maximizing the internal validity of the impact assessment) and possible in principle but still not feasible in practice. The ideal of randomized assignment to groups is occasionally achieved. For example, the income maintenance studies enjoyed random assignment of subjects to different levels of guaranteed income and taxation rates (Robins, Spiegelman, Weiner, & Bell, 1980). In these studies, the subjects were offered a powerful financial incentive to participate in whatever experimental condition was chosen for them and suffered no harm by having to join the control condition. In contrast, in many programs, denial of the intervention to the control group is seen as harmful by the clientele or the staff. Political pressure may extend the apparently desirable new service to those in the control group, thus destroying the possibility of assessing the impact of the intervention. Alternatively, a random assignment plan may be compromised piecemeal by staff who feel that the treatment should be offered selectively to the most needy, whether they were originally assigned to the experimental group or not.

In Conner's (1977) analysis of twelve evaluations, he found several keys to successful randomization. With respect to the planning of the evaluation, he recommends researcher control of the assignment process, fixed randomization with no exceptions, and the blocking of clients prior to random assignment for maximum group equivalence in small samples. With respect to the implementation of the evaluation, he advises a centralized location for assignment, of cases, a single person to implement the assignment, training of this implementer in the requirements of valid randomization, and a monitoring procedure for checking on the success of the randomization.

Random assignment can often be accomplished when the denial of the treatment is not perceived as harmful or when the demand for the treatment far exceeds the available supply. In the latter case, random assignment actually seems most equitable for distributing a scarce service. On ethical and public relations grounds, it is desirable to reward the control subjects for their patience with an offer of the experimental treatment after the evaluation. This delayed equity and the perception that the assignment was "fair" will often ease the pressure to abort the assignment plan. Moreover, the delayed treatment control group lends itself to a multiple time series design in which the first-treated group serves as a control for the later-treated replication (Heath, Kendzierski, & Borgida, 1982).

Assessing Multiple Outcomes. Program evaluation differs importantly from basic research in its concern with unhypothesized effects. The basic researcher typically focuses the outcome measures on the constructs specified in the tested theory and is not obliged to look for serendipitous or unhypothesized findings. In contrast, evaluators expect unhypothesized effects and design their research to capture them. Practical experience has shown that programs often produce desirable and undesirable side effects besides the intended effects predicted from theory. For example, Head Start may not have produced the expected academic outcomes but almost certainly contributed to the nutrition and medical care of the enrolled children through its health screening and lunch requirements. Although health was not a primary goal of Head Start, the initial Head Start program discovered considerable health problems in the children from poor families. Judging the overall value of a program, therefore, requires that all the pluses and minuses be accounted for.

A common observation in impact assessment is that the expected goal was not achieved (Chen & Rossi, 1980). Nevertheless, it seems implausible that a substantial intervention effort should produce no effect. It follows that evaluators must employ more sensitive and more numerous outcome measures to capture the missing effects. One proposed solution, that of ignoring the stated goals in order not to miss the actual achievement (Scriven, 1972), seems impractical. Such goal-free research provides no guidance about what to measure and needlessly ignores the most likely outcomes.

An alternative is to supplement the program's goals with other goals that can be predicted from relevant social theory. Chen and Rossi (1980) call this the multigoal, theory-driven approach. They point to the negative income tax (income maintenance) studies designed to test the disincentive effect of such income on work. Since work and income are linked theoretically to many other variables, the income maintenance experiments were wisely designed to reflect potential changes in variables beyond work incentive—for example, psychological distress, divorce, job satisfaction, and demand for children (see Robins, Spiegelman, Weiner, & Bell, 1980).

EFFICIENCY ANALYSIS

Is the Program Worth the Cost?

Definition. **Efficiency analysis** measures the impact of the project relative to its cost. Two general methods are available to efficiency analysts: cost-benefit analysis and cost-effectiveness analysis. **Cost-benefit analysis** measures both the benefits and the costs of the program in monetary terms and expresses their relationship as a ratio or difference.

Sometimes the benefits of social service programs are intangibles that are difficult to express in monetary terms. In that case, **cost-effectiveness analysis** is appropriate. In this approach, outcome goals or achievements can be expressed in nonmonetary units, and different programs can be compared in terms of the monetary costs for achieving the same ends.

Rationale. Basic research is primarily concerned with testing a causal hypothesis, regardless of the cost of manipulating the cause or independent variable. In contrast, program evaluation seeks the most efficient cause for the desired effect. An intervention that achieves the desired effect but at an exorbitant cost will not be sustained or adopted elsewhere and will, in that sense, be unsuccessful despite its positive impact.

The results of cost-benefit and cost-effectiveness analyses help guide policy decisions in choosing among alternative programs. Cost-effectiveness analysis can guide choices between alternatives for achieving the same outcomes (for example, alternate methods for screening populations for early cancer detection). However, cost-effectiveness analysis cannot guide choices between programs with different targets (for example, whether to invest in a cancer screening program or a preschool education program). Cost-benefit analysis, which can express different outcomes in the same metric (that is, monetary terms) can aid in choosing between otherwise noncomparable programs.

Method

Perry Preschool Cost-Benefit Analysis. Our continuing example of program evaluation, the Perry Preschool Project, also illustrates efficiency analysis (see Barnett, 1985, for the details). This cost-benefit study first accounted the monetary costs per student of providing the Perry Preschool intervention to the experimental students (that is, teachers' salaries, supplies, and overhead). For example, one year of preschool for each student was estimated to cost $4,963 in 1981 dollars.

The accounting of benefits to the Perry Preschool Project illustrates some of the tasks involved in attaching monetary value to the outcomes of social programs. First, it was necessary to identify the multiple impacts of the intervention (that is, ways in which the experimental students differed from the control students). For their efficiency study, the researchers chose to include social benefits (those to the society as a whole) as well as those to the individual student. This choice is appropriate since the costs of public preschool programs are paid by society as a whole. Several types of benefits were accounted from among the many that might have been studied:

1. Savings in child-care time of the parents of the experimental subjects
2. Savings in special education required later by the control subjects but not by the experimental subjects (potentially offset by added educational costs for increased college attendance by experimental over control subjects)
3. Savings in criminal or delinquent behavior (not including estimates of pain and suffering of the victims)

4. Earning differences because of greater employment
5. Savings in welfare and economic dependency

Together, these net benefits were estimated to total $10,077 at age 19 in 1981 dollars for each student given one year of preschool. Based on these costs and benefits, the Perry Preschool Project appears to return a net benefit of $5,114 per student through age 19. Of course, the benefits are not expected to stop at age 19. One estimate of lifelong benefits for one year of preschool shows a net benefit of over $90,000 in 1981 dollars (Barnett, 1985, p. 87).

Before concluding that this cost-benefit comparison proves the value of the Perry Preschool Project, a second task must be done—taking into account the effects of time. Most of the benefits of the Perry Preschool Project occur years after the intervention. A dollar of benefits in 1993 may not be equal to a dollar of costs in 1958 for two reasons: the inflation rate and the interest rate. Because of inflation, a dollar in 1993 would not have the same purchasing power as a dollar in 1958. To adjust for inflation, the Perry Preschool's costs and benefits were evaluated in **constant dollars,** using 1981 as the standard. That is, the estimated future benefits and the earlier costs were translated to their inflation-adjusted equivalent value in 1981. This conversion requires calculating an inflation coefficient for each year relative to the criterion year. For example, if a dollar in 1993 is estimated to be worth half of a dollar in 1981, the estimated 1993 benefits would be multiplied by .5 to set them equivalent to 1981 constant dollars.

A second and more complicated matter is the interest or **discount rate** needed to adjust future benefits for the rate of gain of the same investment placed in some other project or saved in the bank. A bank could loan the money to some borrower for a constructive activity (for example, starting a business or buying a house). If $100 is invested at 5 percent interest (net of inflation), it would be worth $105 one year later. Conversely, $105 of program benefits promised one year from now has a **present value** (that is, discounted by 5 percent) of $100 because $105 would have been returned on $100 placed in a bank at 5 percent. To compare present costs with future benefits thus requires adjusting the future benefits not only for inflation but also by some discount rate. The choice of discount rate is important because the higher the rate, the more future benefits will be diminished and the less beneficial a program will appear. For example, the reported net benefit of $5,114 at age 19 is based on a 0 percent discount rate. Had the discount rate been 3 percent, the net benefit would have been $2,339, and if 7 percent, the benefit would nearly disappear ($40). An alternative method of presenting cost-benefit results is the **internal rate of return** (IRR). The IRR represents the rate at which the investment (the cost) grows in value. For the Perry Preschool Project, the IRR was estimated as greater than 11 percent for one year of preschool based on the lifelong return.

The reason for being concerned with such discounted estimates of return is precisely that funds for all enterprises, including public programs, are scarce. This notion is expressed in the term **opportunity cost,** which is the value of the best alternative use of the project's resources. That is, if the Perry Preschool Project did not spend $4,963 on each student in one year, some other project might have been accomplished. The use of IRR analysis is one procedure for evaluating a program's return against the alternative opportunity of investing the resources elsewhere. However, the discount rate solution to the opportunity cost problem raises another problem, that of selecting a rate.

There is no objective rule for determining this rate. If the discount rate is intended to reflect the opportunity costs of diverting resources from the private to the public sector, one should use the prevailing rate of return to private investment (say, that of long-term, secure bonds, as suggested by Baumol, 1969). The higher this rate, the more we will prefer private investments to investments in social programs. Those who feel we should take a longer-range view and maximize social investments will favor applying a lower **social discount rate** in judging public projects. Obviously, the time preference in selecting discount rates has a large subjective and political component.

Problems in Estimation. The costs of social programs would appear simple to account, since the salaries, materials, and overhead have to be summarized in the program's budget. Even unpriced costs (for example, the value of the time of volunteer staff in a free clinic) can be estimated by using **shadow prices**— their value if purchased in the market place.

Another problem is the accounting for external effects or **externalities.** Internal effects are those that occur between two parties—the provider and the consumer or client. External effects are those that occur to third parties not directly involved in the project. A coal-powered plant, for example, produces electricity, and its costs for construction, fuel, and personnel are all internal costs. They all pertain to the production of electricity and must not exceed the utility bills willing to be paid by the electricity consumers. But suppose that the power plant has costly side effects on third parties—for example, the production of acid rain, which damages forests in other states or even in other countries. From the society's perspective, these external costs are real and must be paid by someone. Ideally, when such external costs are found, they are billed to the project. In other words, the project "internalizes" the costs in order to judge its overall profitability. Although social programs may not have dramatic external costs, their cost-benefit evaluations must try to consider any such externalities.

Just as externalities can add to the true costs of a project, so they can add to the benefits. The Perry Preschool Project, for example, may have produced unaccounted benefits by lowering the school dropout rate, increasing the labor force participation rate, reducing the crime rate, reducing the participation in welfare programs, and so on. Were all these benefits to be evaluated, the intervention might appear even more valuable.

Another problem in efficiency analysis involves intangibles—benefits with no dollar equivalent. Perhaps the extreme case is the problem of placing a monetary value on human life for the purpose of analyzing health or other projects intended to save or extend life. How much should the public spend to save a life (for example, to redesign a highway exit ramp with a high fatality record)? To answer such questions, cost-benefit analysts have attempted to estimate life value. Considered are such monetary aspects of life as the person's future earnings (if he or she survives) and the amount that others would pay for the benefits of the person's life (for example, for friendship). These considerations have produced different life valuation formulas (see M. S. Thompson, 1980, chap. 8). Nevertheless, the difficulties (including the morality) of such valuations argue for the use of cost-effectiveness analysis instead of cost-benefit analysis in such cases.

The attraction of cost-effectiveness analysis is that no monetary value need be attached to the benefits of the intervention. Only the costs of achieving a fixed target vary across competing programs and must be accounted for. For example, suppose it is decided to save lives from accidental death. Alternative programs for preventing accidental death can all be compared on a single value: cost per life saved (see Thompson & Fortess, 1980). For example, two programs delivering counseling to hypertensive patients (regarding factors affecting high blood pressure such as diet, smoking, and stress) were compared. Both programs (clinic and telephone) achieved significant reductions in blood pressure (the nonmonetary outcome target). The cost-effectiveness ratio consisted of the number of patients counseled divided by the total cost of counseling them. This ratio favored the telephone method ($39) over the clinic method ($82). See Bertera and Bertera (1981).

UTILIZATION RESEARCH

How Can the Utilization of Evaluations Be Promoted?

Definition.   How well new information about programmatic innovations is disseminated and used is the concern of the final stage of evaluation. The study of innovation diffusion and **utilization** concerns itself with the characteristics of new knowledge that influence its use. Despite its origins in the older field of social change, the evaluation of utilization is relatively recent (Zaltman, 1979). Although the study of utilization can apply to any type of knowledge, including basic research (Ganz, 1980), our concern is specifically for the application of research to social interventions.

The term *utilization* has different meanings (see Leviton & Hughes, 1981, for a review), but can be distinguished both from *impact* and *utility*. *Utility* means having relevance and value, but useful program evaluation may not necessarily be used. *Impact* means a change in programs, but change depends on political and economic factors as well as on evaluation reports. Thus utilization may occur even when little or no impact is observed. Three categories of utilization have been suggested: instrumental, conceptual, and persuasive or symbolic (Leviton & Hughes, 1981). **Persuasive utilization** includes the use of program evaluation to influence others to accept its implications. **Conceptual utilization** includes presentation of evaluation results as an information base. Like persuasive utilization, conceptual utilization does not entail adoption, but unlike persuasive utilization, it serves by its power to clarify rather than as a tool in an effort to change attitudes. Finally, in **instrumental utilization,** the evaluation is actually used in a decision-making or program-shaping way; that is, it has an impact.

Rationale. The concern with the utilization of evaluation stems from the purpose of evaluation and the widespread view that social research is underutilized. The justification for evaluation research is ostensibly to grade projects so that policymakers can support the successful projects and stop funding the less successful ones and so that project managers can improve continuing projects. If decision makers do not use the evaluation results, there is no reason to continue the evaluations.

Research to determine the rate of utilization of evaluations is not automatically conducted. As a result, our perception of the utilization rate is often based on anecdotes and small samples, and reviews of utilization research present a mixed picture (Davis & Salasin, 1975; Hennigan, Flay, & Cook, 1980). Evaluation and social research generally are not totally ignored, and there may well be occasions of overutilization, as when poorly conducted research is relied on for guiding policy. But the prevailing evidence is that the results of evaluations are seldom used directly and specifically (that is, instrumental utilization) to affect policy. They are more commonly used as general background information (conceptual utilization) or as ammunition for justifying decisions already made (that is, persuasive or symbolic utilization). The widespread perception of underutilization of evaluation has motivated research to identify those characteristics of evaluations that increase the likelihood of utilization.

Method

Examples of Disseminating Evaluations. The successful Perry Preschool Project results described in this chapter have been disseminated widely in published reports, newspaper stories, and workshops. However, there is a widespread perception that compensatory preschool education is ineffective despite the evidence for successful compensatory education reviewed by Schweinhart and Weikart (1980). If effective methods such as those used in the Perry Preschool Project are not being universally adopted, how might greater utilization of a successful program be achieved?

An excellent example of research aimed at answering just such a question comes from Fairweather, Sanders, and Tornatzky (1974). Fairweather and his associates had previously evaluated an innovative program for rehabilitating and sustaining mental patients in community dormitories or lodges (Fairweather, Sanders, Maynard, & Cressler, 1969). The very positive results from this evaluation argued for the widespread adoption of the lodge program by mental hospitals.

Fairweather and his colleagues conducted a national experiment to get mental hospital administrators to utilize this new treatment method.

These utilization researchers studied the effects of three different persuasion techniques in 255 hospitals. Less than 10 percent of the contacted hospitals volunteered to establish the lodge program. The brochure and workshop persuasion approaches were better at gaining initial entry to the hospital. However, after gaining entry, the more active in-hospital demonstration approach had more success in achieving a favorable decision to implement the lodge. A second experiment studied the effect of personal versus written (by manual) consultation in facilitating the adoption of the lodge in 12 matched pairs of adopting hospitals. As might be expected, the personal consultation hospitals made better progress in lodge adoption. This massive study illustrates the potential for sound utilization research. With 12 percent or less of the contacted hospitals adopting the lodge in the most persuasive approach, there is a continuing need for such utilization research.

Aids to Utilization. Numerous hints or rules of thumb for increasing utilization have been based on common sense or on research, ranging from improving the presentation of evaluation results to improving the evaluations themselves (see Posavac & Carey, 1985; Rossi & Freeman, 1985). For example, extensive research on the spacing effect has documented its existence: that for a given amount of study time, spaced presentations yield better learning than massed presentations (Dempster, 1988). Nevertheless, this apparently important finding has not been widely incorporated into educational programs. Dempster, after reviewing various possible hindrances to the application of this effect, concludes that, among other things, it is still not well known among educators. If this is the problem, the solution would seem to be greater efforts to disseminate the finding from the psychological laboratories to the teacher training classrooms.

In other cases, the findings of basic researchers are well disseminated but simply not convincing to practitioners. For example, psychologists have pointed to the adverse effects of crowding in prisons, but corrections officers have remained unimpressed (Ruback & Innes, 1988). Basic researchers may have more success in getting their findings utilized if they change their research to include policy variables (those that are controllable by the corrections officers) and dependent variables of greater relevance to practitioners.

Evaluation results and methodologies are seldom the most important factors in making up the minds of decision makers. For example, the massive income maintenance experiments were designed to test the hypothesis that guaranteed income would lead to substantially reduced work motivation. The results indicated relatively small reductions in work effort by primary wage earners, and the results were well known to Congress. Although these findings could be interpreted as supporting the adoption of a guaranteed minimum income, the results were either ignored or used to reinforce the preexisting sentiment against such a policy (Neubeck & Roach, 1981). In short, program evaluations may be interpreted, used, or ignored to suit the predetermined needs of policy makers.

It has been suggested that evaluation research will be utilized to the extent that it meets three criteria: relevance, truth, and utility (Weiss & Bucuvalas, 1980). It is obvious that the evaluation must be timely and relevant to the user's sphere of responsibility. In a study of the ratings of research reports by 155 decision makers, the truth and utility criteria were each found to have two components. The truth test was based on the perceived quality of the research (that is, the various types of validity) and on conformity to the user's expectations. If the evaluation report was counter to the user's practical experience, the evaluation was judged more critically on its research quality (a double standard).

The utility test was based on feasibility (how possible the proposed change was to make) and challenge to the status quo (whether it meant going against prevailing practice and sentiment). If the evaluation did not challenge the status quo, the feasibility component was given greater attention for the specific steps that might be taken. If the evaluation challenged the status quo, it was of conceptual interest to the decision maker, but it would not facilitate utilization.

Utilization of evaluation depends on two types of factors—those under the control of the evaluators (such as quality of the research) and those not under their control (for example, the political mood and economic resources that constrain the policy maker). When different researchers produce conflicting results, the decision makers will, justifiably, base their policies on factors other than the recommendations from social scientists. When utilization of evaluation and basic research is blocked by contradictory results from opposing scientists, scientists themselves need to help clarify the situation. Ultimately, utilization may be advanced by the establishment of science courts and standing committees made up of disinterested scientists, who could identify the best research and evaluations for the use of decision makers (Hennigan, Flay, & Cook, 1980, pp. 135–143).

SUMMARY

Program evaluation is one type of applied social research. Applied and basic research differ mainly in the degree of emphasis placed on problem solving versus theory testing. Program evaluation differs from other applied or policy-related research such as social impact assessment. Evaluation typically aims at judging the success of an intervention in achieving intentional or unintentional benefits. In contrast, social impact assessment estimates the future consequences of hypothetical interventions, is typically more multidisciplinary, and is more interested in monitoring or forecasting social indicators of the whole society.

Most evaluations include one or more types of evaluation. Needs assessment and program monitoring both employ descriptive methods. The first defines the ends of the project, and the second verifies that the means are being implemented as planned. Program impact evaluation employs hypothesis-testing methods to determine whether the program actually accomplished the stated goals or had other unplanned side effects. Impact research is vulnerable to the same validity threats as basic causal research, but it has additional constraints or problems beyond those encountered in basic research (for example, the bias of clients and staff, the resistance of staff, difficulties in implementing random assignment, and difficulties in measuring all of the effects of the intervention). Efficiency analysis expresses the net impact of a program relative to the monetary cost of the intervention. Finally, utilization research determines whether evaluations are being used and points to the means by which evaluators can increase the use of their findings.

EXERCISES

1. Select a report of a program evaluation. Such reports are concentrated in journals such as *Evaluation Review*. Identify the type or types of evaluation (needs assessment, program monitoring, impact assessment, efficiency analysis, or utilization research). Criticize the report from the standpoint of its validity. Then criticize it from the standpoint of its utility (that is, the feasibility and clarity of the implications and the extent to which they are congruent with preexisting political, cultural, and economic forces for the status quo).

2. Repeat Exercise 1 until you have found and criticized one example of each of the five types of evaluation. If you are feeling more ambitious, locate and criticize a social impact assessment. You might contact your local government to see if a recent environmental impact assessment is available for a proposed development that affects the quality of life in your own community.

3. Finally, if you have entry to an ongoing project, try your hand at program evaluation. Select an appropriate type of analysis from needs assessment (if the project is just being formed) to an evaluation of utilization (if a program evaluation has already been completed and disseminated).

GLOSSARY

Conceptual utilization: Type of use of evaluation research in which the research serves to provide background information or clarification but does not actually guide the policy choices.

Constant dollars: Expression of costs or benefits in monetary terms that are adjusted for inflation.

Cost-benefit analysis: Approach to efficiency assessment that assigns monetary value to the outcomes of a program and then compares them with the monetary costs of the program.

Cost-effectiveness analysis: Approach to efficiency assessment that compares different programs producing the same benefit in terms of their respective monetary costs.

Discount rate: Interest rate used to adjust future monetary benefits for the rate of gain that could be expected by some alternative use of the same funds.

Efficiency analysis: Stage of evaluative research that weighs the program's accomplishments by its costs.

Environmental impact statements: Social and environmental impact assessments required by the National Environmental Policy Act of 1969 to be prepared and discussed before new projects can be initiated.

Externalities: External costs or benefits that occur to third parties not directly involved in the project as provider or consumer. Since these potential costs must be paid for by someone in the society, the overall evaluation of the project requires that they be accounted and paid for, or "internalized," by the project.

Incidence: Number of new cases of a disorder appearing in a given time period.

Instrumental utilization: Type of use of evaluation research in which decision making is actually affected.

Internal rate of return (IRR): Yield in monetary terms of a program investment expressed as an annual rate.

Management information systems (MIS): Record-keeping procedures for a program by which managers or others can routinely monitor its operation.

Needs assessment: Stage of evaluative research that identifies the goals of a program.

Opportunity cost: Value of the best alternative use of the project's resources, that is, the value foregone by the decision to invest in the project.

Persuasive utilization: Type of evaluation research in which the research is used as ammunition to justify decisions already made. Also called symbolic utilization.

Present value: Value of program benefits adjusted downward by some discount rate.

Prevalence: Number of existing cases at some point in or in some frame of time.

Program audit: Nonroutine evaluation by an outsider of a program's operation.

Program evaluation: Social research applied to judgment of a program's success, usually concerning one or more of the following subtypes: needs assessment, program monitoring, program impact, efficiency, or utilization.

Program impact: Stage of evaluative research that determines whether the goals of the program are being met by the program.

Program monitoring: Stage of evaluative research that checks the conformity of the program's operation with its plan.

Shadow prices: Estimated monetary value of program resources that are otherwise unpriced (for example, volunteer time), based on estimated value in the open marketplace.

Social area analysis: Community description based usually on archival records; a common element in needs assessment.

Social discount rate: The discount rate used in adjusting future returns to social programs, usually lower than the prevailing private investment rate of return.

Social impact assessment (SIA): Evaluation of all possible future costs and benefits of one or more intervention plans.

Social indicators: Regular reports on the psychological health and social well-being of the population. Such social accounts would do for social variables what economic indicators such as unemployment rates do for economic variables.

Utilization: Stage of evaluative research that assesses the extent to which the research report is used.

Appendix

Statistics Review

INTRODUCTION

Summarizing and Clarifying

Graphic Summary. Suppose you received a score of 16 on a 20-point quiz and your grade is to be based "on the curve." How would you go about comparing your score to the class's overall effort? If the imaginary class's scores (and other information such as sex, practice test score, and major) were posted alphabetically by initial, they might look something like Table A–1. But how does the score of 16 compare with the group as a whole? With 26 quiz scores spread over the table, it is difficult to see the whole, and if your class had 200 students, it would be even more difficult to make sense of the scores.

To get a clearer picture, you would need to sort the individuals by scores rather than alphabetically. Figure A–1(a) illustrates such a rearrangement of the

Table A–1   Quiz Scores, Sex, Practice Pretest Scores, and Major by Initials

Initials	Quiz Scores	Sex	Practice Scores	Major
B.A.	17	M	18	Yes
D.B.	11	F	10	Yes
J.B.	18	F	18	No
T.C.	9	M	7	No
R.D.	8	M	10	Yes
P.D.	16	F	16	No
F.E.	15	M	16	Yes
G.F.	14	M	13	Yes
T.F.	17	M	17	Yes
R.G.	10	F	15	Yes
C.H.	12	F	10	No
L.K.	14	F	18	Yes
T.M.	17	M	14	No
B.N.	15	M	16	Yes
S.O.	12	F	16	Yes
S.P.	20	F	19	No
J.R.	15	F	14	No
T.R.	17	M	15	Yes
N.R.	13	F	15	Yes
P.S.	16	F	12	No
D.T.	16	M	16	No
P.T.	18	M	19	Yes
K.T.	17	M	15	Yes
S.U.	15	F	14	No
A.W.	16	M	17	Yes
R.Y.	19	F	20	No

(a) Individuals (initials) grouped by quiz scores

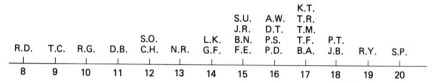

(b) Quiz score histogram

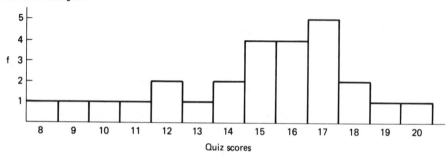

(c) Quiz score frequency polygon

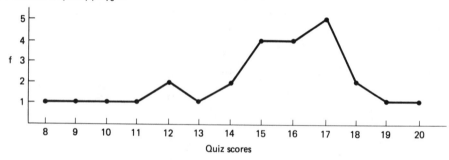

Figure A–1 Frequency distributions.

26 scores in Table A–1. Each set of initials represents one student. Thus, student R.D. got a score of 8, and his initials are located over the number 8. Since his initials are the only ones over the number 8, we know that only one person received that score. Figure A–1(a) is much more helpful than Table A–1 because it shows at a glance how many persons got each score.

Figure A–1(a) could be simplified still further by omitting the initials, which are of less interest than the group's overall performance. Figure A–1(b) is an example of a **frequency distribution**. The frequency (sometimes abbreviated *f*) is the number of occurrences of each score and is indicated on the vertical line, or axis. The scores or categories are indicated on the horizontal axis. The form of the frequency distribution in Figure A–1(b) is called a **histogram**. Another form of frequency distribution is called the **frequency polygon** and is illustrated in Figure

A–1(c). Such displays are helpful because they reduce or remove unnecessary information and organize and highlight the remaining information.

Statistical Summary. Such clarification and abbreviation of data need not stop with frequency distributions. Suppose you wanted to express the performance of the whole section of 26 students in a single number rather than a picture. One simple and commonly used method is the mean. You could simply add up all the individual scores and divide by the number of students. The sum of all 26 quiz scores is 387. Dividing by 26 gives the mean score of 14.88. This number is an example of a **descriptive statistic** because it describes an aspect of a group. You could now locate your score of 16 as being a little more than one point above the mean of the group.

Different kinds of descriptive statistics could be used to summarize different aspects of a group of scores. Some of the most commonly used descriptive statistics will be discussed in later sections of this chapter. Understanding them is essential to understanding reports of social research.

Levels of Measurement

Measurement and Different Types of Variables. Measurement consists of assigning values to observations in a systematic way. A characteristic that can have differing values is called a **variable**. Some variables are regarded as **qualitative variables**, in that observations about them are assigned to different levels or groupings, for example, categorizing persons according to their religion—Catholic, Jewish, Moslem. Often variables have numeric values. When the levels of a qualitative variable have numeric codes, we can think of these codes as naming devices. For example, if we code Catholic = 1, Jewish = 2, and Moslem = 3 for purposes of recording our data, there is no implication that a Moslem is three times a Catholic on any dimension; 3 is just a brief designation for Moslem.

Other kinds of variables are truly **quantitative variables**, in that the numerical values assigned to their observations are intended to reflect different degrees of the measured dimension. For example, when you measure your weight you use a systematic procedure such as stepping on a set of scales, which produces a number for pounds or kilograms. A person weighing 200 pounds is understood to be twice as heavy as one weighing 100 pounds. Measuring weight is understood to be a **continuous measure,** in that a person's weight could be anywhere on the scale, including some fraction such as 133.23 pounds. In contrast to continuous measures, a **discrete measure** could have gaps between possible values. We use a discrete measurement when we count items that cannot have a partial value. To come back to our religious example, it is possible to use a discrete quantitative scale to count the number of individuals with any particular religion, for example, 14 Catholics and 9 Jews in a particular group.

Four Levels of Measurement. It is customary to identify four **levels of measurement** according to the amount of information that is encoded in an observation. In ascending order of the amount of information each level carries, the four measurement levels are nominal, ordinal, interval, and ratio.

In **nominal-level** measurement, observations of the same attribute are grouped together, for example, putting people into religious categories. The only information in nominal-level measurement is that of the equivalence of observations within the separate categories of the variable. This level of measurement is also called the categorical level of measurement and is a clear example of what was earlier termed qualitative.

Ordinal-level measurement goes one step beyond nominal-level measurement in that not only are like observations categorized or grouped together but also the categories are ranked. The meaning of ordinal-level measurement is easy to remember because it involves ordering. An example would be military rank: private versus general. Many social research measures ask for a level of agreement with some statement. For example, the question "Would you rate your social support as very good, satisfactory, or very poor?" asks for an ordinal judgment. Sometimes, ordinal measures use numbers for convenience in coding the answers. In the preceding example, you might have been presented with the answer options "very good (3), satisfactory (2), and very poor (1)," and then been asked to write the number that corresponds to your answer. However, you must remember that using numbers to indicate ordinal categories is only a convenience. When such ordinals are being used as abbreviations or labels, they belong, along with the nominal level, to the qualitative type of measurement. Thus, in the preceding example, you could not conclude that someone answering with a 3 had two units more social support than someone answering with a 1, or three times as much social support as someone answering with a 1. On the other hand, ordinal measures are often used as rough approximations of underlying quantitative realities, and in such cases are often treated much like the next level of measurement.

Interval-level measurement goes one step beyond ordinal measurement. Not only are equivalent observations grouped together in ordered categories, but also the intervals between adjacent categories are equal. The meaning of interval-level measurement will be easy to remember if you think of it as "equal-interval" measurement. The benefit of equal-interval measurement is that numeric labels for different categories are meaningful as numbers and not just as labels. Thus, simple arithmetical operations such as subtraction become appropriate. A good example of an equal-interval measurement is the time of day measured in hours and minutes. The numbers on the clock such as 1 and 3 not only identify which is earlier and later but also indicate that 3 is exactly as much later than 2 as 2 is later than 1. Unlike ordinal measurement, interval measurement establishes the distance between any two levels. However, with interval-level measurement, one cannot say that 100 degrees of centigrade temperature is twice as hot as 50 degrees. The reason is that such a statement would imply that 0 degrees represents no heat. On the centigrade scale, zero does not signify the absence of heat since there is a whole range of negative temperature levels.

Ratio-level measurement is the highest level because it includes all of the characteristics of the interval level plus the additional one of having a true zero point. The advantage of having a true zero is that one can compare different observations by dividing one measure by another. It is easy to remember the meaning of ratio-level measurement because division produces ratios. An example of a ratio measurement is weight. One could weigh oneself (say 150 pounds) and one's pet dog (say 25 pounds) and then express the relationship between the two as a ratio (150 is to 25 as 6 is to 1, or a ratio of 6). Interval and ratio measurements are clear examples of continuous, quantitative variables, and ordinal measures are sometimes treated similarly.

Permissible Statistics Controversy. You may encounter the warning that only certain kinds of statistics can be used with certain levels of measurement and you should, therefore, be aware that a controversy surrounds this matter (for example, Gaito, 1980, opposed this admonition and was rebutted by Townsend & Ashby, 1984). Typically, such guidelines state that ordinal-level data cannot appropriately be analyzed by using statistics (such as the *t* test) supposedly limited to interval-level or ratio-level variables. In practice, such statistics are commonly applied to ordinal-level measures. As the debate has made clear, the decision to use a statistic should be based on the assumptions of the particular statistic, the nature of the underlying construct being measured, and the distribution of the observations (Binder, 1984; Borgatta & Bohrnstedt, 1980; Davison & Sharma, 1988; Maxwell & Delaney, 1985; Michell, 1986).

The remainder of this chapter will present some of the descriptive statistics most commonly seen in the social science literature: first, the statistics used to describe one variable; then a few measures of association between two variables; and finally, a widely used procedure for analyzing three or more variables—multiple regression. There are many more statistics available than can be covered here (for an overview see Andrews, Klem, Davidson, O'Malley, & Rodgers (1981).

UNIVARIATE STATISTICS

Central Tendency and Variability

Statistics that describe one variable are called **univariate statistics.** Two important aspects of a single variable are its **central tendency** (its midpoint) and its **variability** (or dispersion). These two important kinds of univariate statistics will be discussed after reviewing the visual approach of the frequency distribution.

Visual Summaries of One Variable for One Group. A picture of the scores for a whole group of individuals is called a frequency distribution. It combines information about the measurement of the variable (values along the horizontal axis) with information about the number of individuals getting each score (frequency on the vertical axis). The frequency, or count of individuals getting any given score, is a quantitative measure of the type earlier defined as discrete. By using the count, or frequency, it is possible to generate numbers even for nominal- and ordinal-level measurements as well as for interval- and ratio-level measurements. Thus it is possible to derive descriptive statistics for any level of measurement.

Reviewing a frequency distribution such as the one in Figure A–1, we can notice at least four different characteristics. The first is the central tendency of the distribution, that is, the value of the measured variable that is most representative of the group as a whole. A glance at Figure A–1 suggests that the typical person fell in the vicinity of 15 to 17. But "falling in the vicinity of" is too vague, and "typical" can be defined in several different ways (the most common, the middle, or the average). To be more precise, we will need to use one of the descriptive statistics designed to measure central tendency.

The second characteristic is variability or dispersion. Variability refers to the distance of the values from each other. There are different measures of how far apart different observations are from each other, the most common of which are range and standard deviation. Since dispersion pertains to the distance of *ordered* values from each other, it does not apply to nominal measures.

The third common characteristic that can be seen in a glance at a frequency distribution is **symmetry**. If you were to fold the distribution in Figure A–1 on a vertical line down the middle, would the two sides match each other or would one side or tail stretch out farther than the other? If one is longer than the other, the distribution is said to be skewed. **Skewness** is the degree of departure from symmetry. A common skewed distribution is income (with many low incomes but few high incomes). Just as central tendency and dispersion can be expressed precisely by using descriptive statistics, so there is a measure of skewness. The skewness statistic has a value of zero when the distribution is perfectly symmetric (skewness for the variable quiz in Table A–1 = –.64). As distributions are skewed to the left (a longer tail pointing to the lower values), the skewness statistic takes on increasingly larger negative values. Distributions skewed to the right (a long tail trailing off to the larger values) have positive skewness statistics (see Note 3 for the calculation of the skewness statistic).

A fourth characteristic of a distribution also pertains to its shape. Is the distribution relatively flat and spread out or relatively tight and peaked? The name for the degree of peakedness of a distribution is **kurtosis,** and the degree can be measured precisely (see Note 3 for more information about its computation). Often the kurtosis coefficient is adjusted so that a normal distribution has a value of zero, and such moderately peaked distributions are said to be mesokurtic. Negative values of the adjusted kurtosis statistic indicate flatter distributions, called platy-kurtic, and positive values indicate an increasingly peaked shape called leptokurtic. For the variable quiz (Table A–1), the kurtosis is –.28.

Central Tendency. Although the mean is the most commonly seen representation of central tendency, it is not the only such measure and is sometimes inappropriate. For example, it does not make sense to calculate the mean for religious preference in a group of individuals because that expression has no meaning. A measure of central tendency more appropriate for nominal-level variables such as religion is the **mode,** which is simply the value that is most frequently occurring. In the case of Figure A–1, the mode is 17, the value of the highest point of the distribution. Unfortunately, the mode fails to reflect information about the frequency of the other categories. If there is another value that has a high frequency, it is common to report two modes, and such a distribution is called bimodal.

If the level of measurement is at least ordinal, another statistic can be used to describe central tendency. The **median** is the middle value—the one that divides the distribution so that as many observations are above as are below it. In a distribution such as 4, 7, 8, 8, 9, 10, 11, 14, 22, the median is 9 because there are four observations (4, 7, 8, 8) below and four observations (10, 11, 14, 22) above. In Figure A–1 the median is a value not actually observed—it falls between two values. The median for the data in Figure A–1 is 15.5 since 13 scores fall above and 13 scores fall below that value.[1]

The median can be appropriately calculated for ordinal- and higher-level measures but not for nominal measures since for them there is no meaning to the terms *above, middle,* and *below.* The median, unlike the mode, takes into account all of the observations. Unlike the mean, the median does not give any more weight to extreme scores than to more typical scores.

The **mean** (M) is simply the sum divided by the number of observations.[2] It is so commonly seen that it is often abbreviated: either M or $\overline{X}$. Just as it does not make sense to calculate the average religious preference, so it may sometimes not make sense to calculate the mean rank of an ordered variable (for example, among captain, major, and colonel).

The mean takes into account the value of each observation and thus gives proportionally greater weight to *outliers*—those extremely low or high observations that are located far away from the typical scores in a frequency distribution. As a consequence, the mean will often not equal the median and mode. Only if the distribution is symmetric will the mode, the median, and the mean all equal each other. If the distribution is skewed, the extreme scores at the end of the longer tail "pull" the mean toward that end. For example, the mean of the four incomes $1,000, $2,000, $3,000, and $50,000 is $14,000 (pulled far above the lower, more typical incomes). The median will not be pulled so far because it does not respond to the magnitude of the extreme observations and may, therefore, be a better central tendency measure for badly skewed variables. The mode is totally unresponsive to the skew since it remains at the point of the greatest concentration of observations (see Figure A–2).

Variability: Measures of Dispersion. The two most common ways of measuring variability are range and standard deviation. **Range** is simply the span between the lowest and highest observations. Range and other measures of vari-

(a) Symmetric curve

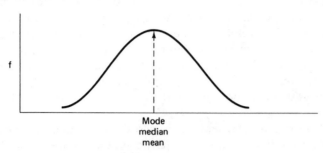

Mode
median
mean

(b) Negative skew

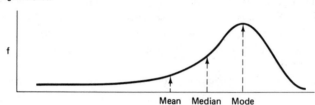

Mean   Median   Mode

(c) Positive skew

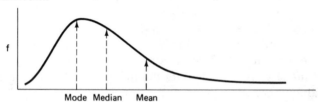

Mode Median   Mean

Figure A–2 Symmetry, skewness, and the location of the mean, median, and mode.

ability are not applicable to nominal measures. Since nominal measures do not have the property of order, it makes no sense to assess the distance from "lowest" to "highest." But range is applicable to ordinal and higher measures. In Figure A–1, the range is from 8 (the lowest score) to 20 (the highest score), or a range of 12.

Range is a very handy but very rough way of describing the dispersion of a group of observations. The range can mislead when the distribution is peculiar (for example, 2, 3, 4, 5, 5, 5, 11, 39). Here the range is from 2 to 39, or 37, but most of the observations are clustered together in the lower part of this wide range (that is, 2 through 5).

The **standard deviation,** symbolized as s or SD, is the most commonly seen measure of variability. The standard deviation takes into account each observation's distance from the mean, not just the values of the two most extreme observations, as in the case of the range. The standard deviation is calculated as follows: First, the difference between each observation and the group mean is obtained. For example, a group of three observations such as 2, 4, and 6 would have a mean of 4—that is, $(2 + 4 + 6)/3 = 12/3 = 4$. Next the mean is subtracted from each observation to yield the deviations from the mean, for example, $2 - 4 = -2$ for the first observation.

The next step is to combine all of these deviations. They could be averaged, but the result would always be zero because the negative and positive values of the deviations would cancel each other no matter how dispersed or concentrated the distribution.

One of the ways to avoid offsetting positive and negative deviations is to square each deviation before averaging. Thus the second step after calculating the deviations is to square each one. For example, the square of the first deviation is $-2^2 = -2 \times -2 = 4$. The third and fourth steps are to calculate the average of the squared deviations by adding them and dividing the sum by the number of observations. In our example, the three squared deviations are 4, 0, and 4, which add up to 8. Divided by 3, this number yields the value of 2.67 for the average squared deviation.

Steps 3 and 4 produce values that have names in their own right. The sum of squared deviations is called, naturally enough, the **sum of squares**. The average of the squared deviations is called the **variance**. The fifth and final step is simply to take the square root of the variance, which in this case is $\sqrt{2.67} = 1.63$. When these five steps are applied to the data in Figure A–1, we obtain a standard deviation [3] of 2.99.

Standard Scores and the Normal Curve

Standard Scores. The **standard** (or *z)* **score** describes an individual's score relative to the group. An individual's raw score is said to be standardized when it is transformed into a z score. First, the group mean is subtracted from the individual's original score. Then this difference is divided by the standard deviation.[4] For example, to return to the original example from the beginning of this chapter, suppose your score was 16. Subtracting the group mean of 14.88, we get a difference of 1.12. Dividing by the standard deviation of 2.99, we get a z score of .37. A z score could be calculated in a similar way for any individual's quiz score.

Standard scores are useful for several reasons. First, the z score summarizes a score's relative position in a group. A z score of .37 indicates two things at a glance. The sign of the z score tells us that the raw score was above the mean of the group. If the z score had been negative, we would have known that the score was below the mean of the group. Second, the magnitude of the z score tells us that the raw score was not very far above the mean—in this case less than 1 standard deviation (.37 of a standard deviation to be precise). A z score of 2 would indicate that the raw score was exactly 2 full standard deviations above the mean, a relatively large amount.

The second benefit of z scores is that they aid in comparing scores from different distributions. Suppose you got the same score of 16 on a later quiz but realized that this later quiz was much more difficult than the previous one. You sense that your score of 16 on the later quiz was a greater accomplishment than the earlier 16. With z scores it is easy to express such comparisons. Suppose that the mean on the later, harder quiz was three points lower (or 11.88) and that the standard deviation was half what it was earlier (or 1.5). In this case, your z score would be (16 − 11.88)/1.5, or 4.12/1.5, or 2.75. Now you can see that your raw score on the later quiz translates into a much larger positive z score, almost 3 standard deviations above the mean. In general, z scores are appropriate for comparing scores from distributions that differ in their means, standard deviations, or both.

A third benefit of z scores is that when a whole group of scores is standardized, the new mean of the group is zero and the new standard deviation is 1. When working with several groups of scores or when handling complicated statistics, it often proves convenient to have groups share the same simple means and standard deviations.

Normal Curve. If you were to observe many frequency distributions, you would find that most would approximate the same shape. This shape in its idealized form is called the **normal curve**. It is symmetrical, neither very peaked nor very flat, and usually described as bell-shaped (see Figure A–3).

So many distributions are roughly similar to this normal curve that we have come to expect groups of observations to be approximately normally distributed, and we take special note of ways in which observed distributions are abnormal (for example, asymmetric, too peaked, or too flat). Some statistics used for drawing conclusions about groups of observations are based on the assumption that the data are normally or nearly normally distributed.

In descriptive statistics, we can make use of a special property of normal distributions—that fixed proportions of observations fall within different sections

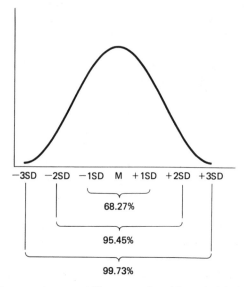

Figure A–3 Normal curve and percent of this area at 1, 2, and 3 standard deviations from the mean.

of the normal curve. For example, just over 2/3 of all scores (68.27 percent to be exact) fall between 1 standard deviation below and 1 standard deviation above the mean. Thus a z score of less than +1 but more than –1 puts that person in the company of the middle 2/3 of the group, assuming that the group's scores are approximately normally distributed. Over 95 percent of all observations fall between +2 and –2 standard deviations, and more than 99 percent fall within ±3 standard deviations (read as "plus or minus 3"). These relationships are summarized in Figure A–3. Recalling these proportions, you will be able to locate your approximate standing in a group if you have your z score (which you can easily calculate from your raw score and the group's mean and standard deviation). For example, if you got a z score on your test of +1, you would know that your performance placed you in the top 1/6 of the class. If your instructor grades on the curve and you know the approximate point on the curve used to distinguish each letter grade (perhaps the top 15 percent get A's), you can estimate your grade.

Single Variable for More Than One Group. This chapter has been devoted, until this point, to the description of one variable in one group. But if you were to sample articles from a recent social science journal, you would probably not see a frequency polygon or a discussion of asymmetry and the relative positions of the mode, median, and mean. Much social research involves many variables or multiple groups or both. Space restrictions make it impractical to print all the frequency distributions that may exist in such studies.

Consequently, the researcher is most likely to summarize information about multiple groups in table or figure form. Only the most important and condensed descriptive information is presented. For example, suppose you were interested in dividing the data of Table A–1 into four groups: male and female majors and nonmajors. After separating the data into the four groups, you could calculate the descriptive statistics and draw the frequency polygons for each of these groups separately. Suppose you then had to select and present just the information that answers the question "Which group did best on the quiz?" You could answer that question in a single table, such as Table A–2.

Table A–2 Quiz Scores by Sex and Major

	MALES		FEMALES		TOTAL	
	n	M	n	M	n	M
Majors	10	15.40	5	12.00	15	14.27
Nonmajors	3	14.00	8	16.38	11	15.73
Total	13	15.08	13	14.69	26	14.88

In this table, *n* stands for the number of observations (in this case, students). The mean for male majors is given in the column labeled *M* under the heading "Males" in the row labeled "Majors": 15.40. This table not only describes the distribution of scores for the four subgroups in question but also gives information about majors and nonmajors, with sexes combined, and about males and females, with majors and nonmajors combined. Notice that the overall or grand mean is given under the vertical column heading "Total" in the row labeled "Total" and is the same value we earlier arrived at for the mean of all the students taking the quiz: 14.88. Implicit in each of the means in Table A–2 is a set of individual quiz scores, which could be arranged into a frequency distribution and for which various other descriptive statistics could be calculated. For example, the standard deviations could have been calculated for each of these subgroups and included in this same table under an appropriate column heading, such as "*SD.*"

The information in Table A–2 could also be presented in graphic form, as in Figure A–4. By convention, the vertical axis is used for the measure itself (in this case, average quiz scores). The horizontal axis is used for the categories or groups falling along one dimension (in this case, sex). When there is a second dimension, as in this case, it can be included by using different lines, as for majors and nonmajors. If there are still more dimensions (for example, class level as upper- and lower-class standing), one would have to make separate figures for each additional category (for example, one for seniors, another for juniors, and so on).

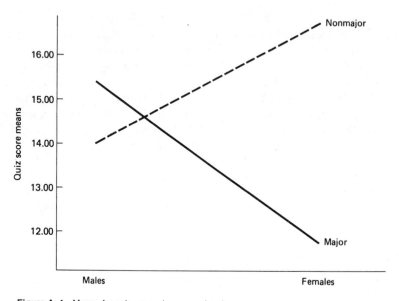

Figure A–4   Means for quiz scores by sex and major.

BIVARIATE STATISTICS

Contingency Tables

Just as distributions of single variables can be displayed graphically and summarized numerically, so can **bivariate statistics** (two-variable) relationships. These methods apply to situations in which each individual in a group has been measured on two different variables.

Cross-Tabulation. When two measures both consist of levels or groupings (such as nominal- or ordinal-level variables), their relationship can be appropriately displayed by cross-tabulation in a contingency table format. **Cross-tabulation** is simply a sorting of individuals into the categories of both variables at the same time. For example, suppose we wanted to cross-tabulate the students from Table A–1 with respect to sex and major status. Each student is either male or female and is also either a major or a nonmajor. The cross-tabulation of students on these two dimensions requires a two-by-two table, as illustrated in Table A–3. This type of tabular display is called a **contingency table** because one can observe whether the sorting of individuals on one dimension (say major versus nonmajor) is contingent on (that is, dependent on) the other dimension (sex).

Every student can be assigned to one and only one of the four cells of the fourfold table. For example, student B.A. would be placed in the upper left-hand cell because he is a male and is a major. One could proceed to assign individuals by initials, as in Table A–3(a). Since the individual designations are not of interest here, it is simpler to count the number of persons in each cell and record them as in Table A–3(b).

This cross-tabulation reorganizes the sex and major data in Table A–1 to permit, at a glance, an assessment of the association of these two variables. In our

Table A–3 Cross-Tabulation of Students by Sex and Major

(a)	Male	Female
Major	B.A., R.D., F.E., G.F., T.F., B.N., T.R., P.T., K.T., A.W.	D.B., R.G., L.K., S.O., N.R.
Nonmajor	T.C., T.M., D.T.	J.B., P.D., C.H., S.P., J.R., P.S., S.U., R.Y.

(b)	Male	Female
Major	10	5
Nonmajor	3	8

hypothetical section, it appears that being a major and being male go together and that being female and being a nonmajor go together. Although this cross-tabulation substantially condenses the raw data about the association of sex and major, it is possible to take one more step. There are statistics that can reduce the information in Table A–3 to a single number, which has the added advantage of expressing precisely the extent to which the two variables "go together" or are associated. Statistics that describe association are generally called **correlation coefficients**.

Proportional Reduction of Error (PRE). Correlation coefficients all approach 1 in absolute value (either +1 or –1) when the association is strong, and they approach zero when the association is weak or nonexistent. Some, but not all, correlation coefficients also tell how much the prediction of one variable is improved by knowing the value of the other. The notion of prediction is used here only as a way of measuring the degree of association. If two variables are not associated, knowledge of one tells us nothing about the other. On the other hand, if two variables are perfectly correlated, knowing the level of one variable tells us the level of the other.

One way of expressing the improvement of prediction is by measuring the **proportional reduction of error** (PRE). Suppose you had to guess whether a student in our hypothetical class was a major or a nonmajor. You know only that out of 26 total students, 15 are majors and 11 are nonmajors. If you had nothing else to go on, you would guess that any particular student is a major since you would be right 15 times and wrong 11 times. If knowledge of another variable reduces our errors in guessing majors, we say that it is associated or correlated with major-nonmajor status. By measuring the proportional reduction of error, we can state precisely how strong the association is.

The proportional reduction of error can be expressed as the difference between the number of errors without knowledge of the other variable (old errors) and with that knowledge (new errors) divided by the number of errors without knowledge: (old errors – new errors)/old errors

If knowledge of the other variable adds nothing to our prediction, old errors will equal new errors and this formula will equal zero. If knowledge of the other variable leads to perfect prediction, there will be no new errors and the formula will equal 1. This formula thus meets our requirement for a correlation coefficient, which approaches 1 as the association strengthens and approaches zero as the association weakens.

Now let us apply this PRE notion to the information in Table A–3, using the sex of the student to reduce our errors in guessing major status. Remember that without knowledge of sex, we would predict or guess that everyone in the section is a major, although we would make 11 errors. This is the old error rate. Now using the information about sex, what predictions would we make about major status and what would our error rate be? Take males first. From Table A–3 we know that of the 13 males, 10 are majors and 3 are nonmajors. If we predict that all males are majors, we will be right 10 times and wrong 3 times. Next, consider females. Of the 13 females, 5 are majors and 8 are nonmajors. If we predict that each female is a nonmajor, we would make just 5 errors. As a result of knowing the student's sex, we would make a total of 8 errors for the section as a whole. Applying the PRE formula, we get $(11 - 8)/11 = 3/11 = .27$

Using this procedure, we can estimate the association of sex and major as .27, which means that knowing the student's sex reduces the error in guessing the major by 27 percent. The name for this particular coefficient is **lambda** (λ). Just as we earlier concentrated the information in Table A–1 about the central tendency of one variable in a single number such as the mean, so we have reduced the information in Table A–3 about the association of two variables to a single number.

Lambda can also be used to express the correlation among ordinal-level measures. However, other kinds of coefficients were expressly designed to capitalize on the extra information contained in ordered variables. One correlation coefficient that is based on PRE and that is often used for ordinal data is called **gamma** (γ). Gamma measures the improvement in predicting the position on one variable (high or low) from knowing the position on the other. A positive gamma indicates that the two variables have like values (both high or both low) rather than unlike values, and a negative gamma expresses the probability of observing unlike values (if high on one variable, then low on the other).

Suppose you wanted to correlate the performance of our students on the most recent quiz with their performance on the practice exam (see Table A–1). One way of organizing the data is to assign letter grades based on scores. This organization could be done in a number of different ways, but let us take 11 and 17 as our dividing points. Failing (F) grades will be assigned to scores up to and including 11. Passing (D and C) grades will be assigned to scores from 12 through 16. Honor (B and A) grades will be assigned to scores of 17 and higher. These categories represent ordinal-level measures because they are ranked, but they have unequal intervals between failing and passing and between passing and honors. We begin by cross-tabulating these two variables (see Table A–4).

We will not concern ourselves with the formula of gamma, but when it is calculated for Table A–4, it is .90. By contrast, the lambda for this same set of data

Table A–4   Cross-Tabulation of Practice Test and Quiz Scores

		PRACTICE TEST		
		Failing	Passing	Honors
Quiz	Failing	3	1	0
	Passing	1	10	2
	Honors	0	3	6

is .46. This difference emphasizes the fact that different types of coefficients will yield different numerical estimates of association for the same data. For the formulas for these and other correlation coefficients consult a standard statistics text.

We will concentrate on the meaning of the coefficient. The gamma was positive, which indicates that like grades (similarly high or similarly low) predominated over unlike grades. A glance at Table A–4 reveals that most students were in the same grade category on the quiz as they were earlier on the practice test: three failed both, ten passed both, and six got honors on both. The opposite kind of association, where a failing practice test would be associated with honors on the quiz, is called an inverse association and would have been indicated by a negative gamma. The gamma was quite large, approaching 1.0, which is the largest possible value, thus indicating that the association was strong.

Unlike ordinal coefficients such as gamma, nominal coefficients such as lambda do not have negative values because nominal variables do not have the property "greater and lesser." Some coefficients such as the lambda are asymmetric. That is, the lambda for predicting major from sex can be different from the lambda calculated for predicting sex from major in our earlier example. In contrast, other correlation coefficients such as gamma are symmetric in that the same value is obtained whether predicting quiz grades from practice test grades or vice versa. This distinction between symmetric and asymmetric correlations is unrelated to the level of measurement. For example, an asymmetric correlation coefficient is sometimes used with ordinal data (Somer's *d*), and you may sometime encounter a symmetric lambda (which consists of a kind of average of the two possible asymmetric lambdas).

Scattergrams and the Pearson Correlation Coefficient

Scattergrams. Sometimes variables take on a large number of different values, as is common with interval- and ratio-level measures. In such cases, cross-tabulation can be very cumbersome. In the previous section, the original scores of the practice exam and quiz combined into two 3-level variables, which were cross-tabulated in Table A–4. Suppose we had cross-tabulated the original raw scores. The box containing all possible combinations of these scores would have had much larger dimensions: 13 (8 through 20 for quiz scores) by 14 (7 through 20 for practice scores), or 182 cells. If we had fractional scores, the number of possible cells could have been enormous.

When displaying the relationship between two interval- or ratio-level variables, the cross-tabulation technique is usually replaced by the **scattergram**. A scattergram uses two axes, as in frequency distributions, and each axis is devoted to one of the two variables in the relationship. Figure A–5 displays the scattergram for the relationship between quiz score and practice score from Table A–1.

Each point in the scattergram represents one student in our hypothetical class. For example, student T.C. has a quiz score of 9 and a practice score of 7. His initials identify the point representing his two scores in Figure A–5. Similarly,

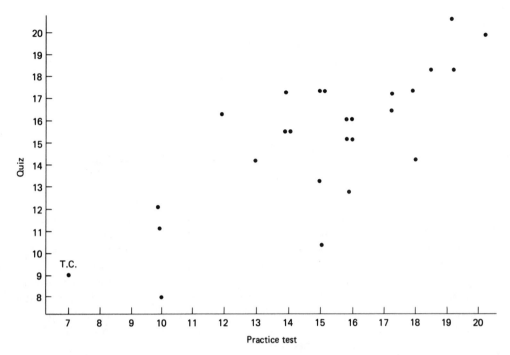

Figure A–5 Scattergram of quiz and practice test scores.

every other student is located by a point signifying two different scores. Since we are not interested in the particular student associated with each point, identifying marks such as initials are omitted from scattergrams. At a glance, the scattergram tells us that the association of the two sets of scores is positive. Small practice scores are associated with small quiz scores just as we had found earlier for the association of grades based on these scores.

Pearson Correlation.   A single number can summarize the association of two variables pictured in a scattergram: the **Pearson product moment correlation coefficient,** represented by the symbol r. The Pearson r is not itself in PRE form. But by a simple transformation—squaring r to r^2—it can be used to express something like the proportional reduction of error. The value r^2 is sometimes called the **coefficient of determination.** Suppose $r = .5$. Then $r^2 = .5 \times .5 = .25$, which signifies that one variable explains 25 percent of the variability in the other.

We need not concern ourselves here with the formula for computing r. The Pearson r ranges from -1 (perfect negative correlation) to $+1$ (perfect positive correlation). Like gamma, r is symmetric in the sense that it has the same value regardless of which of two variables you regard as the predictor. For the practice score and quiz score data for Figure A–5, $r = .76$ and $r^2 = .58$.

Since research reports seldom present scattergrams of associations, it is useful to be able to imagine the appearance of a scattergram by using only the

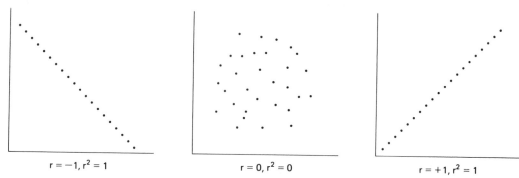

r = −1, r² = 1   r = 0, r² = 0   r = +1, r² = 1

Figure A–6   Examples of scattergrams

information from a correlation coefficient. In Figure A–6 there are three examples of scattergrams corresponding to Pearson correlations of –1, 0, and +1, respectively. Notice that the correlation of $r = 0$ corresponds to a scattergram in which there is no pattern. But the two perfect correlations ($r^2 = 1$) correspond to scattergrams in which all the points fall on a straight line. In the case of negative or inverse correlation ($r = –1$), the line runs from upper left to lower right, indicating that as one variable becomes smaller, the other becomes larger. In the case of the positive correlation ($r = +1$), the points run from lower left to upper right, indicating that as one variable increases, the other also increases.

Other scattergrams would be intermediate between two of these scattergrams. For example, Figure A–5 shows a moderately strong (but not perfect) positive correlation. The points are assembled in a linelike pattern running from lower left to upper right (hence the correlation is positive), but the points are not all exactly on the line (thus the correlation is not a perfect +1). Had the correlation been smaller (say .3), the points would still have formed a pattern running from lower left to upper right, but the line would have been less distinct, with more points falling greater distances from the line. As a correlation becomes smaller and smaller, its scattergram would seem more and more like that of $r = 0$.

Summarizing Many Relationships.   We frequently see the analysis of many variables and many of their possible relationships all in the same report. Suppose there were ten variables that had been collected from the same group of people. Our imaginary class might have, in addition to the practice exam (variable *PE*) and the first quiz (*Q1*), three other quizzes (*Q2, Q3,* and *Q4*) and five homework assignments (assignments *A, B, C, D,* and *E*). Just as we calculated the correlation between *PE* and *Q1* ($r = .76$), we could calculate the correlations between any other pair of these ten variables (for example, *PE* with *Q2, Q3* with *A,* and so forth). It is convenient when presenting many correlations to summarize them in tabular form. A table of correlations is often called a correlation **matrix** (see Table A–5).

The first thing we note in Table A–5 is that much of the space is left blank. The missing coefficients in the upper right half of the table were not forgotten. This

Table A–5 Correlation Matrix for Tests and Homework Assignments

		PE	Q1	Q2	Q3	Q4	A	B	C	D	E
Practice Exam	PE	(1.0)	(.76)								
Quizzes	Q1	.76									
	Q2	.72	.68								
	Q3	.69	.73	.59							
	Q4	.71	.82	.70	.65						
Assignments	A	.38	.37	.30	.29	.33					
	B	.24	.25	.19	.31	.20	.82				
	C	.51	.45	.48	.39	.46	.79	.71			
	D	.09	.05	.15	.11	.10	.65	.48	.62		
	E	.40	.35	.29	.45	.31	.92	.72	.59	.64	

is an example of a symmetric matrix. In symmetric matrices, every coefficient (except the ones on the diagonal) could occur twice. If you folded the matrix along the diagonal from upper left to lower right, you would find that each coefficient was matched with itself. For example, the correlation of PE with Q1 has already been calculated as .76 and can be located in the first column (PE) and second row (Q1). But the correlation could also be located in the second column (Q1) of the first row (PE), as indicated by the .76 in the parentheses. To avoid duplication, the redundant correlations are simply omitted.

The correlations along the diagonal each involve the correlation of a variable with itself, as for example, PE with PE in the first row, first column (indicated by the 1.0 in parentheses). Since the correlation of any variable with itself is always 1.0, all of the diagonal correlations are the same. Instead of printing all these 1's, the diagonal correlations are usually omitted.

Occasionally, you will see a nonsymmetric correlation matrix with values filling all of the rows and columns. In such a case, one set of variables is correlated with another, different set so that no variable is correlated with itself. For example, you can imagine a matrix consisting of the correlations of the practice exam and quizzes (FE through Q4) with the homework assignments (A through E). These correlations would form a full rectangle, as indicated by the box in the lower left of Table A–5.

MULTIVARIATE STATISTICS

Sometimes it is useful to study the association of two or more predictor variables with an outcome variable. Such analyses produce **multivariate statistics,** which have the advantage of describing the association of two variables after adjusting for the effect of the others. Such multivariate analyses can be done with data of any measurement level. For example, nominal or ordinal variables can be studied in multiway contingency tables with as many dimensions as there are variables. Statistical procedures for such cross-classified data are now well developed (for example, loglinear analysis; see Fienberg, 1977). However, the most commonly used multivariate approach in social research is regression analysis. The logic of regression will be presented in the next section, starting with the simplest, two-variable case. The final section will illustrate how regression can be extended for additional variables.

Regression Analysis

Linear Assumption.   Regression analysis is closely related to the kind of correlational analysis described in the prior section. When there are two ordered variables with many levels of each, the nature of their association can be assessed visually in a scattergram, as in Figure A–5. Unlike the Pearson r, which represents this association with a single number, regression describes it with a straight line, which best fits the pattern of points in the scattergram. Implicit in this approach is the **linear assumption**—that the association between the two variables resembles a straight line. If the points form a curving shape such as a U, no straight line can fit well with the data.

The line that is fit to the scattergram's points can be uniquely defined with two numbers. The **intercept** is the value on the vertical axis where the best-fitting line crosses it. The **slope** is the angle of the line. These two numbers are often symbolized by the letters a for the intercept (also called the constant) and b for the slope. The slope tells how much the line rises or falls, expressed in units of the vertical axis for each one unit it extends along the horizontal axis. It is customary to put the outcome variable on the vertical axis and label it Y and the predictor variable on the horizontal axis and label it X. Thus each point in the scattergram can be identified by two numbers, the y value and the x value for the person represented by the point. Because the values on the regression line are estimates, they are labeled $\hat{y}$ (estimated) to discriminate them from the actual values labeled plain y. In summary form, the regression line is defined as: $\hat{y} = a + bx$.

For any possible value of x, the corresponding estimated value of y is the intercept a plus the slope b times x. For example, suppose we know that for each additional hour of weekly study in a course, the average student would probably get an additional five points on the exam and even without study ($x = 0$) would get at least 20 points. How many points would we estimate for the student who studied six hours per week? From our formula, estimated points = 20 (the intercept on the y axis where $x = 0$) plus 5 (slope) times 6 (the given value of x in this case) = 20 + 30 = 50. You can now see that one of the uses of the regression approach is projecting future y values for present x values. For example, a bank economist might regress the number of home loans customers take out (y) on the mortgage rate charged (x). Given the best-fitting line for this regression, the bankers could estimate the demand for home loans for any chosen mortgage rate.

Residual Errors and "Best" Fit. Such hypothetical regression lines are only estimates and seldom fit perfectly with all the points in a scattergram. Other variables—besides the x, which we measure—may also influence y. We can measure some of these other variables and include them in our analysis, but there are always some variables that are omitted from a study. Their omission helps explain why the regression line misses some of the points, that is, why estimated y usually differs at least a little from actual y. Such differences or deviations between actual and expected values are called **residual error,** or residuals.

A regression line is fit to the points in a scattergram in a way that minimizes such error. One could do this visually by drawing first one line and then another to find one that appears closest to all the points. However, computer procedures will perform this function more precisely and quickly by mathematical analysis. Imagine drawing a possible regression line through the points in Figure A–5 and then measuring all of the errors, that is, the distances between each estimated y (the value on the vertical axis of your line for any given x) and each actual y (the value on the vertical axis of the actual point corresponding to the same x). This operation would be equivalent to finding the difference y (estimated) $-y$ (actual) for each x. Graphically this computation would correspond to measuring up or down from your line to each point of the scattergram. Since some of the points are above and some below your hypothetical regression line, these deviations will have both plus and minus values. To convert all these values to positive numbers, it is customary to square them: $(y \text{ estimate} -y \text{ actual})^2$. When all of these squared deviations are added up, we have a term (called the sum of squares) that represents all the errors for this particular regression line. By definition, the best-fitting line is the one that minimizes these errors. For this reason, this approach is also called *least squares regression.*

The least squares line for the data on quiz and practice scores in Figure A–5 is illustrated in Figure A–7. In this case, the intercept (a) is 3.93 and the slope (b) is .73.

Multiple Regression Analysis and Advanced Topics

Adding More Predictors. We have learned that performance on the practice exam is a good predictor of performance on the quiz. Now suppose we were interested in the effects of other, prior variables that might predict exam scores. Perhaps we suspect that women or majors perform better on such tests. To study the effects of each of these variables, we could perform two analyses using quiz as the outcome variable, regressing it first on sex and then on major status. However, if we want to know the effect of each controlling for the other, we would include them both in a single regression. The mathematics of this procedure need not concern us here (for more information on regression, see Berry & Feldman, 1985; Schroeder, Sjoquist, & Stephan, 1986). It is enough to remember that the form of multiple regression analysis is similar to that of bivariate regression. There will still be a constant or intercept value (a), but now there will be two slopes (b_1 and

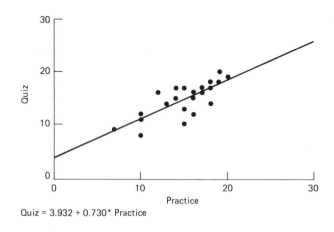

Quiz = 3.932 + 0.730* Practice

Figure A–7   Regression of quiz on practice exam

b_2), one for each predictor. Each describes the increase or decrease in our dependent variable for a unit increase in the predictor. Thus our general regression formula becomes y (estimated) $= a + b_1x_1 + b_2x_2 +. \ldots b_nx_n$, where there are n slope terms, one for each of n predictors.

By converting the information in Table A–1 on sex and major to numbers (1 for males and 0 for females and 1 for major and 0 for nonmajors), these two variables can be analyzed as predictors of quiz scores. The resulting regression gives the following results: $a = 15.42$, b_1 (sex) $= 1.12$, and b_2 (major) $= -1.90$. Of course, multiple regression is not limited to two predictors. We can even include predictors made up of other predictors, such as the product of sex and major. The b for this term tests the interaction between sex and major, that is, whether one sex-by-major combination does better than another. When this term is added, we find that $a = 16.38$, b_1 (sex) $= 12.38$, b_2 (major) $= -4.38$, and b_3 (sex $\times$ major) $= 5.78$. These last results indicate that in these imaginary data the combination of sex and major does affect quiz scores. The nature of this interaction can be seen in Figure A–4, which showed that male majors and female nonmajors did best.

As we add or drop terms from an equation or model, we note that earlier terms may change somewhat. Different models will produce not only different coefficients but also different degrees of fit. We are especially interested in finding a regression model that fits as well as possible. We can judge the overall fit of a regression model by the multiple correlation coefficient R or its square R^2 (similar to the r^2 introduced earlier as the coefficient of determination). You can think of R as the correlation of all of the predictors taken together with the outcome variable. Of course when there is only one predictor, R is the same as the r between the two variables. A large R^2 (approaching 1) indicates that the set of predictors chosen for the model does a good job of accounting for the outcome variable. As we compare one model with another, we can use the change in R^2 to determine how much the addition of more predictors improves the overall fit. In the case of the model with just sex and major, the R^2 was just .09 (leaving over 90 percent of the variability in quiz scores unexplained), but when the interaction between them was added, the

R^2 rose to .28. Although substantially improved, this value still leaves much room for improvement and is not nearly as high as that for the model with practice scores as the predictor ($R^2 = .58$).

Whether the improvement in explanatory power from one model to another is worth noting is the concern of inferential statistics, which are treated in Chapter 8. There you will find an example of a typical tabular presentation of multiple regression results, including tests of whether the observed effect may be due to sampling error or should be considered valid for the population from which the studied sample was drawn.

Advanced Methods in Multivariate Analysis

Other Approaches.   There are a host of sophisticated multivariate statistical procedures, only a few of which can be mentioned in this text. For example, factor analysis (mentioned in Chapter 5) is frequently used in analyzing tests to assess the degree to which various questions measure the same or different concepts. Multiple regression analysis has been applied in path analysis (see Chapter 12), which has been extended to include factor analysis (an approach called structural equation modeling). New computational packages are making these procedures widely available (for example, LISREL and EQS). Another form of regression has been adapted for analyzing experimental designs, called analysis of variance (or ANOVA), and this approach has been extended to cases in which another variable is correlated with the outcome variable (analysis of covariance, or ANCOVA) or there is more than one outcome variable (multiple analysis of variance, or MANOVA).

These techniques increase our ability to study the association of one variable with another while statistically holding constant the effects of other variables. However, these procedures carry with them their own complications, such as additional assumptions about the data, as well as computational complexity. The following section illustrates the nature of this complexity with the problem of analyzing time series data.

Time Series Analysis: An Example.   Data for the same variable(s) at numerous time points are called a **time series**. Several different techniques can be used for time series analysis, the most common being regression analysis. As adapted to the special problems of economic time series, this approach is commonly treated under the label *econometrics* (see Johnston, 1972, for a standard text on econometrics). A more recent but rapidly developing approach is that developed by Box and Jenkins (1976). These and other approaches attempt to determine whether an observed association is due to the influence of some third variable.

This potential for the influence of a third variable is illustrated by the relationship between the number of employed persons and the number of suicides annually from 1900 to 1975. For the United States, this correlation is positive and quite high ($r = .83$, according to Cook, Dintzer, & Mark, 1980, p. 101). One might be tempted to interpret this value as evidence that increased employment causes increased suicide (since it is implausible that increased suicides should lead to increases in employment). However, such an interpretation is so counter to our intuition that we suspect the presence of a third variable.

In the case of employment and suicide, the explanation is readily apparent from a glance at a graph of their relationship over time, as seen in Figure A–8(a). The number of employed persons, the number of suicides, and the number of just about any other aspect of human activity increased steadily from 1900 to 1975 because the population was increasing. That is, the time series relationship between employment and suicide is confounded by the third variable of population growth.

Such a population trend can be removed from the variables before analysis by converting the data to rates (that is, dividing the numbers of suicides and employed by the total number of people). When the trend is removed, the time series is said to be *detrended*. Note that the upward trend of the series in Figure A–8(a) is absent from the detrended series in Figure A–8(b). Detrended employment and detrended suicide are correlated negatively and strongly ($r = -.59$ according to Cook, Dintzer, & Mark, 1980). This finding is consistent with the more intuitive hypothesis that decreases in employment cause increases in suicide.

Sometimes a confounding third variable can be identified and removed, as in the case of population trend. Sometimes the third variable can be measured

(a) Number of employed persons and number of suicides, 1900–1975

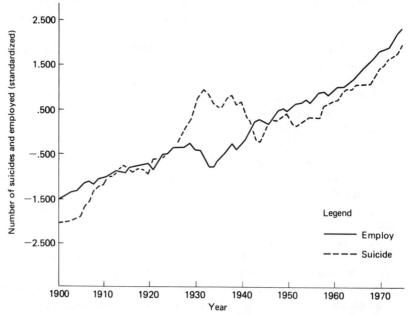

Figure A–8 Concomitant time series relationships with and without trend: Employment and suicide. (From Cook, Dintzer, & Mark, 1980. Copyright © 1980 by Sage Publications, Inc. Reprinted by permission of Sage Publications, Inc.)

(b) Employment rate and suicide rate, 1900–1975.

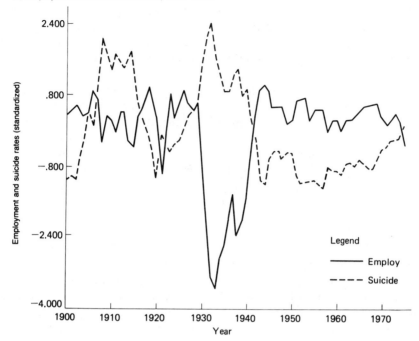

Figure A–8   (Continued).

and included in the analysis in order to assess the partial association of the "cause" and "effect" time series with the third variable being statistically controlled. Other times, the potentially confounding third variable cannot be identified. Nevertheless, we may suspect that some such confounding variable causes some of the shared regularity in the movements of the two time series of interest. If we decide that any regularities in the time series may be due to a confounding but unidentified variable, we can remove these regularities from one or both time series.

The procedures most commonly used to detect and filter out regularities in a time series derive from the Box-Jenkins method (1976). Although statistically sophisticated, the principles underlying the Box-Jenkins analysis are simple enough. When we say that a time series has a regularity or a recurring pattern, we are saying that it contains information about itself. That is, if a pattern recurs (such as a rise in employment every November), this recurrence provides information that allows us to predict what will happen in future Novembers. If we could distill all the information about such regularities, we could apply it to make the best possible predictions about future time points.

The Box-Jenkins method is a technique that distills such information about regularities that can be found within a time series. The method begins with something called an autocorrelogram, which is nothing more than the correlation of a series with lagged versions of itself. For example, a monthly series could be correlated with itself lagged one month, two months, and so on up to 12, 24, or more months. The subsequent statistical procedure goes beyond the scope of this text. But the result is a condensed expression for the type of regularities in the studied time series along with the coefficients for estimating future values. If the estimated values based on this information are subtracted from the actual values, the residuals will have the regularities removed (much as the values expected from an increasing trend can be subtracted from a raw time series to produce a detrended time series). In Box-Jenkins analysis, such a time series of residuals with all regularities and information removed is called **white noise**. If both the "cause" and "effect" time series are reduced to white noise, their subsequent correlation produces a very conservative test of their association. When Cook, Dintzer, and Mark (1980) "prewhitened" both employment and suicide rates, they found the strongest association to be "on time" (that is, no lead or lag), and the magnitude of this best association was still strongly negative ($r = -.59$).

If you were to read reports of time series analysis, you would encounter concern with the problem of **serial correlation**. The most common way of summarizing the magnitude of the relationship between two series is with a correlation coefficient. The test of its statistical significance rests on a number of assumptions, one of which is frequently violated in time series work—namely, the assumption of no serial correlation of residuals. Recall that regression produces such estimates of the actual data that the residuals between the estimates and actual data are as small as possible. One assumption underlying the significance test of the correlation coefficient is that the residuals produced in calculating the correlation coefficient are not themselves correlated. Unfortunately, this assumption is frequently violated in time series analysis, and the problem is called serial correlation. Fortunately, the most common kind of correlated residuals can be detected by the Durbin-Watson (1950, 1951) test, and the serial correlation can be corrected by using a modification of regression called generalized least squares, or GLS (see Hanushek & Jackson, 1977). When you come across references to the Durbin-Watson d statistic and the necessity of utilizing GLS in reports of time series analysis, you are seeing the effort of the researcher to make sure that one of the requirements of the statistical analysis is satisfied. This example illustrates the kind of extra effort necessary for the proper use of such advanced statistical procedures (see Catalano, 1981; Catalano & Serxner, 1987).

SUMMARY

The focus of this chapter has been on reduction and clarification. Descriptive statistics make sense out of raw observations. By grouping the data or isolating selected aspects of the data, we can discover the essential amid the irrelevant. This chapter has presented some of the many ways of summarizing and presenting data. The exploration of data by using descriptive techniques can be a more elaborate process than has been detailed here (see, for example, Tukey, 1977).

The first section dealt with univariate descriptive statistics and visual summary procedures for single variables from single groups. A single variable can be summarized visually by a frequency distribution in such forms as the histogram or the frequency polygon. Descriptive statistics for central tendency (mode, median, and mean) and dispersion (range and standard deviation) may be supplemented by measures of skewness and kurtosis. Finally, the z score was offered as a convenient measure of one observation's relative standing on the assumption of a normal distribution.

The next section dealt with different graphic and statistical techniques of describing relationships between two variables. When the measures are nominal or ordinal, the relationships are commonly portrayed in a cross-tabulation. When the data are ordered and take on many different values, as is often the case with interval or higher-level measures, it is more convenient to present the relationship in a scattergram. Measures of association can be condensed into single numbers or coefficients of correlation. These numbers typically approach 1 (plus or minus) as the relationship becomes stronger and zero as the relationship becomes weaker. Some, but not all, correlation coefficients are based on the idea of PRE—proportional reduction of error. Those coefficients that have the PRE property tell the percentage of improvement in predicting one variable that comes from knowing the other variable.

The final section introduced multivariate statistics, in which two or more predictors can be studied simultaneously in their relationship to an outcome variable. The most widely used multivariate approach, regression analysis, was introduced in the simple, two-variable case and then illustrated with a multivariate example. The numerous advanced statistical procedures were represented by an example from time series analysis, which showed how multivariate procedures are necessary to control for possible confounding by a third variable.

EXERCISES

1. Review each of the visual (frequency distribution) and statistical methods of describing a single variable. For example, use the data in Table A–1 for practice scores to make a histogram or frequency polygon as in Figure A–1. Then calculate the mode, median, and mean as well as the range and standard deviation for this variable.

2. Using the information you have generated about practice scores, compute the standardized, or z, scores for a few individuals. Assess their percentile standing on this test, assuming the distribution is nearly normal. As you take tests in your courses, calculate your own z scores if your instructors provide class means and standard deviations.

3. Review the translation of tabular data into graphic form. Calculate the means by sex and major for practice scores in Table A–1. Then create a graph such as Figure A–4 for the same data.

4. Make a scattergram (as in Figure A–5) of quiz scores and practice scores for just the majors in Table A–1, and then repeat this operation for the nonmajors. Compare these two scattergrams and describe the association in each in terms of direction (positive or inverse) and magnitude. Try drawing a best-fitting straight line through each swarm of points, based on your visual assessment, and estimate the intercept and slope of each.

5. Find a research article with a Pearson correlation matrix (as in Table A–5) or the results of a multiple regression analysis. Select one correlation or regression coefficient from the article and name the two variables involved. Then describe their relationship in ordinary language based on the sign and magnitude of the coefficient.

GLOSSARY

Bivariate statistics: Descriptive statistics for the association of two variables.

Central tendency: Value of the score or category most representative of the group as a whole.

Coefficient of determination: Transformation of r by squaring (r^2), which expresses a relationship in PRE terms, that is, percentage of the variance explained.

Contingency table: Cross-tabulation among two or more variables.

Continuous measure: Type of quantitative variable that can take on any value in its possible range, for example, a person's height, which can be measured in fractions of an inch or meter.

Correlation coefficient: Measure of association, can be the same (symmetric) or different (asymmetric) when predicting one variable from another or vice versa.

Cross-tabulation: Tabular summary of an association in which each individual is assigned to one and only one cell, representing a combination of the levels of the variables.

Descriptive statistics: Class of computed variables that summarize observations.

Discrete measurement: Type of quantitative variable that can take on only certain values between which are gaps, for example, counting the number of students enrolled in a class, for which fractions would be nonsensical.

f: Symbol for frequency.

Frequency distribution: Visual summary of a group of observations in which the number of occurrences of each score (frequency) is indicated on the vertical axis and the value of the score on the horizontal axis.

Frequency polygon: Type of frequency distribution in which a line joins points representing the frequencies of the scores.

Gamma: PRE measure of association for ordinal variables.

Histogram: Type of frequency distribution in which vertical bars represent the frequencies of the scores.

Intercept: In regression analysis, the point on the vertical axis where it meets the regression line, that is, the estimated value of the outcome variable when the predictor variable has the value of zero; usually symbolized by the letter a.

Interval level: Type of measurement that assigns scores on a scale with equal intervals.

Kurtosis: Degree to which the frequency distribution is flat or peaked.

Lambda: PRE measure of association for nominal variables.

Levels of measurement: Categorization of measurement into four types based on the amount of information in the measure: nominal, ordinal, interval, ratio.

Linear assumption: In regression analysis, the assumption that the relationship between the studied variables is best described by a straight line.

Matrix: Table of numbers such as correlations. If the correlations are for one set of variables with itself, the matrix is symmetric (that is, with 1s in the diagonal, and the lower left half is the same as the upper right half).

Mean (M): Measure of central tendency consisting of the sum divided by the number of observations, symbolized by M or $\overline{X}$.

Median: Measure of central tendency consisting of a score with as many observations above as below.

Mode: Measure of central tendency consisting of the most frequently occurring score; if the distribution has two modes, the distribution is called bimodal.

Multivariate statistics: Analytic procedures that can study three or more variables simultaneously, as for example two or more predictors in relation to an outcome variable.

n: Symbol for the number of individuals or observations.

Nominal level: Type of measurement that assigns observations to unordered categories.

Normal curve: Commonly seen, bell-shaped distribution.

Ordinal level: Type of measurement that assigns observations to ordered categories.

Pearson product moment correlation coefficient (r): Non-PRE measure of association best suited for interval or higher variables.

Proportional reduction of error (PRE): Quality of some correlation coefficients that measure association as the degree of improvement in predicting one variable from the other.

Qualitative variables: Type of variable for which observations are assigned to levels rather than given precise quantitative values, for example, religious preference.

Quantitative variables: Type of variable for which observations are assigned measured values, for example, temperature.

Range: Measure of variability consisting of the span between the lowest and highest scores.

Ratio level: Type of measurement that assigns scores on a scale with equal intervals and a true zero point.

Residual error: In regression analysis, the distance or deviation between the estimated value from the regression line and the actual value of the outcome variable for any given value of the predictor variable; also called residuals or deviations.

Scattergram: Graphic presentation of an association in which each point indicates the two scores of each individual.

Serial correlation: Assumption made in the regression analysis of a time series that the residuals or differences between estimated and actual values will be uncorrelated; such a correlation is called the serial correlation of the errors and requires special care in the analysis.

Skewness: Degree of departure from symmetry (that is, one side or tail of the distribution is longer than the other). If the longer tail is to the right, it is called positive skew; to the left, negative skew.

Slope: In regression analysis, the angle of the best-fitting line, that is, how many units on the vertical axis the line rises or falls for each unit on the horizontal axis; commonly symbolized by the letter b.

Standard deviation (SD): Measure of variability; a type of weighted average of distances from the mean of all the observations.

Standard score (z): Individual's score, minus the group mean, divided by the group's standard deviation.

Sum of squares: Sum of the squared deviations from the mean in calculations of variance or from the regression line in assessing its fit.

Symmetry: In a frequency distribution, the degree of similarity of shape of the left and right sides of the distribution.

Time series: Data for a variable at numerous time points, for example, the unemployment rate for each month for several years.

Univariate statistics: Descriptive statistics for one variable.

Variability: Distance of scores from each other; also called dispersion.

Variable: Characteristic of persons, objects, or events that can take on different values.

Variance: Average of the squared deviations from the mean.

White noise: In time series analysis, when the residuals between the estimated and actual values have no correlation among themselves at any lag.

NOTES

1. When the median falls in a class of values, its calculation can be a bit complicated. For example, suppose that the distribution was 4, 7, 8, 9, 9, 10, 11, 14, 22. The value 9 is not the median since there are unequal numbers of observations above (4: 10, 11, 14, 22) and below (3: 4, 7, 8). In this case, the median falls somewhere in the range of values between 8 and 10, that is, between 8.5 and 9.5. The formula for calculating the median in this case is as follows:

$$L + \left(\frac{\frac{T}{2} - B}{M} \right) I, \text{ where}$$

L is the lower boundary of the interval that includes the median, that is, 8.5.
I is the range of the interval that includes the median; that is, $I = 9.5 - 8.5$.
T is the total number of all observations in the distribution, that is, 9.
B is the number of observations below the interval that contains the median, that is, 3: 4, 7, 8.
M is the number of observations in the interval that contains the median, that is, 2: 9, 9. In this example, the median can be found by substituting into the formula

$$8.5 + \left(\frac{\frac{9}{2} - 3}{2} \right) 1 = 8.5 + \frac{4.5 - 3}{2} = 8.5 + \frac{1.5}{2} = 8.5 + .75 = 9.25$$

2. The expression "sum divided by number" is a translation of a mathematical expression: $\Sigma X / N$, where N = total number of observations and Σ is the symbol for summation. ΣX means that all observations, or Xs, are to be added together. The distribution 5, 4, 3, 2 consists of four observations. Each observation may be thought of as an X. Thus $X_1 = 5$, $X_2 = 4$, and so forth. The expression ΣX means $X_1 + X_2 + X_3 + X_4$ or $5 + 4 + 3 + 2$, or 14. $\Sigma X / N$ means 14/4, or 3.5.

3. In the form of mathematical symbols, the standard deviation is

$$SD = \sqrt{\frac{\Sigma (X - M)^2}{N}}$$

Sometimes you will see a slightly different version of this formula, with $N - 1$ substituted for N. The reason for this latter version is that, in small samples, it provides a better estimate of the standard deviation of the population from which the sample came. However, as sample size increases above about 30, the two versions give virtually the same result for practical purposes. Since we are not estimating population variability here, we will use the form with N in the denominator. The expression $(X - M)$ is called a deviation because it measures the distance or deviation of any observation X from the mean. The calculation of the variance requires that each deviation be squared before averaging. But lower and higher powers of this deviation could be taken. The average of the deviations is called the first moment, $\Sigma (X - M) / N$, which is uninteresting because it is always zero. The average of the second power of the deviations is called the second central moment, which is the variance: $\Sigma (X - M)^2 / N$. The averages of the third and fourth powers of the deviations are called the third and fourth central moments, respectively. These higher moments are the basis for calculating the statistics measuring skewness and kurtosis.

$$\text{Skewness:} \quad \frac{\dfrac{\sum (X - M)^3}{N}}{SD^3} \qquad\qquad \text{Kurtosis:} \quad \frac{\dfrac{\sum (X - M)^4}{N}}{SD^4}$$

4. In notation, $z = (X_i - M)/SD$. Here the subscript i represents any individual in the group. For example, if individual number 1 were to have his or her score standardized, i would be 1 (that is, the ith person in this case would the first person), and $z_1 = (X_1 - M)/SD$, where X_1 is the first person's raw quiz score and Z_1 is that person's standardized score. M and SD will be the same for each person from the same group since they describe the group of scores as a whole.

References

ADAMS, J. (1978). Sequential strategies and the separation of age, cohort, and time-of-measurement contributions to developmental data. *Psychological Bulletin, 85,* 1309–1316.

AD HOC COMMITTEE ON ETHICAL STANDARDS IN PSYCHOLOGICAL RESEARCH. (1973). *Ethical principles in the conduct of research with human participants.* Washington, D.C.: American Psychological Association.

AMERICAN ANTHROPOLOGICAL ASSOCIATION. (1979). *Professional ethics: Statements and procedures of the American Anthropological Association.* Washington, D.C.: Author.

AMERICAN PSYCHOLOGICAL ASSOCIATION. (1983). *Publication manual of the American Psychological Association* (3rd edition). Washington, D.C.: Author.

———. (1985). *Standards for educational and psychological testing.* Washington, D.C.: Author.

———. (1987). *Casebook on ethical principles of psychologists.* Washington, D.C.: Author.

———. (1988). *Thesaurus of psychological index terms* (5th edition). Washington, D.C.: Author.

AMERICAN SOCIOLOGICAL ASSOCIATION. (1982). Revised code of ethics. *Footnotes, 10* (23), 9–10.

ANASTASI, A. (1976). *Psychological testing.* New York: Macmillan.

ANDERSEN, R., KASPER, J., FRANKEL, M., & ASSOCIATES. (1979). *Total survey error.* San Francisco: Jossey-Bass.

ANDREWS, F. M., KLEM, L., DAVIDSON, T. N., O'MALLEY, P. M., & RODGERS, W. L. (1981). *A guide for selecting statistical techniques for analyzing social science data.* Ann Arbor, Mich.: Institute for Social Research.

ARMOR, D. J. (1972). The evidence on busing. *Public Interest, 28,* 90–126.

———. (1980). White flight and the future of school desegregation. In W. G. Stephan & J. R. Feagin (Eds.), *School desegregation: Past, present, and future.* New York: Plenum Press.

ASHER, H. B. (1976). *Causal modeling.* Beverly Hills, Calif.: Sage.

ASSAEL, H., & KEON, J. (1982). Nonsampling vs. sampling errors in survey research. *Journal of Marketing, 46,* 114–123.

ATKINSON, D. R., FURLONG, M. J., & WAMPOLD, B. E. (1982). Statistical significance, reviewer evaluations, and the scientific process: Is there a (statistically) significant relationship? *Journal of Counseling Psychology, 29,* 189–194.

BABAD, E. Y., INBAR, J., & ROSENTHAL, R. (1982a). Pygmalion, Galatea, and the Golem: Investigations of biased and unbiased teachers. *Journal of Educational Psychology, 74,* 459–474.

———. (1982b). Teachers' judgment of students' potential as a function of teachers' susceptibility to biasing information. *Journal of Personality and Social Psychology, 42,* 541–547.

BABBIE, E. R. (1973). *Survey research methods.* Belmont, Calif.: Wadsworth.

BAILAR, B. A. (1976). Some sources of error and their effect on census statistics. *Demography, 13,* 273–286.

BALES, J. (1988, November). Breuning pleads guilty in scientific fraud case. *APA Monitor,* p. 12.

BALES, R. F. (1950). *Interaction process analysis: A method for the study of small groups.* Reading, Mass.: Addison-Wesley.

———. (1969). *Personality and interpersonal behavior.* New York: Holt, Rinehart & Winston.

BALTES, P. B., CORNELIUS, S. W., & NESSELROADE, J. R. (1979). Cohort effects in developmental psychology. In J. R. Nesselroade & P. B. Baltes (Eds.), *Longitudinal research in the study of behavior and development.* New York: Academic Press.

BANE, M. J., & ELLWOOD, D. T. (1983). *Dynamics of dependence: The routes to self-sufficiency* (Final Report). Cambridge, Mass.: Urban Systems Research and Engineering. (NTIS No. PB83-258699).

BANGERT-DROWNS, R. L. (1986). Review of developments in meta-analytic method. *Psychological Bulletin, 99,* 388–399.

BARBER, B., & HIRSCH, W. (Eds.). (1962). *The sociology of science.* New York: Free Press.

BARNETT, W. S. (1985). *The Perry Preschool Program and its long-term effects: A benefit-cost analysis.* Ypsilanti, Mich.: High/Scope Educational Research Foundation.

BARTZ, W. R., AMATO, P. R., RASOR, R. A., & RASOR, M. O. (1981). Effects of reducing student anxiety in a statistics course. *Australian Psychologist, 16,* 347–353.

BAUMOL, W. J. (1969). On the appropriate discount rate for evaluation of public projects. In H. H. Hinrichs and G. M. Taylor (Eds.), *Program budgeting and benefit-cost analysis: Cases, text, and readings.* Pacific Palisades, Calif.: Goodyear.

BAUMRIND, D. (1983). Specious causal attributions in the social sciences: The reformulated stepping-stone theory of heroin use as exemplar. *Journal of Personality and Social Psychology, 45,* 1289–1298.

BAUMRIND, D. (1985). Research using intentional deception: Ethical issues revisited. *American Psychologist, 40,* 165–174.

BEALS, R. L. (1969). *Politics of social research.* Chicago: Aldine.

BECKER, H. S. (1958). Problems of inference and proof in participant observation. *American Sociological Review, 23,* 652–660.

BEECHER, H. K. (1970). *Research and the individual.* Boston: Little, Brown.

BEGLEY, S., MALAMUD, P., & HAGER, M. (1982, February 8). A case of fraud at Harvard. *Newsweek,* pp. 89–93.

BENTLER, P. M. (1980). Multivariate analysis with latent variables: Causal modeling. *Annual Review of Psychology, 31,* 419–456.

BENTLER, P. M., & BONETT, D. G. (1980). Significance tests and goodness of fit in the analysis of covariance structures. *Psychological Bulletin, 88,* 588–606.

BENTLER, P. M., & WOODWARD, J. A. (1978). A Head Start reevaluation: Positive effects are not yet demonstrable. *Evaluation Quarterly, 2,* 493–510.

BERELSON, B. (1952). *Content analysis in communication research.* New York: Free Press.

BERGIN, A. E., & LAMBERT, M. J. (1978). The evaluation of therapeutic outcomes. In S. L. Garfield and A. E. Bergin (Eds.), *Handbook of psychotherapy and behavior change: An empirical analysis* (pp. 239–252). New York: John Wiley.

BERKOWITZ, L., & DONNERSTEIN, E. (1982). External validity is more than skin deep: Some answers to criticisms of laboratory experiments. *American Psychologist, 37,* 245–257.

BERRUETA-CLEMENT, J. R., SCHWEINHART, L. J., BARNETT, W. S., EPSTEIN, A. S., & WEIKART, D. P. (1984). *Changed lives: The effects of the Perry Preschool Program on youths through age 19.* Ypsilanti, Mich.: High/Scope Educational Research Foundation.

BERRY, W. D. (1984). *Nonrecursive causal models.* Beverly Hills, Calif.: Sage.

BERRY, W. D., & FELDMAN, S. (1985). *Multiple regression in practice.* Beverly Hills, Calif.: Sage.

BERSOFF, D. N. (1987). Social science data and the Supreme Court: Lockhart as a case in point. *American Psychologist, 42,* 52–58.

BERTERA, E. M., & BERTERA, R. L. (1981). The cost-effectiveness of telephone vs. clinic counseling for hypertensive patients: A pilot study. *American Journal of Public Health, 71,* 626–629.

BINDER, A. (1984). Restrictions on statistics imposed by method of measurement: Some reality, much mythology. *Journal of Criminal Justice, 12,* 467–481.

BIRDWHISTELL, R. L. (1970). *Kinesics and context: Essays on body motion and communication.* Philadelphia: University of Pennsylvania Press.

BISHOP, G. F., OLDENDICK, R. W., & TUCHFARBER, A. J. (1985). The importance of replicating a failure to replicate: Order effects on abortion items. *Public Opinion Quarterly, 49,* 105–114.

BLANCK, P. D., & ROSENTHAL, R. (1984). Mediation of interpersonal expectancy effects: Counselor's tone of voice. *Journal of Educational Psychology, 76,* 418–426.

BLOOMBAUM, M. (1983). The Hawthorne experiments: A critique and reanalysis of the first statistical interpretation by Franke and Kaul. *Sociological Perspectives, 26,* 71–88.

BONJEAN, C. M., HILL, R. J., & MCLEMORE, S. D. (1967). *Sociological measurement: An inventory of scales and indices.* San Francisco: Chandler.

BOOTH, A., & JOHNSON, D. R. (1985). Tracking respondents in a telephone interview panel selected by random digit dialing. *Sociological Methods and Research, 14,* 53–64.

BORGATTA, E. F., & BOHRNSTEDT, G. W. (1980). Level of measurement: Once over again. *Sociological Methods and Research, 9,* 147–160.

BOULDING, K. E. (1966). *The impact of the social sciences.* New Brunswick, N.J.: Rutgers University Press.

BOX, G. E. P., & JENKINS, G. M. (1976). *Time series analysis: Forecasting and control.* San Francisco: Holden-Ray.

BRADBURN, N. M., SUDMAN, S., & BLAIR, E. (1979). *Improving interview method and questionnaire design.* San Francisco: Jossey-Bass.

BREWER, M. B., & COLLINS, B. E. (Eds.). (1981). *Scientific inquiry and the social sciences.* San Francisco: Jossey-Bass.

BROAD, W. J. (1982). Report absolves Harvard in case of fakery. *Science, 215,* 874–876.

BROAD, W. J., & WADE, N. (1982). *Betrayers of the truth.* New York: Simon & Schuster.

BROWNE, J. (1976). Field work for fun and profit. In M. P. Golden (Ed.), *The research experience.* Itasca, Ill.: Peacock.

BUREAU OF THE CENSUS. (1978). *The current population survey: Design and methodology. Technical Paper No. 40.* Washington, D.C.: U.S. Government Printing Office.

BUROS, O. K. (Ed.). (1978). *Eighth mental measurements yearbook.* Highland Park, N.J.: Gryphon Press.

BYRNE, D. G., ROSENMAN, R. H., SCHILLER, E., & CHESNEY, M. A. (1985). Consistency and variation among instruments purporting to measure the Type A Behavior Pattern. *Psychosomatic Medicine, 47,* 242–261.

CACIOPPO, J. T., & PETTY, R. E. (1981). Electromyograms as measures of extent and affectivity of information processing. *American Psychologist, 36,* 441–456.

CAMPBELL, D. T. (1975). Reforms as experiments. In E. L. Struening and M. Guttentag (Eds.), *Handbook of evaluation research, Vol 1.* Beverly Hills, Calif.: Sage.

CAMPBELL, D. T., & ERLEBACHER, A. (1970). How regression artifacts in quasi-experimental evaluations can mistakenly make compensatory education look harmful. In J. Hellmuth (Ed.), *Dis-*

advantaged child, Vol. 3: Compensatory education: A national debate. New York: Bruner/Mazel.

CAMPBELL, D. T., & FISKE, D. W. (1959). Convergent and discriminant validation by the multitrait-multimethod matrix. *Psychological Bulletin, 56,* 81–105.

CAMPBELL, D. T., & STANLEY, J. C. (1963). *Experimental and quasi-experimental designs for research.* Skokie, Ill.: Rand McNally.

CAMPBELL, J. P. (1976). Psychometric theory. In M.D. Dunnette (Ed.), *Handbook of industrial and organizational psychology* (pp. 185–222). Chicago: Rand McNally.

CARMELLI, D., ROSENMAN, R. H., & CHESNEY, M. A. (1987). Stability of the Type A Structured Interview and related questionnaires in a 10-year follow-up of an adult cohort of twins. *Journal of Behavioral Medicine, 10,* 513–525.

CARVER, R. P. (1978). The case against statistical significance testing. *Harvard Educational Review, 48,* 378–399.

CATALANO, R. (1981). Contending with rival hypotheses in correlation of aggregate time-series (CATS): An overview for community psychologists. *American Journal of Community Psychology, 9,* 667–679.

CATALANO, R., & SERXNER, S. (1987). Time series designs of potential interest to epidemiologists. *American Journal of Epidemiology, 126,* 724–731.

CECI, S. J., PETERS, D., & PLOTKIN, J. (1985). Human subjects review, personal values, and the regulation of social science research. *American Psychologist, 40,* 994–1002.

CHAPPLE, E. D. (1949). The Interaction Chronograph: Its evolution and present application. *Personnel, 25,* 295–307.

CHEN, H., & ROSSI, P. H. (1980). The multi-goal, theory-driven approach to evaluation: A model linking basic and applied social science. *Social Forces, 59,* 106–122.

CHU, F. D., & TROTTER, S. (1974). *The madness establishment: Ralph Nader's study group report on the National Institute of Mental Health.* New York: Grossman.

CHUN, K., COBB, S., & FRENCH, J. R. P., JR. (1975). *Measures for psychological assessment: A guide to 3000 original sources and their applications.* Ann Arbor: University of Michigan Press.

CICCHETTI, D. V. (1980). Reliability of reviews for the *American Psychologist*: A biostatistical assessment of the data. *American Psychologist, 35,* 300–303.

CICIRELLI, V. G. (1970). The relevance of the regression artifact problem to the Westinghouse-Ohio Evaluation of Head Start: A reply to Campbell and Erlebacher. In J. Hellmuth (Ed.), *Disadvantaged child, Vol. 3: Compensatory education: A national debate.* New York: Bruner/Mazel.

CICIRELLI, V. G., EVANS, J. W., & SCHILLER, J. S. (1970). The impact of Head Start: A reply to the report analysis. *Harvard Educational Review, 40,* 105–129.

CLEARY, T. A., HUMPHREYS, L. G., KENDRICK, S. A., & WESMAN, A. (1975). Educational uses of tests with disadvantaged students. *American Psychologist, 30,* 15–41.

CLIFFORD, F. (1987, November 27). Worrisome trend: Research funds: Not so scientific. *Los Angeles Times,* pp. 1, 3, 28.

COLE, S., COLE, J. R., & SIMON, G. A. (1981). Chance and consensus in peer review. *Science, 214,* 881–886.

COLEMAN, J. S. (1976). Correspondence: Response to Professors Pettigrew and Green. *Harvard Educational Review, 46,* 217–224.

COLEMAN, J. S., CAMPBELL, E. Q., HOBSON, C. J., McPARTLAND, J., MOOD, A. M., WEINFELD, F. D., & YORK, R. L. (1966). *Equality of educational opportunity.* Washington, D.C.: U.S. Government Printing Office.

COLLINS, B. E., & HOYT, M. F. (1972). Personal responsibility for consequences: An integration and extension of the "forced compliance" literature. *Journal of Experimental Social Psychology, 8,* 558–593.

COMMITTEE FOR THE PROTECTION OF HUMAN PARTICIPANTS IN RESEARCH. (1982). *Ethical principles in the conduct of research with human participants.* Washington, D.C.: American Psychological Association.

COMSTOCK, G. W., & HELSING, K. J. (1973). Characteristics of respondents and nonrespondents to a questionnaire for estimating community mood. *American Journal of Epidemiology, 97,* 233–239.

CONNER, R. F. (1977). Selecting a control group: An analysis of the randomization process in twelve social reform programs. *Evaluation Quarterly, 1,* 195–244.

CONVERSE, J. M., & PRESSER, S. (1986). *Survey questions: Handcrafting the standardized questionnaire.* Beverly Hills, Calif.: Sage.

COOK, S. W. (1985). Experimenting on social issues: The case of school desegregation. *American Psychologist, 40,* 452–460.

COOK, T. D., & CAMPBELL, D. T. (1979). *Quasi-experimentation: Design and analysis issues for field settings.* Skokie, Ill.: Rand McNally.

COOK, T. D., DINTZER, L., & MARK, M. M. (1980). The causal analysis of concomitant time-series. *Applied Social Psychology Annual, 1,* 93–135.

COOK, T. D., & GRUDER, C. L. (1978). Metaevaluation research. *Evaluation Quarterly, 2,* 5–51.

COOK, T. D., & LEVITON, L. C. (1980). Reviewing the literature: A comparison of traditional methods with meta-analysis. *Journal of Personality, 48,* 449–472.

COOPER, H. M., & ROSENTHAL, R. (1980). Statistical versus traditional procedures for summarizing research findings. *Psychological Bulletin, 87,* 442–449.

CORDARO, L., & ISON, J. R. (1963). Psychology of the scientist: X. Observer bias in classical conditioning of the planarian. *Psychological Reports, 13,* 787–789.

CORDES, C. (1984, January). Political pull tips NIE scale: Bank Street cries foul on award to Harvard. *APA Monitor,* pp. 1, 14, 22.

COWLES, M., & DAVIS, C. (1982). On the origins of the .05 level of statistical significance. *American Psychologist, 37,* 553–558.

COZBY, P. C. (1984). *Using computers in the behavioral sciences.* Palo Alto, Calif.: Mayfield.

CRAIN, R. B., & MAHARD, R. E. (1983). The effect of research methodology on desegregation-achievement studies: A meta-analysis. *American Journal of Sociology, 88,* 839–854.

CRONBACH, L. J. (1975). Five decades of public controversy over mental testing. *American Psychologist, 30,* 1–14.

CRONBACH, L. J., GLESER, G. C., NANDA, H., & RAJARATNAM, N. (1972). *The dependability of behavioral measurements: Theory of generalizability for scores and profiles.* New York: John Wiley.

CRONBACH, L. J., & MEEHL, P. E. (1955). Construct validity in psychological tests. *Psychological Bulletin, 52,* 281–302.

DAVIS, H. R., & SALASIN, S. E. (1975). The utilization of evaluation. In E. L. Struening and M. Guttentag (Eds.), *Handbook of evaluation research, Vol. 1.* Beverly Hills, Calif.: Sage.

DAVISON, M. L., & SHARMA, A. R. (1988). Parametric statistics and levels of measurement. *Psychological Bulletin, 104,* 137–144.

DEMPSTER, F. N. (1988). The spacing effect: A case study in the failure to apply the results of psychological research. *American Psychologist, 43,* 627–634.

DEUTSCH, M. (1980). Socially relevant research: Comments on "applied" versus "basic" research. In R. F. Kidd and M. J. Saks (Eds.), *Advances in applied social psychology, Vol. 1.* Hillsdale, N.J.: Lawrence Erlbaum.

DILLMAN, D. A. (1978). *Mail and telephone surveys: The total design method.* New York: John Wiley.

DOOLEY, D., & CATALANO, R. (1980). Economic change as a cause of behavioral disorder. *Psychological Bulletin, 87,* 450–468.

DOOLEY, D., & CATALANO, R. (1986). Do economic variables generate psychological problems? Different methods, different answers. In A. J. MacFadyen & H. W. MacFadyen (Eds.), *Economic psychology: Intersection in theory and application* (pp. 503–546). Amsterdam: Elsevier Science.

DUBIN, R. (1978). *Theory building*. New York: Free Press.

DUNCAN, G. J., & MORGAN, J. N. (1981). Persistence and change in economic status and the role of changing family composition. In M. S. Hill, D. H. Hill, & J. N. Morgan (Eds.), *Five thousand American families—patterns of progress: Volume IX. Analyses of the first twelve years of the Panel Study of Income Dynamics*. Ann Arbor, Mich.: Institute for Social Research.

DUNKELBERG, W. C., & DAY, G. S. (1973). Nonresponse bias and callbacks in sample surveys. *Journal of Marketing Research, 10,* 160–168.

DURANT, W., & DURANT, A. (1961). *The age of reason begins*. New York: Simon & Schuster.

DURBIN, J., & WATSON, G. (1950). Testing for serial correlation in least squares regression: Part I. *Biometrica, 37,* 409–423.

———. (1951). Testing for serial correlation in least squares regression: Part II. *Biometrica, 38,* 159–178.

DURKHEIM, É. (1951). *Suicide: A study in sociology*. (G. Simpson, Ed.; J. A. Spaulding & G. Simpson, Trans.). New York: Free Press. (Original work published 1897).

DURLAK, J. A. (1979). Comparative effectiveness of paraprofessional and professional helpers. *Psychological Bulletin, 86,* 80–92.

EKMAN, P., & FRIESEN, W. (1978). *FACS investigator's guide*. Palo Alto, Calif.: Consulting Psychologist's Press.

ELASHOFF, J. D., & SNOW, R. E. (Eds.). (1971). *Pygmalion reconsidered*. Worthington, Ohio: Charles A. Jones.

ELLSWORTH, P. C., & LUDWIG, L. M. (1972). Visual behavior in social interaction. *Journal of Communication, 22,* 375–403.

ERLEBACHER, A. (1977). Design and analysis of experiments constrasting the within- and between-subjects manipulation of the independent variable. *Psychological Bulletin, 84,* 212–219.

ERON, L. D., & WALDER, L. O. (1961). Test burning: II. *American Psychologist, 16,* 237–244.

ETHICS COMMITTEE OF THE AMERICAN PSYCHOLOGICAL ASSOCIATION. (1988). Trends in ethics cases, common pitfalls, and published resources. *American Psychologist, 43,* 564–572.

EYSENCK, H. J. (1973). *Eysenck on extraversion*. London: Crosby Lockwood Stapes.

FAIRWEATHER, G. W., SANDERS, D. H., MAYNARD, H., & CRESSLER, D. L. (1969). *Community life for the mentally ill*. Chicago: Aldine.

FAIRWEATHER, G. W., SANDERS, D. H., & TORNATZKY, L. G. (1974). *Creating change in mental health organizations*. Elmsford, N.Y.: Pergamon.

FEDERAL REGISTER. (1981, January 26). *46* (16).

FESTINGER, L., RIECHEN, H. W., & SCHACHTER, S. (1956). *When prophecy fails: A social and psychological study of a modern group that predicted the destruction of the world*. New York: Harper & Row.

FIENBERG, S. (1977). *The analysis of cross-classified categorical data*. Cambridge, Mass.: MIT Press.

FINSTERBUSCH, K., & MOTZ, A. B. (1980). *Social research for policy decisions*. Belmont, Calif.: Wadsworth.

FIREBAUGH, G. (1978). A rule for inferring individual-level relationships from aggregate data. *American Sociological Review, 43,* 557–572.

FIREBAUGH, G. (1980). Cross-national versus historical regression models: Conditions of equivalence in comparative analysis. *Comparative Social Research, 3,* 333–344.

FISKE, D. W. (1987). Construct invalidity comes from method effects. *Educational and Psychological Measurement, 47,* 285–307.

FOSTER, S. L., & CONE, J. D. (1980). Current issues in direct observation. *Behavioral Assessment, 2,* 313–338.

FRANK, J. D., NASH, E. H., STONE, A. R., & IMBER, S. D. (1963). Immediate and long-term symptomatic course of psychiatric out-patients. *American Journal of Psychiatry, 120,* 429–439.

FRANKE, R. H., & KAUL, J. D. (1978). The Hawthorne experiments: First statistical interpretation. *American Sociological Review, 43,* 623–643.

FREEMAN, D. (1983). *Margaret Mead and Samoa: The making and unmaking of an anthropological myth*. Cambridge, Mass.: Harvard University Press.

FRIEDMAN, H. J. S., & BOOTH-KEWLEY, S. (1987). The "disease-prone personality": A meta-analytic view of the construct. *American Psychologist, 42,* 539–555.

GAITO, J. (1980). Measurement scales and statistics: Resurgence of an old misconception. *Psychological Bulletin, 87,* 564–567.

GANZ, C. (1980). Linkages between knowledge creation, diffusion, and utilization. *Knowledge: Creation, Diffusion, Utilization, 1,* 591–612.

GELLER, E. S. (1980). Application of behavioral analysis to litter control. In I. D. Glenwick & L. Jason (Eds.), *Behavioral community psychology: Progress and prospects*. New York: Holt, Rinehart & Winston.

GERGEN, K. J. (1985). The social constructionist movement in modern psychology. *American Psychologist, 40,* 266–275.

GHOLSON, B., & BARKER, P. (1985). Kuhn, Lakatos, and Laudan: Applications in the history of physics and psychology. *American Psychologist, 7,* 755–769.

GLASS, G. V., & ELLETT, F. S. (1980). Evaluation research. *Annual Review of Psychology, 31,* 211–228.

GLASS, G. V., McGAW, B., & SMITH, M. L. (1981). *Meta-analysis in social research*. Beverly Hills, Calif.: Sage.

GLAZER, M. (1972). *The research adventure: Promise and problems of field work*. New York: Random House.

GOLDEN, M. P. (Ed.) (1976). *The research experience*. Itasca, Ill.: Peacock.

GOLDMAN, R. N., & WEINBERG, J. S. (1985). *Statistics: An introduction*. Englewood Cliffs, N.J.: Prentice-Hall.

GOTTFREDSON, S. D. (1978). Evaluating psychological research reports: Dimensions, reliability and correlates of quality judgments. *American Psychologist, 33*, 920–929.

GREEN, B. F., & HALL, J. A. (1984). Quantitative methods for literature reviews. *Annual Review of Psychology, 35*, 37–53.

GROVES, R. M. (1979). Actors and questions in telephone and personal interview surveys. *Public Opinion Quarterly, 43*, 190–205.

———. (1983). Implications of CATI: Costs, errors, and organization of telephone survey research. *Sociological Methods and Research, 12*, 199–215.

GROVES, R. M., & FULTZ, N. H. (1985). Gender effects among telephone interviewers in a survey of economic attitudes. *Sociological Methods and Research, 14*, 31–52.

GROVES, R. M., & KAHN, R. L. (1979). *Surveys by telephone: A national comparison with personal interviews*. New York: Academic Press.

GUENZEL, P. J., BERCKMANS, T. R., & CANNELL, C. F. (1983). *General interviewing techniques: A self-instructional workbook for telephone and personal interviewer training*. Ann Arbor, Mich.: Institute for Social Research.

GURIN, G., VEROFF, J., & FELD, S. (1960). *Americans view their mental health*. New York: Basic Books.

HALL, E. T. (1965). A system for the notation of proxemic behavior. *American Anthropologist, 65*, 1003–1026.

HANUSHEK, E. A., & JACKSON, J. E. (1977). *Statistical methods for social scientists*. New York: Academic Press.

HATTIE, J. A., SHARPLEY, C. F., & ROGERS, H. J. (1984). Comparative effectiveness of professional and paraprofessional helpers. *Psychological Bulletin, 95*, 534–541.

HEARNSHAW, L. S. (1979). *Cyril Burt: Psychologist*. London: Hodder and Stoughton.

HEATH, L., KENDZIERSKI, D., & BORGIDA, E. (1982). Evaluation of social programs: A multi-methodological approach combining a delayed treatment true experiment and multiple time series. *Evaluation Review, 6*, 233–246.

HEATHER, N., & ROBERTSON, I. (1983). *Controlled drinking*. New York: Methuen.

HEISE, D. R. (1975). *Causal analysis*. New York: John Wiley.

HENNIGAN, K. M., FLAY, B. R., & COOK, T. D. (1980). "Give me the facts": Some suggestions for using social science knowledge in national policy-making. In R. F. Kidd and M. J. Saks (Eds.), *Advances in applied social psychology, Vol. 1*. Hillsdale, N.J.: Lawrence Erlbaum.

HERSHEY, N., & MILLER, R. D. (1976). *Human experimentation and the law*. Germantown, Md.: Aspen Systems.

HESS, E. H. (1973). Pupillometrics: A method of studying mental, emotional and sensory processes. In N. S. Greenfield & R. A. Sternbach (Eds.), *Handbook of psychophysiology*. New York: Holt, Rinehart & Winston.

HILL, M. S., HILL, D. H., & MORGAN, J. N. (Eds.). (1981). *Five thousand American families—patterns of economic progress: Volume IX. Analyses of the first twelve years of the Panel Study of Income Dynamics*. Ann Arbor, Mich.: Institute for Social Research.

HOFFER, A., OSMOND, H., & SMYTHIES, J. R. (1954). Schizophrenia: A new approach. *Journal of Mental Science, 100*, 29–45.

HOHMANN, M., BANET, B., & WEIKART, D. P. (1979). *Young children in action: A manual for preschool educators*. Ypsilanti, Mich.: High/Scope Educational Research Foundation.

HOLLINGSHEAD, A. B. (1975). *Four factor index of social status*. Privately printed. 1965 Yale Station, New Haven, Conn. 06520.

HOLLINGSHEAD, A. B., & REDLICH, F. C. (1958). *Social class and mental illness*. New York: John Wiley.

HOLSTI, O. R. (1969). *Content analysis for the social sciences and humanities*. Reading, Mass.: Addison-Wesley.

HOROWITZ, I. L. (1973). The life and death of project Camelot. In N. K. Denzin (Ed.), *The values of social science*. New Brunswick, N.J.: Transaction Books.

HOSTETLER, A. J. (1987, May). Investigation: Fraud inquiry revives doubt: Can science police itself? *APA Monitor*, pp. 1, 12.

HOWE, H. L. (1981). Social factors associated with breast self-examination among high risk women. *American Journal of Public Health, 71*, 251–255.

HUCK, S. W., & SANDLER, H. M. (1979). *Rival hypotheses: Alternative interpretations of data based conclusions*. New York: Harper & Row.

HUGHES, J. R., JACOBS, D. R., JR., SCHUCHER, B., CHAPMAN, D. P., MURRAY, D. M., & JOHNSON, C. A. (1983). Nonverbal behavior of the Type A individual. *Journal of Behavioral Medicine, 6*, 279–289.

HUMMEL, C. E. (1986). *The Galileo connection: Resolving conflicts between science and the Bible.* Downer's Grove, Ill.: Intervarsity Press.

HUNT, M. (1985). *Profiles of social research: The scientific study of human interactions.* New York: Russell Sage.

JASON, L. A., ZOLIK, E. S., & MATESE, F. J. (1979). Prompting dog owners to pick up dog droppings. *American Journal of Community Psychology, 7,* 339–351.

JENCKS, C., & CROUSE, J. (1982). Should we relabel the SAT . . . or replace it? In W. Schrader (Ed.), *New directions for testing and measurement, guidance, and program improvement* (pp. 33–49). San Francisco: Jossey-Bass.

JENCKS, C., SMITH, M., ACLAND, H., BANE, M. J., COHEN, D., GINTIS, H., HEYNS, B., & MICHELSON, S. (1972). *Inequality: A reassessment of the effect on family and schooling in America.* New York: Harper & Row.

JENKINS, C. D., ZYZANSKI, S. J., & ROSENMAN, R. H. (1971). Progress toward validation of a computer-scored test for the Type A coronary-prone behavior pattern. *Psychosomatic Medicine, 33,* 193–202.

JENSEN, A. R. (1969). How much can we boost IQ and scholastic achievement? *Harvard Educational Review, 39,* 1–123.

JENSEN, G. (1986). *Dis-integrating integrated theory: A critical analysis of attempts to save strain theory.* Paper presented at the Annual Convention of the American Society of Criminology, Atlanta.

JOHNSON, H. H., & FOLEY, J. M. (1969). Some effects of placebo and experiment conditions in research on methods of teaching. *Journal of Educational Psychology, 60,* 6–10.

JOHNSTON, J. (1972). *Econometric methods.* New York: McGraw-Hill.

JONES, J. H. (1981). *Bad blood: The Tuskegee syphilis experiment.* New York: Free Press.

JORDAN, L. A., MARCUS, A. C., & REEDER, L. G. (1980). Response styles in telephone and household interviewing: A field experiment. *Public Opinion Quarterly, 44,* 210–222.

JORESKOG, K. G., & SÖRBOM, D. (1981). *LISREL V: Analysis of linear structural relationships by maximum likelihood and least squares methods.* Chicago: National Educational Resources.

KASL, S. V., CHISHOLM, R. F., & ESKENAZI, B. (1981a). The impact of the accident at Three Mile Island on the behavior and well-being of nuclear workers: Part I: Perceptions and evaluations, behavioral responses, and work-related attitudes and feelings. *American Journal of Public Health, 71,* 472–483.

KASL, S. V., CHISHOLM, R. F., & ESKENAZI, B. (1981b). The impact of the accident at Three Mile Island on the behavior and well-being of nuclear workers: Part II: Job tensions, psychophysiological symptoms, and indices of distress. *American Journal of Public Health, 71,* 484–495.

KAZDIN, A. E. (1978). Methodological and interpretive problems of single-case experimental designs. *Journal of Consulting and Clinical Psychology, 46,* 629–642.

KIDDER, L. H. (1981). Qualitative research and quasi-experimental frameworks. In M. B. Brewer & B. E. Collins (Eds.), *Scientific inquiry and the social sciences.* San Francisco: Jossey-Bass.

KIESLER, C. A., & LOWMAN, R. P. (1980). Hutchinson versus Proxmire. *American Psychologist, 35,* 689–690.

KIESLER, D. J. (1973). *The process of psychotherapy: Empirical foundations and systems of analysis.* Chicago: Aldine.

KIM, J., & MUELLER, L. W. (1978). *Introduction to factor analysis.* Beverly Hills, Calif.: Sage.

KLOTZ, I. M. (1980). The N-Ray affair. *Scientific American, 242* (5), 168–175.

KOSLOSKI, K. (1986). Isolating age, period, and cohort effects in developmental research. *Research on Aging, 8,* 460–479.

KRAEMER, H. C., & THIEMANN, S. (1987). *How many subjects? Statistical power analysis in research.* Beverly Hills, Calif.: Sage.

KRITZER, H. M. (1977). Political protest and political violence: A nonrecursive causal model. *Social Forces, 55,* 630–640.

KUHN, T. S. (1970). *The structure of scientific revolutions.* Chicago.: University of Chicago Press.

KURTZ, R. R., & GRUMMON, D. L. (1972). Different approaches to the measurement of therapist empathy and their relationship to therapy outcomes. *Journal of Consulting and Clinical Psychology, 39,* 106–115.

LANDY, F. J. (1986). Stamp collecting versus science: Validation as hypothesis testing. *American Psychologist, 41,* 1183–1192.

LeCOMPTE, M. D., & GOETZ, J. P. (1982). Problems of reliability and validity in ethnographic research. *Review of Educational Research, 52,* 31–60.

LEIGHTON, D. C., HARDING, J. S., MACKLIN, S. B., MACMILLAN, A. M., & LEIGHTON, A. H. (1963). *The character of danger.* New York: Basic Books.

LEVENKRON, J. C., COHEN, J. D., MUELLER, H. S., & FISHER, E. B., JR. (1983). Modifying the Type A coronary-prone behavior pattern. *Journal of Consulting and Clinical Psychology, 51,* 192–204.

LEVINE, D. W., McDONALD, P. J., O'NEAL, E. C., & GARWOOD, S. G. (1980). Classroom ecology: The effects of seating position on grades and participation. *Personality and Social Psychology Bulletin, 6,* 409–412.

LEVITON, L. C., & HUGHES, E. F. X. (1981). Research on the utilization of evaluations: A review and synthesis. *Evaluation Review, 5,* 525–548.

LIBRARY OF CONGRESS, SUBJECT CATALOGUING DIVISION. (1986). *Library of Congress subject headings* (9th edition). Washington, D.C.: Author.

LIEBOW, E. (1967). *Tally's corner: A study of Negro streetcorner men.* Boston: Little, Brown.

LIGHT, R. J., & SMITH, P. V. (1971). Accumulating evidence: Procedures for resolving contradictions among different research studies. *Harvard Educational Review, 41,* 429–471.

LILIENFELD, A. M. (1976). *Foundations of epidemiology.* New York: Oxford University Press.

LINEHAN, M. M., & NIELSEN, S. L. (1981). Assessment of suicide ideation and parasuicide: Hopelessness and social desirability. *Journal of Consulting and Clinical Psychology, 49,* 773–775.

LOCANDER, W., SUDMAN, S., & BRADBURN, N. (1976). An investigation of interview method, threat and response distribution. *Journal of the American Statistical Association, 71,* 269–275.

LOETHER, H. J., & MACTAVISH, D. G. (1980). *Descriptive and inferential statistics: An introduction.* Boston: Allyn & Bacon.

LOFLAND, J. (1966). *Doomsday cult: A study of conversion, proselytization, and maintenance of faith.* Englewood Cliffs, N.J.: Prentice-Hall.

———. (1971). *Analyzing social settings: A guide to qualitative observation and analysis.* Belmont, Calif.: Wadsworth.

MCCALL, G. J., & SIMMONS, J. L. (Eds.). (1969). *Issues in participant observation: A test and reader.* Reading, Mass.: Addison-Wesley.

MCCRAE, R. R., & COSTA, P. T., JR. (1983). Social desirability scales: More substance than style. *Journal of Consulting and Clinical Psychology, 51,* 882–888.

MCDILL, E. L., MCDILL, M. S., & SPREHE, J. T. (1972). Evaluation in practice: Compensatory education. In P. H. Rossi and W. Williams (Eds.), *Evaluating social programs: Theory, practice, and politics.* New York: Seminar Press.

MCGARVEY, B., GABRIELLI, W. F., JR., BENTLER, P. M., & MEDNICK, S. A. (1981). Rearing social class, education, and criminality: A multiple indicator model. *Journal of Abnormal Psychology, 90,* 354–364.

MCGUIRE, W. J. (1969). Suspiciousness of experimenter's intent. In R. Rosenthal and R. L. Rosnow (Eds.), *Artifact in behavioral research* (pp. 13–57). New York: Academic Press.

MCKEY, R. H., CONDELLI, L., GANSON, H., BARRETT, B. J., MCCONKEY, C., & PLANTZ, M. C. (1985). *The impact of Head Start on children, families, and communities: Final report of the Head Start evaluation, synthesis, and utilization project.* (DHHS Publication No. OHDS 85-31193). Washington, D.C.: U.S. Government Printing Office.

MAGIDSON, J. (1977). Toward a causal model approach for adjusting for preexisting differences in the nonequivalent control group situation: A general alternative to ANCOVA. *Evaluation Quarterly, 1,* 399–420.

MANICAS, P. T. & SECORD, P. F. (1983). Implications for psychology of the new philosophy of science. *American Psychologist, 38,* 339–413.

MARQUIS, D. (1986). An argument that all pre-randomized clinical trials are unethical. *Journal of Medicine and Philosophy, 11,* 367–383.

MARUYAMA, G., & MCGARVEY, B. (1980). Evaluating causal models: An application of maximum-likelihood analysis of structural equations. *Psychological Bulletin, 87,* 502–512.

MARX, M. H. (Ed.). (1965). *Theories in contemporary psychology.* New York: Macmillan.

MATARAZZO, R. G., MATARAZZO, J. D., SASLOW, G., & PHILLIPS, J. S. (1958). Psychological test and organismic correlates of interview interaction patterns. *Journal of Abnormal and Social Psychology, 56,* 329–338.

MATHEWS, K. A. (1988). Coronary heart disease and Type A behaviors: Update on and alternative to the Booth-Kewly and Friedman (1987) quantitative review. *Psychological Bulletin, 104,* 373–380.

MAUGH, T. H., II. (1988, July 27). Journal probe of lab test results sparks furor. *Los Angeles Times,* p. 3.

MAXWELL, S. E. & DELANEY, H. D. (1985). Measurement and statistics: An examination of construct validity. *Psychological Bulletin, 97,* 85–93.

MEHAN, H., & WOOD, H. (1975). *The reality of ethnomethodology.* New York: John Wiley.

MEIDINGER, E., & SCHNAIBERG, A. (1980). Social impact assessment as evaluation research: Claimants and claims. *Evaluation Review, 4,* 507–535.

MELTON, G. B., LEVINE, R. J., KOOCHER, G. P., ROSENTHAL, R., & THOMPSON, W. C. (1988). Community consultation in socially sensitive research: Lessons from clinical trials of treatments for AIDS. *American Psychologist, 43,* 573–581.

MELTZER, B. N., PETRAS, J. W., & REYNOLDS, L. T. (1975). *Symbolic interactionism: Genesis, varieties, and criticism.* London: Routledge & Kegan Paul.

MICHELL, J. (1986). Measurement scales and statistics: A clash of paradigms. *Psychological Bulletin, 100,* 398–407.

MILLER, D. C. (1977). *Handbook of research design and social measurement.* New York: McKay.

MILLER, N. (1980). Making school desegregation work. In W. G. Stephan & J. R. Feagin (Eds.), *School desegregation: Past, present, and future.* New York: Plenum Press.

MITCHELL, J. V., JR. (1985). *The ninth mental measurements yearbook.* Lincoln, Neb.: The Buros Institute of Mental Measurements.

MITCHELL, S. K. (1979). Interobserver agreement, reliability, and generalizability of data collected in observational studies. *Psychological Bulletin, 86,* 376–390.

MOOS, R. H., & VAN DORT, B. (1979). Student physical symptoms and the social climate of college living groups. *American Journal of Community Psychology, 7,* 31–43.

MORENO, J. L. (Ed.). (1960). *The sociometry reader.* New York: Free Press.

MORRIS, R. J., & SUCKERMAN, K. R. (1974). Therapist warmth as a factor in automated systematic desensitization. *Journal of Consulting and Clinical Psychology, 42,* 244–250.

MORRISON, D. E., & HENKEL, R. E. (Eds.). (1970). *The significance test controversy: A reader.* Chicago: Aldine.

NAGEL, S. S., & NEEF, M. (1977). Determining an optimum level of statistical significance. In M. Guttentag (Ed.), *Evaluation studies review annual, Vol 2.* Beverly Hills:, Calif.: Sage.

NAIRN, A. (1980). *The reign of the ETS: The corporation that makes up minds.* Washington, D.C.: Ralph Nader.

NATIONAL COMMISSION ON EMPLOYMENT AND UNEMPLOYMENT STATISTICS. (1979). *Counting the labor force.* Washington, D.C.: U.S. Government Printing Office.

NEDERHOF, A. J. (1985). A comparison of European and North American response patterns in mail surveys. *Journal of the Market Research Society, 27,* 55–63.

NELKIN, D. (1979). Scientific knowledge, public policy, and democracy. *Knowledge: Creation, Diffusion, Utilization, 1,* 106–122.

NESSELROADE, J. R., STIGLER, S. M., & BALTES, P. B. (1980). Regression toward the mean and the study of change. *Psychological Bulletin, 88,* 622–637.

NETTLER, G. (1959). Test burning in Texas. *American Psychologist, 14,* 682–683.

NEUBECK, K. J., & ROACH, J. L. (1981). Income maintenance experiments, politics, and the perpetuation of poverty. *Social Problems, 28,* 308–320.

NUNNALLY, J. C. (1978). *Psychometric theory.* New York: McGraw-Hill.

O'NEIL, M. J. (1979). Estimating the nonresponse bias due to refusals in telephone surveys. *Public Opinion Quarterly, 43,* 218–232.

ORNE, M. T. (1962). On the social psychology of the psychological experiment: With particular reference to demand characteristics and their implications. *American Psychologist, 17,* 776–783.

————. (1969). Demand characteristics and the concept of quasi-controls. In R. Rosenthal and R. L. Rosnow (Eds.), *Artifact in behavioral research* (pp. 143–179). New York: Academic Press.

ORNE, M. T., SHEEHAN, P. W., & EVANS, F. J. (1968). Occurrence of posthypnotic behavior outside the experimental setting. *Journal of Personality and Social Psychology, 9,* 189–196.

ORWIN, R. G., & CORDRAY, D. S. (1985). Effects of deficient reporting on meta-analysis: A conceptual framework and reanalysis. *Psychological Bulletin, 97,* 134–147.

OSMOND, H., & SMYTHIES, J. R. (1952). Schizophrenia: A new approach. *Journal of Mental Science, 98,* 309–315.

PALIT, C., & SHARP, H. (1983). Microcomputer- assisted telephone interviewing. *Sociological Methods and Research, 12,* 169–189.

PATTERSON, M. L. (1976). An arousal model of interpersonal intimacy. *Psychological Review, 85,* 235–245.

PATTON, M. Q. (1980). *Qualitative evaluation methods.* Beverly Hills, Calif.: Sage.

PAYNE, J. S., MERCER, D. C., PAYNE, R. A., & DAVISON, R. G. (1973). *Head Start: A tragi-comedy with epilogue.* New York: Behavioral Publications.

PENDERY, M. L., MALTZMAN, I. M., & WEST, L. J. (1982). Controlled drinking by alcoholics? New findings and a reevaluation of a major affirmative study. *Science, 217,* 169–174.

PETTIGREW, T. F., & GREEN, R. L. (1976). School desegregation in large cities: A critique of the Coleman "white flight" thesis. *Harvard Educational Review, 46,* 1–52.

PETTIGREW, T. F., USEEM, E. L., NORMAND, C., & SMITH, M. (1973). Busing: A review of "the evidence." *Public Interest, 30,* 88–118.

PHILLIPS, D. P. (1979). Suicide, motor vehicle fatalities, and the mass media: Evidence toward a theory of suggestion. *American Journal of Sociology, 84,* 1150–1174.

PLATT, J. R. (1964). Strong inference. *Science, 146,* 36–42.

POPPER, K. (1987). Science: Conjectures and refutations. In J. A. Kourany (Ed.), *Scientific knowledge: Basic issues in the philosophy of science* (pp. 139–157). Belmont, Calif.: Wadsworth.

POSAVAC, E. J., & CAREY, R. G. (1985). *Program evaluation: Methods and case studies.* Englewood Cliffs, N.J.: Prentice-Hall.

POUPARD, P. (Ed.). (1983). *Galileo Galilei: Toward a resolution of 350 years of debate—1633–1983.* (I. Campbell, Trans.). Pittsburgh: Duquesne University Press.

POWELL, L. H. (1987). Issues in the measurement of

the Type A Behaviour Pattern. In S. V. Kasl & C. L. Cooper (Eds.). *Stress and health: Issues in research methodology* (pp. 231–282). London: John Wiley.

RAFFEL, J. A. (1985). The impact of metropolitan school desegregation on public opinion: A longitudinal analysis. *Urban Affairs Quarterly, 21,* 245–265.

RAPPAPORT, J., CHINSKY, J. M., & COWEN, E. L. (1971). *Innovations in helping chronic patients: College students in a mental institution.* New York: Academic Press.

RAVITCH, D. (1978). The "white flight" controversy. *Public Interest, 51,* 135–149.

REDONDI, P. (1987). *Galileo heretic.* (R. Rosenthal, Trans.). Princeton, N.J.: Princeton University Press. (Original work published 1983).

REED, J. G., & BAXTER, P. M. (1983). *Library use: a handbook for psychology.* Washington, D.C.: American Psychological Association.

REYNOLDS, P. D. (1979). *Ethical dilemmas and social science research.* San Francisco: Jossey-Bass.

———. (1982). *Ethics and social science research.* Englewood Cliffs, N.J.: Prentice-Hall.

RICH, C. L. (1977). Is random digit dialing really necessary? *Journal of Marketing Research, 14,* 300–305.

RIST, R. C. (1970). Student social class and teacher expectations: The self-fulfilling prophecy in ghetto education. *Harvard Educational Review, 40,* 411–451.

ROBINS, P. K., SPIEGELMAN, R. G., WEINER, S., & BELL, J. G. (Eds.). (1980). *A guaranteed annual income: Evidence from a social experiment.* New York: Academic Press.

ROBINSON, J. P., ATHANASIOU, R., & HEAD, K. B. (1969). *Measures of occupational attitudes and occupational characteristics.* Ann Arbor: University of Michigan Press.

ROBINSON, J. P., RUSK, J. G., & HEAD, K. B. (1968). *Measures of political attitudes.* Ann Arbor: University of Michigan Press.

ROBINSON, J. P., & SHAVER, P. R. (1973). *Measures of social psychological attitudes.* Ann Arbor: University of Michigan Press.

ROBINSON, W. S. (1950). Ecological correlations and the behavior of individuals. *American Sociological Review, 15,* 351–357.

ROETHLISBERGER, F. J., & DICKSON, W. J. (1939). *Management and the worker.* New York: John Wiley.

ROGERS, C. R. (1957). The necessary and sufficient conditions of therapeutic personality change. *Journal of Consulting Psychology, 21,* 95–103.

ROGERS, T. F. (1976). Interviews by telephone and in person: Quality of responses and field performance. *Public Opinion Quarterly, 40,* 51–65.

RORER, L. G. (1965). The great response-style myth. *Psychological Bulletin, 63,* 129–156.

ROSENBERG, M. J. (1969). The conditions and consequences of evaluation research. In R. Rosenthal and R. L. Rosnow (Eds.), *Artifact in behavioral research* (pp. 279–349). New York: Academic Press.

ROSENTHAL, R. (1976). *Experimenter effects in behavioral research.* New York: Irvington.

———. (1978). Combining results of independent studies. *Psychological Bulletin, 85,* 185–193.

———. (1979). The "file drawer problem" and tolerance for null results. *Psychological Bulletin, 86,* 638–641.

ROSENTHAL, R., BLANCK, P. D., & VANNICELLI, M. (1984). Speaking to and about patients: Predicting therapists' tone of voice. *Journal of Consulting and Clinical Psychology, 52,* 679–686.

ROSENTHAL, R., & JACOBSON, L. (1968). *Pygmalion in the classroom.* New York: Holt, Rinehart & Winston.

ROSENTHAL, R., & ROSNOW, R. L. (1969). The volunteer subject. In R. Rosenthal and R. L. Rosnow (Eds.), *Artifact in behavioral research* (pp. 139–155). New York: Academic Press.

ROSENTHAL, R., & RUBIN, D. B. (1971). Pygmalion reaffirmed. In J. D. Elashoff and R. E. Snow (Eds.), *Pygmalion reconsidered* (pp. 139–155). Worthington, Ohio: Charles A. Jones.

———. (1978). Interpersonal expectancy effects: The first 345 studies. *The Behavioral and Brain Sciences, 3,* 377–415.

———. (1982). A simple, general purpose display of magnitude of experimental effect. *Journal of Educational Psychology, 74,* 166–169.

ROSS, S., KRUGMAN, A. D., LYERLY, S. B., & CLYDE, D. J. (1962). Drugs and placebos: A model design. *Psychological Reports, 10,* 383–392.

ROSSELL, C. H. (1975–1976). School desegregation and white flight. *Political Science Quarterly, 90,* 675–695.

ROSSI, P. H. (1978). Issues in the evaluation of human service delivery. *Evaluation Quarterly, 2,* 573–599.

ROSSI, P. H., & FREEMAN, H. E. (1985). *Evaluation: A systematic approach.* Beverly Hills, Calif.: Sage.

ROSSI, P. H., WRIGHT, J. D., & WRIGHT, S. R. (1978). The theory and practice of applied social research. *Evaluation Quarterly, 2,* 171–191.

ROTTER, J. (1966). Generalized expectancies for internal versus external control of reinforcement. *Psychological Monographs, 80* (1, Whole no. 609).

ROZENSKY, R. H., & HONOR, L. F. (1982). Notation systems for coding nonverbal behavior: A review. *Journal of Behavioral Assessment, 4,* 119–132.

RUBACK, R. B., & INNES, C. A. (1988). The relevance and irrelevance of psychological research: The example of prison crowding. *American Psychologist, 43,* 683–693.

RUBIN, Z. (1975). Disclosing oneself to a stranger: Reciprocity and its limits. *Journal of Experimental Social Psychology, 11*, 233–260.

RUSSELL, B. (1945). *A history of western philosophy.* New York: Simon & Schuster.

———. (1948). *Human knowledge: Its scope and limits.* New York: Simon & Schuster.

RUSSELL, D., PEPLAU, L. A., & CUTRONA, L. E. (1980). The revised UCLA Loneliness Scale: Concurrent and discriminant validity evidence. *Journal of Personality and Social Psychology, 39*, 472–480.

SAMELSON, F. (1980). J. B. Watson's Little Albert, Cyril Burt's twins, and the need for a critical science. *American Psychologist, 35*, 619–625.

SANDERS, J. R., & KEITH-SPIEGEL, P. (1980). Formal and informal adjudication of ethics complaints about psychologists. *American Psychologist, 35*, 1096–1105.

SARASON, S. B. (1981). *Psychology misdirected.* New York: Free Press.

SCARR, S., & WEINBERG, R. A. (1976). IQ test performance of black children adopted by white families. *American Psychologist, 31*, 726–739.

SCHAIE, K. W. (1965). A general model for the study of developmental problems. *Psychological Bulletin, 64*, 92–107.

SCHEIRER, M. A. (1978). Program participants' positive perceptions: Psychological conflict of interest in social program evaluation. *Evaluation Quarterly, 2*, 53–70.

SCHERER, K., & EKMAN, P. (Eds.). (1982). *Handbook of methods in nonverbal behavior research.* Cambridge, Eng.: Cambridge University Press.

SCHERVITZ, L., BERTON, K., & LEVENTHAL, H. (1977). Type A assessment and interaction in the behavior pattern interview. *Psychosomatic Medicine, 39*, 229–240.

SCHRAGER, R. H. (1986). The impact of living group social climate on student academic performance. *Research in Higher Education, 25*, 265–276.

SCHROEDER, L. D., SJOQUIST, D. L., & STEPHAN, P. E. (1986). *Understanding regression analysis: An introductory guide.* Beverly Hills, Calif.: Sage.

SCHUMAN, H., PRESSER, S., & LUDWIG, J. (1981). Context effects on survey responses to questions about abortion. *Public Opinion Quarterly, 45*, 216–223.

SCHWARTZ, H., & JACOBS, J. (1979). *Qualitative sociology: A method to the madness.* New York: Free Press.

SCHWEINHART, L. J., & WEIKART, D. P. (1980). *Young children grow up: The effects of the Perry Preschool Program on youths through age 15.* Ypsilanti, Mich.: High/Scope Press.

SCRIVEN, M. (1972). Pros and cons about goal-free evaluation. *Evaluation Comment, 3*, 1–4.

SEWELL, W. H., & SHAH, V. P. (1967). Socioeconomic status, intelligence, and the attainment of higher education. *Sociology of Education, 40*, 1–23.

SIEBER, J. E., & STANLEY, B. (1988). Ethical and professional dimensions of socially sensitive research. *American Psychologist, 43*, 49–55.

SIEGMAN, A. W., & FELDSTEIN, S. (1987). *Nonverbal behavior and communication.* Hillsdale, N.J.: Lawrence Erlbaum.

SILVERMAN, I. (1977). *The human subject in the psychological laboratory.* Elmsford, N.Y.: Pergamon.

SINGER, H., GERARD, H. B., & REDFEARN, D. (1975). Achievement. In H. B. Gerard & N. Miller (Eds.), *School desegregation: A longitudinal study.* New York: Plenum Press.

SMART, B. (1976). *Sociology, phenomenology, and Marxian analysis: A critical discussion of the theory and practice of a science of society.* London: Routledge & Kegan Paul.

SMITH, M. L., & GLASS, G. V. (1977). Meta-analysis of psychotherapy outcome studies. *American Psychologist, 32*, 752–760.

SMITH, M. S., & BISSELL, J. S. (1970). Report analysis: The impact of Head Start. *Harvard Educational Review, 40*, 51–104.

SMITH, T. W. (1987). That which we call welfare by any other name would smell sweeter: An analysis of the impact of question wording on response patterns. *Public Opinion Quarterly, 51*, 75–83.

SNYDER, S. H. (1974). *Madness and the brain.* New York: McGraw-Hill.

SOCIOLOGICAL METHODS AND RESEARCH. (1977, November). (Special issue) *6* (2).

SROLE, L. (1975). Measurement and classification in socio-psychiatric epidemiology: Midtown Manhattan Study (1954) and Midtown Manhattan Restudy (1974). *Journal of Health and Social Behavior, 16*, 347–364.

SROLE, L., LANGNER, T. S., MICHAEL, S. T., OPLER, M. K., & RENNIE, T. A. C. (1962). *Mental health and the metropolis: The Midtown Manhattan Study. Vol. 1.* New York: McGraw-Hill.

STOKOLS, D., NOVACO, R. W., STOKOLS, J., & CAMPBELL, J. (1978). Traffic congestion, Type A behavior, and stress. *Journal of Applied Psychology, 63*, 467–480.

STOUT, C. C., THORNTON, B., & RUSSELL, H. L. (1980). Effect of relaxation training on students' persistence and academic performance. *Psychological Reports, 47*, 189–190.

STOVE, D.C. (1982). *Popper and after: Four modern irrationalists.* New York: Pergamon.

SUDMAN, S. (1976). *Applied sampling.* New York: Academic Press.

———. (1983). Survey research and technologicalchange. *Sociological Methods and Research, 12,* 217–230.

SUDMAN, S., & BRADBURN, N. M. (1982). *Asking questions: A practical guide to questionnaire design.* San Francisco: Jossey-Bass.

SUINN, R. M. (1969). The STABS, a measure of test anxiety for behavior therapy: Normative data. *Behavior Research and Therapy, 7,* 335–339.

SURVEY RESEARCH CENTER. (1976). *Interviewer's Manual.* Ann Arbor, Mich.: Institute for Social Research.

THALER, R. E. (1985, May). Fieldnotes case resolved; Scholars' rights supported. *Footnotes,* p. 1.

THOMPSON, J. J., CHODOSH, J., FRIED, C., GOODMAN, D. S., WAX, M. L., & WILSON, J. O. (1981). Regulations governing research on human subjects: Academic freedom and the institutional review board. *Academic, 67,* 358–370.

THOMPSON, M. S. (1980). *Benefit-cost analysis for program evaluation.* Beverly Hills, Calif.: Sage.

THOMPSON, M. S., & FORTESS, E. E. (1980). Cost-effectiveness analysis in health program evaluation. *Evaluation Review, 4,* 549–568.

THOMPSON, W. C. (1989). Death qualification after Wainwright v. Witt and Lockhart v. McCree. *Law and Human Behavior, 13,* 185–215.

TINSLEY, H. E. A., & WEISS, D. J. (1975). Interrater reliability and agreement of subjective judgments. *Journal of Counseling Psychology, 22,* 358–376.

TOBIAS, S. (1978). *Overcoming math anxiety.* New York: W. W. Norton.

TOWNSEND, J. T. & ASHBY, F. G. (1984). Measurement scales and statistics: The misconception misconceived. *Psychological Bulletin, 96,* 394–401.

TRICE, A. D. (1987). Informed consent: IV. The effects of the timing of giving consent on experimental performance. *Journal of General Psychology, 114,* 125–128.

TROLDAHL, V. G., & CARTER, R. E. (1964). Random selection of respondents within households in phone surveys. *Journal of Marketing Research, 1,* 71–76.

TUCHFARBER, A. J., & KLECKA, W. R. (1976). *Random digit dialing: Lowering the cost of victimization surveys.* Cincinnati: Police Foundation.

TUKEY, J. W. (1977). *Exploratory data analysis.* Reading, Mass.: Addison-Wesley.

TULL, D. S., & ALBAUM, G. S. (1977). Bias in random digit dialed surveys. *Public Opinion Quarterly, 41,* 389–395.

TURNER, C. W., & SIMONS, L. A. (1974). Effects of subject sophistication and evaluation apprehension on aggressive responses to weapons. *Journal of Personality and Social Psychology, 30,* 341–348.

VEATCH, R. M. (1981). Protecting human subjects: The federal government steps back. *The Hasting Center Report, 11,* 9–12.

VEROFF, J., DOUVAN, E., & KULKA, R. A. (1981). *The inner American: A self portrait from 1957 to 1976.* New York: Basic Books.

VINE, I. (1971). Judgment of direction of gaze: An interpretation of discrepant results. *British Journal of Social and Clinical Psychology, 10,* 320–331.

WEBB, E. J., CAMPBELL, D. T., SCHWARTZ, R. D., & SECHREST, L. (1966). *Unobtrusive measures: Nonreactive research in the social sciences.* Skokie, Ill.: Rand McNally.

WEBER, R. P. (1985). *Basic content analysis.* Beverly Hills, Calif.: Sage.

WEEKS, M. F., JONES, B. L., FOLSOM, R. E., JR., & BENRUD, C. H. (1980). Optimal times to contact sample households. *Public Opinion Quarterly, 44,* 101–114.

WEIGEL, R. H., & PAPPAS, J. J. (1981). Social science and the press: A case study and its implications. *American Psychologist, 36,* 480–487.

WEIKART, D. P., EPSTEIN, A. S., SCHWEINHART, L., & BOND, J. T. (1978). *The Ypsilanti Preschool Curriculum Demonstration Project: Preschool years and longitudinal results.* Ypsilanti, Mich.: High/Scope Press.

WEISS, A. T. (1975). The consumer model of assessing community health needs. *Evaluation, 2,* 71–73.

WEISS, C. H., & BUCUVALAS, M. J. (1980). Truth tests and utility tests: Decision-makers' frames of reference for social science research. *American Sociological Review, 45,* 302–313.

WELCH, F. (1987). A reconsideration of the impact of school desegregation programs on public school enrollment of white students, 1968–76. *Sociology of Education, 60,* 215–221.

WERNER, O., & SCHOEPFLE, G. M. (1987a). *Systematic fieldwork, volume 1: Foundations of ethnography and interviewing.* Beverly Hills, Calif.: Sage.

WERNER, O., & SCHOEPFLE, G. M. (1987b). *Systematic fieldwork, volume 2: Ethnographic analysis and data management.* Beverly Hills, Calif.: Sage.

WESTINGHOUSE LEARNING CORPORATION & OHIO STATE UNIVERSITY. (1969). *The impact of Head Start: An evaluation of the effects of Head Start on children's cognitive and affective development. Vols. I and II.* (Order No. PB 184329). Springfield, Va.: Clearinghouse for Federal Scientific and Technical Information, U.S. Department of Commerce.

WHEATON, B. (1980). The sociogenesis of psychological disorder. *Journal of Health and Social Behavior, 21,* 100–124.

WILLIAMS, B. (1978). *A sampler on sampling.* New York: John Wiley.

WILLIAMS, W., & EVANS, J. W. (1972). The politics of

evaluation: The case of Head Start. In P. H. Rossi & W. Williams (Eds.), *Evaluating social programs: Theory, practice, and politics.* New York: Seminar Press.

WILSON, F. D. (1985). The impact of school desegregation programs on white public-school enrollment, 1968–1976. *Sociology of Education, 58,* 137–153.

———. (1987). A reply to Finis Welch. *Sociology of Education, 60,* 222–223.

WILSON, W. J. (1987). *The truly disadvantaged: The inner city, the underclass, and public policy.* Chicago: University of Chicago Press.

WOLF, F. M. (1986). *Meta-analysis: Quantitative methods for research synthesis.* Beverly Hills, Calif.: Sage.

WORD, C. O., ZANNA, M. P., & COOPER, J. (1974). The nonverbal mediation of self-fulfilling prophecies in interracial interaction. *Journal of Experimental Social Psychology, 10,* 109–120.

ZALTMAN, G. (1979). Knowledge utilization as planned social change. *Knowledge: Creation, Diffusion, Utilization, 1,* 82–105.

ZIMBARDO, P. G. (1975). Transforming experimental research into advocacy for social change. In M. Deutsch & H. A. Hornstein (Eds.). *Applying social psychology: Implications for research, practice, and training* (pp. 33–66). New York: Lawrence Erlbaum.

ZIMBARDO, P. G., HANEY, C., BANKS, W. C., & JAFFE, D. (1975). The psychology of imprisonment: Privation, power, and pathology. In D. Rosehan & P. London (Eds.), *Theory and research in abnormal psychology.* New York: Holt, Rinehart & Winston.

Glossary Index

Below is a list of glossary terms and the chapters in which they appear and are defined.

Name Index

Subject Index